Inclusion Strategies for Students with Learning and Behavior Problems

Inclusion Strategies for Students with Learning and Behavior Problems

Perspectives, Experiences, and Best Practices

EDITED BY PAUL ZIONTS

pro·ed
An International Publisher
8700 Shoal Creek Boulevard
Austin, Texas 78757-6897
800/897-3202 Fax 800/397-7633
Order online at http://www.proedinc.com

© 1997 by PRO-ED, Inc.
8700 Shoal Creek Boulevard
Austin, Texas 78757-6897
800/897-3202 Fax 800/397-7633
Order online at http://www.proedinc.com

Library of Congress Cataloging-in-Publication Data

Inclusion strategies for students with learning and behavior problems
  / [edited] by Paul Zionts.
     p.   cm.
  Includes bibliographical references and index.
  ISBN 0-89079-698-X (soft cover : alk. paper)
    1. Mainstreaming in education—United States. 2. Learning
  disabled children—Education—United States. 3. Problem children-
  -Education—United States. I. Zionts, Paul.
LC4031.I525 1997
371.9'046—dc20   96-21574
                                                    CIP

This book is designed in Palatino.

Printed in the United States of America

4   5   6   7   8   08 07 06 05 04 03 02

Contents

Unit 2

Best Practices

Chapter 12

Chapter 13

Chapter 14

Chapter 15

Perspectives and Experiences

CHAPTER 1

Inclusion: Chasing the Impossible Dream? Maybe

Paul Zionts

T he issue of integrating students with differences has existed since the turn of the century and the advent of compulsory education laws, which state that *all* children must be educated. Clearly, public schools in the United States have reflected the dreams and ideals of a melting pot society, adjusted through litigation and legislation. No longer is it legal to segregate a U.S. citizen from a free and appropriate public education because of race, creed, or religion. No longer is it legal to deny a citizen an education because of a disability. Herein lies the crucial debatable issue of full inclusion: Is denying an individual with a significant disability full access to the general education setting, a setting that may deny the person an appropriate public education, *the same* as forced segregation? Is the dual system of general and special education *the same* as the "separate but equal" doctrine that has been declared unconstitutional for students with disabilities?

This debate, some of which is discussed in this chapter, will not be resolved soon. The intention of this book is not to add to the debate, but rather to assist those who are currently attempting to implement their version of inclusion. In fact, it is safe to assume that readers of

I thank Richard Simpson, Laura Zionts, Suzanne Shellady, Barry Alford, and Pamela Pruitt for their comments and contributions to this chapter.

this book are expecting, because of its title, practical strategies that will enhance their efforts. Thus, it is important that the reader be aware of the definition of inclusion used in this book and some of the salient aspects of the current debate. Thousands of teachers and students are being thrust, willingly and unwillingly, into implementing various versions of inclusion. As discussed later, the simple terms *inclusion* and *full inclusion* mean different things to different people. The following is a functional (one of many, to be sure) definition for inclusion that will be used in this book:

> Simply stated, inclusion is the implementation of the *least restrictive environment* dictum as originally stated in Public Law (P.L.) 94-142, the Education for All Handicapped Children Act of 1975. Inclusion means providing a free and public education to all students with disabilities in an environment that is as close to the general education setting as possible. It means ensuring that students with disabilities will not be handicapped, no matter what supports have been implemented, because of the environmental constraints that are imposed upon them.

It should be noted that Osborne and DiMattia (1994) have argued that the law has been interpreted only for those with mild disabilities, but perhaps it was really intended for all students with disabilities (see Yell, 1995b). They correctly observed that times are changing. The critical issue revolves around how appropriate it is for those students with moderate and severe disabilities to be educated in general education classes.

In my opinion, it is the issue of the least restrictive environment, as outlined in the above definition, that needs to be addressed. Heretofore, it has been the practice of educators to (a) adopt a "within-child" perspective by diagnosing and labeling those children and youth who are different from the norm and (b) determine that it is the children's "problem." This practice prevents these children with disabilities from being educated in the general education setting. With (mostly) good intentions, educators have pulled these students out of the general education classroom, away from their peers, and placed them in special education settings for part or all of the day. The purpose of this pull-out practice was to allow these students to receive Individualized Education Programs (IEPs) that would allow them to maximize their potential in their educational settings. It is recognized that this was not merely agenda. Many educators hoped that those individuals with disabilities would be cured and eventually become freely integrated upon their return to the general education setting. Others wanted these students removed from general education students because of the difficulties associated with their differences, academic and/or behavioral. However, as recognized by many critics of special education (Sailor, 1991; S. Stainback & W. Stainback, 1988; S. Stainback, W. Stainback, & Ayres, 1996; Wang, 1989), the special education students' inability to be integrated was not always their fault. In fact, they were being closed off from a system that was becoming increasingly intolerant of differences. The hue and cry of the educational reform movement for higher standards, to go back to "the basics," and for classroom management were at its highest, and those who could not fit were excluded. For the most part, the special education critics' words met with deaf ears.

The era of "school reform," regardless of its meaning, is on the minds of legislators, educators, and parents alike. Changes seem to be occurring at a rapid pace. As a result, curricular and instructional changes, seemingly made "for change's sake," has left many teachers wary about the logic of any move from the status quo. Unfortunately, this reluctance may in fact hinder students from receiving an education in the least restrictive environment.

Clearly, most teachers and parents wish that all students could have their academic, social, and emotional needs met in the general education setting. However, this wish meets with conflict: How can inclusion be accomplished and when is it appropriate? In response to the inclusion movement, the National Information Center for Children and Youth with Disabilities (NICHCY) has received many practical questions that seem to be concerned not with the debate, but rather with how to better integrate those students not currently in the general education setting. NICHCY (1995) reported that callers want to know the following:

- what the pros and cons are of including children with disabilities

- how to include

- how to plan for inclusion

- how to adapt the general education curriculum to meet the special education needs of each included student

- how to evaluate student performance

- how to train teachers

- where to find or reallocate the financial resources to provide the aids and supports students with disabilities may need
- what types of accommodations can and should be made
- where successful inclusive programs are located
- what effective practices exist
- where materials can be found
- what the elements of collaboration are (p. 1)

As discussed in the forthcoming chapters, an important first step for all involved will be to determine the definition and philosophy of inclusion. The answers to the above-stated questions will surely aid in the quest.

Why Inclusion?

The arguments for the inclusion of special education students in the general education classroom are both academic and social. Some professionals are dissatisfied with special education's being identified as academically inferior to general education. Others maintain that students educated solely in special education classes miss crucial social and academic interactions and experiences with their general education peers that will forever exclude them from the mainstream of society.

Proponents of reform believe that evidence is unclear that special education works (Carlberg & Kavale, 1980). Lipsky and Gartner (1991) contended that "the current system of special education needs to be changed for a basic reason: It does not work. That is, it fails to serve well the students. Although particular practices are faulty, the cause is not in practice but in basic conception" (p. 43). For example, Reynolds, Wang, and Walberg (1992) contended that students in special education actually receive less general instruction and less reading instruction than if they were placed in regular education settings. Further, Safran and Safran (1987) suggested that special educators are not any more tolerant of inappropriate behaviors than are regular educators. W. Stainback and S. Stainback (1984) have argued since the early 1980s that if there are no differences in these important areas, then regular education can and should make the modifications to include all people.

In short, these educators suggest that perhaps it is time for schools to recognize that all students have individual needs and to suggest that one type is regular and one type is special is a false and discriminating assumption (W. Stainback & S. Stainback, 1984). They further stress that special education is both academically and fiscally inefficient. They conclude that it is more expensive to operate the current dual system (due to testing, staffing, etc.).

A more cynical belief was espoused by Reynolds (1990), who suggested that special education advocacy groups are simply territorial and are concerned mainly with protecting their jobs. This appears to be the major point of contention espoused by the professionals discussed in the next section. They believe that the population with learning and behavior problems has distinctly different characteristics and needs that will not be served with full inclusion.

Concerns About Inclusion

The thrust of this book is to present strategies that may be implemented in inclusive settings. The contributors to this text firmly believe, because of research results and perhaps faith, that these practices will enable many students to become integral members of general education environments. Nevertheless, it would be unfair and disingenuous to ignore the concerns about inclusion. Clearly, inclusion engenders a wide variety of emotions. Professionals on both sides of the inclusion debate argue with both research and their hearts.

The following reporting of these concerns about inclusion as reported in the literature may seem weighty within the context of this chapter, but it remains minor within the overall context of this book. Hopefully, the tactics addressed within this book will allow more, although probably not all, students with special needs to become active members of the general education community.

Although it is important for both regular and special educators to share the responsibilities of educating learners with disabilities, many educators have expressed a pessimistic view regarding the impacts of such previous educational reforms. Algozzine, Ysseldyke, Kauffman, and Landrum (1991) expressed concern that, "Depending on how the issues are framed, the reform movement may leave students with behavior problems particularly vulnerable to neglect" (p. 10). Nevertheless, the inclusion movement is upon us. The majority of the concerns discussed in the following paragraphs relate to inclusion defined as full-time attendance in the general education setting. Remember, not all authors agree upon this definition of inclusion as fitting within the least restrictive environment. As discussed later, this particular definition of inclusion has been and continues to be open to debate.

Walker and Bullis (1991) argued against mainstreaming for the sake of mainstreaming: "Nor do we believe that mere placement in the regular classroom is in any way equivalent nor synonymous with best practice when implemented in the absence of other critical considerations such as the design and delivery of an appropriate educational program" (p. 75). In addition, they contended that "the hope that the student will progress academically and benefit socially from mere placement in a regular classroom setting will likely not be realized; in fact, the opposite set of outcomes (lack of teacher acceptance, rejection by nonhandicapped peers, and academic failure with concomitant decrements in self esteem) are far more likely" (p. 76) (see also Gresham, 1982). They further argued that the above-stated claims about the purported failure of special education are false. In fact, Walker and Bullis (1991) suggested that it is the regular education settings in public school that have failed the populations of students with learning and behavior problems. They questioned any evidence that would suggest that there have been major attitude changes of public school personnel that would call for an inclusive atmosphere (see also Pappanikou, 1979).

In refuting the notion that the regular education setting is more appropriate for the social growth of all students, research and literature have been highly suggestive that nonhandicapped peers reject students with learning and behavior problems (Konopasek, 1990; Larrivee & Horne, 1991; Roberts & Zubrick, 1993; Sarbonie, 1987). In fact, Larrivee and Horne (1991) also found that nonhandicapped students in low-reading groups were less accepted by their peers. This information, however, conflicts with research conducted by Walker and Bullis (1991), which found peer acceptance of students with learning disabilities (LD). Nevertheless, even within the LD research, conflicting results have been reported. Sale and Carey (1995) found in an inclusive school of mostly white students that those with (unlabeled) mild disabilities were still perceived in a negative manner by their peers. If "formally labeled," these students would be identified as having LD. The authors concluded that "Putting students together for 100% of the day in this school did not change how they are reported to be liked or disliked by their same-aged peers" (p. 17). These conclusions differ little from those arrived at by Gresham (1982), who called for the need to train students in the area of social skills. There is a wide gap between the ways peers accept students with learning disabilities and students with learning and behavior problems (Sarbonie, Kauffman, Ellis, Marshall, & Elksnin, 1987–1988).

Research has suggested that teachers do not like having disturbing students in their classrooms (Gable & Laycock, 1991; Landrum, 1992; Lewin, Nelson, & Tollefson, 1983). Besides the obvious reasons, classroom researchers have suggested that teachers perceive the concept of inclusion as more work; are unsure of their own abilities to teach this population; and are unsure of the possible benefits (Carter, 1991; Gersten, Walker, & Darch, 1988; Landrum, 1992). It is not surprising that teachers feel this way, as research has suggested that colleges and universities are not delivering or requiring the coursework that will inform preservice teachers to integrate students with disabilities. How can teachers have good attitudes about teaching students with learning and/or behavioral problems, if they do not know how to help them (Kearney & Durand, 1992)?

The sanctity of the regular education setting was also called into question by Gable, Hendrickson, and Rutherford (1991) who concluded, following their review of the literature, that "not all students with behavior disorders are best served in regular classroom situations" (p. 27). They also identified factors that should be situationally considered:

1. Knowledge of demands of LRE
2. Climate for collaboration
3. Level of administrative support
4. Complexity of required programming
5. Intrusiveness of required programming
6. Duration of required programming
7. Acceptability of programming demands
8. Possible side effects of programming
9. Teacher motivation
10. Student motivation (p. 28)

Each of these factors is addressed fully in Unit 1 of this book.

As mentioned earlier, one criticism of the professionals who address these concerns is that they are being protective not only of students with learning and behavior problems, but also of their own jobs. Braaten, Kauffman, Braaten, Polsgrove, and Nelson (1988) refuted this claim by suggesting that "BD [behavior disordered] students placed in regular classes present particular problems because their character-istics demand additional instructional resources, including specially trained staff to manage extremely disruptive and dangerous behavior. Other students' rights to a safe and supportive learning environment are neither minor nor moot when the assumption that nobody should be segregated forces the integration of BD students" (p. 23). Their assertion has been supported in the courts. Yell (1995a) noted the case of *Clyde K. and Sheila K. v. the Puyallup School District,* which involved the issue of the full inclusion of a student with emotional and/or behavioral problems. The school system did not want the student included because of the difficulties he would cause in the classroom. Yell noted that although most court decisions have been in favor of full inclusion, most of those cases were concerned with individuals with moderate disabilities. Again, the notion of adequate support and the effect of inclusion on the education of the individuals *or their peers* was Yell's focus of discussion. Yell contended that support is implied in the law in its provision of such help as management plans, teacher training, and behavioral aides. If these types of support do not work, then more restrictive placements must be necessary.

The implementation of wholesale (full) inclusion involves three assumptions: that the behaviors of students with learning and behav-ior problems are simply a function of being labeled as such, and when integrated with others, they will no longer have these problems; that teaching students with learning and behavior disabilities is identical to teaching regular education students; and that regular education teachers now possess the necessary skills and attitudes to teach stu-dents with learning and behavioral disabilities (Braaten et al., 1988).

It has been argued that students with learning and behavior prob-lems are an underrepresented population with regard to support and advocacy. Certainly, there is little sympathy for these individuals when they are exhibiting their disabilities. Further, no national parent support groups exist to advocate for the rights of these children. There is a concern that wholesale inclusion will result in children and youth with learning and behavior problems being suspended, expelled, pushed, or elbowed out of school.

Diamond (1993) cautioned that "If we regard inclusion as a reli-gious principle, if we disregard the differences among the students we consider disabled, if we continue to insist that the least restrictive environment is some absolute standard rather than a continuum of variability that has truth only for each individual in question, we will lose some of the most valuable and creative and lovable citizens in our community" (p. 6).

Needless to say, there is no simple answer to this complex problem. Is it true, as Lipsky and Gartner (1991) contended, that the Education for All Handicapped Children Act of 1975 was right for its time and has now assured access for all? More important, are those teachers "in the trenches" also excited about this movement? The Executive Committee of the Council for Children with Behavioral Disorders has contended that these movements are the agenda of "certain government officials and highly vocal minority of special educators and school administrators" (Council for Children with Behavioral Disorders, 1989, p. 203) (see also Kauffman & Hallahan, 1994). Certainly, the past does not suggest success with a "single system of education." Has education progressed to the point that only one system can be effective?

Special education law does not mandate these movements. It does, however, require that students must be placed in the least restrictive environment.

Inclusion: What Do We Do?

Commenting on the strength of the full inclusion movement in special education, Kauffman and Hallahan (1994) described the movement as "special education's largest bandwagon ever, one having gathered such great mass and momentum that it seems to many unstoppable" (p. ix), and as a movement whose "size, velocity, and direction have become potentially fatal not only to those on board but to the entire special education community through which it is traveling" (p. ix). Others have cautioned that the full inclusion movement lacks a scientific foundation (Kauffman, 1993) and "that it is often based on references to the 'moral and just thing to do' rather than scientifically established benefits" (Simpson & Sasso, 1992, p. 3). In this regard, Simpson and Sasso (1992) criticized the underpinning of much of the inclusion movement:

> The full inclusion debate has too often been reduced to superficial arguments over who is right, who is moral and ethical and who is a true advocate for children. Much of this simplistic posturing obscures the real issue (i.e., what is best for children) via claims of moral and ethical "high ground" and denouncements of "nonbelievers" as not

knowing what is best and not caring about children with disabilities. While perhaps effective in the short term, this process can lead to results that are directly opposite to those intended, including impediments to maximally effective programs for children and youth with autism. We are of the opinion that full inclusion . . . is the right thing to do only if it benefits students with disabilities, their normally developing peers, or (ideally) if it is beneficial for both groups. That is, "the right thing to do," in our estimation, is that which provides the most benefits, not something that someone or some group deems appropriate because it fits their value system, is congruent with a fashionable trend, or appears to be a suitable, albeit unsupported alternative. (p. 4)

Those who strongly advocate for full inclusion believe it to be the next logical step in the progression of securing appropriate services for children and youth with disabilities (Sailor, 1991; S. Stainback & W. Stainback, 1992). In this regard, advocates of integration and inclusion have observed that service provision outside general education has been associated with discontinuity in instruction (Wang, Reynolds, & Walberg, 1986), reduction of curricular options for students with exceptionalities (W. Stainback & S. Stainback, 1984), and impediments to children and youth with disabilities in gaining skills and knowledge that facilitate their full-time reentry into general education (Sailor et al., 1989). By-products of pull-out and other segregated programs purportedly include self-concept and self-esteem problems for students with disabilities (H. Rogers & Saklofske, 1985); impaired social skills (Madden & Slavin, 1983); and lack of preparation for adulthood, as evidenced by a high rate of unemployment among persons with disabilities (Reynolds, Wang, & Walberg, 1987; Will, 1984).

One bellwether of public opinion is the Gallup Poll. A recent poll examined the attitudes of parents toward inclusion (Elam & Rose, 1995). Interestingly, their comments reflect the desire for the status quo with regard to current practices. In fact, if anything, parents believe that the federal government's role in providing services to those students with disabilities should be increased when compared with the responses of parents polled in 1977. Further, parents of non–public school children had similar beliefs about federal government involvement. The results to four questions posed by Elam and Rose are provided in Table 1.1. The results of these questions also reflect another belief. There are different opinions regarding inclusion, different, real, honest opinions that can be turned and twisted to support or deny the inclusion movement.

TABLE 1.1
Results of Survey of Parents' Attitudes Toward Inclusion
(Given as Percentages of Respondents)

	Survey Group			
	National	No Children in School	Public School Parents	Non–Public School Parents
Response	1995 1977	1995 1977	1995 1977	1995 1977

1. Services for physically and mentally handicapped students cost more than regular school services. When the local schools are required to provide these special services by the federal government, should the federal government pay the extra cost, or not?

Yes should	84	82	82	80	89	85	89	84
No should not	12	11	14	12	9	9	10	14
Don't know	4	7	4	8	2	6	1	2

2. In your opinion, should children with learning problems be put in the same classes with other students, or should they be put in special classes of their own?

Yes same	26	—	25	—	29	—	25	—
No special	66	—	68	—	62	—	66	—
Don't know	8	—	7	—	9	—	9	—

3. Do you think that including children with learning problems in the same classrooms with other students would have a powerful effect on the other students, a negative effect, or would it not make much of a difference?

Positive effect	23	—	21	—	25	—	26	—
Negative effect	37	—	38	—	35	—	39	—
Little difference	36	—	37	—	35	—	34	—
Don't know	4	—	4	—	5	—	1	—

4. How about children with learning problems themselves? Do you think including them in classes with other students would have a positive effect on the children with learning problems, a negative effect, or would it not make much difference?

Positive effect	38	—	35	—	44	—	42	—
Negative effect	40	—	43	—	35	—	43	—
Little difference	17	—	17	—	16	—	11	—
Don't know	5	—	5	—	5	—	4	—

Note. From "Of the Public's Attitude Toward the Public Schools," by S. M. Elam and L. C. Rose, 1995, *Phi Delta Kappan, 77,* pp. 41–56.

The contributors of this book are of the strong professional opinion that imprudent placement of all students with disabilities in general education settings is inappropriate. However, we believe that many children and youth with disabilities may be successfully assigned to general education settings, given the right conditions. Before embarking on a discussion of how to facilitate appropriate inclusion of students with disabilities, it is important that the issue of terminology be addressed. We are of the opinion that dialogue related to inclusion and integration will be productive only insofar as individuals with an interest in these topics have a shared understanding of basic terminology. Accordingly, I present a brief discussion of major terms associated with the debate and movement. Once common ground is attained in understanding inclusion-related terminology, it is possible to discuss how to facilitate the education of children and youth with disabilities in general education settings.

Basic Terminology

A major issue associated with the inclusion debate relates to the variations in terminology used by professionals and parents. For example, a workshop recently attended by one of the authors involved presentation of a "full inclusion model," which nevertheless excluded students with behavior disorders and severe disabilities and consisted of having all students in the program spend at least 2 hours daily in a special education resource room.

An additional lexical problem is that leaders on the subject of inclusion have, in some instances, radically altered their integration and inclusionary positions over time, without altering their use of terminology. For example, in the mid-1980s W. Stainback and S. Stainback (1984) recommended that inclusion of students with disabilities in general education classrooms should be encouraged; however, they noted that "students would still need to be grouped, in some instances into specific courses or classes according to their instructional needs" (p. 108). In a later writing, these same authors reversed their earlier moderate position, noting that "an inclusive school or classroom educates all students in the mainstream" (S. Stainback & W. Stainback, 1992, p. 34).

For the purposes of this text, contributors will be referring to or basing comments on five basic terms: least restrictive environment, regular education initiative, integration, mainstreaming, and inclusion. Clarification of these terms is needed to correctly comprehend the book's content, as well as to fully understand the current inclusion debate.

The *least restrictive environment* (LRE) component of the Individuals with Disabilities Education Act (IDEA, 1990) requires that children and youth with disabilities be educated along with students who do not have disabilities to the maximum extent *appropriate*. IDEA requires that placement decisions relating to students with disabilities begin with a consideration that the child or youth be educated in a general classroom setting. If the team commissioned to make a placement decision for a student with a disability believes that the student cannot be satisfactorily placed in a regular classroom, that team may recommend an alternative setting, selected from a continuum of alternative placements. However, even these alternatives should provide for contact with peers without disabilities, to the maximum extent appropriate. The most significant element of the least restrictive environment concept is that it must include a range of services and environmental alternatives capable of meeting students' individual needs. Thus, LRE does not mean that all students with disabilities will receive their education in a general education classroom, even though there is a preference (whenever appropriate) for general education classrooms.

The term *regular education initiative* (REI), often used in the 1980s (Reynolds et al., 1987), directly preceded the inclusionary movement. REI proponents challenged the assumption that general and special education programs should be independent. Accordingly, the REI movement advocated for the creation of a single educational system capable of responding to all students' needs. Indeed, a basic element of the REI movement was that the existence of separate general education and special education systems created barriers to effectively responding to the needs of students with disabilities. These purported barriers were also thought to be the reason that educational systems were unable to accommodate students without disabilities who were experiencing educational problems.

With reference to inclusion, *integration* is a general term referring to placement of students with disabilities in settings attended by their peers without disabilities. Integration and inclusion are not synonymous terms. Integration often refers to contact between disabled and nondisabled groups in other than shared classroom activities. For instance, integration may refer to shared experiences in a lunch room, hallway, or school commons area that occur between general education students and students with disabilities who are assigned to a self-contained special education classroom. This definition of integration is the most commonly understood. What needs to be addressed is that integration—that is, "bringing together as a whole"—occurs only when deliberate attempts are made by teachers to have students engage in social and/or academic interactions with nondisabled peers. For example, a student with mental retardation is in a self-contained class of students with emotional and/or behavioral disorders who eat lunch together, at their own table, with general education peers surrounding them. This is not integration. Simply occupying the same physical space is not integration.

Mainstreaming is a term that is commonly used when considering placements of students with disabilities in general education settings. It frequently has been used to refer to the selective placement of students with disabilities in one or more general education classes. However, in many instances the placement of these students has not been selective. In fact, driven by a social reform mentality or perhaps the relieving of the economic burden of financing special education, educators have often placed students with little, if any, support in general education. When attempted with the best intentions, mainstreaming has as an underlying assumption that students with disabilities should generally have the necessary knowledge and skills to benefit from the general education curriculum. Thus, with individualization and adaptation, students who are mainstreamed are thought to be able to progress with their nondisabled peers in regular classroom settings.

Inclusion refers to a commitment to educate children and youth with disabilities in general education classrooms, to the maximum extent possible. Inclusion involves transporting support services to students in general classrooms, as opposed to pulling students out for services. Moreover, unlike mainstreaming, inclusion requires only that students profit from being in a general education classroom (e.g., social benefits are accrued), and not that they must compete with their nondisabled peers. Inclusion can be full or selective.

Full inclusion is built on several basic principles. First, and most important, full inclusion is designed to accommodate all students with disabilities in general education classrooms (it is a "zero reject" model). Second, children and youth in full inclusion programs receive their education at the same attendance center as other same-age students in their neighborhood. Third, students with disabilities are placed in general education classrooms at a rate consistent with disability incidence statistics. That is, no more than one to three students with disabilities are in any one general education classroom. Fourth, students with disabilities receive their education alongside their chronological-age classmates. Fifth, regular classroom teachers and other general education personnel assume primary responsibility for educating students with disabilities; and special education personnel and related services staff (e.g., speech–language specialists, physical therapists) support these regular education personnel. Finally, general education experiences are designed to develop and enhance peer relationships and to enhance social development, regardless of each individual's ability and overall intellectual functioning.

Selective inclusion, on the other hand, is a term used to refer to partial general education class placement of students with disabilities (i.e., some students some of the time). The assumptions of selective inclusion are that the general education placement is not appropriate for all students with disabilities; that inclusion is only one option on the continuum of services; that inclusionary program options may not be available at every attendance center; that some students with disabilities may benefit from receiving at least a portion of their instructional services from special education and related services personnel; and that multidisciplinary IEP teams determine the extent to general education placement of students with disabilities. To determine if a student is to be included, educators should try to address the following questions:

- What are the reasons that the student cannot be provided his or her educational program in the general education classroom?

- What supplementary aids and services are needed to support the student in the special education setting?

- Why can these aids and services not be provided in the general education classroom?

- What is the continuum of alternate placements available to these students?

A Few Steps Forward

As previously discussed, the early results of inclusion are clearly inconclusive. Although anecdotal reports seem positive, actual classroom research has been unequivocal. Zigmond and Baker (1995) visited six schools in five states and concluded that students with learning disabilities who were fully included in regular education classrooms were not being adequately served. They contended that for many schools inclusion is about placement and not instruction. They do not believe that inclusive placements, by themselves, are going to provide equal opportunities for students with learning disabilities. It is important to note that these authors found that many changes have occurred: "In Kansas, teachers had developed thematic units that integrated reading, language arts, science, and social studies instruction. In spite of these changes, though, we did not see evidence of practices that truly addressed individual student needs" (p. 246). They concluded that "special education for students with LD will, in the future need *more* resources, not fewer" (p. 247), and that "in most cases, current reform of special education into full inclusion deprived the students with Individualized Education Programs of the *special* services to which they were entitled by law" (p. 250). I agree wholeheartedly that individuals with disabilities need to be situated in an academically and affectively barrier-free environment and am discouraged by those who argue that the affective domain is the only area that needs to be addressed. We need to care about both the affective and cognitive domains to consider inclusion a success. Yet, I also admit to being extremely encouraged by Zigmond and Baker's findings that general education teachers were implementing many of the "best practices" that have been found to be effective in reaching more students (many of which are found in this book).

As you read this book, consider the variables that constitute a viable inclusion program. Peruse and use the chapters that will help you answer these questions. Ask yourself if the following questions, as listed by J. Rogers (1993), need to be addressed in your school:

1. Do we genuinely start from the premise that each child belongs in the classroom he or she would otherwise attend if not disabled (or do we cluster children with disabilities into special groups, classrooms, or schools)?

2. Do we individualize the instructional program for all the children whether or not they are disabled and provide the resources that each child needs to explore individual interests in the school environment (or do we tend to provide the same sorts of services for most children who share the same diagnostic label)?

3. Are we fully committed to maintenance of a caring community that fosters mutual respect and support among staff, parents, and students in which we honestly believe that nondisabled

children can benefit from friendships with disabled children and disabled children can benefit from friendships with nondisabled children (or do our practices tacitly tolerate children teasing or isolating some as outcasts)?

4. Have our general educators and special educators integrated their efforts and their resources so that they work together as integral parts of a unified team (or are they isolated in separate rooms or departments with separate supervisors and budgets)?

5. Does our administration create a work climate in which staff are supported as they provide assistance to each other (or are teachers afraid of being presumed to be incompetent if they seek peer collaboration in working with students)?

6. Do we actively encourage the full participation of children with disabilities in the life of our school including co-curricular and extracurricular activities (or do they participate only in the academic portion of the school day)?

7. Are we prepared to alter support systems for students as their needs change through the school year so that they can achieve, experience successes, and feel that they genuinely belong in their school and classes (or do we sometimes provide such limited services to them that the children are set up to fail)?

8. Do we make parents of children with disabilities fully a part of our school community so they can experience a sense of belonging (or do we give them a separate PTA and different newsletters)?

9. Do we give children with disabilities just as much of the full school curriculum as they can master and modify it as necessary so that they can share elements of these experiences with their classmates (or do we have a separate curriculum for children with disabilities)?

10. Have we included children with disabilities supportively in as many as possible of the same testing and evaluation experiences as their nondisabled peers?

Each of these factors needs to be fully operationalized. For example, regarding number 3, the differentiating between accepting and respecting differences needs to be explored. To implement this, ask parents in your community how their needs would best be met. Perhaps receiving/attending general education news/events is as important as having a source of support within their realm of meeting their children's unique needs. Or number 4 may not (should not?) imply that all children need to be asked or expected to learn from the same resources. For example, in high school, not all students will experience a long-term benefit from the core curriculum. They may need intensive reading, math, or social skills instruction.

Conclusion and Overview of Book

Earlier in this chapter, many of the questions asked of NICHCY were offered. Through a careful review of the literature, this agency concluded that for inclusion to be successful the following components must be demonstrated: a philosophy that supports appropriate inclusionary practice; extensive planning; involvement of the principal as a change agent; involvement of parents; development of disability awareness of staff and students; training for staff; provision of adequate support; structure and support for collaboration; a planning team for each included student; implementation of adaptations; and policies and methods for evaluation of student progress and for the entire inclusion program. The basic principles of inclusion are too important to be minimized as a fad or bandwagon. Clearly there are concerns that need to be addressed.

I remember hearing many lecturers claim that good special education is good general education. Clearly, one does not need to have a special education endorsement or certification to learn and teach these methods. I also remember hearing that students with mild handicaps can learn in a similar manner and that many of these students learn in a manner similar to those who are "lower achieving." It seems that the message inherent to these lecturers is that it is now time for educators to stop the bickering and devote time and energy to practicing interventions—that is, to do something. The purpose of this text is to contribute to this process.

The remainder of Unit 1, Perspectives and Experiences, is an examination of the administrative considerations of inclusion. In Chapter 2, Jo Webber outlines the key components for success in this endeavor. Jo highlights the concept of *responsible* inclusion. Responsible inclusion means that educators have to consider both the ideals of inclusion and the realities of their environment. The critical premise of this concept is that the development and implementation of a philosophy of inclusion and the delineation of the roles that all individuals will undertake is prerequisite to any success. These factors, coupled with the main goal of delivering a sound educational program, should enhance any inclusion program.

It goes without saying that the most important factor integral to any inclusion effort is the building of collaboration teams. In Chapter 3, Nancy Mundschenk and Regina Foley provide the step-by-step process that will allow the development and maintenance of teams. Nancy and Regina have been involved in an inclusion project in East Saint Louis and share how they are attempting to deal with many of the problems that we see in the literature.

The authors of Chapters 4 and 5 outline their inclusion efforts, providing specific ideas about how to implement inclusion with and without support from colleagues and administrators. In Chapter 4, Lisa Matts and Paul Zionts describe how to overcome and in some cases ignore obstacles. It seems that many educators are reluctant to implement new ideas until "everyone is on board." The philosophy presented in Chapter 4 is that if one person believes in inclusion, then important progress can be made. The authors provide specific techniques and personal anecdotes regarding successes and failures.

In Chapter 5, Jennifer Gildner and Laura Zionts provide a wide variety of activities that have proven successful. Their approach is less political than that in Chapter 4; their message is that the more activities the teacher attempts, the greater the opportunity for one or more of them to succeed.

In Chapter 6, Sandra Keenan presents the administrator's perspective of inclusion. Sandra discusses the initiation of inclusion programming in Westerly, Rhode Island, and the specific tactics that she employed to successfully implement a model inclusion program. Her story is rags to riches. She was involved with a school system that was fraught with noncompliance issues 7 years ago, but has evolved into one that is currently viewed as having a model program. She asserts that the inclusion efforts in her town were reflective of major changes within the system, not only in the area of special education.

It is imperative that the perspectives of the consumers—that is, the students and their parents—be understood as inclusion efforts are attempted. Chapters 7 and 8 present, respectively, first-person experiences from Timothy and Nancy Hartshorne, parents of a student with a disability, and Mark Tovar, a student with a disability. Their stories and their advice to educators must be considered.

Unit 2, Best Practices, is a more formal presentation of the strategies that facilitate inclusion. In Chapter 9, Richard Simpson, Brenda Smith Myles, and Janice DePalma Simpson discuss behavioral and classroom management strategies to be used in general education set-tings. The authors describe staff roles, as well as specific strategies to implement in the general education setting. They stress that imple-mentation of these tactics can be accomplished only with an under-standing of how the physical environment must be considered in order to prevent maladaptive behaviors from occurring and in order to encourage a positive learning environment. Simple and easy to use techniques are provided for the classroom teacher.

Many of the classroom management strategies presented can be effective for group instruction. Nevertheless, there will be occasions when individualization will be needed. For specific remediation to occur, a careful assessment must take place. In Chapter 10, Gary Sasso, Linda Garrison Harrell, and Jane Doelling describe the process of functional assessment and its subsequent treatment. Proper functional assessment suggests that there is a purpose behind the behavior exhibited by students, and when that purpose is under-stood, appropriate interventions can follow. While this relationship would seem obvious to the reader, its practice is rare. The authors provide an easy to follow, step-by-step process and practical treat-ment suggestions.

In Chapter 11, John Maag offers an insightful and sometimes humorous approach to managing those students who are described as resistant. While the more overt occurrences of behavior certainly receive (and deserve) attention, resistant students may be the more frequent cause of teacher and student stress. These oppositional behaviors can break the spirit of even the most optimistic and dedi-cated teachers. John provides the suggestions and techniques neces-sary to allow teachers to combat these troublesome problems.

Simply removing inappropriate behaviors will not prepare many students for their inclusion into general education settings. These students may never have developed the emotional and/or behav-ioral repertoire to succeed with others. In Chapter 12, Linda Garrison Harrell, Jane Doelling, and Gary Sasso explain social interaction interventions that can be used to effectively teach students. These strategies—cooperative learning and peer networking—better enable students with behavior and learning problems to interact in a posi-tive manner with their general education peers.

The importance and, more important, the application of facilitat-ing academic instruction for students in all settings are discussed by Christine Ormsbee, Sharon Maroney, and Linda Meloy in Chapter 13. The techniques presented demonstrate a clear message:

Learning academic subject matter is crucial and may be attained by modifying the manner in which educators teach. Most of the strategies in their chapter may be utilized in any classroom environment.

When one speaks of the context of inclusion among educators, the bringing together of those with and without disabilities is brought to mind. In Chapter 14, Laura Zionts and Pamela Baker examine the realities of teaching in many classrooms today. They suggest that any discussion of inclusion must include all students who are different, that is, diverse. Diversity is the consideration of not only disability, but also color, socioeconomic status, culture, and language. The authors detail many activities and references that promote both social and academic growth that can be used in the classroom for the purpose of teaching students with differences.

In Chapter 15, Pamela Pruitt describes the philosophy and techniques necessary to include preschool students with disabilities both socially and (pre)academically. Following the theme presented throughout this book, Pam firmly asserts her belief that inclusion can be achieved only through the careful planning of activities designed to bring students together as a community.

References

Algozzine, B., Ysseldyke, J. E., Kauffman, J. M., & Landrum, T. J. (1991). Implications of school reform in the 1990s for teachers of students with behavior problems. *Preventing School Failure, 35*, 6–10.

Braaten, S., Kauffman, J. M., Braaten, B., Polsgrove, L., & Nelson, C. M. (1988). The regular education initiative: Patent medicine for behavior disorders. *Behavioral Disorders, 55*, 21–27.

Carlberg, C., & Kavale, K. (1980). The efficacy of special class versus regular class placement for exceptional children: A metaanalysis. *The Journal of Special Education, 14*, 295–309.

Carter, J. F. (1991). REI: What regular educators are saying. In R. B. Rutherford, Jr., S. A. DiGangi, & S. R. Mathur (Eds.), *Severe behavior disorders of children and youth* (Vol. 14, pp. 11–17). Reston, VA: Council for Children with Behavioral Disorders.

Council for Children with Behavioral Disorders. (1989). *A proposed definition and terminology to replace "serious emotional disturbance" in Education of Handicapped Act.* Reston, VA: Author.

Diamond, S. C. (1993). Special education and the great God, inclusion. *Beyond Behavior, 4*, 3–6.

Education for All Handicapped Children Act of 1975, 20 U.S.C. §1400 *et seq.*

Elam, S. M., & Rose, L. C. (1995). Of the public's attitudes toward the public schools. *Phi Delta Kappan, 77,* 41–56.

Gable, R. A., Hendrickson, J. M., & Rutherford, R. B., Jr. (1991). Strategies for integrating students with behavioral disorders into general education. In R. B. Rutherford, Jr., S. A. DiGangi, & S. R. Mathur (Eds.), *Severe behavior disorders of children and youth* (Vol. 14, pp. 18–32). Reston, VA: Council for Children with Behavioral Disorders.

Gable, R. A., & Laycock, V. K. (1991). Regular classroom integration of adolescents with emotional/behavioral disorders in perspective. In S. L. Braaten & E. Wild (Eds.), *Programming for adolescents with behavior disorders* (Vol. 5, pp. 1–19). Reston, VA: Council for Children with Behavioral Disorders.

Gersten, R., Walker, H., & Darch, C. (1988). Relationship between teacher's effectiveness and their tolerance of handicapped students. *Exceptional Children, 54,* 433–438.

Gresham, F. M. (1982). Misguided mainstreaming: The case for social skills training with handicapped children. *Exceptional Children, 48,* 422–433.

Individuals with Disabilities Education Act of 1990, 20 U.S.C. §1400 *et seq.*

Kauffman, J. M. (1993). How we might achieve radical reform of special education. *Exceptional Children, 60,* 6–16.

Kauffman, J. M., & Hallahan, D. P. (1994). Preface. In J. M. Kauffman & D. P. Hallahan (Eds.), *The illusion of full inclusion* (pp. ix–xi). Austin, TX: PRO-ED.

Kearney, C. A., & Durand, V. M. (1992). How prepared are our teachers for mainstreamed classroom settings? A survey of postsecondary schools of education in New York State. *Exceptional Children, 59,* 6–11.

Konopasek, D. E. (1990). Priests on my shoulder. In R. B. Rutherford, Jr., & S. A. DiGangi (Eds.), *Severe behavior disorders of children and youth* (Vol. 13, pp. 11–17). Reston, VA: Council for Children with Behavioral Disorders.

Landrum, T. J. (1992). Teachers as victims: An interactional analysis of the teacher's role in educating atypical learners. *Behavioral Disorders, 17,* 135–144.

Larrivee, B., & Horne, M. D. (1991). Social status: A comparison of mainstreamed students with peers of different ability levels. *The Journal of Special Education, 25,* 90–101.

Lewin, P., Nelson, R. E., & Tollefson, N. (1983). Teacher attitudes toward disruptive students. *Elementary School Guidance and Counseling, 17,* 188–193.

Lipsky, D. K., & Gartner, A. (1991). Restructuring for quality. In J. W. Lloyd, N. N. Singh, & A. C. Repp (Eds.), *The regular education initiative: Alternative perspectives on concepts, issues, and models* (pp. 43–56). Sycamore, IL: Sycamore.

Madden, N. A., & Slavin, R. E. (1983). Mainstreaming students with mild handicaps: Academic and social outcomes. *Review of Educational Research, 53,* 519–569.

NICHCY News Digest (Special Issue). (1995). 5(1).

Osborne, A. G., Jr., & DiMattia, P. (1994). The IDEA's least restrictive environment mandate: Legal implications. *Exceptional Children, 61,* 6–14.

Pappanikou, A. J. (1979). Mainstreaming. *Teacher Education and Special Education, 2*, 51–55.

Reynolds, M. C. (1990). Noncategorical special education. In M. C. Wang, M. C. Reynolds, & H. J. Walberg (Eds.), *Special education: Research and practice: Synthesis of findings* (pp. 57–80). Oxford, England: Pergamon.

Reynolds, M. C., Wang, M. C., & Walberg, H. J. (1987). The necessary restructuring of special and regular education. *Exceptional Children, 53*, 391–398.

Reynolds, M. C., Wang, M. C., & Walberg, H. J. (1992). The knowledge bases for special and general education. *Remedial and Special Education, 13*(5), 33–43.

Roberts, C., & Zubrick, S. (1993). Factors influencing the social status of children with mild academic disabilities in regular classrooms. *Exceptional Children, 59*, 192–202.

Rogers, H., & Saklofske, D. H. (1985). Self-concepts, locus of control and performance expectations of learning disabled children. *Journal of Learning Disabilities, 18*, 273–278.

Rogers, J. (1993). The inclusion revolution. *Research Bulletin* (issue 11), 1–6.

Safran, J. S., & Safran, S. P. (1987). Teachers' judgments of problem behaviors. *Exceptional Children, 54*, 240–244.

Sailor, W. (1991). Special education in the restructured school. *Remedial and Special Education, 12*(6), 8–22.

Sailor, W., Anderson, J., Halvorsen, A. T., Doering, K., Filler, J., & Goetz, L. (1989). *The comprehensive local school: Regular education for all students with disabilities.* Baltimore: Brookes.

Sale, P., & Carey, D. M. (1995). The socioeconomic status of students with disabilities in a full-inclusion school. *Exceptional Children, 62*, 6–19.

Sarbonie, E. J. (1987). Bi-directional social status of behaviorally disordered and nonhandicapped elementary school pupils. *Behavioral Disorders, 13*, 45–57.

Sarbonie, E. J., Kauffman, J. M., Ellis, E. S., Marshal, K. J., & Elksnin, L. K. (1987–1988). Bi-directional and cross-categorical social status of learning disabled, behaviorally disordered and nonhandicapped adolescents. *The Journal of Special Education, 21*, 39–56.

Simpson, R. L., & Sasso, G. M. (1992). Full inclusion of students with autism in general education settings: Values versus science. *Focus on Autistic Behavior, 7*(3), 1–13.

Stainback, S., & Stainback, W. (1988). Educating severe disabilities in regular classes. *Teaching Exceptional Children, 21*, 16–19.

Stainback, S., & Stainback, W. (1992). *Curriculum considerations in inclusive classrooms: Facilitating learning for all students.* Baltimore: Brookes.

Stainback, S., Stainback, W., & Ayres, B. (1996). Schools are inclusive communities. In W. Stainback & S. Stainback (Eds.), *Controversial issues confronting special education* (2nd ed., pp. 31–43). Needham Heights: MA: Allyn & Bacon.

Stainback, W., & Stainback, S. (1984). A rationale for the merger of special and regular education. *Exceptional Children, 51*, 102–111.

Walker, H. M., & Bullis, M. (1991). Behavior disorders and the social context of regular class integration: A conceptual dilemma? In J. W. Lloyd, N. N. Singh, & A. C. Repp (Eds.), *The regular education initiative: Alternative perspectives on concepts, issues, and models* (pp. 75–93). Sycamore, IL: Sycamore.

Wang, M. (1989). Accommodating student diversity through adaptive instruction. In S. Stainback & W. Stainback (Eds.), *Educating all students in the mainstream of regular education* (pp. 183–197). Baltimore: Brookes.

Wang, M. C., Reynolds, M. C., & Walberg, H. J. (1986). Rethinking special education. *Educational Leadership, 44,* 26–31.

Will, M. (1984). Let us pause and reflect—But not for long. *Exceptional Children, 51,* 11–16.

Yell, M. L. (1995a). Clyde K. and Sheila K. v. Puyallup School District: The courts, inclusion, and students with behavioral disorders. *Behavioral Disorders, 20,* 179–189.

Yell, M. L. (1995b). Least restrictive environment, inclusion, and students with disabilities: A legal analysis. *The Journal of Special Education, 28,* 389–404.

Zigmond, N., & Baker, J. M. (1995). Concluding comments: Current and future practices in inclusive schooling. *The Journal of Special Education, 29,* 245–250.

CHAPTER 2

Responsible Inclusion: Key Components for Success

Jo Webber

T he practice of integrating special education students into general education classrooms, known as inclusion, has caused much controversy. The practice has appeared in federal mandates and has been espoused by zealous advocates. On the other hand, many educators and parents oppose the practice as a matter of policy. The practice is especially controversial when applied to students with emotional or behavioral disorders who have the potential of becoming aggressive and/or noncompliant. To assure that students are educated in places best suited for their educational progress, integration decisions must be made in a responsible manner. In this chapter I review the forces behind the practice of inclusion, discuss historical implications for integration programs and current roadblocks to their success, and delineate a planning process and decision points for use by school personnel. If school personnel understand the concept of inclusion and prepare inclusion programs in a responsible manner, then it is very likely that all special education students will be served appropriately.

A Historical Perspective

The current inclusion movement is one of several integration efforts instigated on behalf of students with disabilities since the early 1970s.

The first notable movement resulted in the federal law, currently called the Individuals with Disabilities Act of 1991 (IDEA), which states that students with disabilities will be pulled out of a general education classroom only when their education cannot be achieved satisfactorily in that classroom, even with special services and aids. Advocates for students with disabilities were instrumental in conceptualizing this law, and they promoted the subsequent "mainstreaming" movement. This movement included massive training of general education teachers, special education teachers, and parents. States and local school districts assured a full continuum of services for students with disabilities and guaranteed Individualized Education Programs (IEPs).

Despite this cogent effort by special educators in the late 1970s, general educators were not ready to accept ownership of students with disabilities; they saw no incentive for struggling to educate them; and they generally viewed special education as a place to send students who were not progressing in their classrooms (Bradfield, Brown, Kaplan, Rickert, & Stannard, 1973; Webber, Henderson, & Seifert, 1993). Meanwhile, special educators established a separate system with differential teacher training and certification standards. Pull-out programs for students with disabilities became commonplace. In the mid-1980s, yet another integration movement occurred. This movement, again from the special education ranks, was on behalf of those students with mild and moderate disabilities who were spending much of the school day in special education classrooms. The movement was known as the regular education initiative (REI) (Reynolds, Wang, & Walberg, 1987). It was pointed out that students with mild and moderate disabilities were not making adequate academic progress in special education settings, and that mainstreaming had not worked. Proponents recommended funneling special education funds to general education, providing general education teachers with training in adaptive techniques, and changing the special educator's role to that of a consultant. In this way, they said, students with mild and moderate disabilities would improve their academic achievement.

Many special educators were skeptical that a system (general education) which had already failed to educate these students could, or would, do so at this point, and argued that mainstreaming had not totally failed (Davis, 1989). In any case, general educators were still not ready to adopt a new philosophy of integration and little change occurred as a result. In fact, general educators had yet to be included in any meaningful dialogue about goals for students with disabilities.

Currently, another special education integration movement is under way. This movement, known as full inclusion, is not as clear as previous attempts in terms of goals, justification, terminology, or accountability. The full inclusion movement was initiated by special education advocates who represent individuals with severe disabilities (i.e., The Association for Severe Handicaps, The Association for Retarded Citizens). They are pushing for full integration of special and general education. These advocates state that *all* students with disabilities will benefit socially (they seldom mention academic achievement) from full immersion into general education if provided with appropriate support services (Stainback & Stainback, 1991). Their zealous philosophy has been criticized because of their apparent disregard of the IDEA mandates to individualize educational decisions (including placement) and their rather arrogant "one-place-fits-all" view (Kauffman, 1993). The result has been the widespread "dumping" of special education students into general education classrooms and, in many cases, a reduction in the continuum of special education services (Smelter, Rasch, & Yudewitz, 1994; Baines, Baines, & Masterson, 1994).

To further complicate matters, general education is in the midst of its own reform movement. Fortunately for special educators, this movement is based on a broad view of who should be educated and a comprehensive definition of education. Furthermore, reformers are advocating educational strategies that had been recommended by special education during their mainstreaming and REI periods (e.g., cooperative learning, multimodal presentations, multilevel instruction, peer assistance, performance assessment) (Association for Supervision and Curriculum Development, 1994). This general education reform movement is often referred to as the "inclusive schools" movement. It appears that, in their attempt to educate the wide variety of students now attending public schools, general educators might finally be ready to participate in the responsible integration of students with disabilities.

Historical Implications

Special education's reform history provides useful information regarding the integration of students with disabilities. For example, it has become clear that mandating integration has not worked. Additionally, the assumptions that general education practices would change for a few students and that general education curriculum is appropriate for all students have not been validated. Furthermore, short-term inservice training has not resulted in highly trained teachers, and accountability for all students learning what they need to learn has been lacking. Using this knowledge of what has failed in the past can assist us in the present. The following paragraphs offer some general suggestions for avoiding ineffective practices and for facilitating successful integration activities.

1. *Reform curricula.* If general educators are to "own" students with disabilities, it is imperative that they buy into a philosophy of "education for all" and a broader view of public education goals than merely the transmittal of subject matter content. Public education should also include the development of cognitive processes (e.g., problem solving) and a curriculum of self-actualization (e.g., reaching one's full potential).

2. *Collaborate rather than mandate.* History shows that dictating, mandating, and demanding that integration occur have not worked well. A better strategy might be for special educators to join general education in school reform, for special educators to share their expertise for working with difficult students, and for special educators to preserve and develop various instructional options for all students. It would be wise to move cautiously and thoughtfully in order to finally operationalize IDEA in the manner in which it was intended. This may also mean resisting zealous reformers and continuing to advocate for individual students.

3. *Clarify integration goals.* Special educators need to be very clear about why integration is best for students with disabilities. In many instances, integration has become the goal—the curriculum, as it were. Perhaps integration is merely one strategy for achieving individual academic, social, cognitive, and mental health goals. If students are placed in general education classrooms only for social development reasons, it is important to impart this information to the general education teacher. Teachers who think they are to teach the core curriculum to individuals who are not ready to learn it might become easily frustrated and give up. If, on the other hand, teachers understand that academic achievement is not the primary goal, they may be willing to arrange various opportunities to encourage social development and, subsequently, feel more successful and keep trying.

4. *Redefine educators' roles.* If the goal for special education students in general education classrooms is academic achievement, then special educators must give up their own classrooms and become

strategy and behavior management specialists in order to assist general educators in their task. Most special education students with mild and moderate disabilities have already failed to learn academics in general education classrooms. This means that special educators not only need to overcome a history of failure but also need to assist general educators in reconceptualizing the way schools do business. This would best be done through a consultation and collaboration model (Idol & West, 1991). This collaborative process also implies that special educators have, themselves, mastered effective instructional methods, curriculum development, strategy adaptations, behavior management techniques, and crisis management. Unfortunately, this is not always the case.

5. _Match preparation and training to the job_. Another implication of this historical perspective for special educators has to do with training. For integration efforts to be successful, administrators and general education personnel need information regarding student characteristics, effective instructional and behavior management strategies, consultation skills, and individualized instruction. The original mainstreaming and REI literature is replete with training models for preparing general educators for the integration of students with disabilities (e.g., Meyen, Vergason, & Whelan, 1975). We need to dust off these training packages and adapt them for the 1990s. We need also to consider preservice training that produces "special" general educators, maybe in the form of dual certification programs. Additionally, special educators need to be trained as "experts." Many university programs have watered down their teacher preparation curricula in order to create "generic" special educators, resulting in fewer specialists. The collaborative models recommended for inclusion campuses assume a partnership between special education and general education. When special educators fail to offer specialized expertise, they run the risk of being relegated as glorified teaching assistants.

6. _Define "success."_ The final implication is one of accountability. IDEA mandates an individualized, appropriate education for students with disabilities. In order to assure this, educators must document each student's progress. Special education students who are not making progress in general education classrooms may need alternative programming. Special education has provided many students with effective programs since its inception. It would be best not to "throw out the baby with the bathwater" in this latest integration movement. Educators need to continue doing those things that work

and engage in ongoing evaluation activities to assure each student's progress. The first step to assuring accountability for special education programming is to establish clear curricular goals for each student for which progress can be measured and documented. Indeed, curriculum concerns have presented and will continue to present one of the most formidable obstacles to successful integration.

The Curriculum Roadblock

For the purposes of this discussion, curriculum is defined as "what the student needs to learn." Curriculum, usually in the form of goals and objectives, should drive all other educational decisions for students. Educators clearly need delineated goals and objectives before commencing any discussion about placement, instructional strategies, materials, or personnel allocation. Part of the reason why curriculum is so important to integration is that special educators have adopted integration as a goal—that is, part of the curriculum (Pugach & Warger, 1993). As a result, special educators have concentrated on strategies to mainstream students while ignoring mastery of the core academic curriculum. Failing to master the general education core curriculum probably has been the most common reason for referral to special education. General education, with its lockstep structure of graded schools and its standardized assessment and curricula, has resulted in a system for sorting and tracking students who cannot keep up. Thus, special education students, by definition, have been "pulled out" of general education because they cannot master the designated academic goals. Historically, special educators who chose alternate curricula, or who watered down the core curricula by eliminating some content or by spending less time teaching it, have found it very difficult to mainstream their students. This will continue to be the case. Pugach and Warger (1993) stated that true integration will work only when general educators reform their curricula to include goals for reaching autonomy, mastering social competence, and developing lifelong learning strategies. These authors maintain that if all children are to be educated in this country, curricula need to become more humanized and accessible to a diverse population. Until educators reform the standard curriculum, integrating special education students into general education classrooms might continue to result in students' failure to master what their peers can achieve (particularly at the secondary level), to learn important "life skills" material, and to experience appropriate social interaction (since general educators find the core curriculum most efficiently taught through direct instruction, teacher-driven methodologies).

The current core academic curriculum should be open to inspection and question. Why do all children in the United States need to learn geometry? Does mastery of the core curriculum correlate with good citizenship and adult contentment? Should there be even higher standards set on seemingly outdated and irrelevant content? If general education continues to grasp a "back to basics" view of curriculum, it will become increasingly difficult to integrate those students who either do not need to learn that material or cannot master it at the traditional pace. Thus, key curricular questions to be considered in an integration model are as follows: "What are reasonable educational goals for students designated as requiring special education? . . . Should these goals differ from those set for non–special education students in the mainstream?" (Pugach & Warger, 1993, p. 126). Under what conditions will the student best master the designated goals?

To answer these questions, school personnel might consider what they view as important for students to learn. Should students be taught cognitive strategies (e.g., organization, study strategies, thinking strategies) that can be applied to any type of content? Or might it be more important to stress a developmental curriculum that promotes self-growth and personal autonomy? The IEP team may decide that the goals of socialization and citizenship are most important, or that transmitting common content knowledge is most important for a particular student (Eisner & Vallance, 1974). For students with severe disabilities, the team may decide that learning skills for independent living and working is most important. This is a very different curriculum from that for general education students. After the curricular decisions have been made, it becomes much easier to make decisions about strategy modifications and placement.

Reforming the current general education curriculum into one that is relevant and interesting, and that incorporates core content and cognitive strategies within a context of social interaction in a learning community, will form a foundation for successful integration. It will also be necessary to realize that those special education students who need a very different curriculum (i.e., life and vocational skills) may be integrated into general education classrooms only for social reasons. Bear in mind that the curriculum for individuals with severe disabilities may be compromised if the goals are not clear to everyone concerned. The ability to address goals for a wide diversity of learners is a necessary component for inclusive schools.

If it is decided by the IEP team that students who were previously kept in special education classrooms could more effectively attain their curricular goals through general education placement, then administrators and teachers need to engage in a multifaceted planning process. This chapter includes several key components to consider during this process. Some of the recommendations are recycled ideas from past integration movements. Some are simply good planning strategies. Not much of the inclusion literature presents new ideas; rather old principles are being applied to a new situation. Responsible inclusion means considering the historical implications and viewing a vision for the future. Planning and preparation are pivotal to its success.

Planning for Inclusion

The success of any school program greatly depends on the amount of planning and preparation that precedes its implementation. If a team is expected to conduct the program, then it is best to have that team involved in the planning. If the program involves all school personnel, then it is best to include everyone in initial discussions. Thoughtful, deliberate decisions will usually emerge from a productive process. Establishing a quality inclusion program requires two essential components: (a) setting the stage for a planning process and (b) addressing all pertinent issues.

Set the Stage

Develop a Philosophy

An initial step to ensuring a successful integration program is to develop a philosophy pertaining to all students in the school. The philosophy statement should be developed by the school administrators in conjunction with the entire faculty. This will require some meeting time, but the process itself tends to accomplish consensus and result in general agreement regarding the school's goals. A useful philosophy statement probably needs to be child centered, and refer to the fact that everyone in the school is responsible for educating all students in the school. It might further reflect the notion that education should address cognitive, social, physical, and emotional develop-ment, implying that curricular options and instructional strategies may need to be flexible. Finally, the statement may mention that "stu-dents with disabilities should have the same access to knowledge, growth, achievement, success and belonging as do students without handicaps" (Murray, 1993, p. 171).

Establish a Transition Team

Once the philosophy has been developed, it might be best to appoint a transition team. A transition team can be effective only if the school administrators are knowledgeable about inclusion and support the integration movement. It may even be necessary to have central office personnel meet and discuss issues if a very different structure is recom-mended (Roach, 1994). Special educators, general educators (from each grade level), and at least one administrator should be members of the transition team. The team might be responsible for some of the following:

1. Facilitating communication among all stakeholders regarding IEP decisions, particularly curricular goals for individual stu-dents

2. Researching the most promising inclusion models and instruc-tional strategies

3. Making necessary decisions regarding support and training to facilitate inclusion and soliciting faculty and administrator sup-port

4. Designing an accountability system to assure progress for each special education student and monitoring the program

5. Becoming an ongoing "referral team" to solve behavioral and instructional problems encountered by specific students

Members of the transition team will need flexible schedules in order to meet frequently (at least once a week). Training and incen-tives should also be provided to team members. The more informed they are, the more likely their decisions will be good ones. Incentives can be in the form of conference participation, special recognition, and flexible time. Also, a plan is needed for achieving the most effec-tive instruction for each student. This plan will entail discussions about curriculum, instructional modifications, delivery models, job descriptions, support services, and accountability. Ten planning deci-sions are listed in Table 2.1 as a guide to school personnel who are planning to include only one previously segregated student, or who are planning a comprehensive inclusion program. This list is not exhaustive, and the order of the decisions is not necessarily imperative. However, decisions about curricular design and instructional modifications will impact subsequent decisions. Important considerations for each decision are discussed further in the following text.

Make Decisions

Decide What the Student(s) Need(s) To Learn

Because a fairly lengthy discussion has already been offered regarding curriculum decisions, only a few issues remain to be addressed. By law, curricula for special education students must be developed by an IEP team. Unfortunately, those teams rarely include anyone skilled at curriculum development. Special education teachers are usually not well versed in curriculum domains and organization; rather, they tend to be strategy specialists. Thus, IEPs are very seldom a well-developed curriculum. In most instances, IEPs are lists of possible

TABLE 2.1
Ten Decisions for Developing Inclusion Programs

1. Decide what the student(s) need(s) to learn.

2. Decide which instructional modifications are necessary for the learner(s).

3. Conceptualize the best delivery model for accommodating the student(s) in the least restrictive environment.

4. Decide the general and special educators' roles.

5. Decide if the student(s) need(s) a behavior management plan.

6. Decide what support is needed from the administration (e.g., schedule changes, space utilization, personnel allocation, materials acquisition, training).

7. Decide what support from outside agencies (e.g., mental health, juvenile justice) might be necessary.

8. Decide how best to validate that goals and objectives were met for each student.

9. Decide the best way to evaluate the program.

10. Decide the best methods for communicating with parents, with the central office, with other schools, and with stakeholders within the school.

goals that are often hastily marked by team members for the purpose of complying with the law. However, if inclusion is "to work" for special education students, everyone must be clear about precisely what an individual student needs to learn and for what purpose he or she needs to learn it.

Curricular decisions for individuals with severe disabilities are clearer than for students with mild and moderate disabilities. For students with severe disabilities, goals and objectives should be developed that will enhance their independent functioning inside and outside school. One method of developing a functional curriculum for these students was delineated by Brown et al. (1979). Known as environmental assessment, it is recommended that the teacher and the parent prepare several lists:

1. List of major environments (e.g., home, school) in which the individual must function

2. List of subenvironments (e.g., classroom, hallway, kitchen, bathroom) of each environment

3. List of activities to be performed in each subenvironment

4. List of skills necessary to conduct each activity, including language and social skills

The resulting list of skills first becomes the assessment instrument. Once it is determined which skills the student has not yet mastered, those skills are checked for social validity. Those skills and activities that significant people in the student's life agree are necessary and useful for eventual employment and independent living then become the curriculum. Language and social skills necessary for the activities are also assessed, and the entire curriculum is checked for age appropriateness.

It is much more difficult to make curricular decisions for individuals with mild and moderate disabilities. Many of these students display one or more of the following: a lack of social skills, severe behavioral disorders, oral and written language deficits, academic achievement deficits, low self-esteem, poor decision-making and problem-solving strategies, and poor attending and memory skills. These students differ from those with severe disabilities in that they do not require basic self-care and language skills. However, they are not prepared to function independently in the world of work, and they cannot achieve at a level appropriate for college-track students. So, what is to be done for these students?

For older students for whom a higher education track is not an option, a vocational curriculum may need to be considered. All special education students may need to learn cognitive strategies, coping strategies, and some social skills. However, for each designated goal and objective chosen that does not match those of the standard academic curricula, an academic goal must be forsaken. For example, if it is deemed necessary that a special education student needs to learn "study skills," then time must be taken from the general education curriculum for the learning-strategy instruction. Over time, the special education student will receive less and less of the core curriculum. This, in turn, will make it more difficult for him or her to master the content taught in general education classrooms.

Current recommendations for inclusion models presume that many of the social and cognitive goals and objectives will be taught concurrently with the core curriculum (e.g., Salend, 1994; T. E. C. Smith, Polloway, Patton, & Dowdy, 1995). This seems easier to accomplish in elementary classrooms where tool subjects prevail and socialization is accepted as a worthwhile goal. However, in secondary schools, where academic content is stressed, fewer techniques exist that will easily mesh instruction in social, cognitive, emotional, and academic curricula. In any case, careful consideration should be given to developing a relevant and functional curriculum for each student. These decisions will impact students for their entire lives. If academic curricula are forsaken in favor of a more functional curriculum, then the student will never achieve at grade level and will probably always meet eligibility for special education. If, on the other hand, students are forced into the core curriculum for "inclusion's" sake, then a more functional curriculum may be sacrificed, and the student may be unemployable after graduation.

Each student's team should do the following to determine an appropriate curriculum:

1. Choose relevant curricular areas (e.g., academic content areas; tool subjects; cognitive strategies; social skills; coping strategies; prevocational/vocational skills).

2. List long-term goals in each curricular area.

3. Assess the student for current level of functioning in each area.

4. Using discrepancy analysis, devise a sequence of instructional objectives at appropriate levels of learning.

5. Reassess the student using the curriculum list.

6. Pinpoint appropriate target objectives and check for social validity.

Learning levels might correspond with Bloom's (1956) taxonomy or with a response hierarchy (Alberto & Troutman, 1990). The resulting scope and sequence not only will provide a clear guide, but will provide a basis for formative assessment. Once clarity about the curriculum has been achieved, the remaining decisions become easier.

Instructional Modifications

For those special education students with mild and moderate disabilities who have failed to learn the core curriculum in traditional classrooms, strategy modifications are recommended. For the purposes of this chapter, strategies refer to "ways to teach." It is believed that if content were taught in different ways, these students could learn it at an acceptable pace. Thus, for students with mild and moderate disabilities, the student's team might decide *not* to modify the general education curriculum, but to make modifications in the way it is taught. For those students with severe disabilities, both curriculum and instructional strategies probably need modification. Most school district special education programs compile lists of instructional modifications to be considered during IEP meetings. These lists include strategies for modifying the environment, for modifying the presentation of material, for utilizing multimodal approaches, for modifying the pacing of material, for modifying testing and grading, and for organizing classroom procedures and materials. A summary of some types of instructional strategies is provided in Table 2.2.

For example, one instructional modification often recommended for use in general education classrooms to improve both social skills and academic achievement is cooperative learning (Johnson, Johnson, & Holubec, 1991). Students, grouped in triads, are organized in such a way as to promote interdependence. This organization may be designed around content (i.e., each student has a piece of the content so that the total lesson can be completed only when all learn their part) or may include teaching roles (i.e., one participant reads, one interprets, and one writes, so that the task cannot be completed unless each member performs his or her role effectively). Organizing students to be interdependent allows the stronger students to assist those students who need extra help. At the same time, this strategy promotes collaboration and cooperation—both worthy goals.

TABLE 2.2
Sample Instructional Modifications

Modification of Lesson Presentation

1. Present content in shorter segments with more practice of each small chunk.
2. Teach concrete concepts before teaching abstract.
3. Tell the student what will be taught and why it is important to learn it.
4. Provide advance organizers.
5. Use vocabulary that the student can understand.
6. Check for understanding with signal, choral, and individual responses frequently.
7. Use tape recorders, computers, calculators, typewriters, and projects as appropriate.
8. Use highlighting, underlining, oral tests, and simple formats.
9. Repeat often, use additional examples, give frequent feedback, and reward correct responding.
10. Present material at the students' instructional level.

Modifications to Materials

1. Provide lecture notes ahead of time.
2. Highlight and/or underline important sections in materials.
3. Keep workspace clear.
4. Avoid copying from the board; use boxes and arrows; and show relationships on boards and transparencies.
5. Give information in print and orally.
6. Use manipulative, hands-on activities whenever possible.
7. Use visual aids (charts, maps, pictures) whenever possible.
8. Rework textbook and workbook material to be easily understood.
9. Avoid cluttered, crowded worksheets by using blocking (block assignments into small segments) and cutting/folding (cut/fold worksheets into sections and provide one problem per section).
10. Provide notebooks with organized sections, a calendar, homework assignments, class notes, study guides, and to-do lists.

Modifications to the Environment

1. Arrange desks to communicate expectations (e.g., discussion, lecture, individual work).
2. Use student carrels for focused work.
3. Keep classroom free of distracting noises and visual stimulation.
4. Provide opportunities for movement.

(continues)

TABLE 2.2 *Continued*

---

5. Label shelves with materials and keep things in their place.
6. Set a routine and teach the procedures.
7. Have necessary materials in the classroom and ready.
8. Provide trays, folders for completed work.
9. Provide regular times to clean desk, organize notebooks, and so on.

Modifications to Time Demands

1. Use timers to indicate the amount of time to complete work, the amount of time before the period is over, the amount of free/reward time, and so on.
2. Reduce the amount of work or length of test rather than increase amount of time.
3. Space short work periods with breaks or change of task.
4. Specify time periods for each assignment.

Cooperative learning, however, may not work well with students who have low cognitive and language abilities.

Determining specific instructional modifications for particular students requires comprehensive assessment and analyses. The recommended strategies should match learner characteristics. This means that special educators need to gather information about (a) learning styles (modality preferences, class structure preferences, environmental preferences); (b) behavior functions of excessive behavior (why a student behaves inappropriately); (c) specific errors in academic performance (error analysis), especially the tool subjects; (d) cognitive strategy deficits (study skills, organizational skills, memory skills, self-talk, listening skills, self-monitoring); and (e) the student's attitudes (attribution style, self-efficacy, prejudices). Once assessment information has been examined in light of the desired goals, a plan to modify instructional strategies can be developed. Utilizing a comprehensive list of instructional adaptations, the student's team should delineate which strategies need to be implemented for each student. At this point, decisions about placement and personnel roles will be easier to determine.

Conceptualize a Delivery Model and Delineate Roles

After deciding what is important for students (both special education and general education) to learn and choosing which instructional modifications might be necessary, the student's team should consider where and how the educational plan might best be delivered. The team also should consider what types of related services might be necessary for students. This may impact delivery decisions. It is best to consider a full range of delivery options (see Salend, 1994, for a discussion of the full continuum of services). If students with disabilities are to receive educational services in general education classrooms, then there are several implementation models for educators to consider. This should not preclude creating a combination of several models or inventing one that meets student and staff needs. Table 2.3 provides a list of possible integration models for consideration.

Currently, one of the most popular models is the consultation model (Idol-Maestas, 1983). Specialists (often special education teachers) may assist the general education teacher to adjust, redesign, and monitor classroom strategies for individual students. The specialists could provide behavioral observations, diagnostic assessment, coaching, collaborative planning, and actual resources necessary for the student to succeed educationally. Effective consultation depends on good communication and effective problem-solving strategies. Good consultants need to be able to work well with other adults, have expertise in some area, develop and clarify goals, be accountable for progress, and allow others to succeed.

Recently, the consultation model has been expanded to include team teaching (T. E. C. Smith et al., 1995). Teaming means the special educator and general educator plan and implement lessons jointly or parallel to each other. Each teacher may be responsible for one aspect of the lesson. This concept has been modified into a supported education model whereby special educators who are strategy specialists and/or behavior management specialists team with academic content teachers to teach core content in an integrated classroom. This is particularly effective at the secondary level, where special education teachers lack academic content expertise. In this model, the teachers plan together, may take turns teaching various lessons, assist each other with behavior management, or teach simultaneously (e.g., one teacher presents information while the other writes or draws the information on overhead transparencies). During guided practice the two adults may each assist small groups of learners so that the student–teacher ratio is greatly reduced. This model works best when both teachers are effective instructors and they have developed a productive working relationship. For more information on consultation models, see Zins, Curtis, Graden, and Ponti (1988).

TABLE 2.3
Sample Inclusive Delivery Models

Special Class Placement with Partial General Education Placement

The student's primary placement is in a special education classroom, usually because of the student's need for structure, low stimulation, extra support, and low student–teacher ratios. However, general education students may come to the special education classroom, in a reverse mainstreaming effort, or the student may be placed in general education classes when deemed appropriate. These classes are usually nonacademic classes.

General Class Placement with Resource Room Assistance

The resource teacher often provides direct instruction to special education students in a separate classroom in order to support the student's receiving primary instruction from general educators. Rather than a parallel class, this model works best when the resource teacher provides instruction in school survival skills and cognitive strategies while providing assistance to general educators in terms of instructional modifications. One example of this type of model is the Content Mastery Model in Texas (Jenkins & Sileo, 1994).

General Class Placement with Itinerant Specialist Assistance

The student is placed primarily in general education classes, with the support of an itinerant specialist. This may be a counselor, a speech–language therapist, occupational or physical therapist, or specialist in vision or hearing. The teacher may provide the support in the general education classroom or another room in the building, and work with the classroom teacher to integrate special techniques for the student.

General Education Placement with Consulting Teacher Assistance

The consultation model has been widely adopted as the best model for full integration of students with disabilities. The consulting teacher works with the general education teacher to plan and teach lessons, adapt strategies, manage behavior, and develop materials. *Team teaching* is a variation of this model, whereby the consulting teacher plans and implements lessons jointly with the general education teacher. There may be several special education students included in this type of classroom. A second variation is referred to as *supported education*, in which most of the instruction is presented by the general education teacher. The consulting teacher conducts activities in the classroom (writes on overhead, writes on board, makes handouts) that reinforce the instruction. In *complementary instruction*, two lessons are taught simultaneously—a lesson within a lesson (e.g., notetaking and social studies). *Parallel instruction* implies that the special education teacher teaches a small group separately while the teacher works with the rest of the class. This model is often recommended for students with severe disabilities.

(continues)

TABLE 2.3 *Continued*

General Education Placement with Few or No Support Services

The general education teacher is totally responsible for instructing the special education student. This teacher may receive training in instructional modifications and may use some various methods to ensure success. There may also be support available, if necessary. One variation of this is a *crisis intervention center*, perhaps available to all students in the school, for times of emotional or behavioral crisis. This classroom is staffed with a counselor. Students are allowed to spend time in this classroom to regain composure, receive counseling, work quietly, or plan self-management strategies. Additional support may come in the form of tutoring services or mentors. Another way to provide support to general educators is through *paraprofessionals*. Some students with severe emotional disturbance, physical and sensory impairments, or severe cognitive deficits may need additional assistance to be able to participate in the general education classroom. Paraprofessionals can provide that assistance and help other students as well.

Another important concept in the consideration of service delivery models is that of behavior management. If special education students have disorders of conduct, the student's team should plan ahead. Schools might consider establishing a crisis intervention center—some place for the student to receive high structure and counseling. This center may be used to prevent behavior problems by allowing students to visit the center at the first sign of frustration. The crisis specialist may be responsible for teaching social skills, developing token systems and contracts, counseling, crisis intervention, and planning with the students. During times when no students are in the center, the crisis specialist can act as a behavior specialist for the entire school.

One way to ensure the success of any delivery model is to formulate a group to monitor progress and make decisions. This group acts as an oversight committee, as it were, for all students who are struggling. This group may be the transition team or may be another group referred to as prereferral teams (Fuchs, Fuchs, & Bahr, 1990; Mastropieri & Scruggs, 1994) or teacher support teams (Murray, 1993). The concept is that special educators, other specialists, and general educators meet to discuss specific students for the purpose of providing appropriate services. Thus, the team engages in a collaborative effort to share information, problem solve, and plan. The support team may also include community members (e.g., church personnel, agency personnel, local police officer). This particular group can be of great assistance by solving learning and behavior problems, by accessing internal and external resources, and by coordinating various intervention components.

The process of conceptualizing the delivery model will facilitate identifying personnel roles. The transition team may need to consider the strengths of existing personnel while developing the delivery model, but be wary of compromising the model due to personality quirks. Sometimes school personnel are reluctant to take on new roles if they feel they cannot adequately implement the expected duties. It is important to provide training to all personnel, to provide necessary materials, and to reinforce everyone for success. In some cases, it may be necessary to hire new personnel (as in the case of a crisis intervention specialist). It is important to include all stakeholders in the development of the model so that all feel invested in its success.

The tasks needed to develop an inclusion model are listed in Table 2.4.

Decide If the Student Needs a Behavior Management Plan

Some students have been referred to special education because they exhibit behavioral disorders and are disruptive in the general education classroom. For students with mild and moderate disabilities who experience failure and frustration, acting out might be a way of coping. For students with severe disabilities (e.g., autism), bizarre behavior may be a way to communicate. For these students, success in general education classrooms will depend on effective behavior management.

TABLE 2.4
Developing an Inclusion Model

1. Study various inclusion models in the literature and at other schools.
2. Consider behavior management and related service needs of "included" students.
3. Consider the strengths of existing personnel.
4. Keep sight of the program goals.
5. Provide all necessary training and promote teaming.
6. Develop a unique model to meet specific needs.
7. Promote personal investment in the model.
8. Formulate an oversight or support team.

Generally the best way to manage student disruptive behavior is to simultaneously remediate social deficits and eliminate behavioral excesses. For example, a student with severe disabilities who screams may need to be taught to ask for what he or she wants, while receiving an overcorrection technique for screaming. Or a student with mild disabilities who is noncompliant may need to be reinforced for following directions, as well as "fined" for not following directions. It is beyond the scope of this chapter to delineate all possible behavior reduction techniques, but I recommend that someone in the school develop a working knowledge of these strategies. Refer to Alberto and Troutman (1990), Rhode, Jenson, and Reavis (1992), and Webber and Scheuermann (1991) for techniques that can be used in general education settings.

One method of directly addressing behavior problems is to instruct students in social skills and school survival skills. This instruction may be delivered in the general education classroom for all students by the counselor, the special education teacher, or a teacher team; alternatively, small groups of students might be pulled out of the general education classroom to receive instruction. It is best to have appropriate role models available either on a video or as role-play examples. See Mastropieri and Scruggs (1994) for a review of social skills curricula. After the students have acquired basic social skills, teachers may want to use behavioral contracts, token systems, and self-monitoring strategies to assure the maintenance and generalization of these behaviors. Behavioral contracts are agreements between the teacher and the student about behavioral expectations and subsequent consequences. Token systems simply provide some type of symbolic reward that can later be turned in for desirable items and privileges. The rewards are contingent upon appropriate classroom behavior or upon the absence of inappropriate behavior. Self-monitoring is a technique whereby the student keeps a tally of his or her own behavior to be later rewarded. Various self-monitoring forms are available for this type of tally, and self-monitoring techniques have been found to greatly assist mainstreamed students. (See Young, West, Smith, & Morgan, 1993, for a discussion of self-monitoring techniques.) Table 2.5 summarizes some suggestions for managing disruptive behavior in general education settings.

Students with disabilities who are disruptive often behave better in general education settings. Perhaps this is due to the appropriate role models, or perhaps the students come under the influence of their non-

TABLE 2.5
Suggestions for Managing Disruptive Behavior
in General Education Settings

1. Conduct a functional assessment of the disruptive behavior.

2. Teach students social skills, school survival skills, and alternate methods of communication.

3. Manipulate classroom variables (e.g., structured lessons) in order to solicit appropriate behavior.

4. Establish token systems for rewarding "key" behaviors (e.g., following directions).

5. Use point cards and self-monitoring techniques.

6. Provide many *appropriate* peer role models.

7. Protect student from extreme frustration, ridicule, and rejection.

8. Add counseling and punishment techniques as necessary.

9. Provide a safe place for students to practice self-control.

handicapped peers. To assure that this effect occurs, students who are at risk for behavior problems should be placed in classrooms where most other students display appropriate behavior. It is also important to place students who may have a "bad" reputation in classrooms where the students do not have a history with that student. Even if the special education student acts appropriately, peers may reject the student due to his or her reputation.

If it is determined that a student needs a behavior management plan, the individual or team who knows most about behavioral change techniques can design a plan in conjunction with the classroom teacher. The plan ought to be designed around a functional assessment (Foster-Johnson & Dunlap, 1993) and should include reinforcement for alternate prosocial behavior. If a punisher is to be used, it should be one that can be delivered and tolerated in general education classrooms. General education students could be traumatized by watching adults "restrain" another student. The special education student should be taught about the behavior management program, and it should be implemented as early in the transition as possible. It is much easier to prevent behavior problems than to try to eliminate them after people are angry and frustrated.

Decide What Support Is Needed

After most of the implementation decisions have been determined, the next planning decision addresses program support. Support may come in the way of training, schedule changes, space utilization, materials acquisition, or agency support (e.g., counseling or protective services). If the school principal has been included in the decision-making process, decisions about support will be easier. Arranging adequate meeting times for teacher support teams or collaborative teacher teams is crucial to the success of the program. Training (conference attendance, staff development opportunities, video training, college courses) may require funding and need to be timely. For various delivery models, additional classroom space may be required. If teachers and paraprofessionals are to change their roles, additional personnel may be needed and job descriptions rewritten. Perhaps the teachers will need additional materials (e.g., social skills curricula).

The principal will most likely need to be creative in his or her attempts to obtain the funding and make the necessary changes for an inclusion program to work. Funding might be obtained through state and federal grants, through community donations, or by shifting existing resources. It would be best for the principal to communicate regularly with the central administrative personnel in order to receive their support throughout the process. It is also wise to include the entire school faculty on any decisions that affect others in the school. One or two individuals might be able to sabotage the most well-conceived program.

In addition to school-based support, it might be determined that outside agency support is necessary. This is particularly important for students who may benefit from health, mental health, juvenile justice, rehabilitation, or social services (e.g., Malone-Fenner, 1994). These services could be provided by agency personnel who have offices in the school or via regular visits from mental health and rehabilitation counselors, public health nurses, or probation officers. Depending on the size of the school and the needs of the students, health clinics and day-care centers could be established, job fairs organized, counseling groups for students and families formed, and public assistance programs administered on the school grounds. In this way, services to students and their families are better coordinated and evaluated. Most educators know that simply instructing students who have a multitude of personal problems is not enough. Adopting a preventative, ecological view of "education" demands persistence and collaboration, but it is well worth the trouble if student problems are alleviated.

Decide the Best Way To Evaluate Progress

At least two major components of an inclusion program are in need of evaluation. First, it must be determined whether students are making progress toward their designated goals. If it was decided that students should be included in general education classrooms for the purpose of improving academic achievement, then systematic academic assessment needs to be incorporated. The teacher teams may design informal tests, or may choose to readminister some of the initial assessments in order to document progress. This progress might be displayed in several interesting ways. It might be compared with the student's level of functioning before the new model was established; it might be compared with an average student's achievement in the inclusive classroom; and/or it might simply illustrate progress for the student over several weeks or months. If evaluation questions are developed at the program's inception and evaluation tasks are assigned, it is more likely that useful evaluation data will be collected.

If students are included in general education classrooms for purely social reasons, then it would be necessary to collect data regarding social skills. Observational recording and curriculum-based or standardized social skills instruments may be used. It would be interesting to note whether other (i.e., academic, functional) skills are also improving. Many educators and parents feel that functional curriculum for students with severe disabilities is sacrificed for the notion of inclusion, so it is important to prevent that from happening. It might also be necessary to assess emotional indicators for psychologically fragile students and to survey the students themselves regarding their perceptions of the inclusion program. Various types of formative assessment can alert teachers to skill deficits, psychological problems, and individual progress.

The program as a whole forms the second component needing evaluation. Making changes in school programs necessitates a method of accountability. The evaluation plan might include an evaluation of teacher attitudes toward special education students, toward the delivery model, and toward the original philosophical statement. It would be interesting to note whether teachers and paraprofessionals felt supported and whether they thought the students fared better in the new model. Other stakeholders (e.g., parents, support personnel) should be surveyed as well. Additionally, a program evaluation might include an analysis of the effectiveness of various program elements. Has the transition procedure worked well? Are personnel being used in the most cost-effective way? Has staff development resulted in better performance? Are support services adequate? Which of the program elements seem to be most important for determining success for students (e.g., team teaching, crisis management specialist, teacher support teams)? For more information regarding inclusion program evaluation, see M. L. Smith and Noble (1993). Quality evaluative information will formulate the basis for ongoing decisions regarding effective school programming. The components of inclusion programs that need to be evaluated on an ongoing basis are listed in Table 2.6.

Decide the Best Methods for Communicating

Communication permeates the entire decision-making process. A planning process necessitates communicating with stakeholders within the school (faculty and staff) and within the school system as a whole (central office, sister schools), with parents, with external agency personnel, and with the students themselves. Communication implies imparting and receiving information, so the best methods for establishing a network offer opportunities for input as well as dissemination. Communication with faculty and staff is usually done through meetings. This implies frequent meeting time, and training

TABLE 2.6
Components for Program Evaluation

1. Compare student academic achievement data.

2. Compare student social skills performance data and emotional indicators.

3. Compare functional skill performance in several settings.

4. Evaluate student perceptions of program implementation.

5. Evaluate teacher perceptions of student progress and program implementation.

6. Evaluate support personnel perceptions of student progress and program implementation.

7. Evaluate parental attitudes of student progress.

8. Assure that all program components are in compliance with current law.

9. Analyze various program components for cost-effectiveness, personnel performance, and impact on successful outcomes.

for personnel about consensus decision-making, collaboration, and communication skills. Printed communication (memos, newsletters) can also be helpful, but may not encourage two-way communication. A notecard system (Salend, 1994) may allow several teachers to communicate with each other regarding particular students. This same system could be used to obtain teacher feedback regarding various aspects of the program (an administrative–faculty network).

Communication with students can be accomplished through student interviews, student surveys, and student meetings. Since students are grouped throughout the day, most communication can be accomplished during class time. It is important to inform general and special education students about expectations and to give them feedback concerning outcomes. Student attitudes toward each other can be a determining factor in the success or failure of an inclusion model. (See Salend, 1994, and T. E. C. Smith et al., 1995, for methods of preparing general education students for inclusion.) Communication with parents is also important. PTA meetings, special training sessions, coffee meetings, and home visits provide opportunities to discuss the impact of the inclusion program on children. Individually, parents can receive and provide information through daily report cards, interactive notebooks, home–school contracts, and regular telephone calls. Parents are important stakeholders in special education programming and must be included in all phases of program development.

It is also imperative that the principal maintain an open communication with the school district administrative offices. In this way, there might be extra resources designated for the project or newspaper coverage as the program establishes itself. For those schools serving the same students, it would be wise to share evaluation information. Each school may formulate a different model, so sharing information about what works and what does not work can save much time and many resources. Ideally, all stakeholders need to be given evaluation findings. Thus, it is important to compile evaluation data into graphs and/or pamphlets so that the information can be easily understood. If the inclusion model is a comprehensive one, and unique to the school district, a newsletter might be developed to provide updates on progress. The newsletters can be sent to community agency personnel. These people can also be kept informed regarding program development by way of multidisciplinary meetings. By including as many stakeholders as possible in the planning process, and by establishing a systematic method of communicating, opposition to various aspects of the program might be prevented and/or alleviated. Allowing everyone to succeed, acknowledging a job well done, supporting effective instruction, documenting progress, and advocating for the students are important for program success.

Possible Pitfalls

Even the best intended program may suffer problems. To prevent problems from occurring, school personnel should periodically check the program and the planning process for possible pitfalls. Table 2.7 lists possible impediments to successful inclusion planning. These

TABLE 2.7
Impediments to Successful Inclusion Programming

1. No clear curricular decisions. Teachers are unclear about what needs to be taught to special education students.
2. General education teachers are not adequately prepared.
   a. They are not aware of the program philosophy or program goals.
   b. They do not agree with the philosophy or the program goals.
   c. They are not given adequate training.
   d. There is no incentive for succeeding with tough-to-teach students.
3. Students are not adequately prepared.
   a. General education students have not been prepared to accept individual differences, and to assist special education students.
   b. Special education students have not been taught basic school survival skills, social skills, or attending skills.
4. The schoolwide and classroom behavior management systems are inadequate or nonexistent.
5. Administration is not supportive.
   a. School administrators are not aware of program components and goals.
   b. School administrators offer no flexibility in scheduling and funding.
   c. School administrators eliminate pull-out options.
   d. School administrators are not responsive to faculty input.
   e. No systematic program evaluation is conducted.
6. Personnel are unclear regarding their roles.
7. Communication and collaboration are ineffective or nonexistent.

impediments hinge around inadequate decision making, poor personnel preparation, ineffective instruction for students, ineffective discipline programs, ineffective program administration, and poor communication. Problem prevention is much easier than trying to repair negative perceptions and feelings of failure later in the process. Because any one of these items could derail program development, it is important to assure that all pieces of the puzzle are addressed in an efficient manner. Comprehensive program planning demands attention to detail, a global vision for the future, effective problem-solving mechanisms, creative resource development, positive attitudes and communication styles, and caring energetic people. Good programs develop when people are willing to take a risk and try something new. Programs grow and maintain when various program variables are addressed in a systematic and thorough way. Inclusion is a concept of integrating students with special needs into their local schools. By avoiding the pitfalls, and attending conscientiously to each of the decision points listed, school personnel can develop effective inclusion programs and have fun doing it.

References

Alberto, P. A., & Troutman, A. C. (1990). *Applied behavioral analysis for teachers* (3rd ed.). Columbus, OH: Merrill.

Association for Supervision and Curriculum Development. (1994, October). Making schools more inclusive: Teaching children with disabilities in regular classrooms. *Curriculum Update*, pp. 1–8.

Baines, L., Baines, C., & Masterson, C. (1994). Mainstreaming: One school's reality. *Phi Delta Kappan, 76,* 39–40, 57–64.

Bloom, B. S. (Ed.). (1956). *Taxonomy of educational objectives handbook I: Cognitive domain.* New York: David McKay.

Bradfield, R. H., Brown, J., Kaplan, P., Rickert, E., & Stannard, R. (1973). The special child in the regular classroom. *Exceptional Children, 39,* 384–390.

Brown, L., Branston, M. B., Hamre-Nietupski, S., Pumpian, I., Certo, N., & Gruenwald, L. (1979). A strategy for developing chronological age-appropriate and functional curricular content for severely handicapped adolescents and young adults. *The Journal of Special Education, 13,* 81–90.

Davis, W. E. (1989). The regular education initiative debate: Its promises and problems. *Exceptional Children, 55,* 440–446.

Eisner, E., & Vallance, E. (1974). *Conflicting conceptions of curriculum.* Berkeley, CA: McCutchan.

Foster-Johnson, L., & Dunlap, G. (1993). Using functional assessment to develop effective, individualized interventions for challenging behaviors. *Teaching Exceptional Children, 25,* 44–50.

Fuchs, E., Fuchs, L. S., & Bahr, M. W. (1990). Mainstream assistance teams: A scientific basis for the art of consultation. *Exceptional Children, 57,* 128–139.

Idol, L., & West, J. F. (1991). Educational collaboration: A catalyst for effective schooling. *Intervention, 27,* 70–78.

Idol-Maestas, L. (1983). *Special educator's consultation handbook.* Rockville, MD: Aspen.

Individuals with Disabilities Education Act of 1991, 20 U.S.C. §1400 *et seq.*

Jenkins, A. A., & Sileo, T. W. (1994). The Content Mastery Program: Facilitating students' transition into inclusive education settings. *Intervention in School and Clinic, 30,* 84–90.

Johnson, D. W., Johnson, R. T., & Holubec, E. J. (1991). *Cooperation in the classroom* (rev. ed.). Edina, MN: Interaction.

Kauffman, J. M. (1993). How we might achieve the radical reform of special education. *Exceptional Children, 60,* 6–16.

Malone-Fenner, S. (1994). Building mental health services into the public school. *Journal of Emotional and Behavioral Problems, 3*(3), 45–48.

Mastropieri, M. A., & Scruggs, T. E. (1994). *Effective instruction for special education.* Austin, TX: PRO-ED.

Meyen, E., Vergason, G., & Whelan, R. (Eds.). (1975). *Alternatives for teaching exceptional children.* Denver: Love.

Murray, L. B. (1993). Putting it all together at the school level: A principal's perspective. In J. I. Goodlad & T. C. Lovitt (Eds.), *Integrating general and special education* (pp. 171–201). New York: Macmillan.

Pugach, M. C., & Warger, C. L. (1993). Curriculum considerations. In J. I. Goodlad & T. C. Lovitt (Eds.), *Integrating general and special education* (pp. 125–143). New York: Macmillan.

Reynolds, M., Wang, M. C., & Walberg, H. J. (1987). The necessary restructuring of special and regular education. *Exceptional Children, 53,* 391–398.

Rhode, G., Jenson, W. R., & Reavis, H. K. (1992). *The tough kid book: Practical classroom management strategies.* Longmont, CO: Sopris West.

Roach, V. (1994, November). The superintendent's role in creating inclusive schools. *The School Administrator,* pp. 20–27.

Salend, S. J. (1994). *Effective mainstreaming: Creating inclusive classrooms.* New York: Macmillan.

Smelter, R. W., Rasch, B. W., & Yudewitz, G. J. (1994). Thinking of inclusion for all special needs students? Better think again. *Phi Delta Kappan, 76,* 35–38.

Smith, M. L., & Noble, A. J. (1993). Toward a comprehensive program of evaluation. In J. I. Goodlad & T. C. Lovitt (Eds.), *Integrating general and special education* (pp. 149–170). New York: Macmillan.

Smith, T. E. C., Polloway, E. A., Patton, J. R., & Dowdy, C. A. (1995). *Teaching children with special needs in inclusive settings.* Boston: Allyn & Bacon.

Stainback, W., & Stainback, S. (1991). A rationale for integration and restructuring: A synopsis. In J. W. Lloyd, N. N. Singh, & A. C. Repp (Eds.), *The regular education initiative: Alternative perspectives in concepts, issues, and models* (pp. 226–239). Sycamore, IL: Sycamore.

Webber, J., Henderson, K., & Seifert, E. H. (1993). Current perceptions of school administrators regarding the implementation of P.L. 94-142. *Journal of Research for School Executives, 2,* 86–95.

Webber, J., & Scheuermann, B. (1991). Accentuate the positive . . . Eliminate the negative! *Teaching Exceptional Children, 24,* 13–19.

Young, K. R., West, R. P., Smith, D. J., & Morgan, D. P. (1993). *Teaching self-management strategies to adolescents.* Longmont, CO: Sopris West.

Zins, J. E., Curtis, M. J., Graden, J. L., & Ponti, C. R. (1988). *Helping students succeed in the regular classroom: A guide for developing intervention assistance programs.* San Francisco: Jossey-Bass.

CHAPTER 3

Collaboration: Strategies for Building Effective Teams

Nancy A. Mundschenk
and Regina M. Foley

C reating environments in which all students strive toward challenging outcomes with the necessary supports and services can seem like a task that would daunt even experienced teachers. Many general education teachers express anxiety that they lack the time, professional training, and for some, even the inclination to provide effective instruction for students with disabilities (Bradley & West, 1994). To deal effectively with the increasing diversity found in integrated classrooms, teachers will need to combine their professional skills, and begin to utilize the expertise of a range of school and community personnel and resources. Collaboration is gaining recognition as a critical element in the inclusion of students with behavior disorders into general education classrooms (see Table 3.1). Collaboration has been defined as a style for direct interaction between two or more equal parties who voluntarily engage in shared decision making to achieve a common goal (Friend & Cook, 1992). In this sense, engaging in collaboration activities is more than being cooperative or amiable with colleagues. Effective collaboration is based on the underlying assumption that general educators and special educators can work as equal partners, combining their individual skills to develop and implement effective instructional programming. These combined efforts are directed toward a common goal. In inclusive classrooms, one goal shared by general and

TABLE 3.1
Benefits of Collaboration for Included Placements

---

1. The ongoing planning, evaluation, and modification necessary to ensure the success of included placements can be facilitated with collaboration.

2. Collaboration enables general education classrooms to meet the needs of students with and without disabilities in new and exciting ways.

3. Collaboration can provide the personal and professional support of highly skilled colleagues.

4. Working collaboratively with others can result in personal and professional growth for all participants.

5. Collaboration helps teachers identify ways to access the skills, knowledge, and expertise of other teachers.

---

special educators may be for all teachers involved with that program to share responsibility for all students. Another shared goal may be to establish an environment in which students with learning and behavior disorders are full members of the classroom community, not merely guests.

Characteristics of Effective Collaborators

Pugach and Johnson (1995) identified five basic qualities observed in teachers who are effective collaborators. These qualities are obvious prerequisites for professional interactions designed to promote the successful inclusion of students with learning and behavior disorders into general education classrooms. First, effective collaborators recognize that the goal is complex and requires joint effort. The changes that may be required in philosophy, curriculum, teaching strategies, and structural organizations are well beyond the scope of one or two "inclusion meetings." Collaboration, like inclusion, is a process, not an end. Ongoing planning, evaluation, and modification are necessary to ensure the continued success of included placements. Success may not occur immediately, and inclusion may be achieved in incremental steps. The commitment of teachers to continue to collaborate and problem solve is vital.

Second, effective collaborators acknowledge the creativity generated by working collaboratively. Combining the effectiveness of teachers skilled in content and curriculum with those adept at classroom modifications and adaptive teaching strategies will enable general education classes to address the individual needs of students, with and without disabilities, in new and exciting ways. This kind of synergism benefits all teachers who participate in the process.

Joint problem solving is by definition a social activity. The third quality of effective collaborators is that they participate willingly because they value the positive professional interactions that are part of collaborative activities. Many teachers feel overwhelmed with the myriad tasks and concerns they must address, often within the isolation of their single classroom. Others are attempting new and innovative techniques with their students and wonder if their experiences are similar to those of other teachers. In both cases, these teachers welcome the personal and professional support of highly skilled colleagues.

Teachers engage in collaborative problem solving first because it facilitates achievement of the shared goal. The fourth quality of effective collaborators is that they also recognize and value the personal growth that results from collaborative problem solving. In addition, professionals who collaborate value the stimulation and intellectual growth that takes place as a result of working with others.

Finally, effective collaborators are reflective about their own educational practices. Teachers who expend time and energy in collaborative activities are not satisfied with the status quo. They look for more effective and efficient ways to deliver instruction to their students. This requires them to evaluate their own teaching competencies, and identify personal areas of strength and weakness. They are then able to identify ways to access the skills, knowledge, expertise, and support of other colleagues, in order to provide comprehensive programming for all students in the program. As a result of this reflection, effective collaborators strive to improve their individual performance, and support improvement in their colleagues as well. This does not mean that they jump on every educational bandwagon. Quite the contrary. With their colleagues, they critically analyze the possible benefits and negative side-effects of any proposed plan or methodology, and evaluate the possible outcomes for their students. No plan for inclusion of students with learning and behavior disorders into general education classrooms can be successfully implemented without ongoing evaluation of teacher effectiveness and student outcomes.

Facilitating Effective Collaboration

A number of factors have been identified that directly and indirectly affect the success of collaborative interactions. Effective collaboration requires a change in teachers' roles, and a move from isolation to collaboration in professional practice (West, 1990). Some teachers have expressed concern about role clarification, working out expectations, and working effectively with others—sometimes in the same classroom (Bradley & West, 1994). In addition, barriers to effective communication can arise that interfere with collaborative interactions, and foster miscommunication (Pugach & Johnson, 1995). While working with groups of general and special education teachers on collaboration training activities, Mundschenk and Foley (1994) identified several critical factors during problem-solving sessions that should be considered in order to facilitate collaborative planning for inclusion.

Parity-Based Relationships

For the most part, teachers are accustomed to being in charge, in control of what goes on in their classrooms. They assume responsibility for the students assigned to them, and they use the skills and talents they have to do the best possible job. A sense of territoriality inherent in public school structures (Bradley & West, 1994) suggests that each teacher is an expert in his or her own classroom and, as such, the best person to plan and execute effective instruction. If teachers are going to pool their professional skills and expertise to provide quality instruction in general education settings, a parity-based relationship must be established. This means that all teachers recognize and appreciate the unique talents and skills that their colleagues can bring to a collaborative relationship. It requires moving away from the consultant–consultee situation, in which the special educator advises the sixth-grade teacher how to accommodate Joshua in the class, to a parity-based relationship, in which both teachers sit down together as equal partners to plan the best program for Joshua. Both take responsibility for the successes and failures resulting from their decisions, and they continue to work together to adjust and refine the educational program. Because working with another teacher as a co-equal can be difficult at first, it is probably a good idea to begin collaborating with someone with a similar teaching style, or one with whom a positive relationship already exists. For example, Warren recognized that many of his students were failing the unit math tests, but he did not know how to remediate the weak areas without losing valuable instructional time for the entire class. His special education colleague, Barb, explained her method of conducting short but frequent probes on the math lessons and reteaching concepts that a significant number of students had failed to master. Her concern, however, was that her probes might not include all of the key concepts that students would need to know for future math courses. During collaborative planning, Warren identified the critical concepts for each lesson, and Barb was able to help develop the assessment probes.

Operationally Defined Problems

When teachers come together to jointly address an issue or problem, the lack of a common language base becomes obvious. Special education teachers feel comfortable in dialogue replete with acronyms such as IEP, BD, and IDEA. General educators may feel distanced by this cryptic language and less inclined to enter into a problem-solving session. Collaborators need to be sensitive to the background and training of their colleagues, and ensure that their conversations promote a shared language to describe and analyze classroom events (Glatthorn, 1990).

Once a common language base has been established, classroom events or problems must be operationally defined in order for educators to proceed through the process of problem solving. This can be a challenge for general educators who often lack the training in systematic methods of behavioral observation and definition. General education teachers may report on the effects of the behavior on the entire classroom or on their instruction, rather than focusing on the specific observable and measurable aspects of the behavior. Special educators must be prepared to follow up on a teacher's expressed concern with questions that identify the parameters of the behavior, such as frequency, setting, conditions, consequences, and other students involved. In addition, special educators should realize that their frame of reference may be more clearly focused on programming for individual students, whereas their general education colleagues are concerned with programming for a large group. One teacher exclaimed, "I know this behaviorally disordered kid is going to end up in my classroom, so how do I deal with his bad attitude?" In this case the educators need to operationally define "bad attitude," and look at the student's behavior in relation to student performance expectations of that teacher, management and instructional strategies, and curriculum (Idol, Paolucci-Whitcomb, & Nevin, 1987). In another case, several teachers were complaining about their students' lack of motivation. When prompted to more clearly define the problem, a range of issues arose, including students being late for class after lunch, not answering teacher academic questions, and not completing homework assignments. Clearly, the problem solution is contingent upon the specific problem, not a broad category of issues.

Alternative Solutions

In an attempt to be helpful, some teachers may respond to the statement of a problem with their advice as to the appropriate solution. Although specific suggestions are often welcomed by teachers, collaborators distinguish between giving advice too quickly and helping to generate alternative solutions. When teachers give advice without engaging in joint problem solving, they run the risk of promoting their status as "experts," which is contrary to the parity-based interactions of effective collaborators. This can negatively affect shared goals, such as mutual responsibility for students, when some teachers are viewed as having greater expertise and, therefore, greater responsibility for students with disabilities. In addition, giving advice assumes that the receiving teacher is comfortable with the suggestion, and skilled at fully implementing it. If a teacher simply takes the advice and the solution ultimately is ineffective, that teacher may be less inclined to ask for additional help. We know that teachers are more likely to incorporate methods that they think are valid and beneficial to their students (Nowacek, 1992). If special educators approach problem solving with general educators as an opportunity to help identify strategies acceptable to them and either already in their repertoire or supported by special educators or related service providers, the outcomes are more likely to be effective. Table 3.2 summarizes factors to consider during problem solving between special and general educators.

Dismissed Problems

Effective collaborative colleagues are willing to discuss any and all problems without making value judgments regarding the worth of each problem (Pugach & Johnson, 1995). This means that it is inappropriate to tell a general education teacher not to worry about "minor

TABLE 3.2
Factors to Consider During Problem Solving

---

1. Teachers need to realize and appreciate the unique talents and skills of their colleagues.

2. It is best to begin collaborating with someone with a similar teaching style, or one with whom you already have a positive relationship.

3. Special education teachers may need to help general education teachers specify the exact nature of the problem.

4. General education teachers may need help in incorporating interventions for individual students into whole-class instruction.

5. Giving advice too quickly without engaging in joint problem solving is contrary to collaboration.

6. Collaborators should be willing to deal with any and all problems, even small ones.

7. Utilizing even short time periods for collaborative problem solving can facilitate the entire process.

8. Failure to follow up on implemented solutions is a critical flaw in many attempts at collaborative problem solving.

---

problems" when programming for students with learning and behavior disorders. Rather, the teacher should be helped to gain a greater understanding of the problem, and to generate potential solutions. This willingness to deal with even small problems can be an important support for teachers. Consider the fact that many school districts employ "one-shot" inservice programs in which teachers learn "all" they need to know about a new methodology in one session. If, after being exposed to a 3-hour session on cooperative learning strategies, a third-grade teacher has a question on how to manage the transition time to and from group activities, a response such as "Weren't you at the inservice on Tuesday?" probably will not tempt that teacher to seek out the expertise of her colleagues on a different occasion. Sometimes teachers try to eclipse one another by presenting *their* problem as being clearly more challenging than the last one mentioned. This one-upmanship may be interpreted as meaning "Your problem or concern is not as important—or at least not as significant—as mine."

Occasionally catharsis may be helpful, but simply a list of increasingly more difficult problems is not productive. Problems or concerns should be dealt with one at a time, and an environment should be fostered in which input from colleagues can be sought on any issue, large or small.

On the other hand, viewing issues as insurmountable can also be problematic. Teachers may be faced with significant challenges when integrating students with learning and behavior disorders into general education classes. Rather than allowing themselves to be overwhelmed by the scope of the problem, effective collaborators address large problems systematically, identifying smaller components and generating effective solutions.

Systematic Selection of Solutions

To engage in systematic problem solving, educators must first operationally define the problem and generate an exhaustive list of potential solutions. Then they must evaluate each solution in terms of possible benefits and drawbacks if implemented. Finally, they must determine feasibility of, and teacher preference for, each solution (Friend & Cook, 1992). This process may be almost automatic for skilled collaborators, but for teachers just beginning to establish collaborative relationships, or for those working on particularly complex issues, the process may require more time and effort. Because sufficient time is a crucial issue, teachers can become stymied by articulating the problem and possible solution but never being able to conclude the process. Certainly teachers should work to obtain flexible scheduling and released time for collaborative problem solving. However, utilizing small windows of opportunity—such as passing in the hall, lunchtime, or meeting at the faculty mailbox—to get colleagues thinking about the issue can help limit the time needed to introduce the problem once the planning session begins, thereby facilitating the entire process.

Teachers should also guard against embracing quick fixes or accepting the first possible solution. Because of the pressures to find and implement effective solutions quickly, teachers may be tempted to adopt any feasible solution. This may seem like an appropriate course of action; however, valuable time and effort may be wasted by implementing interventions that further analysis would show to be ineffective or unsatisfactory. Several possible solutions should be thoroughly evaluated so that the chosen solution is not only effective, but the most appropriate under the specific circumstances that define the situation.

Follow-Up

Failure to follow up on implemented solutions is a critical flaw in many attempts at collaborative problem solving. Even when teachers engage in very effective problem-solving activities and identify solutions that they are convinced will have positive results, they fail to articulate the procedures that will be used to evaluate the effectiveness of the intervention. This means that they have not established a procedure to gather data for decision making about any changes that might be needed in the implementation. Considerations include whether the chosen intervention was ineffective and a new intervention should be selected, whether the chosen intervention needs to be modified, or whether the problem has been resolved. This lack of follow-up procedure is a problem found in the interactions between general and special educators, between teachers and supportive service staff, and among administrators, teachers, and parents. Another issue is the importance of recognition and credit given for ideas and accomplishments that result from collaborative problem solving. In one case, a science teacher and an art teacher combined their skills to develop a series of hands-on science activities that were appropriate for students with limited science background. The activities were so successful that the teachers were recognized at a regional competition for science programs. The recognition that these teachers received from their peers highlighted that collaborative activities can have positive results, and increased the likelihood that others will share their knowledge and time in collaborative relationships. In sum, follow-up procedures are a requisite part of effective problem-solving processes.

Establishment of Collaborative Teams

A number of collaborative structures have been used to facilitate the inclusion of students with disabilities into the general education program (Dettmer, Thurston, & Dyck, 1993; Friend & Cook, 1992; Pugach & Johnson, 1995). These include team teaching, peer coaching, teacher assistance teams, child study teams, and grade-level teams. Common to all of these structures is the pooling of professional expertise and resources to meet the demands of a variety of situations. Typically, these collaborative structures are composed of a group of professionals who voluntarily form interdependent units or teams for the purpose of directly working to achieve a common purpose or goal (Friend & Cook, 1992).

The team approach provides a number of benefits for teachers that can impact service delivery for students with and without disabilities. Peer coaching teams (Joyce & Showers, 1982; Morgan, Menlove, Salzberg, & Hudson, 1994) have been effectively used by teachers in assisting one another to use new instructional techniques, thereby developing new professional skills. Collaborative teams may serve as a support mechanism for teachers when integrating students with diverse needs into general education classrooms (Pugach & Johnson, 1995). Finally, teams may be employed to address schoolwide concerns, such as curricular issues and school governance (West, 1990).

The success of collaborative teams hinges on a number of key elements. These elements, described below, include (a) organizational structure of teams, (b) team goals, (c) team resources, (d) communication, and (e) evaluation activities. Table 3.3 lists the strategies for the development of effective teams, which are described in detail in the remainder of this chapter.

Team Organizational Structure

Collaboration-based teams benefit from the diversity of the professionals' expertise, and from the structure that organizational elements can provide. Membership, leadership, and organizational processes contribute to the success of the team.

Team Membership

Each established team should comprise individuals who are interested in the outcomes or who are directly involved in the process to achieve program goals. The size of the team depends on the purpose and the decisions to be made by the team. For instance, a grade-level team at a secondary school requires the inclusion of educators from each major content area (e.g., science, social science, mathematics) to meet the student's educational needs and goals. Similarly, elementary school teams may include general educators from two or more grade

TABLE 3.3

Strategies for the Development of Effective Teams

---

1. Limit team size to a manageable number of from 6 to 10 people.

2. Select a team format that matches the goals, expected outcomes, and available resources of the school.

3. Establish written guidelines for the role and responsibilities of a team leader.

4. Establish written procedures for the ongoing documentation and dissemination of team activities.

5. Translate team goals into behavioral objectives.

6. Use the objectives to guide the selection of instructional activities, curriculum, and other resources.

7. Use data to guide instructional and program decision making.

8. Work with administrators to obtain common planning time for team members, and a quality staff development program.

9. Use ongoing and frequent communication to promote cooperation and support among team members, parents, administrators, and colleagues outside the team.

10. Evaluate the team's progress toward the established goals and objectives.

---

levels, as well as representatives from special education or other related service providers. However, it is preferable that teams be limited to a manageable number of from 6 to 10 persons (Ulschka, Nathanson, & Gillan, 1981).

Team Format

The current school infrastructure may guide team format (e.g., grade-level teams, teacher assistance teams) (Phillips & McCullough, 1990; West, 1990). The feasibility of different options is reflective of the (a) current routines, such as class and lunch schedules and transportation requirements; (b) current resources, including financial resources, teaching and support personnel, and availability of time; and (c) educational philosophy of administrators and educators.

Prior to the selection of the format, the involved stakeholders (e.g., administration, faculty) need to review several key components. First, the purposes for a collaboration-based team should be considered, ranging from teams serving as a resource to teachers with students experiencing academic and/or behavioral difficulties, to grade-level teams responsible for the instructional services for students with and without disabilities. Second, desired outcomes for both teachers and students are decided. Possible student outcomes include improved academic performance, decreased number of disciplinary referrals, or increased integration of students with behavioral disorders into general education classrooms. Plausible teacher outcomes are improved professional skills, such as increased use of alternative instructional and/or behavior management strategies. Finally, the availability of resources to support a collaboration-based team is a consideration. Attention should be paid to time constraints, as well as the accessibility of financial and personnel resources (e.g., paraprofessionals, related service providers). In sum, the selected format should match the purpose, the expected outcomes, and the available resources (West, 1990).

Team Leader

An initial organizational task is to select a team leader who possesses strong leadership skills, including the ability to organize group activities, create a comfortable and communicative environment, and synthesize group outcomes (Pugach & Johnson, 1995). It is also critical that the leader have a clear understanding of the group's purpose. Team leaders have been reported as beneficial for facilitating the collaborative activities and, subsequently, increasing the team's outcomes (MacIver & Epstein, 1991).

Procedural guidelines are necessary to guide the nomination and selection of the team leader. The procedural issues to be addressed include voting procedures; length of tenure of the position (e.g., one semester, one academic year); and the team leader's responsibilities, including organizational, leadership, and administrative tasks. These procedures should be written guidelines that convey to all members the expectations and responsibilities of the team leader.

Documentation of Team Activities

The team needs to develop procedures to guide and document its activities, such as developing meeting agenda and recording minutes of team meetings. This will facilitate effective communication among team members and other stakeholders, and ensure that the team remains focused on its purpose.

A set agenda assists the team by directing attention to a given set of topics. A meeting agenda should include strategies for coping with urgent situations (e.g., student in crisis), routine issues (e.g., instructional planning), short-term goals (e.g., planning a parent meeting), and long-term goals (e.g., curriculum development). For example, the daily meeting agenda may be set by team members' listing of agenda items and assigning of priority status (e.g., urgent, high, low) on a dry-erase board; these items form the agenda for the next team meeting. When time does not allow for the discussion of low priority items, those items may be assigned to the following day's meeting agenda with their priority status upgraded or included as an agenda item for topical team meetings (e.g., evaluation meetings, curriculum meetings). Likewise, team discussion of short- and long-term goals may be accomplished by designating specific meetings to discuss certain issues (e.g., curriculum, integration strategies). For instance, the team may set aside meetings on the first and third Fridays for curriculum development activities, and on the second and fourth Fridays for reviewing evaluation data and making modifications in curricula or behavior management practices. The remaining daily meetings are dedicated to handling urgent and routine activities. The use of such strategies avoids the team's being continually consumed with crisis and routine activities during daily meetings, and not having time available for addressing critical short- and long-term issues.

The routine recording of the minutes of team meetings is of utmost importance. First, team meeting minutes provide a permanent record for members to review their decisions and activities, thus facilitating effective communication among team members. Second, accountability for team activities is established through the meeting minutes. Team minutes furnish district- and building-level administrators with information to document use of personnel and time resources as well as a description of the outcomes of the team process (e.g., summaries of students' academic success, curriculum modification).

The team member who is selected to record the minutes has the responsibility of recording, preparing (e.g., typing, copying), and distributing the minutes to the appropriate stakeholders. As for the team leader, procedures should be developed to guide the nomination and selection of the team recorder. For example, the guidelines may call for the rotation of the recorder position among team members. The written guidelines should include processes for the selection of the recorder, including the term of appointment, appointment cycle, and a detailed description of the recorder's responsibilities. Specific procedures are critical to the communication of the role and expectations of the team recorder.

Team Goals

The setting of team goals enhances the effectiveness of the group (Pugach & Johnson, 1995) by identifying specific outcomes and focusing team efforts (Friend & Cook, 1992). Furthermore, the established goals guide the development of objectives and strategies necessary to achieve desired outcomes.

Needs Assessment

Team goals and objectives are derived from needs assessment activities, which may take several forms, including surveys of consumers (e.g., students, parents, colleagues), interviews of key stakeholders of team activities (e.g., school administrators, teachers, parents, community service providers), and review of permanent product data (e.g., number of disciplinary referrals, standardized test scores, number of school dropouts). It is important that the data be summarized using methods (e.g., percentages, rankings) that illustrate the strengths and deficits in assessed domains (e.g., instructional competencies, parent involvement). For example, data summarized by the percentage of educators reporting their competence at one of three levels—no skill, average skill, or highly skilled—is more valuable for identifying faculty members' skill strengths and weaknesses than computing an average or mean rating of each item across all faculty members.

Long- and Short-Term Goals

Using the results of the needs assessment, the next step is for the team to delineate its goals. To illustrate this point, a group of high school educators was charged with the responsibility of reorganizing the delivery of instruction to students from a departmental structure to grade-level teams. Upon review of the academic achievement records, disciplinary records, and content area curricula, the educators established five student-oriented program goals: (a) to develop a foundation of academic and technological skills; (b) to develop a social and personal awareness of the democratic ideals of the country; (c) to develop a positive personal, social, academic, and vocational well-being; (d) to develop career awareness activities and career opportunities; and (e) to establish the link between education and community, national, and global career and educational opportunities. For each goal, the educators developed a set of behavioral objectives. These objectives, in turn, guided the selection of instructional activities, curricula, and other available resources (e.g., community resources).

Systematic Monitoring

Systematic monitoring of the team's progress toward its established goals and objectives has a number of advantages. First, the use of systematic data collection and monitoring procedures results in data that guide instructional and program decision making. For example, if students are having difficulty developing fluency on basic math facts, the team may allocate additional instructional time to fluency-building activities. Second, the maintenance of ongoing records for each program goal and its objectives provides accountability for team activities. Also, it provides a baseline from which new program goals and objectives can emanate. For instance, from ongoing data summaries, the team can account for the use and success of specific interventions to accomplish program goals. Third, systematic monitoring can be extended to individual students. By summarizing an individual student's performance, the team can monitor the student's progress toward mastery of a specific skill. Therefore, as students move through the stages of skill acquisition, the team can respond with appropriate instructional activities. As an example, biology students who have mastered the instructional objectives covering the human circulatory system may be advanced to the next instructional unit, the central nervous system. These data are valuable for communicating each youngster's progress to parents and other professional colleagues.

The record-keeping system should be incorporated in the team's goal-setting and planning activities. The record-keeping system will have several components. An example of a program and objective planning guide is presented in Figure 3.1. The first component of the planning guide is the program goal statement, which is taken from previous team goal identification activities. The second item listed on the planning guide is the objective. This objective is for a specific skill

PROGRAM GOAL AND OBJECTIVE PLANNING GUIDE

Date: 9/1/95

Program Goal: Students will develop a foundation of academic and technological skills.

Objective: Students will bring to class three materials—pen/pencil, paper, book for 6 periods per day.

Outcome Measure	Assessment Technique	Intervention	Persons Responsible	Target Completion Date	Outcome Summary
Number of students who attend class without pen/pencil, paper, and book each week.	Direct observation and recording the number of students without materials each class period.	First week of class instruct students in the necessary materials needed for class.	Each team member.	10/10/95	Reports/6 periods Wk 1 = 25 reports Wk 2 = 23 reports Wk 3 = 10 reports Wk 4 = 8 reports Wk 5 = 9 reports Wk 6 = 1 report
		Deliver study skills curriculum during homeroom period.	Each team member during homeroom period.		

FIGURE 3.1   Program goal and objective planning guide.

or behavior that is part of a sequence of skills or activities that culminate in obtaining the program goal. The goal, in this case, was to require students to bring required materials to class.

The third set of items requires the team to identify the outcome measure, assessment technique, intervention, persons responsible, target completion date, and outcome summary. The measure is an observable and measurable behavior that can be reliably recorded to evaluate students' progress toward mastery of the objective. For this sample objective, each team member counted the number of students without one or more materials (pen or pencil, paper, book) for each class period. The assessment technique refers to the methodology used to collect the data. In this case, it was direct observation of the students' possession of required class materials.

For each objective, the team identifies the instructional strategy and/or materials used to deliver instruction to the students. For this example, the intervention strategy was two-pronged. The first part of the intervention was a statement of expectations by each teacher to his or her group of students; the second part was the delivery of a study skills curriculum.

Three additional items on the program guide require the team to identify individual persons responsible for the delivery of the intervention, establish a target completion date, and record the outcome summaries. The outcome summary requires the team to record the findings on a frequent basis. In this instance, the team recorded the frequency of the students' lacking one or more materials on a weekly basis.

Other data-recording strategies include the use of logs to record behaviors such as the frequency of contacts with parents, administrators, and related service providers. Students can also record their own progress for individual academic and behavioral objectives with monitoring of accuracy from team educators, and the use of computer-based data summary applications (e.g., spreadsheets, grade books) can speed data summary activities.

Team Resources

A number of critical resources have been identified for successful collaboration-based teams. The required resources include (a) common planning periods, (b) adequate meeting space, and (c) professional development opportunities.

Time and Space

Common planning time among team members has been repeatedly identified as the foremost element to successful team functioning (e.g., MacIver & Epstein, 1991; Phillips & McCullough, 1990; Walsh & Shay, 1993). Scheduling of sufficient team planning time requires both the support of school administrators and the identification of multiple scheduling options. Potential options include staggering lunch and extracurricular activity schedules, extending the instructional day, reorganizing the daily sequence of courses and teacher planning periods, and/or providing team teachers with multiple planning periods.

A comfortable meeting place is another critical element of successful teams. Meeting areas should provide an environment with sufficient privacy to foster open communication among team members (Friend & Cook, 1992). Administrative support should be solicited to secure an adequate meeting area.

Collaboration Skills Training

Previously, others have noted the inadequacy of preservice preparation of general and special educators to participate as team members in the planning and delivery of instruction to students with and without disabilities (Friend & Cook, 1990; Simpson, Whelan, & Zabel, 1993). Thus, an essential team resource is a quality staff development program to provide the needed training in collaborative planning and problem solving (West, 1990; Zins, Curtis, Graden, & Ponti, 1988). It has been suggested that the programs focus on three skill areas: (a) communication, interaction, and collaborative problem-solving skills; (b) effective teaching and instructional practices for educating all students; (c) skills in system change, team facilitation and management, organizational and individual resistance, and program evaluation (West, 1990). Staff development programs should incorporate proven training procedures, such as detailed demonstrations, opportunities for practice, and instructional activities to promote transfer of skills to typical situations presented in included classrooms.

Other Resources

The availability of other resources, such as flexible schedules, instructional materials, audiovisual equipment, and other technology (e.g., computers, interactive laser discs), affect the team's collaborative efforts. Teams may seek the assistance of administrators and others to obtain the necessary materials. For example, teams have collaborated to solicit local community business leaders to obtain necessary materials and resources. The teams have received donations of equipment (e.g., computers), services (e.g., computer training), instructional support materials and services (e.g, speakers, field trip sites, videotapes), and professional development opportunities (e.g., workshops).

Communication

Effective teams establish clear communication links among team members and between the team and critical stakeholders. Ongoing and frequent communication promotes cooperation and support among team members and key supporters (Friend & Cook, 1992). Besides the team, three important stakeholders of collaborative activities are (a) students' parents, (b) district- and building-level administrators, and (c) colleagues outside the team.

Parents of Students

Parents, as consumers of the educational process, have concerns about the quality of educational services for their children, particularly in times of educational reform. Thus, it is imperative that educators inform parents of changes in educational structures and the associated impact on their children's education.

An initial step to establishing communication with parents is to invite them to an informational meeting. The parents' invitation should describe the meeting's activities, including the types of information (e.g., program goals, student's schedule, names of student's teachers) that will be shared with parents. Furthermore, the meeting should be held on a day and time that will encourage parents' attendance. For example, an option selected by one team was a Saturday morning meeting. At this meeting, parents were (a) furnished with descriptions of the teaming process (including schedules) by the teachers, counselors, and administrators, followed by a question-and-answer period; (b) given opportunities to meet with the educators of their child's assigned team; (c) provided tours of the physical facilities (including computer labs, group project meeting rooms); and (d) encouraged to volunteer for specific classroom activities (e.g., speaker, tutor, classroom aide, field trip supervisor). Each parent was given a packet of material that included the team program goals, team class schedules, team rules, a listing of the team teachers and their time periods available for parent contact, and a phone number. Careful records were maintained of parents who attended the meeting. Parents not in attendance were sent the materials with an invitation to visit and be involved in school activities. The combination of a detailed invitation and a program oriented toward parents' needs resulted in an overwhelming number of the parents attending the meeting. Certainly, successful team efforts to establish a strong and positive relationship with parents will assist team members in meeting the diverse needs of their students with and without disabilities.

The second task is for the team to maintain ongoing communication with parents. Besides parent–teacher conferences, valuable communication strategies include a biweekly newsletter of team activities mailed to parents, frequent personal contact with parents either by phone or mail to discuss student outcomes that are both positive (e.g., via Good News Notes on school letterhead) and negative (e.g., by asking parents to meet with team to discuss student difficulties), and continued recruitment of parents to be involved in their children's education.

District- and Building-Level Administrators

District- and building-level administrators are key contributors and stakeholders in the success of collaboration-based teams. First, administrative personnel are often responsible for approving schedule revisions necessary to secure the required planning time, allocation of funds for materials and other school-related activities, and the provision of staff training. Second, building-level administrators may be asked to account for the activities of restructuring efforts (e.g., teams) to district-level administrative staff. Thus, a strong communication pathway between administrators and team members is vital to the continued support of district- and building-level administrators.

Several communication strategies are offered to establish and maintain communication ties with administrative personnel. First, administrative personnel should be invited regularly to participate in team meetings. Several benefits arise from administrators' participation in these meetings, including insight from a different educational perspective or the securing of additional resources. Perhaps the foremost benefit is that the administrator witnesses the team members interacting and sharing their expertise and resources to improve the quality of education to diverse learners.

Second, administrators may be kept informed of the team's activities by distributing copies of the team minutes to them. Subsequently, administrators have an ongoing record of the team's activities and outcomes (e.g., revisions in behavior management practices; integrated curriculum activities). The stream of information to administrators engages their cooperation and support by keeping them adequately informed of the team's activities.

Finally, each team should share the results of their evaluation activities with the administration. The data are valuable for identifying the strengths and weaknesses of the team process. The data showing strengths serve as measures of accountability for the restructuring and utilization of finite resources. Data such as increases in academic performance of students with and without disabilities are valuable for maintaining administrators' and other decision-makers' support of a collaboration-based team approach. The data showing weaknesses afford opportunities for teams to secure additional support for the collaborative process, such as additional planning time, material resources, and/or professional development activities.

Colleagues

Regular communication between team members and colleagues outside of the team should be established, particularly as changes are being made in the delivery of educational services to students. Keeping nonparticipating colleagues informed of the activities and successes of pilot programs influences their support and increases the likelihood of their participation in the event of program expansion. Examples of information-sharing opportunities with colleagues include providing oral progress reports at school faculty meetings and distributing copies of team newsletters and program evaluation summaries to faculty members.

Program Evaluation

Evaluation procedures are an integral part of collaboration-based teams. Evaluation activities may include (a) measuring the collaboration teams' progress toward program goals, (b) evaluating the success of specific intervention strategies, (c) assessing the level of consumer satisfaction, (d) determining the cost-efficiency of the program, and (e) disseminating program evaluation results.

Program evaluation activities are beneficial for several reasons. First, evaluation activities indicate areas of program improvement. For example, parent contact or study skills instruction may be identified as program weaknesses. Assessing the viability of expanding collaboration-based teams is another benefit of evaluation. The success of a pilot program often influences whether the approach is permanently integrated into the educational program. Finally, positive and significant outcomes of a program may lead to the replication of the program in other settings. If other schools or districts learn of the positive results (e.g., increased integration of students with disabilities), the approach may be adopted by other districts.

Program Goals

Generally, program goals are directed at global outcomes, such as student achievement, disciplinary reports, and dropout rates. Systematic evaluation procedures for each goal are included as a significant part of the goal-setting process. For instance, reducing the absence rate of students was one team's program goal. The identified outcome measure was the number of students absent for more than one class period per school day. Absence rates were calculated for each week and month, as well as for quarter and semester grading periods.

Student Outcomes

The second set of evaluation measures describes individual student progress. Thus, an ongoing evaluation system should be established to (a) determine students' present skill level, (b) monitor students' progress toward skill mastery, and (c) measure students' maintenance and generalization of learned skills. One proven approach that provides a reliable and valid technology for ongoing evaluation is curriculum-based assessment (CBA) (Deno, 1985). CBA is guided by the behavioral objectives of the curriculum. For each objective, a series of short probes is generated to measure students' skills. The probes are integrated into the instructional process as pretest measures of student skill, measures of student progress, and posttest measures. From summaries (e.g., graphs, charts) of students' performance, educators are provided data to guide instructional decisions (e.g., reteach the content, proceed to next objective). Because this system is based on behavioral objectives, modifications of curriculum content and academic expectations can be made and monitored easily. Furthermore, the system is easily adapted to a diverse group of learners present in an integrated classroom.

An ongoing evaluation system provides documentation for several evaluation issues. First, parents, students, and other consumers are provided with frequent measures of student performance rather than several comprehensive measures (e.g., quarter or semester exams). Second, the data guide instructional and curriculum modification for students with a broad range of skills and abilities. For example, if a student has limited skills, key content objectives can be selected to reduce the amount and the complexity of the instructed content. Finally, the data contribute to program evaluation efforts. A review of students' progress may identify specific academic and behavioral skill deficits across all students or groups of students (e.g., high-performing, low-performing, disabled students), and describe the effectiveness of alternative instructional approaches (e.g., cooperative learning groups; peer tutoring).

Consumer Satisfaction

Consumer satisfaction, or the degree to which the program met individuals' perceived needs, is a critical component of the evaluation process. In this case, it is important to determine whether the stakeholders (i.e., parents, students, support personnel, administrators) were satisfied with general and special education services offered by a collaboration-based team of educators. These data are valuable for identifying positive and negative aspects of the program (e.g., discipline policies; parent contact) that may influence the level of participation and/or interest of students, parents, and colleagues.

Surveys, interviews, or rating scales may be used to assess parents', students', and other concerned persons' degree of satisfaction with collaboration-based teams. These measures may ask respondents to identify positive and negative aspects of the program, to suggest modifications or changes in the program, and to provide an overall evaluation of the program. For example, concerned stakeholders may respond to questions evaluating the quality of instructional services, the accessibility of team members, and the effectiveness of communication strategies. Certainly, this information, combined with other outcome measures (e.g., test scores, individual student outcomes), will provide the team and other stakeholders with a multidimensional evaluation.

Cost-Efficiency

The basic question answered by a cost-efficiency analysis is whether the personnel and the related expenditures (e.g., materials, planning time) were worth the obtained outcomes. For example, a district may want to make a comparison between the performance of students in collaboration-based teams and those in traditional classrooms. Other analyses may include the comparison of the academic and behavioral skills or student subgroups, such as students with disabilities, being provided services under two different instructional programs (e.g., team-based vs. traditional approaches).

Dissemination of Program Evaluation Results

Upon completion of the evaluation, summaries of the results should be prepared and communicated to key stakeholders, such as the team members, administrative personnel, and parents. For each group, the shared information should be geared to their information needs. For example, administrators charged with responsibility for the allocation of financial resources should receive the cost-analysis information, whereas parents may be more interested in the overall academic and behavioral gains made by students, the number of parent contacts made by the educators, or the types of resources contributed by community businesses. In all cases, the information should be communicated in a clear and straightforward manner.

References

Bradley, D. F., & West, J. F. (1994). Staff training for the inclusion of students with disabilities: Visions from school-based educators. *Teacher Education and Special Education, 12*(2), 117–128.

Deno, S. L. (1985). Curriculum-based measurement: The emerging alternative. *Exceptional Children, 52*(3), 219–232.

Dettmer, P., Thurston, L. P., & Dyck, N. (1993). *Consultation, collaboration, and teamwork for students with special needs.* Boston: Allyn & Bacon.

Friend, M., & Cook, L. (1990). Collaboration as a predictor for success in school reform. *Journal of Educational and Psychological Consultation, 1*(1), 69–86.

Friend, M., & Cook, L. (1992). *Interactions.* New York: Longman.

Glatthorn, A. A. (1990). Cooperative professional development: Facilitating the growth of the special education teacher and the classroom teacher. *Remedial and Special Education, 11*(3), 29–39.

Idol, L., Paolucci-Whitcomb, P., & Nevin, A. (1987). *Collaborative consultation.* Austin, TX: PRO-ED.

Joyce, B., & Showers, B. (1982). The coaching of teaching. *Educational Leadership, 40,* 4–8, 10.

MacIver, D. J., & Epstein, J. L. (1991). Responsive practices in the middle grades: Teacher teams, advisory groups, remedial instruction, and school transition programs. *American Journal of Education, 99,* 587–622.

Morgan, R. L., Menlove, R., Salzberg, C. L., & Hudson, P. (1994). Effects of peer coaching on the acquisition of direct instruction skills by low-performing pre-service teachers. *Journal of Special Education, 28,* 59–76.

Mundschenk, N. A., & Foley, R. M. (1994, October). *Improving instruction: Strategies for building effective teams.* Paper presented at the Fourth Annual Iowa–Illinois Conference, Bettendorf, IA.

Nowacek, E. J. (1992). Professionals talk about teaching together: Interviews with five collaborating teachers. *Intervention in School and Clinic, 27*(5), 262–276.

Phillips, V., & McCullough, L. (1990). Consultation-based programming: Instituting the collaborative ethic in schools. *Exceptional Children, 56,* 291 304.

Pugach, M. C., & Johnson, L. J. (1995). *Collaborative practitioners, collaborative schools.* Denver: Love.

Simpson, R. L., Whelan, R. J., & Zabel, R. H. (1993). Special education personnel preparation in the 21st century: Issues and strategies. *Remedial and Special Education, 14*(2), 7–22.

Ulschak, F. L., Nathanson, L., & Gillan, P. G. (1981). *Small group problem-solving: An aid to organizational processes.* Reading, MA: Addison-Wesley.

Walsh, K. J., & Shay, M. J. (1993). In support of interdisciplinary teaming: The climate factor. *Middle School Journal, 24*(4), 56–60.

West, J. F. (1990). Educational collaboration in the restructuring of schools. *Journal of Educational and Psychological Consultation, 1*(1), 23–40.

Zins, J. E., Curtis, M. J., Graden, J. L., & Ponti, C. R. (1988). *Helping students succeed in the regular classroom.* San Francisco: Jossey-Bass.

CHAPTER 4

Implementing Inclusion in a Middle School Setting

Lisa Matts and
Paul Zionts

Why Begin an Inclusion Program? Debunking Some Myths

Simply stated, initiating an inclusion program is the job for people who truly perceive it as a solution to the problems of servicing special education students who currently receive all or most of their education in pull-out programs. In our experience, contrary to popular belief, individual teachers can make a difference by more fully integrating students with special needs into general education settings. Granted, in the ideal world, the school administration, general and special education colleagues, parents, and most important students will be philosophically and instrumentally behind the changes that may need to be implemented. However, cooperation and assistance from these important parties are not always available.

In other words, we have found that, if a teacher believes in inclusion and is relatively alone in this commitment, it still can be accomplished. This may mean that the teacher needs to move ahead with plans for inclusion even if it means doing so alone. The support of administration is helpful *but not imperative*. Planning for inclusion with all of the general education staff would be nice *but not completely necessary*. Inservice workshops for general and special education teachers on how to set up inclusion can greatly assist the process *but are not crucial.* For example, my principal wanted me (Matts) to "team" with a teacher who needed some help with his special education students. This teacher was reluctant to attempt any modification in his teaching. The thought of trying to work with a teacher who was not willing to change worried me. I realized that we did not have a chance for success. After meeting with the teacher, my fears were confirmed. I then spoke to my colleague, the other language arts teacher, who agreed to work as a team with me and our current and the transferred students. I met with the guidance counselors and we changed the students' schedules. Although my principal was not aware of the changes until they were complete, his goal was met because the students' needs were being met. I am still not sure if my principal truly cared *how* I met his goal.

Teachers can make inclusion work, regardless of the political realities of their settings. My team teacher and I did not have formal planning periods, so we used lunchtime for planning. We did not officially call it planning, but we talked about the progress and future programming of our students as we ate lunch. It was not an ideal situation, but a necessary accommodation.

Although schools may "talk inclusion," they may provide little real support for the endeavor. Inclusion inservice workshops tend to be too general to meet an individual teacher's needs. Teachers have to remember that each individual student may still need a specific plan to be integrated into the general education classroom. For example, a teacher's time might be better spent collaborating with a teaching partner, sharing both general and special education information on the best practices of inclusion. This can be obtained from a myriad of sources: conferences, inservice workshops, the literature, and, most important, practical, personal successes. We recognize that inclusion is uniquely interpreted by most school systems (and individual schools). However, we also know that the more individualized the methods for servicing students, the better inclusion will work. Also, grouping students who will respond best to these methods is integral to successful inclusion. We believe that inservice training is best if it emanates from within the school.

Isolationism can certainly be a barrier of inclusion. A teacher who is without formal support must try to locate teachers who may be willing to work with him or her. It was not an easy task convincing most of my future partners that inclusion would work. I promised them support and cooperation. I took every opportunity to enlist another teacher. When one teacher was on maternity leave, I worked with her substitute teacher and became an important addition to the classroom. When the teacher returned, she welcomed me as an equal partner.

Clearly, motivation for undertaking inclusion must exist. What are the personal benefits to the teachers who may participate? To the students? To their parents? In each case, the answers may be different. We believe that the positives of including students with behavioral and learning problems with general education students far outweigh the negatives. We also believe that the ideas that have been generated (and have yet to be generated) during this movement will better meet the needs not only of students with special needs but also of students who are low achievers. The more time special education students can be with and learn with students who are considered typical learners, the more all will learn. We realize that many of these students have learning and behavioral needs that many general education teachers are unable or unwilling to accommodate. These students and teachers need the support of special education teachers.

For inclusion to work, special education teachers must be in the general education classroom. There are many ways for special education and general education teachers to work together. In some cases, the special education teacher can coteach with the general education teacher, sharing equally in the teaching of the content material. The two teachers approach each lesson using different delivery systems, thus giving all students an opportunity to be actively engaged. The two lessons may be simultaneously delivered, with each educator teaching the same content in different ways. We do not mean to imply that all students *will* be actively engaged, but that instruction will be presented so that all students will have the opportunity to learn. No learner will be discriminated against because of a learning or behavioral handicap.

Another collaborative method may be that the general education teacher presents the material and the special education teacher monitors behavior. This approach, while better than nothing, is not recommended because it sets up a dual instructional system. The temptation for special education teachers to become behavioral specialists or monitors delineates their role in a nonteaching manner. Further, it will probably set up a system within a system. The "monitoring" teachers will most likely interact only with special education students.

In all cases, it is important that the entire class views both adults as teachers. For example, one way to start the school year is to have the general education teacher teach the class rules and the special education teacher teach the student handbook. This way the students see both teachers as equal partners. Another strategy is to have both teachers agree to work with each other when they have something to contribute to the conversation. If one teacher is asked a question by a student, the other teacher might politely interrupt and help give the specific information that the other might not know. The message to the students is obvious: We are *both* here to help you. The message to each other is also clear: I trust you to help me in this classroom; we are partners. We also recommend as much self-disclosure as reasonable by both teachers in the classroom; it is important for each to talk about his or her own experiences, allowing the students to perceive them as "people."

Structural Factors

An important factor to consider in making inclusion work is the total number of students who will be in the class. This determination can depend upon many variables and adequate teacher planning. For example, the students who require the most time should be combined with students who can work independently. Our experiences suggest that no more than 20% of the students in a classroom should have special needs. Further, of those students, no more than half (10% of the total) should have significant emotional and/or behavioral problems. Once again, the need to individualize this process must be stressed. The constitution of the class is crucial to its success. We truly believe that, with the right attitude and the willingness to modify current approaches to teaching, the inclusion of almost any number of students with special needs will be successful. For example, we once had four students with emotional and behavioral disorders (EBD) in a math class of 28 work well because of the individualized nature of math. In a language arts class, four students with emotional and behavioral disorders were integrated successfully because of the group work that was endemic to the pedagogy of that environment. Also, each student in both classes had either in-class support or content-specific study halls.

Simply placing students with disabilities in the general education setting will not make these students into typical students. Specific academic and emotional–behavioral programming may be necessary for the entire class. Constant instruction and reminders of acceptable behaviors are integral to an exciting and well-managed classroom. It seems to be an unfortunate reality that the initial "bottom line" on the success of an inclusion program is the appropriate behaviors of the students involved. We agree with many of the practices described in this book and would like to personally highlight some specific points that we believe are crucial.

If assimilating socially is one of the key benefits of inclusion, it would follow that not only a constant monitoring of students' behavior is necessary, but also instruction to help them gain the social skills deemed requisite for success. Clearly, many students with emotional and behavioral disorders will need more than the routine application of rules and consequences. For example, they may need a rationale for behaving other than rules and punishments that the general education classroom provides. We spend a lot of time talking to students who have behavior differences about the expectations of the general education teachers. We discuss their differences and how they will need to adapt to those differences. Sometimes they understand better if we explain it as "playing the game."

Many of these students may not behave for other reasons (e.g., the issue of compliance). They challenge authority figures and are compliant with those teachers whom they perceive as less threatening. Sometimes students find that rules in the classroom are diametrically opposed to those in their homes. Rewards may be given to these students for behaving well in their more difficult classes.

Teachers need to provide an environment in which students can learn to succeed with respect. They should not be humiliated because of their behavior. Horror stories abound. We know of a student who was forced to write 500 times, "I will act normal in gym." One can only guess how a student will feel after 3 days of writing this sentence! One teacher would continually harass special education students for not completing their work on time, although some general education students in the same setting were not completing their work. The teacher would say to the special education students, "You boys work with Mrs. Matts on that story." Sensing unfairness, the students complained about their treatment (the general education students who were in the same predicament were ignored by the teacher). After airing their complaints, I volunteered to help both the special and the general education students. The teacher was relieved and stopped focusing her attention on the special education students.

Although appropriate classroom behavior seems to occupy the minds of teachers and administrators alike, a shared responsibility for interactions must also take place. Many times, students inappropriately behave when work is too hard or too easy for them. Teachers must assume instructional responsibility by carefully tailoring each lesson. It seems as if teachers need to relearn their introductory education classes and implement those truisms that are presented in university classes, conferences, and inservice workshops: Many students may need assignments broken down into sections, and they may need advance organizers for content work.

Practicing What I (Matts) Preach

I had a group of very difficult eighth-grade boys in a categorical program for students with emotional and behavioral disorders. In January of that year, they pleaded with me that they just wanted "regular" math. I told them if they could take math seriously and realize that it was their behavior that kept them out of the general education classroom, they could be in general math the next year. We spent the rest of the year playing "catch-up" in the eighth-grade book. Their motivation to be like the general education students, to attend classes with them, and to learn with them spurred these students to attend to their task. It also took everything that I had to rise to the challenge to teach them what they needed to know so that they could exit the pull-out program. I did not realize that the work I put into that year would pale next to the effort required of me if inclusion for these students was going to be successful.

As mentioned above, for students to succeed, their behaviors must improve and/or become more tolerated by the general education teachers. One of the most important things to do in an inclusive setting is to review all the behavioral change methods. Many behaviors need to be monitored when special education students are put into a general education classroom, especially when the work is hard for them. There are many interventions from which to choose. The best idea is for teachers to look at all the methods and decide which ones meet the needs of their students. Also, the program may need to be modified as the school year progresses. One intervention may work well for a short time, and another one may work all year.

I was constantly making changes. I changed my lunch hour three times in one year. If students needed more time, I gave it to them. One of two special education students in a language arts classroom moved away. The other student was doing well, so I started an affective class for all students who needed it. I constantly changed reinforcers in both quality and quantity; some students reacted well to long-term "powerful" rewards and others reacted well to continual "minor" rewards.

Teachers need to routinely ask, "Is the behavior improving?" If not, it is time to review the program. In many cases, the best behavior intervention is the teacher. If the student respects the teacher and feels good about himself or herself, his or her behavior may improve. Once, I had a student on my caseload whom I saw only occasionally. His teacher sent him to me after his first real crisis; I tried to talk to him, but he did not know me and was not going to cooperate with me. I did persuade him to visit me later that week. I allowed him to bring a friend, which made him feel more comfortable. We began to establish a relationship and, when subsequent problems occurred, he was more open to my help. He needed to know that someone cared about the way he was feeling and that any solution would not be easy. Taking time to develop a relationship with each student helps when there is a crisis situation. If a teacher develops a positive relationship with students, they will know they can trust the teacher if problems occur. I am not saying that students are doomed without me, but I do know that my work to develop relationships has helped students to get through many troubles.

Our version of inclusion provides the students with a support class each day. This class provides the teacher an opportunity to help the students with assignments and to teach affective, social, and behavioral skills. In some cases, this class may simply entail a discussion of students' current problems and helping them arrive at possible solutions. Topics might include problems that occur during lunch or recess, with the general education teachers, with rules, and with problems at home. Often, other students in class serve as valuable resources for the students having problems by giving suggestions or agreeing to help the students with their problems.

When students have no specific problems to discuss, we utilize a formal social skills program to teach them particular skills that would better enable them to succeed. This is one of the areas where a special education teacher's training and expertise can be most beneficial.

Interventions

The behavioral interventions discussed in the following subsections can be used in an inclusion setting to help general education teachers improve their overall management plans. Many of these techniques have been used specifically for individual students who have learning and behavioral problems and who are experiencing difficulties in the classroom.

Self-Monitoring

Self-monitoring is a procedure whereby a student is given verbal and visual prompts to represent on-task behaviors. As the name implies, the students record their own progress. This intervention works best with students who are working independently or on very structured activities. It has been particularly effective when students can be taught the procedure in a special education class first and then transfer the procedure to general education classes. It helps students feel more accepted by others. A visual reminder chart (see Figure 4.1) can be used as a prompt for students. It represents the behaviors expected by the classroom teacher: Stay in your seat, keep eyes on your work, do not interrupt, and raise your hand. The teacher merely points to this chart, even from across the room, to remind any student of the behavior that may need to be exhibited. Students may use this chart to remind themselves of appropriate behaviors required in the setting.

Time-Out

When one thinks of the traditional special education setting, the concept of time-out as an intervention comes to mind. Many forms of time-out, however, also can be successfully implemented in general education settings. Time-out refers to the removal of the source of reinforcement (e.g., an activity in the classroom, peers, or even the teacher). If a student is behaving in an inappropriate manner in the teacher's presence, the teacher may choose to leave her alone and tell her that when she is ready for help and can behave correctly, the teacher will be back to help. It may not take long for the student to realize she wants help and stop the inappropriate behavior. This works especially well if the student knows that if she does not get help on the assignment, there will be other predetermined consequences (e.g., loss of participation in group activity).

The more traditional use of time-out involves the removal of a student from the classroom. If a student's behavior is extremely disruptive and it is interrupting the learning of other students, a temporary time-out from the classroom can help. Time-out works best if it takes place in an area near the classroom.

FIGURE 4.1   Example of a visual prompt chart.

Time-outs normally last from 5 to 10 minutes. This intervention is meant to be a concrete reminder that students need to refocus on work or maybe that they just need to calm down. Teachers should not use the time-out period as the time to discuss the misbehavior. Typically, students are not ready to discuss their behaviors at this time. Also, engaging in discussion with the students during these times can serve as a positive reinforcement to students who might opt for time-out to get more attention.

At most, teachers should simply remind the students of the rules they have violated. One of the teachers, or an aide if available, should stay with the student during time-out. The intervention is most effective if it is used by both teachers, thus avoiding the stereotyping of roles (e.g., special education teachers are in the room to enforce rules, whereas general education teachers are in the room to teach). Consequently, the students learn that both teachers expect them to be members of the class without interrupting the others' chance to learn. It is extremely important to have contingencies in the setting that hinge upon the time spent in class. In other words, if the student is missing time in class for any reason, it follows that the time missed will result in yet another consequence (incomplete assignment, lowered grade, loss of reward). This communicates to the students that the time spent in class is valuable and time missed can result in the loss of additional privileges.

Token Economy

Token economy is a system that involves awarding or removing points contingent upon a student's display of specified behaviors. These points or tokens are redeemed for activities, objects, or privileges. This works well in either the general or the special education setting, and either teacher can complete the record sheet. The other students in the class do not have to be aware of the contract. The rewards may be given at a later time, perhaps in the special education class. An example of a behavior contract that uses token economy to improve behavior is presented in Figure 4.2.

Response Cost

Response cost is another behavioral intervention that can be successful in both general and special education settings. This intervention involves taking away privileges from students who exhibit inappro-

BEHAVIOR CONTRACT

Student _____   Class _____

Teacher _____   Date _____

Goals (Circle one)	Not Acceptable	Could Be Better	Good	Excellent
Demonstrates appropriate interaction with other students.	1	2	3	4
Comments _____				
Demonstrates appropriate care and handling of others' property.	1	2	3	4
Comments _____				
Demonstrates appropriate behavior on the school grounds.	1	2	3	4
Comments _____				

Total _____

Tally Sheet

Each Day: 70 points = successful day

Hour	Task	Total Points
1	Language Arts	_____
2	Support	_____
3	Social Studies	_____
4	Lunch	_____
5	Math	_____
6	Science	_____
7	Computers	_____
8	Flex	_____

Parent signature: _____

FIGURE 4.2   Example of a behavior contract.

priate behaviors. The message to students is clear: All privileges are for all students, unless a student demonstrates that he or she cannot behave like all students. Response-cost consequences in classrooms are similar to those used in society through fines, penalties, and so forth. When classroom rules are broken, something is taken away from the student, such as free time, computer time, group time, tokens, or points being saved for a specific reward. The teacher might explain to students that the only way some people stop speeding is to get a large fine; response cost is a similar system that may enable students to understand why they must change their behaviors.

Token economies and response cost seem to be most effective when used in combination. For example, one student had a contract that included rewards for doing his work and punishments for not doing it. He earned points for free time and lunch with me if his work was done. He also received detentions and other consequences if his work was incomplete. This intervention required daily monitoring and support from parents and administrators.

These interventions do not work for everybody. If a student begins to lose more points than he or she earns, the program should be promptly modified. Also, many students function well in a small, special class with the aid of a token economy, but when put into general classrooms, their behavior may deteriorate. These interventions are generally best used with students who have significant problem behaviors. We cannot overemphasize the need to constantly monitor behaviors, paying close attention to levels of maintenance and generalization. Another tip is to change the criteria and rewards so that the students' growth continues and the consequences remain enticing.

Peer-Mediated Interventions

A method that works well to improve behavior and includes the cooperation of general education students is peer-mediated interventions. An example of this is when the special education teacher explains to the general education students the nature of emotional disturbance and how it affects a particular student who will be entering the class. Teachers may be candid about these descriptions (after notifying parents of special education students of this tactic) and ask the students for their help. In fact, it helps to tell the class that the student will be successful in the classroom only with the help and cooperation of all the classmates. Teachers also can give specific assignments for certain students, such as asking them to encourage the special education student to do a good job and tell him or her what he or she is doing wrong. The students can monitor behaviors, and let the teacher know if serious behaviors occur. Teachers can then reinforce the general education students with rewards, such as an extra recess, a field trip, or treats. The special education student may also participate in receiving the reinforcer. This method is particularly effective with students in the upper elementary grades, as students in this age group seem to enjoy helping their peers.

Behavioral Contracts

One method that we have found to be very successful in monitoring behavior is the use of behavior contracts. The benefits of behavior contracting are (a) to manage behavior when the teacher is not present, (b) to include all people who work with the student, (c) to provide clear goals with consequences and rewards for the student, and (d) to provide a means for all adults to use the same language when dealing with the student. The following are some suggestions for writing a behavior contract:

1. Write specific observable goals (preferably with the student).
2. Decide who will be involved (involve parents only if they will follow through).
3. Define the roles of those involved in the contract.
4. Determine the criteria. How often does the student need to meet the goal?
5. What will be considered successful?
6. Choose the reinforcers: short term (for achieving incremental gains) and long term (for completing the goal).
7. Decide upon consequences that can be enforced.
8. Prepare a chart to monitor success.
9. Type the contract.
10. Have all parties involved sign the paper.
11. Be consistent and follow through.

Although each contract is developed with the best intentions, not every contract can be achieved. If all attempts fail, the teacher(s) and student may have to modify the contract or even determine that it cannot be completed. One student who was working on a contract was not doing very well with it. Her behavior was erratic and the reinforcers were not working. Her counselor started a program with her mother than included a daily note home from teachers reporting the behaviors on the contract. The mother agreed to reward her daughter for her appropriate behaviors. This was far more successful than the contract. As with almost everything addressed in this chapter, constant monitoring, flexibility, and evaluation are crucial.

Different types of contracts can be used in an inclusion program. A *home–school contract* is one in which the parents have agreed to reward the student at home for behavior at school. The contract must state exactly what the student must do in order to earn the reward. An example of a home–school contract is in Figure 4.3. In this case, the parent agreed to base the student's allowance on his daily behavior. The agreement was found to work best if the student's day was divided into halves; if the student had a bad morning, he knew he could improve his behavior and still earn the afternoon allowance. Another factor that worked well was to send home only the student's point total because the mother was upset by the comments from the teachers describing the inappropriate behaviors on the daily comment sheets. It was important to focus on the good behavior with this particular student.

Another type of contract is the *individual contract*. This contract is written with the student and includes the desired behavior and rewards and consequences. An example of this type of contract appears in Figure 4.4.

One type of contract that can be used to monitor all the special education students in the general education classroom at the same time is a *group contingency contract*. This contract makes monitoring behavior much easier than having individual contracts with each student. When using this type of contract, a reward is given to the student who earns the most points. For example, the reward for one contract was to have lunch with the teacher. One student wanted to know who was paying for the lunch because he was sure to win it if the general education teacher was paying. "I will make that sucker pay," he said. It is amazing what is rewarding to some students.

An example of a group contingency was used successfully in an inclusion math class where four students with emotional and behavioral disorders were being monitored by the special education teacher. The general education students did not know about the contract, which was discussed only in the special education classroom. Specific

---

HOME–SCHOOL CONTINGENCY CONTRACT

Student _____

Teacher _____

Date   _____

The student will (Goals):

1. Use appropriate language.
2. Control anger.
3. Complete work to teacher's satisfaction.

Rewards:

- Free time when work is complete
- Each successful day earns a candy bar
- 8 out of 10 successful days earns a model (Mustang) or cassette tape
- Next 8 out of 10 successful days earns a lunch with the counselor, teacher, principal, or Mrs. Matts

The parent will:

- Give positive feedback.
- Encourage good behavior.
- Give $.50 per successful day ($.25 for morning and $.25 for afternoon).

I agree to this contract:

Student _____

Parents _____

          _____

Teacher _____

FIGURE 4.3   Example of a home–school contract.

CONTRACT

Student _____

Teacher _____

Date   _____

The student will (Goals):

1. Listen to and follow directions. Know the assignment.
2. Make an attempt to do the work, ask questions, complete work.
3. Use time wisely.

The teacher will:

- Actively listen.
- Give alternatives/help solve problems.
- Record daily progress.

Rewards:

- Each day 7–9 checks = candy bar
- Each week all checks = $.05
- $2.00 worth of points = a reward from Mrs. Matts's closet

I agree to this contract:

Teacher _____

Student _____

($\checkmark$ = yes; check the box below that applies)

	M	T	W	TH	F
1. Listen to and follows directions. Knows the assignment.					
2. Makes attempts to do work, asks questions, completes work.					
3. Uses time wisely.					
Date _____ Total					

FIGURE 4.4   Example of an individual contract indicating desired behavior and rewards and consequences.

behaviors on the contract included homework completion, class participation, recording of assignments, beginning work promptly, and paying attention to tasks.

Another type of group contingency is called *marbles in the jar.* This works for all students in a class to improve behavior. When the entire class is working hard or following all the class rules, marbles are added to a clear jar. A predetermined reward is earned when the jar is full. The reward could be free time, a movie, a special treat, no homework, and so on. This intervention works even with middle school students, and benefits both general and special education classes.

Conclusion

Inclusion has worked for us because we have used the behavioral interventions and the academic strategies found in this chapter. The best advice is for each teacher to choose the intervention that works in his or her situation. Teachers must be flexible and willing to change. We are still struggling with certain aspects of inclusion. Although our program is working well, we have encountered the following difficulties:

- Students may not perceive the special education teacher as the "real" teacher. Students may ask the teacher, "What do you teach?" It further complicates matters if the school lists a teacher as a special education teacher. A simple remedy is to list special education teachers under the grades that they teach.

- Some teachers do not understand special education students and, even when they are successful, label and treat them in a discriminatory manner.

The many advantages to implementing inclusion in our school have included the following:

- Our being in the classroom with the students, which allowed us to know firsthand the requirements of the general education settings. It made it easier for developing Individualized Education Program goals and objectives that are necessary for successful transition.

- We did not have to chase teachers to find out what they were doing in their classes. When a student is in another teacher's inclusion class, we obtain the class requirements from the special education teacher who teams with that teacher. I (Matts) had a student who was not in my inclusion class for science. Because he had another teacher, it was difficult to help him prepare for tests and assignments. Another special education teacher who was teaming with that science teacher gave me the notes for that class, and I would give them to my student. Without sharing, I could not possibly keep up with all of the teachers my students had in one day.

- Team teaching provides a means for sharing of ideas between general education and special education teachers. We found that sharing ideas created more opportunities for success.

- The general education students increased their level of under-standing of students with disabilities. I think they were surprised to find that the special education students were not significantly different from themselves.

- Students do better. We have found that students learn more and behave better in the general education classroom than in the tra-ditional pull-out special education format. They developed a sense of responsibility and increased their self-esteem.

After much hard work, we believe that inclusion can be a very effective placement for most students. Although teachers must constantly think of ways to improve things and make constant changes and modifications, the results are well worth the effort.

CHAPTER 5

Planning for Inclusion in an Elementary Setting

Jennifer Gildner and
Laura Zionts

The job of teaching is far more complex than simply delivering content.
—MARCIA KALB KNOLL

Vision

In 1990, the passage of the Individuals with Disabilities Education Act (IDEA; P.L. 101-476) did not provide a definition for the term *inclusion*. Rather, it mandated that children be provided an education in the least restrictive environment and receive support services that allow them an appropriate education. For many children who have learning and behavioral challenges, these criteria can be met within the regular classroom alongside their peers. That is what educators commonly refer to as inclusion. Although a unified definition for inclusion has not yet been developed, many professionals have been working to devise a definition that works well for the student and the school. As one example, also in 1990, Michigan developed a statewide definition for inclusion as a placement of children with handicaps in a setting with their nonhandicapped peers in general education classrooms supported by special education teachers and services.

The term *support* can be defined uniquely by every school or by every team. Each child receiving "support" through special education can receive different services. *That is the beauty of inclusion:* Each child can be served as an individual. Time, teachers, students, and research have all demonstrated that students who have mild disabilities (e.g., behavioral disorders, learning difficulties) and are educated in

101

the regular education classroom make similar academic progress to students in special education settings, *and* they make added social–emotional gains as well. Any person who believes in these ideals and is willing to work by this measure of success can make inclusion happen at his or her school.

The primary teacher quality required in a classroom that includes all students is flexibility, or willingness to change. A successful inclusion program is composed of several components: vision, an action plan, teaching and collaboration skills, and student incentives. A teacher's flexibility is crucial to each component. Through the introduction of this chapter, I (Gildner) have described my vision for schools that embrace diversity among youth. In the following three sections, I address the remaining components. This chapter is an integration of my personal perspectives and experiences with current research and literature.

An Action Plan

Establishing Teams

Currently, many models for inclusive schools are meeting with success. The key to making a successful match between a particular model and an individual school district seems to be administrative support. Collaborative teaming (the pairing of general and special education teachers for planning and teaching) seems to work best when the teachers have the active support of their building and district administrators. However, it is important to note that any team can make inclusion work, without fancy training or finances, and even without wholehearted administrative support. Although these professional supports are certainly advantageous, the drive to provide an opportunity for all students to learn is the most important ingredient when developing an action plan.

Establishing teams of regular and special educators can be a challenge (see Aefsky, 1995; Baker, 1995; Kansas State Board of Education, 1993; Ventura, 1993; Zigmond, 1995). Optimally, general and special educators will work closely together to establish one classroom environment. By nature of the task, these professionals need to form a comfortable relationship. As for any partnership, trust, communication, and honesty are imperative. Also, team organizers should consider the teaching styles of the teachers, which will contribute to a more successful team. Promoting the idea of team members who choose each other is often a good policy because, then, all team members have chosen to participate in the process of inclusion. Likewise, they have chosen to work toward this goal together.

The teaching profession presents many opportunities for educators to work collaboratively. Many feel that it is most pleasant to work closely with someone whose personality and approach to teaching complements one's own, but one also has the opportunity to learn from teachers with very different teaching styles. One year, I worked with two new teachers who were extremely different. One was very organized and liked her desks in a row; the other liked activities occurring all the time. I learned from both of these teachers.

Developing the Action Plan

After teaching teams have been formed, the true development of an action plan can begin. It is best for the collaborative general and special educator team to meet and establish a plan of action from the beginning (see National Education Association, 1992; Stainback & Stainback, 1992; Ventura, 1993). It is essential to the success of an inclusion program that the teachers take every opportunity to communicate with each other about the global and specific goals for the students, the classroom environment, and the appropriate division of labor. The majority of conflicts that arise in an inclusive model of education are in the areas of academic instruction, behavioral management, lesson design and delivery, and classroom environment. Because these areas are trouble spots for general educators and special educators in segregated settings as well, inclusion brings to teachers the added benefit of collaborative problem solving. Many collaborative teams have emphasized the advantages of the general educators' training in large group instruction and management issues, and the special educators' knowledge of individualization techniques.

There are many successful ways for the general and special educators to divide their roles and responsibilities based on what the individual teachers are comfortable implementing. Communication and honesty (with oneself and the other teacher) will guide this division of labor. Teachers may choose to take on a role for a week or a unit at a time, and then change places. Regardless, an important consideration is that curriculum planning, behavioral expectations and consequences, and evaluation procedures must be mutually determined and consistently implemented. This is critical to ensuring a beneficial educational experience for the students. Planning for specific activities and lessons is most effectively done together, but if planning time is restrained, then turn-taking can be successful. In this event, however, the teacher who did the planning must provide constant and thorough information to the other teacher.

Teams that establish a regularly scheduled planning time are most effective (and sane). If that is not possible, teachers must be creative in their efforts to find actual "professional collaboration" time. Ideas for "stealing time" to collaborate and plan together include the following: bartering goods or teaching time with another educator in exchange for temporary coverage; examining effective uses of paraprofessionals; using computer systems to communicate, document, and organize ideas, plans, and content; meeting over dinner at a restaurant once a month; and meeting with the building administrator to determine where flexibility exists in the school schedule (many administrators are supportive in this regard).

When establishing a plan of action, it is important that the team teachers agree on answers to at least the following questions (and probably others that will arise in the process):

1. *Who plans what and when?* How much time does each educator spend in class?

2. *When will planning occur?* Options include meeting regularly at lunch, once a week, before or after school, or partway through preparation period. Other possibilities are use of floating substitute teachers within the school to allow multiple teams to have planning time during one day, or a sign-up sheet in the faculty workroom on which teams agree to provide coverage for each other at requested times.

3. *Who will teach what areas? How?* Options that teachers should consider include content areas, study skills, large groups/small groups, cooperative learning groups, and centers.

4. *How will the team teachers share the work environment?* The teachers need to determine how to share furniture, storage space, and desks.

5. *How will the teachers grade and evaluate student progress/achievement, and how will they document this?*

6. *How and when will the teachers evaluate their collaborative endeavors and inclusive classroom procedures?* The teachers need to consider the following: What is working and what needs to be revised from the teachers' standpoint? What is working and not working for students? What is working and not working for parents?

7. *What classroom routines will be established?* Considerations include hall passes, consequences, student expectations, and classroom procedures and policies.

8. *What will the classroom environment be?* The teachers need to determine an acceptable noise level, and consider use of paired and small group or large group instruction.

9. *How will the paraprofessional(s) be used?* How much time is required of the paraprofessional(s) in another regular education classroom? How often should this person be scheduled in the team-taught classroom, freeing the special educator for Individualized Education Program meetings or consultations with other teachers? How much time will the paraprofessional(s) work directly with students?

Many inclusive classroom models have been used effectively. The following is a partial list of models:

- One general educator and a full-time aide teach a class of no more than 24 students.

- Special educators consult with all general educators in a school to modify and adapt curriculum, materials, and presentation to students with special needs.

- The general educator teaches all students, and a paraprofessional trained to deliver direct instruction to students identified by the teacher as in need of skill acquisition during specified, reserved parts of the day.

- General educator, special educator, and paraprofessional all collaborate in one classroom.

- All lower functioning students are placed in one classroom with full-time teaming from the special educator.

- A special educator is assigned to collaborate with two to four general educators by spending specific parts of each school day in each class.

Teaching and Collaboration Skills

Teachers who choose to build an inclusive classroom also require flexibility in collaboration and teaching skills. I discuss what I believe this means in two subsections: collaboration skills and teaching skills. The topics are grouped under one category because both involve the teachers' need to employ critical professional skills that can make or break a successful program.

Collaboration Skills

One productive model for providing support consists of a certified general educator and a certified special educator collaboratively teaching full days in one classroom. In this model, there are typically no more than 25% to 30% identified at-risk and special education students in a classroom. Paraprofessionals provide support to other general educators, who are assigned smaller numbers of special education students. The team members determine between themselves the roles and responsibilities each will assume. When it comes to collaborating to create an inclusive classroom, teachers may use many different types of activities depending on the needs of the students. The flexible team will interchange their roles to fit the demands of the students, the curriculum, and the daily lesson.

In the following paragraphs I provide some ideas and suggestions that a team might try. There are many other possibilities that might work well.

A special educator may teach learning strategies, study and organizational skills, and/or social skills to the large group or to a group of targeted students. He or she may search out and recommend materials to support the core curriculum of the school district or state; or model a specific teaching technique; or observe and make recommendations about a particularly challenging student, subject, or time of day (the team designates the problem, establishes the variables to be observed, and devises solutions). The special educator may conduct study sessions to enable classroom learners to review material before a test. Although he or she may be responsible for individualized planning and documentation of progress toward a student's Individualized Education Program, once a team is established, the special educator should begin to release *sole* ownership of actually meeting the student's educational goals.

Some teams are able to work effectively with one teacher taking a leading role and the other a more supportive role. For example, the general educator conducts each daily lesson as the special educator monitors behavior, keeps all students on task with proximity and visual or verbal reminders, reteaches small groups, and reads text aloud and administers tests. A second idea along these lines is known as *Speak and Chart*. This model is most effective for meeting the needs of the visual and auditory learners in the classroom. While one teacher is lecturing or giving directions, the other teacher is at the board note-taking or using visual organizers. He or she simplifies and organizes the information presented to fit an outline or other structure. When teaching elementary or middle school students to take notes, modeling is extremely effective. It also aids any child who has trouble processing verbal cues quickly by providing a visual image.

A very natural collaborative technique is referred to as *Speak and Add*. In this procedure, while one instructor is speaking, the other may politely interject an added point or experience to enhance the other teacher's lesson. The students benefit by having the added knowledge and insight from two people instead of only one.

Station Teaching works well for teachers who like to use cooperative learning groups within their classroom. In this technique, students are divided into small groups who report to a specific teacher for each lesson or activity. Another use for this method is when one of the teachers delivers the lecture or directions and then the students report to their small group stations to complete their independent work. The student–teacher contact time is increased greatly with both variations of this technique.

Some circumstances allow for a trio of teachers. I was once involved in a double classroom of about 60 students with two general educators and me, the special educator. Within this teacher trio, we rotated the roles frequently. One of us would write and conduct the lesson for about a week, while the other two monitored the classroom by walking around, assisting some of the students who had difficulty keeping up, and managing behaviors. Often we divided students into three small groups and read material aloud, or conducted parallel lessons. Through shared observation and evaluation, we identified students who did not understand a concept or had failed to master a new skill. These students and any who had been absent from instruction were assembled for a small group activity for reteaching of the lesson(s). The rest of the class participated in an enrichment activity to enhance their understanding of the lesson. Because the participants in the small group varied, students did not feel singled out or embarrassed.

The environment that the teachers set up in their teamed classroom is of vital importance. In the interest of having students with learning and behavioral disabilities "fully included" on a social level with their peers, the labels of special education teacher and special education student(s) should be avoided. Respect of individual differences must be modeled by the teachers on every level. Teaching all students to recognize in themselves what they do well and what circumstances help them perform best is a challenging task; however, doing so helps all students receive the gifts of self-awareness and self-advocacy. My team has an "expertise" poster board displaying the areas in which each child feels he or she is expert. Children with questions seek out others who claim expertise in an area.

Dealing with a student's disability can be tricky at times; most teachers appreciate the need to balance discretion and respect for the student's privacy with honesty and open acceptance of the student as a whole person. Often it is effective for the teachers to privately ask each student how he or she prefers to publicly address (or not address) his or her disability. Emphasize within the class every student's opportunity to successfully learn new skills rather than which students need special help. It would be difficult for almost any person to walk into a room each day where everyone else knew about and openly focused on his or her greatest weaknesses (be they punctuality, balancing a checkbook, overeating, or losing one's temper). When teachers accept and respect each person in the class, eventually the students will also.

Creating an inclusive environment requires a great deal of flexibility from the adults who will work in that classroom. Identifying personal biases and constructing ways to learn acceptance (or in some cases simple tolerance) of difference and diversity will be one of the most beneficial investments of teachers' time in preparing for inclusion.

Teaching Skills

Content delivery in an inclusive classroom is a challenge for even the best of teachers. The diversity that teachers are working hard to respect and celebrate can seem overwhelming when looking at academic capabilities. When I first started an inclusion class for eighth-grade students with learning disabilities and emotional disorders, I was afraid that they all would fail. The pace was fast and information assumed. Through great communication with the general education teacher, we came up with a plan. We began adjusting Mastery Learning (for more information, see Barnes, 1993; King-Sears, 1994) to fit our needs. To make it work for us, we planned each unit using a table of specifications, which was a written summary including every concept, vocabulary word, and expectation we had for each student to understand about the unit (see Figure 5.1). If we were planning to teach it, it was on that table.

The unit was taught as usual, with experiments, group work, independent work, and the like. Whenever we did group work, we found it most productive to group the students in threes: two general education students and one special needs student. Thus, the pressure of being partnered with a more challenging person was a shared responsibility. After teaching the unit completely, we administered a test, which we called Formative A. All information requested on the test was taken directly from the table of specifications. The students received immediate reinforcement by receiving their grades that day. We got their scores to them quickly by using multiple-choice or fill-in formats. Students who earned 80% or better on the test spent the following 2 days with one teacher doing enrichments. These included extra experiments, movies, or fun activities that had to do with the topic but were not essential. This was a motivation for the students. However, students have to want to earn the enrichment activities chosen by the teaching team.

Students who did not receive 80% or better reported to the other teacher for correctives; this provided students a second chance to learn the information that they had not mastered on the test. On the day following Formative A, they looked at their mistakes and were retaught key information. They reviewed and rewrote individual answers. Instruction was individualized or given in small groups. Students concentrated on the concepts or vocabulary that they missed on Formative A. The next day, students in the corrective group took Formative B, which covered the same material as did the first formative, but with different, reworded questions. Most students passed Formative B with an 80% or better.

The general education teacher and I decided together when a student warranted modifications to the test or grading procedure. Not all concepts were expected of all students. We agreed upon these issues when first establishing the table of specifications. The success for all students increased greatly when there was no guessing game regarding what information would be tested or how the test was to be written. The students understood what was expected from them, and they were motivated to succeed. Following the tests, we gave students certificates of merit for completing and mastering each unit. All students who mastered the content, whether it took them one or two tries on the formatives, received a certificate of achievement.

The following are some other ideas that seem to help students

TABLE OF SPECIFICATIONS

Course: _____

Unit: _____

		Knowledge of		Translations	Applications	Analyses and Syntheses
Terms	Facts	Rules and Principles	Processes and Procedures			

FIGURE 5.1   Sample table of specifications.

learn well together. Teachers can use various graphic organizers to assist students in visually and conceptually organizing information presented in class (Adger, 1995; Bellanca, 1992). For example, when starting a new unit or concept, a strategy such as Know–Want–Learn (KWL) can assist students in making a link between the topic or skill and the knowledge or experiences that the students already have related to that area. Using the KWL strategy (Mandeville, 1994; McAllister, 1994), students note the information on a given topic that they already *know,* then list what they *want* to know. At the conclusion of the unit or activity, the students write all the things that they have *learned.* This various information can be written in three columns on one sheet of paper. Depending on the students' ages and skill levels, this activity can be done as a large group, in several small groups, or in pairs. It works best, however, in some form of collaborative effort. Students often come to the classroom with differing levels of knowledge and varied experiences. By completing this activity together, students have the opportunity to share ideas and levels of understanding about a topic. The students can use the resulting lists as a ready-made review for a project or test.

Other graphic organizers include charts or partial outlines that organize information found within literature (e.g., themes, crisis/turning points, settings, characters, points of view, resolutions), science (e.g., how a seed grows into a plant), or social skills (e.g., the key points to remember when asking appropriately for help). When asked to read a section or chapter of a text independently, students who have learning or behavioral difficulties find it challenging to remain on task, read for information, and process the language used within the passage. By encouraging use of a graphic organizer to be completed as students read, or as information is read to them, the teacher can better assume that all students will understand or retain some information. Students can use these organizers as study guides for tests and quizzes. Story pyramids and character maps, brainstorming, and Venn diagrams are effective ways of beginning the prewriting process. These maps can serve as an aide to help students select a topic on which to write. Visual organizers are also good projects for pairs of students.

Cooperative learning groups are effective in any inclusion program because the students share their unique knowledge and skills. Forethought and care should be given to forming groups or pairs of students. Teachers who would like to use cooperative learning in their classrooms should be aware that it is trickier than it seems.

Teachers must watch the students carefully before planning any activity. The students need to have certain social skills before they begin working together in learning groups. When students have not developed skills such as taking turns, giving compliments, and appropriately giving and receiving criticism, disaster can happen very quickly. I am not saying that if the students do not have these skills, then teachers should abandon the idea of cooperative learning. Because this approach has many benefits, it is worth pursuing. However, the teachers need to provide direct teaching of the requisite social skills before beginning any cooperative assignment. Some teachers have said they teach the prerequisite social skills for up to the first half of the school year before they begin using full-blown cooperative learning groups. Other groups of students do not need that much time to learn the skills. It takes some long-range planning by the teachers, but cooperative learning groups are very effective with learners who have diverse academic abilities.

When ready to divide students into cooperative groups, teachers need to keep the following tips in mind:

1. Assign the groups yourself. Students may not choose the partners with whom they will be most productive.

2. Assign a specific job for each student in the group. As students become more comfortable with cooperative learning, you can simply list the responsibilities and let them divide the tasks as they choose.

3. Rotate group members from activity to activity or from unit to unit so that students gain experience in working with all of their class members. They get to know and appreciate each other and their abilities.

4. Give precise and clearly stated information about the project requirements and the project goal, including how it will be evaluated. Include some form of evaluation of project completion (their incentive to work together) and individual accountability (their incentive to work at all).

5. Model positive praise and support each team.

Student Incentives

Whenever a potpourri of abilities and personalities is mixed, challenging behaviors will arise. At the action plan phase, the collaborative team needs to determine how to consequent positive and negative behaviors. The decisions should be listed, and then discussed and modified or added to very frequently. Consistency and communication are vital. Classroom rules and consequences that are established for all may need to be supplemented or individualized for some. Some students require more motivation, more consequences, and more attention. The role of designing behavior modifications is usually filled by the special educator, but it can be handled effectively as a team as well, particularly by experienced teachers.

When trying to motivate students to make appropriate choices, the team must offer consequences that the student finds particularly reinforcing (or nonreinforcing as the case may be). A simple "interest inventory" can be completed by students (e.g, at the beginning of each grading period). The teacher sets up a reward system for the individual student to earn points (or whatever commodity) for using appropriate behaviors in the general education classroom based on his or her interests. For example, Bobby is frequently off task and out of his seat, disrupting other students during independent work time. Bobby has listed several things he enjoys (going down the hall to quickly say hi to a favorite adult or student, baseball cards, brand new pencils because he loses his often and he wants to come to class prepared, and mixing the paints for art). When either of the teachers sees Bobby working on task and not disrupting his neighbor, that teacher walks over to him and whispers that he is making good choices about his behavior and that he will earn a bonus point, which may be recorded on a clipboard that the teacher carries around. On Fridays, the points are totaled and, when he has earned the correct number of points, Bobby may choose the reinforcer he prefers from his list (older students may choose reinforcers such as time with the social worker, extended homework time during school time, or shortened assignments). The reinforcement schedule can be altered by changing the time frame from hourly, to daily, to weekly, to biweekly (whatever makes a student successful) and gradually extending it over time.

Small groups of students or whole classes also can be rewarded or compete for a reward. An example of a classwide reinforcement technique that can be used by team teachers is called Marbles in the Jar. Every time any student performs the targeted behavior, a marble is placed in a clear, glass jar. The class hears the noise and sees the marble going in the jar, and can imitate the appropriate behavior. Teachers can adjust the pace at which the reward is earned by attaching specific criteria, such as earning a marble only during a challenging time of day (e.g., returning quietly to their seats after recess and assemblies) or only if the entire class demonstrates the behavior (when students are becoming proficient at it). Choosing the material to record the behavior can be a creative adventure as well. For example, if marbles are unavailable, perhaps large, uncooked noodles can be used instead.

Remaining positive and treating all students fairly is the job of the team teachers. Fair does not always mean "the same." Getting the students to understand this is sometimes a difficult task. However, when teachers model acceptance of all differences and respect for each student, the students will learn to do the same. Being able to change with the students and adapt to their changing needs is a wonderful ability of a team on its way to success.

Conclusion

Making the decision to establish an inclusive classroom is one step toward a goal of full inclusion of people who have learning and behavior disabilities in communities. Having flexibility will be the foundation upon which that goal can be met. An educator who chooses to take on this goal has a big job ahead. However, the educator is in a uniquely wonderful place to promote acceptance. When people work together toward a common goal, they are more likely to change their attitudes about each other and to become more accepting of differences and more tolerant of individuality. The educator can provide these opportunities for students in a supportive and nurturing environment by setting up the students to succeed in joint learning and social interactions through appropriate instruction, support, and reinforcement. The educator can create lifelong positive changes in the lives and attitudes of the people who pass through his or her classroom for the school year.

References

Adger, C. T. (1995). *Engaging students: Thinking, talking and cooperating.* Thousand Oaks, CA: Corwin Press.

Aefsky, F. (1995). *Inclusion confusion: A guide to educating students with exceptional needs.* Thousand Oaks, CA: Corwin Press.

Baker, J. M. (1995). Inclusion in Virginia: Educational experiences of students with learning disabilities in one elementary school. *Journal of Special Education, 29*(2), 116–123.

Barnes, S. K. (1993, March). *Creating the quality school for all students by implementing outcome-based education.* Paper presented at the Annual Conference on Creating Quality Schools, Oklahoma City.

Bellanca, J. (1992). *The Cooperative Think Tank II: Graphic organizers to teach thinking in the cooperative classroom—K–adult.* Palatine, IL: Skylight.

Individuals with Disabilities Education Act of 1990, 20 U.S.C. §1400 *et seq.*

Kansas State Board of Education. (1993). *Collaborative teaming for inclusion-oriented schools: An introduction and video guide.* Topeka, KN: Author.

King-Sears, M. E. (1994). *Curriculum-based assessment in special education.* San Diego, CA: Singular.

Mandeville, T. F. (1994). KWLA: Linking the affective and cognitive domains. *Reading Teacher, 47*(8), 679–680.

McAllister, P. J. (1994). Using KWL for informal assessment. *Reading Teacher, 47*(6), 510–511.

National Education Association. (1992, May). *The integration of students with special needs into regular classrooms: Policies and practices that work.* Washington, DC: Author.

Stainback, S., & Stainback, W. (Eds.). (1992). *Curriculum considerations in inclusive classrooms: Facilitating learning for all students.* Baltimore: Brookes.

Ventura, E. (1993). A kindergarten through second grade multiage classroom. *Insights into Open Education, 25*(5), 9.

Zigmond, N. (1995). Inclusion in Kansas: Educational experiences of students with learning disabilities in one elementary school. *Journal of Special Education, 29*(2), 144–154.

CHAPTER 6

Program Elements that Support Teachers and Students with Learning and Behavior Problems

Sandra M. Keenan

One of the most difficult challenges in education today is effective programming for students with behavioral and learning problems. Most practitioners would agree that little has been done to change service delivery models for this very visible student population. The latest initiative described as inclusive education has not produced enough information about these students' needs and the types of supports that would be necessary to provide appropriate programming. Some would argue that *appropriate* and *inclusive* do not exist in education for some of these students. It seems that special education has been a system based on the notion that first a student must fail to get appropriate services. A label designating a student as disabled has been required to access those services.

My intent in this chapter is to provide the reader with a summary of program elements that have produced great change in a service delivery system in one school district. It is crucial to note that this district was ready for change. In 1988, district leadership changed as a result of many concerns regarding noncompliance with state regulations. Part of the compliance agreement was to make improvements in many of the areas discussed in this chapter. A new director of special education was hired, and then I was hired as assistant director. At the same time, the district was experiencing change in site-based management, decision making, and educational reform. The train had left the station, so to speak; we just added another car.

This chapter does not supply multiple references to research or other published works. It does, however, supply practical information about the daily process of change. I am, first and foremost, a practitioner. I am an administrator, once teacher, who still believes that one person can make a difference in a student's life. I hope that this information will be helpful for other districts, schools, or teachers involved in including all students, especially those who have emotional or behavioral needs.

After I define the population, I discuss the planning, supports, personnel, and training that are necessary to provide successful programming. Mental health statistics stated that 7% to 8% of school-age students have emotional or behavioral disorders that require special services; 3% have severe behavioral disorders; and only 1% are currently identified. Twenty percent of those identified are arrested while in school, and an additional one third will be incarcerated within 2 years of leaving school. These students fail more courses and have more retentions than typical students. Approximately 17% of the students identified as severely emotionally disturbed are instructed in regular classrooms, 29.2% in resource rooms, 35.8% in separate classes, 13.3% in separate schools, 3.5% in residential settings, and 1.5% in homebound or hospital settings (U.S. Department of Education, 1993).

There are few prevention programs and fewer attempts to screen for those who may be at risk. An analysis of national programs (U.S. Department of Education, 1993) shows limited access to academic vocational opportunities, an overemphasis on behavior management and control, and little opportunity for socializing with peers. Historically, services have been fragmented. There are programs for adjudicated youth, violent and aggressive youth, dropouts, at-risk students, and special education students.

There have been very few examples of comprehensive services for all of these populations that school districts can replicate. The recruitment of new teachers and retention of existing service providers continues to be a problem. The teaching expectancy for teachers of those with emotional and behavioral disorders is 3 to 4 years (Smith-Davis, Burke, & Noel, 1983). During the 1991–1992 school year, 4,724 special education teachers were needed for students labeled seriously emotionally disturbed.

Philosophy Development on Inclusion

I believe that it is crucial to develop a philosophy statement before implementing any educational program. Educators need to answer the question, What are we attempting to achieve? Any philosophy statement should begin with the important dictums set forth by the Education for All Handicapped Children Act of 1975 (P.L. 94-142), renamed after two rounds of amendments as the Individuals with Disabilities Education Act of 1990 (IDEA; P.L. 101-476). Our school district examined such maxims as the following from IDEA:

- "Unless a child with disabilities individualized educational program requires some other arrangement, the child is educated in the school which he or she would attend if not handicapped." [300.552(c)]

- "Each child with a handicap has an educational placement as close as possible to the child's home." [300.552(a)(3)]

- "That special classes, separate schooling or other removal of children with handicaps from the regular educational environment occurs only when the nature or severity of the handicap is such that education in regular classes with the use of supplementary aids is unsatisfactory." [300.550(b)(2)]

- "That to the maximum extent appropriate, children with handicaps, including children in public or private institutions or other care facilities, are educated with children who are not handicapped." [300.550(b)(1)]

Several national organizations have taken positions regarding inclusion. For example, the Council for Exceptional Children (1993) wrote that students "with disabilities should be served whenever possible in general education classrooms in inclusive neighborhood school and community settings. Such settings should be strengthened and supported by an infusion of specially trained personnel and other appropriate supportive practices according to the individual need of the child."

The full inclusion movement has proposed that all students with handicapping conditions should be integrated into general education settings. However, those students who have emotional disturbances or behavioral disorders seem to be among the least included. It is important to implement the practice of inclusion when possible because it has an anticipated benefit of providing opportunities for identified students to interact with their nonidentified peers. This is less likely to occur once the student is placed in a restrictive environment (Knitzer, Steinberg, & Fleisch, 1990). This interaction is important because, as suggested by Strain and Shores (1983), some skills can be taught only in the social context in which they are practiced (the regular classroom). Stainback and Stainback (1982) also stressed that this interaction is beneficial to both "special and regular" students. The "special" students gain an extended, more normalized learning experience, while the "regular" students gain an understanding about human similarities and differences.

Several variables seem to be common in programs or systems where successful inclusion has occurred. They include the consideration of attitudes and beliefs, services and physical accommodations, school support, collaboration, and instructional methods (ERIC: Clearinghouse Views, 1993).

Inclusion is misused when it means reducing special education services, expecting all children to learn the same way, or expecting general education teachers to teach all children who have disabilities without needed support. Inclusion is best utilized when all children are participating in all aspects of school. This occurs when instruction emphasizes collaboration of special and general education personnel and resources, and when strategies are used to accommodate the varied learning styles of all children. Consequently, all children will have opportunities to interact and develop friendships and there will be the necessary support of general education teachers who have students with special needs in their classrooms.

Attitudes and beliefs are not easy to change. With a system that has communicated for 20 years that separate education is better and that special education personnel have some "special way" of dealing with children, general educators are reluctant to suddenly believe that their classrooms are the best place to educate all students. In addition, many are reluctant to believe that they have or can be trained to have the necessary skills to make it work. The initial steps in this change process require that all stakeholders develop a philosophy and delineate beliefs. Teachers, administrators, and individuals in communities must ask the following questions:

- What do I need to acknowledge in order to accept all children into the classroom?

- What are my beliefs about learning?

- What are my beliefs about students?

- What role does the curriculum play?

- What are my beliefs about teaching?

- What is my role as a teacher, administrator, parent, or community member?

- What is the school's role in the life of the student, family, or community?

- What are the rewards of teaching and learning?

- What are my beliefs about authority and decision making?

- How many modifications or individual programs are too many?

- What behaviors should not be accepted in schools, no matter what supports are in place?

In our school district, this process involved many meetings and the development of a task force. Individual schools met to have various discussions on inclusion with representatives from all levels of personnel, parents, and community members. Each school was at a different point on the readiness continuum for inclusion. Therefore, those schools that felt the most comfortable began the process first. The following are examples of beliefs developed in our system in 1990:

- All students can learn.

- All students should be as much a part of "their" school and class as possible.

- There is a need for change and the time is right.

- We should and could do what is right for students, personnel, and families.

Our goals included:

- To gradually (over 3 years) incorporate change and success that would lead to more inclusive programs, especially programs for our students with behavior disorders.

- To provide teachers and school personnel with support and resources to improve programs.

- To rebuild trust and communication with students, teachers, parents, and the community.

Inservice and Staff Development

For inclusion to be successful, a school district must value ongoing staff development and training opportunities. All levels of service providers should be a part of the training. Administrators need to participate, not only to learn the content, but to reinforce the philosophy and commitment to change and to inclusion. Support personnel, such as aides, secretaries, janitors, bus personnel, and parents should all be invited to share in this process. Once again, this involvement of everyone reinforces the philosophy and commitment to change.

As our system was undergoing change, we planned specific staff development opportunities, inservice training, consultant visits, and site visits to other schools. Initially, sessions focused on a basic understanding of inclusion, collaboration, and building common beliefs among staff, parents, and the community. As the training became more specific to handicapping conditions (e.g., emotional and behavioral disorders, mental retardation), the intent was not only to develop new skills but also to dispel fear. Unless a system is ready to acknowledge the fear and empower teachers, barriers will continue to arise. General educators who have never experienced a student with an Individualized Education Program (IEP) in their classroom may assume that all students with IEPs have emotional–behavioral problems or that all are developmentally delayed. It is not difficult to see why those teachers do not feel adequately prepared to work with students who have special needs and why they fear change toward inclusion.

Although each school system has unique training needs, the specific training that we developed may serve as a framework for others. We began with an overview of all the handicapping conditions and legal obligations under IDEA and Section 504 of the Rehabilitation Act of 1973. We presented extensive information on learning disabilities, behavior disorders, and other disorders from the *Diagnostic and Statistical Manual of Mental Disorders, Fourth Edition* (DSM–IV) (American Psychiatric Association, 1994), such as oppositional defiant disorder, anxiety disorder, and attention-deficit/hyperactivity disorder. Special education teachers who successfully were using these methods presented curriculum modifications and instructional strategies. We presented data regarding numbers of students with IEPs and their handicapping conditions. Within smaller groups, such as grade-level teams, we reviewed specific student profiles that contained strengths, weaknesses, behavioral data, formal evaluation information, and learning profiles.

Behavioral intervention and prevention were priorities. We were in the process of returning several students who had been placed in more restrictive programs outside of the district. The community, school, and personnel needed a basic understanding of behavior and how behavior is acquired. We examined functions of behavior, including frequency, duration, and intensity. Interventions such as reality therapy, crisis intervention, restraint training, and avoiding power and control issues were also presented. This training was conducted in groups of 20 to 30 people in order to enable interaction and role playing.

Only those people who would have daily direct contact with those students who were returning to the district, as well as support personnel, were trained in restraint techniques. We solicited assistance from the staff of the out-of-district facility where the students had been attending. They had the best working knowledge of the needs of these students, and they knew the antecedent behavior that might occur before crisis incidences. We felt it was not advisable to train an entire faculty. We thought that many people might have a problem touching a child for any reason and may be concerned about liability issues. We also did not want holding a student to be the first or only response to inappropriate behavior.

Scheduling training sessions can be problematic because of district and local professional contracts. We utilized 2 to 3 release days per year, a summer training institute, and after-school sessions, and provided substitutes in order to release teachers. Compensation for summer hours, after-school hours, and substitutes was provided through grant funding. In the first 2 years of our system change, several state and federal grants funded these activities. In some cases, individualized training was provided as needed or as outlined in an IEP.

Advocacy and Public Relations

Once planning was under way for the eventual return of the out-of-district students, meetings with the School Committee were held to discuss funding for the new programs. Parents, members of the community, and board members needed to understand the types of supports necessary in the district in order to accommodate these returning students. In the first year, there was no budget increase, only a transfer of funds from an out-of-district tuition account to the local operating budget. We did, however, realize that at some point, program transition may cost more, depending on the number of students and the degree of severity of their disabilities. In the initial phase, local funding was appropriated for new program development and transitions from the outside programs. In the second year, additional personnel were funded through the procurement of grants. Since our third year, all new expenditures have been funded by local budgets.

As we were attempting to bring back those students with serious behavioral needs, we began to receive positive recognition from a variety of sources regarding our inclusion programs for other students with disabilities. Students with multiple handicaps, severe speech and language needs, and mental retardation were all being included in our schools. Many students were attending neighborhood schools. A reporter from our local newspaper wrote an article detailing several of the programs; the state department of education began to use our staff for their state training sessions; and several organized parent groups visited the programs and provided positive feedback to other groups. As a result, other schools became more receptive about inclusion.

While planning the new components of the program for our students with behavioral and emotional needs, we felt it was important to begin dialogue with community agencies regarding the array of services needed for these students and their families. Many of these agencies were already involved with some of these families, and it was important to not duplicate or complicate their efforts. Members of our staff joined community task forces and boards, and participated in several new initiatives at the state level. Although the school system will probably never have all the services it needs, this outreach effort resulted in improved relationships and improved services. In addition, we were able to put faces with names and to have a direct link to the agency if a problem or conflict should arise. During this time, various state agencies were developing interagency agreements that would affect service delivery models in the near future.

After serving as a staff member of a residential treatment center for many years, I knew it was important to establish an advisory group for our new programs serving students with behavioral problems. We needed the advice, approval, and "conscience" of our community in establishing the practices that would be used in these programs. We knew that, as the programs began implementing services, other parents and community members would raise questions and concerns. Therefore, the support and advocacy that this advisory group could provide would be very important.

We sought additional parent involvement through parent–teacher organizations, site councils, and our district special education advisory group. While providing inservice training to our school staff, we provided similar information to these other groups.

Instructional Strategies

The organizational structure that I have outlined will undoubtedly fall short unless appropriate educational strategies are used in the presentation of content and skills. According to Guetzloe (1994), in determining an appropriate curriculum for a student with emotional and behavioral disorders, the following must be considered:

- The curriculum should provide for each student's unique social, emotional, behavioral, and academic needs, as well as the school's traditional educational demands.

- The curriculum should focus on the specific facts that caused an individual student to be eligible for special education services. These factors should be addressed as goals and objectives in the student's IEP.

The curriculum must be implemented by a confident and well-trained staff. According to ERIC: Clearinghouse Views (1993, p. 66),

- Teachers have the knowledge and skills needed to select and adapt curricula and instructional methods according to individual student needs.

- Teachers foster a cooperative learning environment and promote socialization.

In addition to these stated priorities, we have found other instructional strategies to be vital to the success of inclusive programming. They include cooperative learning, peer tutoring, related services in an inclusionary model, curriculum modifications, and collaborative teaching. While many of these strategies are explained in depth elsewhere in this book, I believe that it is important to illustrate the parts that they played in our school system.

Following districtwide training in 1990, cooperative learning groups are used in all of our schools. This method is almost mandatory for inclusionary classrooms, because it allows students to participate in the group activity based on their strengths, not their weaknesses. It also provides the opportunity to teach social skills such as team building, leadership development, sharing, taking turns, and appropriate peer interactions.

The tutoring of peers utilizes student strengths and allows the student to build positive self-esteem. We use peer tutoring in many of our inclusive classrooms. Further, we use cross-grade and/or cross-school tutoring. Some of the best success stories with our students who have behavioral problems involve those who have tutored younger students. Some of our students who have behavioral difficulties have strong academic skills. Teaching reading or math to a younger student is rewarding and helps lift their self-esteem.

In most cases related services can be effectively delivered in an inclusionary model. Speech–language pathologists, occupational therapists, physical therapists, and social work services can benefit not only the identified students with special needs but many students in an inclusive classroom. Examples of collaborative teams using related services are a speech pathologist coteaching a language arts class, an occupational therapist coteaching a penmanship class, a physical therapist coteaching a physical education class, or a social worker coteaching a group social skill session or a creative writing unit.

Although an entire chapter could be written on curriculum modifications, I list here some consistent modifications we use in our inclusion programs. We have a four-page attachment with 80 different modifications, which are divided into the following categories: presentation of materials, environment, time demands, materials (visual motor integration, visual processing, language processing, organizational), and grading. This attachment is included in IEPs, in 504 accommodation plans, or with some students as a prereferral intervention.

Collaborative or team teaching is viewed by many as the cornerstone of inclusion. One teacher has knowledge of content, while the other has knowledge of instructional modifications. In 1990–1991, we began with two collaborative teams in the district. Inservice training continued, and the number of teams increased to 10 in 1991–1992, 40 in 1992–1993, 45 in 1993–1994, 56 in 1994–1995, and over 80 in 1995–1996. The number of self-contained classes (historically, classes in which students with special needs are completely separate all day) have decreased from 13 in 1990 to 2 in 1994. Also, the schools are meeting the needs of students with moderate to severe disabilities in more inclusive ways. Thus, every student in kindergarten through 12th grade has access to a general education homeroom and is part of a social unit in that class. The goal is to gradually increase the time students spend in that unit while appropriately meeting their educational needs. The most important qualities each teacher must bring to a collaborative relationship are flexibility and the ability to effectively communicate. All initial teams began on a voluntary basis. In the past several years, we have recruited new partners. In 1995–1996 an entire school incorporated collaborative teaching across all teams.

Environmental Accommodations

There are five major factors in environmental accommodations in our programs. They are flexible scheduling, flexible programming, ability to increase or decrease program restrictiveness, appropriate space, and appropriate materials. Scheduling students, especially at the middle and high school levels, can be difficult for any system. However, the addition of inclusionary programs, specific to certain teachers or teams, can make the job seem impossible. In grades 5 through 8, two or four teachers team together, with 26 students per teacher. A collaborative teacher rotates among the teachers. In organizing our inclusion programs, we developed a database with student information regarding primary disability, academic levels, and need for support services. That information was then sorted by grade, and severity of need. We then distributed those students using a heterogeneous grouping for a grade-level team. For example, a team of four general education teachers and one special education teacher were assigned 20 students with IEPs and a total of 104 students as follows:

Class	Total Students	Students with IEPs	Collaborative Special Education Teacher's Division of Time
1	26	12	50%
2	26	3	10%
3	26	2	10%
4	26	3	10%
Pull-out direct or planning time			20%

The 20 students with IEPs were assigned to the following primary eligibility categories:

Learning disabilities	12	Mental retardation	2
Behavior disorders	2	Speech–language disabilities	0
Other health impaired	2	504	2

The daily service profile for special education services for students was as follows:

7 students (historically self-contained)	More than 2.5 hours of service
5 students (extended resource)	Up to 2 hours of service
6 students (resource)	Up to 1 hour of service
2 students (monitored)	Up to 1 hour per week of service

As this information indicates, we have mixed eligibility categories, degrees of severity, and regular education students. We have mixed our certified staff to be part of these collaborative teams. In our state, special education teacher certifications are in the areas of severe/profound, mild/moderate, and resource. We have applied for waivers from our state, so that any one certification may be used in these mixed collaborative classes. We also have had to deal with regulations on caseloads. In our state, resource teachers may service a maximum of 30 students, while mild/moderate (self-contained) teachers may service a maximum of 10 students (with one aide). By mixing the student population, which is comprised of both categories, we had an agreement with our staff not to exceed 20 students per special needs provider or per team.

Students having speech–language disabilities were scheduled into a separate grade-level team from our other IEP students. (Thus, none were listed on the primary eligibility list for teams described previously.) This enabled us to focus the speech pathologist team's time on only one or two classes per grade, so collaborative sessions could be scheduled. The speech pathologist team teaches in language arts classes, reading classes, English classes, and writing workshop classes. There is still time in the speech pathologist's schedule for private or small group therapy sessions.

Although our elementary schools use many different models of inclusion, the same philosophy exists. Students by degree of need are mixed with a heterogeneous class and a collaborative teacher is assigned. The amount of collaborative teaching directly reflects the number of IEPs in the grade or school. For example, a teacher may spend half of his or her day in a first-grade classroom and half in a third-grade classroom. If that collaborative teacher has a classroom aide, the aide may be assigned to the third grade and then the first grade, so that the special education students receive continuous services in the regular classroom. This enables those students with IEPs to spend the entire day with their peers.

At the high school, each special education teacher is assigned to a department, and team teaches several classes in that department. For example, the special needs teacher assigned to the English department has 7 periods in her day. She team teaches 4 periods of English and 1 or 2 periods of resource room and has 1 or 2 periods of planning and monitoring. Because students at the high school may have three or four different service providers, we have developed a program facilitator model. Every student in special education has a program facilitator. That staff member is primarily responsible for communication, scheduling meetings or IEP reviews, and having the best knowledge of that student's learning profile in order to effectively advocate for him or her.

The second major area is flexible programming. The very nature of special education mandates individualized programs; therefore, the system must be flexible. There are always new factors impacting an existing program, such as new students being identified, student transfers, IEP changes, and students exiting the special education program. Consequently, it is helpful to look at data from the last 3 or 4 years and make some estimates. We found that at least 3 to 4 students per grade at the elementary level and 2 to 3 at the secondary level were either newly identified or transferred during any given year. We attempt to leave a few openings in our collaborative classes for that reason. However, we would not support changing a student's entire schedule if we were already into the second or third quarter of a year. Other features of flexible programming at our schools include having altered days, late starts, early dismissals, after-school programs, or our Saturday Academy (described later). All of these options are individualized and depend on an IEP decision.

The third major area is the ability to increase or decrease the restrictiveness of the program. At our middle school and high school, we have one or two teachers who provide a variety of services. For instance, a teacher may serve the one classroom in the district that appears to be self-contained. Although most of this teacher's students spend time in the general setting, a few spend a large portion of their day with this teacher. If necessary, they may spend the entire day (we have arranged coverage for that possibility). This is the setting where a student may begin when he or she has transferred from a more restrictive program, such as a special day or residential program for students with emotional and/or behavioral problems. The transition time may be as short as necessary, and the student would move out to one of the grade collaboratives where there is another special service provider. A similar process would occur if a student in a regular class is having much difficulty. The student could be placed in the special setting for a few weeks. A new transition plan will be developed with no interruption of services.

The fourth area of environmental accommodations is appropriate space. This may not be an issue in some districts where facilities have been developed with demand; however, many schools do not have space to provide alternative settings or a center where support personnel can service students. We have created student planning centers and resource centers, and have plans for creating a Child Opportunity Zone in our high school. The student planning centers are places in a school where a student can go to calm down, manage anger, talk with someone, develop a plan to return to class, have access to a phone or an outside agency, and receive help with academic demands. Resource centers are classrooms with multiple computers, as well as several service providers (a special education teacher, literacy personnel, bilingual personnel, aide, volunteers) who are available to assist with academic support. A Child Opportunity Zone is a space provided in a school building, where community services operate in the school and are easily accessible for students and families.

For these centers to be effective, they need to be in an appropriate location with appropriate supplies and materials, which is the fifth major area of environmental accommodation. Confidentiality should be respected when choosing a location for these centers. Spaces for private discussions, phone conversations, and group interactions are needed. A telephone and locking file cabinet are essential, especially in the planning centers. If the school plans to allow students who may be angry or losing control to be in this area, the safety of the staff must be ensured.

Transition Plans and Overlap of Services

A transition for a student with emotional and behavioral needs can be very difficult, not only for the student, but for the family. The student may remember the general education classroom (or in our case, the public school) as the place of failure, embarrassment, and ridicule. The family may remember it in much the same way, but with added memories of guilt or anger. Therefore, it does not make sense to be in one classroom (or out-of-district school) on a Friday and back in the general education classroom (or public school) on Monday, with no other steps made for the transition.

We have tried with as many students as possible to have a transition plan that allows for overlap of services for a given time period so both the student and the family feel supported. First, we have staff for the public school visit the out-of-district placement. They conduct observations, meet with other staff, and review records. Then staff from the out-of-district placement visits the public school. They meet our staff, administer observations in the planned classroom(s), and provide feedback to the district on training issues, environmental accommodations, or curriculum modifications that will be needed. A detailed learning profile is developed with strengths, weaknesses, behavioral history, and a list of antecedent behaviors.

The parent and student visit the public school and observe in the classroom. They usually choose to do this with a staff member from the private school whom they trust. We usually plan a second visit to the classroom, for a longer period of time. Next, we assign a buddy or mentor who is a classmate who will show the student around. If the student or family has been involved in counseling with the private school, and counseling is still recommended, we will help the family find a local provider 1 to 2 months prior to discharge. It is important that the student and family feel they have a support base in the local community to assist with any issues.

In some cases, we have implemented gradual transfers, such as beginning with 4 days in the out-of-district setting and 1 day with us, and progressing to 2, 3, 4, and then 5 days at our school. In other cases, we have made an immediate transfer, directly following the visits and after the support systems are in place. With a few students, we have maintained a therapist or staff member from the private school for a month or so after the transition; these transitions have been very successful. It is important to negotiate this cost with the private school.

Behavioral and Emotional Support Systems for All Students

In our elementary schools, we use a consultation model with personnel who share responsibility in four elementary schools. They consult with the classroom teachers, conduct observations, write behavior intervention plans, contact families, and interact with outside agencies if needed. In our middle school, we use a student planning center and support services team, with cooperative services as needed through the community agencies. We have a full-time position at this school for a behavior specialist who runs the planning center and coordinates the programs of all students who receive these services. In our high school, we utilize a student assistance center and support services team, with cooperative services through community agencies and an area psychiatric hospital. Once again, a behavior specialist manages the student assistance center and coordinates programs.

The middle school planning center was developed to be used by students with behavior disorders and those who have been identified as at risk. A student does not require an IEP in order to receive support at the center. In fact, after 3 years of programming, statistics show that about 50% of the students serviced by the center had not been identified as special education students. The center is an alternative space within the school that provides a temporary cool-down period. The goal is to assist students in learning how to manage and take responsibility for their own behavior, including academic achievement.

This program is a building-wide support program and is open to all students, whether or not they have IEPs. Each student involved in this support program has an individual behavior plan developed by the support services team. The team comprises a school psychologist, a school social worker, a behavior specialist, and a school administrator. The team reviews referrals once a week and conducts individual program reviews on a scheduled basis. Team members consult with teachers or parents and administer classroom observations. They communicate with area agencies, physicians, and therapists, and provide feedback to teachers and staff within the school. It is their view that the diverse expertise of the professionals involved with the team have helped to create an academically stimulating and behaviorally sound environment for the students involved with the support services team.

Each member of the support services team makes a contribution to the prevention model. The school psychologist responds to teacher concerns, conducts observations, processes screenings, administers reevaluations, communicates with physicians, conducts parent and child counseling, and serves as a member of the multidisciplinary team. The school social worker completes social histories; assists with home issues; conducts social skills groups, individual counseling, and changing family groups and support groups; and serves as a member of the multidisciplinary team. The behavior specialist provides the framework for the planning center program. He or she performs all aspects of the center as previously described, as well as engaging in consultations with classroom teachers, coordinating all communications regarding students in the center, and providing many schoolwide and districtwide training activities.

The planning center provides many resources in one room: student support, emotional time-out, crisis intervention, individualized academic support, and a social network. Some students come to the center at scheduled times for academic assistance, organizational assistance, relaxation training, anger management training, or reality therapy. No single philosophy is followed. We use whatever works for each student. When a student uses the room, the professional present records the reasons why the student is in the room. This documentation is the basis of the quarterly report summarizing how well the students have been using the center, how often they come to the center, and which interventions or recommendations are beneficial for the continuation of the program.

During the first year of the planning center, many issues had to be resolved. The center looked much more like a crisis center or a detention hall. Students were sent to this area for almost any minor infraction that occurred in the classroom. No communication was being exchanged between the classroom teacher and the planning center. Simultaneously, however, we were conducting meetings, holding inservice training, and developing team procedures. After the first semester, the planning center settled down as communication systems and procedures were created and followed. Processes were developed for referral, for sending a student out of class to the center, and for contacting administrators or parents if needed. By the second year, the operations were running very smoothly.

Currently, the results of our program are clearly evident. Truancies, suspensions, retentions, failing grades, and major aggressive episodes have decreased, whereas passing grades, school attendance, number of special needs students who made honor roll, student mediation, and satisfied staff and parents have increased. This support program is truly viewed as a schoolwide support service and prevention model, and not as a special education program.

Our high school program has a student assistance center and a support services team which function very much like those in the middle school model, with the addition of a student assistance counselor, guidance counselor, and a teacher. The program goal is to enable each student to take responsibility for his or her actions. More placement options are built into the program, such as flexible schedules, partial days, vocational placements, extended days on site, extended days off site, short-term day treatment, short-term hospitalization, and on-call psychiatrist. These features allow for more individualization of programs, and the ability to move to more or less restrictive environments with better transitions.

This continuum of options did not occur overnight. A representative from an area psychiatric hospital was invited to participate on a planning committee for the high school program. He listened to the needs of the staff and gaps in our service delivery system. Also, he helped develop other program options. One true asset in our program is the opportunity for a student to move very quickly if a change in placement decision is made. There are very few situations that require a student to wait for more than a few days to a week for a more restrictive placement. Because parental involvement is valued and encouraged, parents have been cooperative partners with the school system in making these placements. Improved partnerships with area mental health agencies have also contributed to more timely responses to crisis situations and less abuse of the system. True collaborative partnerships have been formed and all parties continue to nurture them.

Other aspects of the emotional and behavioral support systems that we provide include integrated social skill lessons, behavior plans, alternative disciplinary responses, student mediation, and mentoring. School social workers work with many students through group or individual counseling. In some schools, the social worker serves as a collaborative teacher, integrating social skills lessons into language arts class, recess, or health activities. This has become an increasingly popular option among the classroom teachers.

All of our support personnel are involved in developing behavior plans as needed in each of the schools. The middle and high school are very structured in their approach due to the planning centers; however, there are still options at the elementary level. Some plans call for alternative disciplinary responses; these might include an altered school day or schedule, time before school in the planning center, time after school in a study group, Saturday Academy, community service, restrictions, or shadowing.

Saturday Academy is a schoolwide option, provided for students who have been assigned detention, have failed to show up, or have had repeated difficulties completing homework assignments. It is held on Saturday mornings and is staffed by an administrator and a teacher. Parents have been very supportive of this activity.

An integral component of the behavior plan is the use of positive reinforcers. This intervention may differ for each student. For some students, a token economy system may be used. For others, reinforcers may include a special outing or field trip, time with a special adult, a special lunch, extra computer time, additional time in the center, or maybe a "day off."

Community service is usually assigned for some violation of a major school rule that would normally earn a student suspension days. The student's parent must support this option; otherwise, the student is suspended. The student is assigned to perform community service for a number of hours equal to a 1- to 3-day suspension. This service must be completed during evenings or the weekend. Sites for service have included the library, senior center, cable company, or newspaper. On several occasions, after the commitments have ended, the school has received calls requesting that the students continue their participation. Obviously, a positive connection has been made between the two parties. For many of these students, it may be the first such connection in the community. We believe that it is then up to the parent (or advocate) and student to decide whether to continue the relationship.

Using students as mediators has been a practice in our middle school for 2 years. It has had a very positive effect on many students, and the results can be seen in the student's daily interactions. Although only a few arrangements have been made for mentoring situations, these have been very positive and we would like to expand this practice to involve more community members. In most situations, the mentor has been a Drug Abuse Resistance Education (police) officer, a staff member, or a counselor.

Active Communication Network

Communication seems to be an area that could always use improvement. Historically, at least in our system, general education teachers received little information about students once they were identified as having special needs. The students would leave the general education classroom for some specified period of time and return with little or no information shared. There may be many school districts where this is not the case; however, being faced with this, as a system, we needed to do things differently to prepare teachers for inclusion.

The first thing we did was to make IEPs and evaluations available for classroom teachers. It was hard to imagine that some teachers had taught 20 years and had never seen an IEP. We provided them with information regarding confidentiality and provided a secure area for keeping the records. We answered questions regarding formal evaluations and their responsibilities in this area.

Special education providers set up regular scheduled feedback networks for teachers, some of whom requested daily updates, some weekly, and some biweekly. Special education teachers developed status/summary sheets to detail progress in various areas. These summaries were sent to teachers, and to parents if requested. Each student was assigned a designated person to coordinate all communication and to serve as the contact person for the teacher and parent.

For some students, parents and teachers are not the only ones involved in their lives. Courts, mental health agencies, physicians, police, and child protective services may also be involved. Although it can be very time-consuming, coordination of services and communication with the agencies are vital to successful intervention. This is especially true with students who have attention-deficit/hyperactive disorder or another condition that requires medication. Successful treatment depends on frequent feedback from parent and school to the physician. In our program, a school psychologist, social worker, or behavior specialist is the program facilitator for these students.

We have also tried to meet a couple of times a year with a group representing all the outside agencies who deal with our students. Representatives from the police, courts, mental health agencies, private counselors, YMCA, child protective services, and physicians, meet for 2 hours and give each other a "report card." We identify what we are doing well, and what areas need improvement. This has been very useful in setting goals for the next year.

Support for Teachers

Many of the topics discussed previously could be listed in this section because all aspects of the program need to support teachers in their objective of educating all children. Several, however, need to be highlighted. Teachers need to have access to information on all of their students, and to be able to use this information. If they do not know how to use this information, then specific training should occur. Everyone needs a working knowledge of various systems and agencies or at least the resources to seek that knowledge.

Personnel need to be available in each building for consultation and for directing the teacher to the appropriate resources. There has to be built-in planning time and meeting time in teachers' schedules. We have pursued grant funding that pays for substitute teachers to cover classes while collaborative partners meet for planning or attend IEP meetings.

Teachers need to feel like part of a team. When meetings are held regarding a student with two teachers, both teachers should be invited. All correspondence should be forwarded to both teachers. If we expect general education teachers to accept responsibility for all students in their classrooms, then they should be included in all information sharing.

Conclusion

It has been a true challenge to participate in the change process of a whole district. One cannot isolate one or two aspects of the program without considering all the variables that have contributed to the changes. We have a dedicated staff of professionals, a supportive school committee and administration, cooperative unions, and enthusiastic parents who have all worked very hard to improve services. We have a student body that has embraced diversity and included all peers as part of one community of learners. It has been the most satisfying experience for me after 20 years in education. This is a very exciting time to be in education, and I am pleased to share information that may help change the way educators deliver services to students with emotional and behavioral needs.

References

American Psychiatric Association. (1994). *Diagnostic and statistical manual of mental disorders* (4th ed.). Washington, DC: Author.

Council for Exceptional Children. (1993). *CEC policy on inclusive schools and community settings.* Adopted by the CEC Delegate Assembly, San Antonio.

ERIC: Clearinghouse Views. (1993, Fall). Including students with disabilities in general education classrooms. *Teaching Exceptional Children,* pp. 66–67.

Guetzloe, E. (1994). Inclusion of students with emotional and behavioral disorders: Program considerations for designing appropriate services. Designing effective services for students with emotional behavioral problems: Perspectives on the role of inclusion. *Highlights from the Working Forum on Inclusion* (p. 5). Denton, TX: The University of North Texas' Institute for Behavioral and Learning Differences.

Individuals with Disabilities Education Act of 1990, 20 U.S.C. § 14 *et seq.*

Knitzer, J., Steinberg, Z., & Fleisch, B. (1990). *At the schoolhouse door: An examination of programs and policies for children with emotional and behavioral problems.* New York: Bank Street College of Education.

Smith-Davis, J., Burke, P., & Noel, M. (1983). *Personnel to educate the handicapped in America: Supply and demand from a programmatic viewpoint.* College Park, MD: University of Maryland, Department of Special Education.

Stainback, W., & Stainback, S. (1982). Integrating seriously emotionally disturbed students with non-handicapped students. *Prise Reporter,* p. 14.

Strain, P., & Shores, R. (1983). A reply to "Misguided Mainstreaming." *Exceptional Children, 50,* 271–273.

United States Department of Education. (1993). *Fifteenth Annual Report to Congress on the Progress of Education for all Handicapped Children Act.* Washington, DC: United States Government Printing Office.

CHAPTER 7

But He's Severely Disabled! How Can He Be in Kindergarten?

Timothy S. Hartshorne and
Nancy S. Hartshorne

A s professionals in school psychology, we have always been sympathetic to the idea of inclusion and welcomed its emergence as a popular practice. However, when we thought about our own child, we dismissed inclusion as applicable to a child with so many disabling conditions. Nancy, the practitioner, was particularly dismissive. How could he get what he needs in a regular classroom? Tim, the professor, was more open, remarking, "Well, if he could have the same program he has now in a regular classroom, that would be fine. I don't particularly care where his program is carried out."

Let us introduce ourselves. Nancy has been a practicing school psychologist for 3 years. Tim has been a trainer in the field for 17 years. Jacob is 5 years old. He was born prematurely as Nancy was completing her school psychology practicum. Jacob has been diagnosed with CHARGE syndrome. CHARGE is an acronym for the various anomalous conditions these children have. Jacob is profoundly deaf and visually impaired. He has significant developmental delays. Although he responds to a few signs, he has very little language. He does not yet walk independently, as his sense of balance is impaired. He also has some autistic-like behaviors, such as self-stimulation, routinized behaviors, and some preference for objects over people.

Jacob's History

Jacob began receiving home-based school services when he was 5 months old. His services were provided by a teacher–consultant, occupational therapist, physical therapist, and speech–language pathologist. When he was 2 years old, a psychologist friend of ours gave us a book on deaf–blindness, and we recognized a lot of Jacob's characteristics. That led us to make contact with the state's consultant for the deaf–blind. That led in turn to an evaluation by the deaf–blind program at the Michigan School for the Blind, and then a meeting between local school personnel and three consultants, the state deaf–blind consultant, a teacher from the School for the Blind, and a teacher for a preschool deaf–blind program in Detroit. These consultants made a strong case for Jacob's needing a full-time classroom program. The school personnel agreed to try a half-day program, and Jacob was placed in a classroom for children with severe multiple impairments. After about 3 months, his program was extended to a full day.

The goals of Jacob's program were largely physical. He continued to receive occupational and physical therapy, and the staff worked on his tactile defensiveness so that he came to tolerate and even enjoy human touch, and he made progress with his motor skills, particularly using a walker. Although he received speech, as well as consultation from the state's deaf–blind consultant on language development, less progress was noted in this area.

The school that Jacob attended initially housed only special education programs. However, in response to concerns about segregation, the local school district opened kindergarten, first-grade, and second-grade classrooms in the building at the start of Jacob's second year there. Some children in those classrooms who knew Jacob from other settings began greeting him when they saw him in the building. We were amused to hear reports of children bragging to each other about being Jacob's friend. That was when we began to seriously consider the problem of Jacob's social development. Because he was the most highly functioning child in his classroom, he was not experiencing appropriate social models there.

At the start of the 1993–1994 school year, we asked if Jacob might at least go out on the playground when the nondisabled children went out. This had not previously been addressed, as Jacob was still preschool age at that time. His playground visits were extremely successful, as the children would crowd around Jacob, help him go up and down the slide, and argue over who got to push him in his wheelchair. A second-grade teacher invited Jacob to sit in on her classroom any time, and so this component was added. Several times a week Jacob would go to this classroom for about an hour, usually during storytime, and sit on the laps of various children.

Could Jacob Be Included?

Several years earlier, Nancy had started attending the annual conference of The Association for Persons with Severe Handicaps (TASH). This organization tends to be rather radical in its educational philosophy, which means that many exciting and cutting-edge ideas are presented. In the fall of 1993, Nancy attended a number of presentations on deaf–blindness, and learned that national experts considered full inclusion to be the best practice for educating these children. She saw several videotapes of inclusion programs, and returned home very enthusiastic about an inclusion program for Jacob.

We found several things persuasive. First, and most important to Tim, there was no reason why Jacob could not receive the same program he was getting in the segregated classroom in a regular kindergarten. All of the services, such as occupational, physical, and speech therapies, could still be provided. Most essential would be a high-quality full-time paraprofessional aide to work with Jacob to implement his program and facilitate his inclusion. Second, and most important to Nancy, Jacob would have a chance to become a part of his community. We wanted Jacob to attend his neighborhood school and become a part of the regular school experience there. In growing up with his typical peers, Jacob would more likely become an accepted member of the community, with a broad network of friends. This could potentially help him with future employment and housing, as some of his peers may one day be the business and civic leaders of our community.

To make this inclusion happen for Jacob, we realized that several steps had to be taken. The first was to get positive responses to the idea from his current teacher and program administrator, from the director of special education for our local school district, and from the principal of our neighborhood school. We received positive responses, but with varying degrees of enthusiasm, from all of these individuals. A theme that ran through the responses we got was to consider this issue carefully and make sure that we do what is right for Jacob, and not simply implement an inclusion program because it is part of the current bandwagon. As professionals, we could not agree more with that sentiment. As parents, we worried that this was a way to temper our enthusiasm, and give the administrators a way out.

The first formal planning meeting for Jacob's potential inclusion took place in February 1994. Present were the administrator from his current school; his current teacher; his occupational and physical therapists and speech pathologist; the principal of his neighborhood school; the special education and kindergarten teachers for his neighborhood school; the state deaf–blind consultant; the director of special education for the school district; Jacob; and ourselves. We met in the special education resource room at his neighborhood school.

It was apparent at this meeting that there are different definitions of inclusion. Nancy's view was that Jacob should participate in everything his nondisabled peers do, and that all of his services should be provided in the regular classroom, with no special pull-out. Several of the support services personnel questioned whether Jacob's goals in their areas could be achieved in the regular classroom. Some of them felt he would still need some pull-out. This led the special education and kindergarten teachers to speculate as to whether Jacob should receive some time in the special education resource room. When Nancy and I resisted this idea, some suggestion was made that it might be a good idea to be somewhat flexible in our definition of inclusion.

How much time Jacob should be in the kindergarten classroom became the first critical question. There were several concerns. First, how would he adjust to being with so many other children in an organized, but constantly changing environment? Could he tolerate this for a whole day? Second, since two groups of kindergartners at this school attend for whole days, every other day, and alternate Fridays, should Jacob attend with one group or both groups? It was agreed that Jacob should continue to receive a full-time educational program, but it was suggested that he could attend kindergarten half time, and return to his previous school half time. One concern related to Jacob's schedule was that special education students in regular classrooms are counted as two students by this school district. Thus, if each kindergarten section normally enrolls 25 children, with Jacob in the classroom that meant 24 actual bodies. If Jacob attended both kindergartens, that would mean he was taking the places of four children in total. Because this particular elementary school is highly regarded in the community, that could mean that three children would be denied admittance to this school and have to attend kindergarten at another elementary school. A third concern was whether Jacob should attend regular kindergarten or developmental kindergarten, where the children would be somewhat younger and not as far advanced.

These questions were not resolved at this meeting. The principal and special education director agreed that they needed additional information from central administration. The neighborhood school teachers wanted some time to consider various issues, and asked us to do the same. The state consultant indicated that she would consult with an inclusion expert from another state. With that, another meeting was scheduled and this one adjourned.

The second meeting was in April. The neighborhood school staff reported that they had carefully considered whether Jacob should attend regular or developmental kindergarten, and had decided in favor of regular. They had concerns that some of the children in the developmental classroom might have difficulties that would detract from Jacob's program. They also thought the children in regular kindergarten would be better role models for Jacob. They were uncertain, however, as to whether Jacob could tolerate full-time kindergarten, and thought perhaps he should continue half time with his current program.

The state deaf–blind consultant reported that she had consulted with a woman from another state who strongly argued against a split program for Jacob. This person emphasized the need for stability in his day and in his program. The state consultant also said that she was bringing this person to Michigan, and she would be available the next month to consult with us about Jacob and his program. The meeting was generally positive, and we agreed to meet the next month to see what this consultant had to say.

The consultant spent 2 full days in town. She observed Jacob in his current placement, observed the kindergarten classroom, and consulted with the principal and teachers. Nancy and Tim took her to dinner. Her consultation seemed to allay most of the concerns that people had about a full-time program in the regular kindergarten.

One final meeting was held prior to the end of the school year. It was agreed that the local school district where Jacob would attend regular kindergarten would hire an aide who would start work in August with Jacob in his current placement (a 12-month program), and then move with him to kindergarten at the start of the new school year. Jacob's current teacher agreed to call together staff presently working with Jacob to outline his current program in a way that the kindergarten and special education teachers at his new school could seek to implement. To further facilitate Jacob's transition from one program to the other, his future kindergarten and special education teachers were invited to our house to see Jacob in his home environment. The state deaf–blind consultant invited them to Michigan School for the Blind to observe the deaf–blind program there. They also agreed to spend a day observing at Jacob's present classroom. Prior to school's starting, Jacob was allowed to explore the kindergarten room to familiarize himself with its space.

Hiring an aide for Jacob was the next major step. A job description was developed by the director of special education with input from the principal, kindergarten and special education teachers, and us. A critical condition was the willingness to deal with bodily fluids, as Jacob is not toilet trained and frequently vomits. Also the person needed to be physically able to lift him for transfers. Third, the aide would need to learn to feed him through his gastrostomy button. Additionally, the aide would need to be able to work well as a part of a team and to implement and facilitate Jacob's participation in kindergarten. A final issue was a willingness to consider working with Jacob in the summer. What to do for Jacob during the summer following inclusion had been briefly discussed at the various meetings, but not resolved. Several options were considered, and it was decided to delay any decisions until early 1995.

Four individuals were interviewed. All of them were quite good. The interview team consisted of the individuals listed above as having developed the job description. The director of special education noted as an aside how unusual it was to have such a large interview team for an aide position. It demonstrated just how critical the school district viewed the position to the success of Jacob's inclusion. Lisa was the unanimous choice of the committee. She already knew Jacob, as she had worked part time on his school bus and had been a substitute aide in his classroom. She is a college student, hoping to go on in special education, but progressing rather slowly in order to support herself. She was enthusiastic about working with Jacob, and thought she could be available for at least 3 years.

In July, Lisa and Nancy attended a meeting for parents of children with deaf–blindness sponsored by the state. Although most of the parents present had older children, it was a good introduction for Lisa to some of the issues and problems Jacob confronts. In early August, the kindergarten and special education teachers, Nancy, and

Lisa went to Michigan School for the Blind to observe the deaf–blind program. Right after that, Lisa began work in Jacob's classroom, and on August 30, 1994, Jacob started kindergarten at his neighborhood school.

The First Months

Our biggest concern about the start of the year for Jacob was how he would be accepted by his peers, and by the parents of his peers. The reaction from friends and acquaintances up to this point had been largely positive, although one person asked Nancy, "What makes you think your son deserves to be in the regular classroom? He doesn't walk does he? What's he going to do all day?" Some friends whose daughter was going to be in Jacob's class invited us over for dinner so that their daughter could get better acquainted with him.

Jacob's initial reception was very positive. Children asked questions about his wheelchair and walker, and were curious about his feeding and toileting, but generally shrugged it off and just accepted him. Within the first few weeks, several children could be identified as his friends, and he was invited to a birthday party. Nancy attended the school open house, and tried to meet as many parents as she could, and answer any questions about Jacob that they might have. Few questions were asked, but a number of the children made it a point to come over and greet Jacob, or point him out to their parents as their friend. Lisa reported after the first month that Jacob was the coolest kid in the classroom. One of Tim's students was working at an after-school day care, and reported that a kindergarten child was looking through a collection of photographs of his fellow students. He paused at one picture and then kissed it and said, "I love this boy." It was the picture of Jacob.

Jacob's core team, consisting of his teacher, special education teacher, aide, therapists, and us, began meeting every other week. The principal and the state deaf–blind consultant also attended some meetings. During the fall, the primary issues discussed were Jacob's schedule, communication, and health.

Schedule

A problem was to fit Jacob and his needs into the regular kindergarten schedule. When would he use the toilet? What would he do during free time? What would he do at the various learning centers in the room? When would his specialists work with him? The special education and regular classroom teachers, along with Lisa, worked on this together. They created a master schedule for the week for Jacob that matched the regular children's schedule, and then each day wrote down what Jacob did during each period of the day. This schedule is sent home every Friday, so that we can see what Jacob did during the week. There were very few difficulties with the scheduling. Probably the most difficult was scheduling breaks and lunch for Lisa. When this was finally worked out, the first day Lisa was leaving the room for lunch, some of the children asked her where she was going. Then they asked who was going to take care of Jacob. Lisa told them the special education teacher was coming over. The children asked, "Is she nice?" They were already feeling very protective of Jacob.

Communication

A very important goal for Jacob is to learn to communicate. He responds to a few signs such as "milk" and "up," but shows little expressive language. With consultation from the state deaf–blind consultant, a schedule board was created for Jacob. This is a plastic clipboard on which Velcro strips are glued. On these are fastened a clamp from one of his feeding tubes to represent mealtime, a small hook to represent hanging up his coat, and several other objects representing different parts of his day. Before he hangs up his coat in the morning, Lisa has him grab the hook off the board and take it to where the coats are hung. We created a similar schedule board for use at home. While this system has not been particularly successful yet, it is a beginning, and we are investigating other methods.

Health

Although Jacob is generally healthy, he is susceptible to colds, partly because he explores everything with his tongue. Colds are easily managed, but two other conditions are more difficult. Jacob goes through periods where he often vomits after a meal. When this happens it can create mucus in his throat, making him more likely to vomit with the next meal. We are quite used to this, and had warned the school about the potential problem, but the first time Jacob threw up on the bus, concern was expressed that perhaps he was too sick to be in school that day. His vomiting was compounded by his falling asleep that particular day. It was difficult for the school to know whether this meant Jacob needed to be home, or whether he could stay in school.

A second condition is that occasionally Jacob becomes agitated. He may cry, toss his toys, crawl around in circles, and generally make himself disagreeable. He seems during these times to be in pain, but he gives no clues as to where he hurts. One day when Jacob behaved this way, the school called and asked us to take him home. Nancy took him from school across the street to his pediatrician's office. The doctor could find nothing physically wrong with Jacob.

At our next team meeting, considerable time was spent addressing the problem of identifying when Jacob needs to be home and when he can function in school. The problem is that we know Jacob, and are used to identifying when something is wrong. As the school has come to know him better, they are managing most of these conditions very well at school.

Circle of Friends

Because one of our major reasons for having Jacob included was socialization, we decided to form a Circle of Friends for him. A Circle of Friends is a social support network that meets to help a person with disabilities and his or her family to meet their goals. We are both a part of a circle for a 30-year-old woman in our community, so we were familiar with the process as applied to adults. A friend of ours who is trained to facilitate circles volunteered to establish one for Jacob, although her experience and training was only with adults. Thus, Jacob became the first child in our area to have a circle.

The idea was for the circle to consist of both adults and children who know Jacob. We thought children in his classroom and perhaps their parents might be added later as they became identified as his friends. During the summer, with our facilitator, we created a map of those who are significant people in Jacob's life, and then invited them to a meeting at our house. Attendance was light, but we began outlining our dreams and nightmares for Jacob, and then what we felt was needed to make his inclusion work.

These outlines were presented to Jacob's professional team, and the list of needs actually formed the basis for the initial organization of his program. Several members of his team agreed to join the circle, and it was decided to have the circle meet at Jacob's school once a month.

We are still in the process of trying to understand how to make the circle into an effective tool for Jacob. A core group of people come to circle meetings, but it is a very small group. The circle has been effective in facilitating the donation of adaptive playground equipment for Jacob, organizing a Christmas party, and is now helping to plan a party for Jacob to give for his friends at school. We have both attended workshops on circles, but very few circles have been established for kindergartners. Because Jacob has been successfully socialized into his classroom, it has not seemed necessary to organize a particular circle from among his classmates. For the time being, the present circle has decided to function as a support system for us, to help us with including Jacob within the larger community. Meetings are likely to be moved to our house and scheduled for a later time of day, in hopes that more people will be able to attend. We will continue to monitor Jacob's socialization at school, and may begin a circle of children when Jacob is a little older and socialization is more difficult.

The Future

Three critical issues face Jacob's team during this second half of the school year. These are curriculum adaptation, retention versus promotion, and a summer program.

Curriculum

At the fall TASH conference, Nancy attended several workshops and talked to a number of people about making curricular adaptations to facilitate inclusion. She has recently presented a model to Jacob's team, which will be carefully reviewed. At issue is how to more fully adapt what the children without disabilities are doing so that Jacob is doing something similar that meets specific educational goals for Jacob. For example, if the class is working with numbers, what could Jacob be doing that would be geared toward quantitative goals for him? At the present time Jacob's Individualized Education Program does not include academic goals, so the curricular adaptations that are made are not terribly focused. Jacob's teacher and Lisa have been working on this all year, but it may be time to be more deliberate in identifying and fine-tuning academic goals for Jacob.

Retention/Promotion

Developmentally, Jacob is far behind his class peers. Does it make sense to promote him to first grade, or keep him in kindergarten another year? Nancy and I until recently tended to favor promotion. Jacob is likely to always be developmentally behind his peers. He has developed some friendships this year, and while he might not notice their absence next year, many of the children would notice that Jacob was not also promoted. In fact one girl in his class has already expressed concern that she might not be in Jacob's class next year. Also favoring promotion is the question of how much more Jacob could benefit from an additional year in kindergarten. More of the same is not necessarily useful.

However, at our last team meeting, several important considerations were expressed that now have us leaning toward retention. The most important is that Jacob may in the next year learn to walk, and he may be toilet trained. Both of these would be a big advantage to his inclusion in first grade a year later. Socially he will make new friends next year, and will also have friends in first grade. That could help with his greater inclusion in the larger school. A final decision has yet to be made.

Summer Program

The third issue is a summer program. Jacob is eligible for a summer program, as he really needs year-round schooling given the extent of his disabilities. Lisa is available to work with him through the summer, and the district is willing to fund this. The question is what kind of summer program to establish. Jacob could return to his previous classroom, but that seems like a step backwards. The alternative we favor right now is the Summer Remedial Clinic for children with language disabilities operated by the Department of Communication Disorders at Central Michigan University. It runs all day for 6 weeks, which is educationally equivalent to his previous classroom, which runs half days for 12 weeks in the summer. Perhaps with intensive therapy, we could make progress on communication with Jacob. We are applying for the program, as well as exploring other options.

Beyond Kindergarten

We are both extremely pleased with our decision to include Jacob. The school continues to be very positive, and his teacher reports continued progress in Jacob's development. Will inclusion be the right thing for Jacob for the next 12 years? That is hard to predict. While we both believe that inclusion is the ideal program for Jacob, we are also committed to his having the best educational plan and intervention possible.

Assuming Jacob spends 2 years in kindergarten, we do not antici- pate his repeating any other grades. The key to his success will be his paraprofessional and the teachers to whom he is assigned. Lisa will likely be his aide for 2 more years, and then she will be too involved in her own education to continue a full-time position. However, now that we have some experience, we have a much better idea of what is needed in an aide, and should be able to make the position much more descriptive and the interview process much more focused. Jacob will need an aide for the rest of his educational career; however, there will likely be a shift in what the aide does. Our hope is that Jacob's inclu- sion will be co-facilitated by the other children in his classroom. They may increasingly be able to make the adaptations Jacob needs to par- ticipate. This will be particularly the case where cooperative learning models are utilized. To the extent this happens, the aide may be able to function in a more consultative role with the other students. The advantage of this is that Jacob's community will learn to adapt to his needs, with the potential of this generalizing to his postschool life.

Much of the success that Jacob continues to experience will be due to his having a classroom teacher who is enthusiastic about his inclu- sion, and open to trying new methods of intervention. We hope that the enthusiasm of his current teacher will infect other teachers in the school, or at least one per grade. As the curriculum becomes more academic, so must Jacob's program. It may be acceptable for Jacob to roll around on the carpet in kindergarten, but by fourth grade accep- tance may be more difficult. Allowance must be made for Jacob's par- ticular needs and abilities, but considerations must also be given to general experience within the classroom. It will take a skilled teacher, in conjunction with the special education teacher, to work this out.

There may come a time when all of Jacob's needs cannot be pro- vided for in a regular classroom setting, or when a different setting may be more effective for his learning, and we may have to explore other options. By high school we will need to be exploring vocational training. However, we feel that with appropriate planning, Jacob should be able to receive most of his educational program alongside his nondisabled peers. Jacob's education has always been on the cut- ting edge, and we expect to keep it there.

Coping with Parents Like Us

Because we are both school psychologists, we are not the typical parents of a child with disabilities. However, in many ways we are typical. We are parents. We have had to deal with the birth of a child who was not "normal." We have had to deal with our grief over that event, with our worries over Jacob's health and well-being, and with our concerns for the future. At times we are discouraged, angry, and defensive. At times the school is the cause of these negative feelings, and at other times the school receives the brunt of them.

Here is some advice for school personnel on how to deal with parents like us. Recognize parents as experts. We are not all teachers, or therapists, or principals, but we know our child better than anyone else. Grant us that expertise. Treat our suggestions seriously; do not simply dismiss even the most "ridiculous" suggestion out of hand. And just because you do not "see it at school" does not mean we are making up what we see at home. If we believe all children can be included, we need to extend that to parents as well; they too can be included. Make them a part of the team.

Do not become defensive. This is very hard to avoid, as parents may be aggressive and angry at times. But when you become defensive, you tend to lash back at the parents, which only makes them more angry and aggressive. Avoid defensiveness by following these steps. First, interpret the parents' "rude" behavior as being based on worry and concern. Parents are often scared. Their anger may be directed at you, but more than likely you are not the source. Second, spend some time just listening to what the parents have to say. Try not to respond except to ask for additional clarification of the concern. Reflect back to the parents what you understand is their concern or issue. Sometimes parents just need to know they are being listened to. Third, try to find some area where you agree with the parents. It may be that you too are worried about the child, or a particular aspect of the program, or an action taken by the school. Let the parents know of your agreement. Skip over for now those areas where you disagree. Fourth, suggest some kind of action, such as meeting with other school personnel, gathering additional data, or making an appropriate referral. Once parents feel school personnel have really listened to them, they will usually be much more open to other points of view.

There are times when the school is right and the parents are wrong. The conventional wisdom seems to be to just tell it to the parents straight. This has some appeal, but avoids recognizing the emotional investment of the parents in their child. By and large parents do not mind being wrong; what they mind is being misunderstood. Before you tell parents that the school is right and they are wrong, make sure (a) that you really understand what the parents are advocating; (b) that you have communicated to the parents that you really understand what they are advocating, and why they are advocating it; and (c) that you really are right. You can avoid this problem altogether by making sure parents are involved in all aspects of the child's program as team members.

There are times when the right answer is very murky. You will not succeed in such cases by pretending to the parents that the answer is clear. Perhaps this is well illustrated by the initial discussions regarding Jacob's inclusion. Should he be in the regular kindergarten full time? We thought so, but we had our private doubts. If school personnel had pretended that they knew the right answer, and it had been different from our own preference, the situation could have become hostile. We never would have confessed to our own doubts. But instead the school people admitted they did not know the right answer, and agreed to seek additional input and data. That made us much more open to consider alternatives.

Finally, the key to making this work is the simple concept of goal alignment. It should be the case that both parents and school personnel want exactly the same thing. They both want the best possible program for the child. We all need to put aside our suspicions of the other, and trust that we share this goal. But parents will ask this first of the school, because parents have to watch out for their own child. When parents hear that certain things are not possible due to budget or personnel or programmatic or administrative difficulties, parents do not trust that the school has the same goal for the child. School personnel need to first make sure they have communicated their desire to create the best possible program for the child. Then they can open up the discussion to problem solving the budgetary and administrative difficulties. Parents can appreciate those problems *if* the parents first feel they and the school share the same ultimate goal.

School personnel sometimes disagree among themselves. Certainly at times they will disagree with parents. However, if parents are included as team members with expertise, in most cases these disagreements can be experienced as normal and expected, and as based on honest differences regarding the best interests of the child. Then it is unlikely for these disagreements to escalate into anything more.

CHAPTER 8

Insights on Teaching and Raising a Child with a Disability

Mark Tovar

Future Aspirations

My future aspirations from where I now stand,
seem so far ahead though still part of my plan.

Aspirations are not only what you hope to achieve,
but a blending of your parent's hopes, dreams, and beliefs.

For every step that I take to make my future aspirations bright,
illuminates another path that doesn't seem quite right.

The path that never seems quite right will not be fixed today,
because of fear that tomorrow's storm will wash it all away.

It's not only the storm itself of which I am afraid,
for a path that gets washed out by storms can always be remade.

The thing that I fear most is not failing at my task,
but that I will be hurt too badly to continue on my path.

How am I to obtain these aspirations that I lack?
For when I look into the mirror a child still looks back.

As I travel along will I meet the aspirations in my life?
Or will there always be a path that doesn't seem quite right?

My purpose in this chapter is to describe many life experiences that I have had as a person with cerebral palsy. I hope to share some obstacles that a child with cerebral palsy or a similar disability might face. I will also suggest ways to deal with these situations. Although these suggestions are not ways to cure a person's disability, they are the best ways I have found to live with it.

To my knowledge there have been very few things written on young people living with cerebral palsy. When I was born in 1975, my parents raised me using what I call the "trial 'n' error method." I call it this because they did not have many books to read on the subject or people to talk to about their expectations. They were unsure of what seem to be the most obvious tasks. They were not sure at first how to apply discipline, dress, or even play with me. Their approach was to attempt a variety of things until they found something that worked. I hope that by reading this chapter, teachers will have an increased insight on children who have disabilities and share this chapter with parents.

Discovering the Disability

I was supposed to be born in March of 1975. Instead, I was so eager to begin my life that I was born on January 9 of that year. Being 2 months premature is what caused me to have cerebral palsy. It caused parts of my brain that are used for motor skills, balance, coordination, speech, and perception to be damaged. My parents were not aware of this "surprise" until some months after my birth. My mother noticed that I was not making the effort to start to walk like other children. She noticed that when she sat me up, I would fall to the side, unable to balance myself. She knew there was something wrong even when some doctors insisted that I was just a late bloomer. They said I would "come around" if she would give me a little more time. Time passed and with it my parents' optimism that they had a healthy baby boy. Finally, one more trip to the doctor's office confirmed my parents' fears: Their son had cerebral palsy.

It was then that each of my parents became overwhelmed with questions such as "Why me?" "How can I possibly raise this child?" "Do I have the patience to raise this child?" "What if I fail?"

What followed in the coming years was an attempt to understand and treat my newly discovered disability. We took hundreds of trips to the doctors, attended therapy sessions, and spent hours at home, with my mom working as my personal therapist and tutor. From the time I was 3 years old until I was 12, I had therapy about twice a week. By the time I reached my mid-teens, I had had seven orthopedic surgeries, about once every 2 years. The majority of my childhood was spent learning to walk the best I could, so that the doctors could judge what was needed for the next surgery. When I reached my full potential from my last surgery and learned to walk, I would be scheduled for another surgery and had to start all over. It took very little time for me to become upset about my doctor appointments. During this time my parents were constantly having to move me, entertain me, bathe me, and carry me to the toilet. (Carrying an 11-year-old boy in a partial body cast to the toilet is not an easy task.) After I began to attend school, we discovered that I had learning disabilities as well as cerebral palsy.

It is important to communicate to parents that it is common to have to spend an incredible amount of time with their children who have disabilities. While this may seem obvious, this constant reinforcement is crucial. Simply stated, children with disabilities often need twice the support of a "normal" child. On the positive side, I believe that parents and children with disabilities establish extremely close relationships because they are dependent on each other for many things. It has been my experience that children with disabilities are less likely to get into serious mischief because they are physically close to the parents and teachers much of the time and not the best at leaving the scene of the crime quickly.

Teaching a Child To Live with a Disability

Starting at the age of 5, I began to notice that there was something very different about me. My parents began to explain to me how I was different, that I had a disease called cerebral palsy (CP). They told me that CP would mean that I would have to try a little harder at school and do physical activities a little differently. They explained that there were some things I would discover along the way that I would not be able to do. They never once told me what these things were; they only said "When you have tried your hardest and still cannot accomplish it, you will know what we mean." I learned what they meant when I tried to ride a bike at 10 years of age (Crash!). My point is that one should never tell a child with a disability what he or she will not be able to do. With a disability such as CP, one can never truly know the extent of each person's capabilities. Let these individuals try something first, and when or if they fall flat on their face, they will come to the realization that this is one of the things that they will not be able to accomplish.

If children are old enough to ask questions about their disability, parents (or teachers) owe them an honest answer. Children will confront enough people who take pity on them. These (well-intentioned) people often try to answer questions with what they think is best suited for a person with a disability to hear. Sometimes, however, they unintentionally insult the children's intelligence.

As I reached the age of 7, the wise words of my mother and father began to have more meaning. I needed to work very hard on the things that were in my control to compensate for the effect of my disability on other things. I remember coming down the stairs one morning dressed for school. I made it to the kitchen, where my mother took a half look at me as if I was crazy and said, "Get yourself upstairs and change into something more suitable for school." When I questioned why I could not wear what I had on, she said, "Mark, you have cerebral palsy. That is already one strike against you. If people see you dressed like that, you will give them another reason to push you to the side." I remember thinking, "What a grouch," but as I grew older I began to see the wisdom and profoundness in my mother's words that morning.

I truly believe that people who care will always push children with disabilities to do all that they can, including the way they dress, act, eat, read, and most important communicate. This power will serve well to lessen the cruelty of this world. For example, we played the "word game" whenever we were driving or during idle time. In this game my parents introduced a new vocabulary word to me and explained it. Before long, I began to use these words in my everyday activity. By the age of 10, I had a very extensive vocabulary. Communication ability is important because, although physically children with disabilities may make bad first impressions, they can redeem themselves if they can hold an intelligent and witty discussion. These children need to be encouraged to read and to participate in daily discussions. I remember sitting at the table with my parents at age 10 talking news, politics, or whatever they talked of that day. Although some people think that children should be seen and not heard, except for extreme cases this rule should not apply to children with disabilities. Stifling the natural curiosity of children will only hurt them later in life. To help them develop confidence, adults need to entrust them with intelligent discussion and teach them when it is time to speak and whom to speak to. Spoken communication has been my greatest equalizer of all. If a child is vocal and intelligent, try as people may to ignore people with disabilities, the child will never be overlooked.

Frustration

As I progressed through school (in special education until sixth grade), I began to come face to face with the learning challenges of my CP. In the fourth grade, my class began to learn the multiplication tables. Every day after lunch our teacher made us write them out and we were timed. No matter what I did, I could not get them done. This is my earliest recollection of my mother as tutor. She came home after a full-time job and sat at the table sometimes from 5:00 in the evening until 9:00 at night. These hours were filled with my constant questions of why I had to do this "stupid crap." No one else in the neighborhood had to do this. She would answer, "You are not everyone else." I do not wish to leave you with the impression that my mother was the most angelic mother in the world and never became frustrated. I can remember times when she got angry at my constant whining and said, "Shut your mouth and finish." Many nights ended with me so incredibly frustrated that I cried myself to sleep. One thing that everyone should understand about children with disabilities is that frustration is a common emotion.

Parents and teachers must be careful not to fall into the timetable of expectations that society commonly places on students. For example, my parents often heard such comments as "Your child should be able to do this at exactly this time in his life." However, it is not unusual for students with disabilities to take quite a bit longer, depending on the severity of one's disability. I believe that there is less pressure on students with disabilities when they are enrolled in special education classes. I was not able to tie my shoes until I was 8, tell time until I was 10, and count money until I was 13. At 20 years old, I still cannot draw a decent stick man, color without going out of the lines, put a small puzzle together in less than 3 hours, or remember directions well enough to get from one place to the other without having to constantly be reminded. I have my CP to thank for all of this. Parents need to be careful not to use this as an excuse to let their child slide too far. There is a fine line between being understanding and being too demanding, and many teachers like to specify where that line is drawn. A parent or a teacher of a disabled child will know the majority of the child's limitations. These people must be ready to fight for the child. At some point in life, it will be necessary to disagree with a teacher, counselor, doctor, or psychologist who claims to know all there is to know about the student's capabilities. However, simply because these professionals have titles before their names, they are not the "Ever-powerful and all-knowing Oz." Some are mistaken more than they care to admit.

A Taste of the Real World

After years of consideration and consternation, my parents and the school system decided that the beginning of my sixth-grade year would be the year I would start general education classes. All those nights at the table in tears and the utter frustration finally began to show justification. Was I ready? I had always been told what to expect by my special education teachers, but I never expected what was to follow.

I approached the first morning of general education with much excitement about the new things that I would find. I remember leaving my house that morning with a smile. Little did my parents know that it was the last smile they would see for a month. I arrived home that evening with the same tears and frustration that I had previously experienced. When my parents asked me what was wrong, I explained to them that it was too hard and not the place that I belonged. The reason I felt this was because my special education classes were taught at a much slower pace, with a lot fewer children in the classroom. I told my mother that I was not going back and that she would just have to find another school. I was more than merely uncomfortable with my surroundings; I despised them. I talked it over with my parents and then I agreed to give it another shot. The same results followed day after day until it came to the point that I was on my knees begging them not to make me go. I would actually get physically ill. I was convinced that my parents were punishing me. I even remember questioning their allegiance to me, "How could you do this to me? I thought you loved me?" They answered me with, "This is something that you have to do sometime in your life. Changing schools will not solve anything. We are here to help you with anything you need, but you will stay at school."

I cannot say exactly what it was that I felt. It was the most frightening, helpless feeling that I had encountered to that point in my life. While I knew that my parents were going to help me in any way they could, the fear of failure would not leave me. In a month's time, the fear was gone and I was fully participating in the general education classroom. My parents had proved to me that I was capable of success in the real world.

I will never understand how my parents had the strength to hold to their convictions as I pleaded with them to stop putting me through hell or how they knew that it was all going to work out. I found out years later as we laughed about it that they did not know if it was going to work out. They just hoped for the best. I believe that their handling of this event made it possible for me to be successful throughout the rest of my life. It is the reason that I never looked back longingly on special education classes, and I have a 3.2 grade point average in my first 2 years at college.

A Word to the Teachers

In this section I provide a little insight on the things that I think helped me or in some cases may have hindered me in school. The first thing I would say is that it is all right for teachers to be uncomfortable around children with disabilities when first meeting them. It is perfectly natural. Teachers must, however, become acclimated rather quickly because it is their job. It is important to do this as fast as possible because, if a child is being integrated, the teacher must be comfortable with the child if he or she hopes to convey unconditional acceptance to fellow students. The students in the class will notice if the teacher is uncomfortable with the situation.

Once the child with a disability is part of the class, one of the most important things that will set the tone for the rest of the year is the seating arrangement. Often the child is placed at a table or special desk in front of the class. This is a trend that I experience even in college. If children with disabilities are supposed to be part of the class, they should not be singled out and put at the very front of the class. I often felt like the child who is being punished for bad behavior and made to stand in front of the class in the corner. I recommend moving desks so that the child with a disability is sitting next to fellow students. I soon became able to transfer from my wheelchair into a normal desk and was happy because I could sit next to my friends.

It is okay for teachers to talk about the student's disability to the rest of the class if the student seems to be comfortable with it. Only a couple of times throughout my school experience has a teacher used me and my wheelchair in a story problem or example of some sort. It made me feel great that they were acknowledging who I was. The rest of the time, teachers did not incorporate my disability into anything they spoke of, perhaps for fear of alienating me. The message that I believe was sent to some of my classmates was that, because the teacher did not ever speak of the disability in class, the topic must be taboo.

I would also suggest that teachers not constantly ask, "Can I help you with this?" I know that it is important to provide assistance; however, teachers may unintentionally communicate to students with disabilities that they are not capable of the task. Pretty soon, the students may actually believe them. When children with disabilities need help, they should learn that, like everyone else in the class, they must ask for it. Another unintentional, yet frequent uninviting behavior is when teachers have students with disabilities line up for lunch first or do things before other students. This may create resentment in other students, or may eventually spoil the children with disabilities into thinking that they are entitled to things strictly because of their disability. The phrase that has been beaten to death over the ages still rings true today: Treat others as you would want to be treated.

Focal Points

Children with disabilities undoubtedly will face one if not more of what I call "focal points" in their lives. Focal points are instances in a child's life that will determine future success or failure. Hindsight is 20/20, so teachers and parents must treat with care all situations in which the child shows discomfort with an issue of acculturating into the nonchallenged world. Adults must use what they know about the child to make an educated guess on how to handle each situation (as thousands of parents of children with disabilities do on a daily basis).

During my last year of high school, I was encouraged by my parents to prepare to move out of our home. They thought since I was going away to college and had depended on them so much, it would be a good idea if I got a taste of the real world. They were right. I moved only 5 miles away from home and my parents helped me financially. With their help and the money I got from Social Security for having a disability, I set out to see if I could live independently. I had to shop, cook, clean, and manage for myself. I had a great time, and this prepared me for college life. This is yet another example of a focal point that was both dependent on previous experiences and a building block for the future. I urge parents to allow their child this experience if the child is capable and the parents can find the means. Training for independent living should begin as early as possible because it does require much responsibility on the part of the child and the ability to let go on the part of the parent and teacher.

Another very important point for teachers and parents to keep in mind is that many people with disabilities rely on routines. We tend to find ways of doing things that work for us and then exclude all other possibilities. The positive aspect of routines is that when they are successful, they can be the building blocks for a very resolute work ethic. The danger of routines is that they force one to become accustomed to certain ways of doing things, increasing stress when it comes time to assimilate into the nonroutinized, nonchallenged world.

Younger Siblings and Children with Disabilities

People's attention often gravitates toward children with disabilities, even in the presence of their siblings. This can be especially difficult for younger children. Whether people are paying attention to the child because they are truly interested in that child or because they are intrigued by the child's disability, the fact remains (in the eyes of the younger sibling) that the disabled child receives more attention.

I cannot begin to count how many times my younger sister Erica (who is 5 years younger than I) has been overlooked by people in conversation or otherwise because my disability overshadowed all. We would go out on Halloween and on our return, I would have a garbage bag full of candy as opposed to my sister's pillowcase full. People simply felt sorry for me and gave me twice as much. She grew up to be very shy about talking in public and still is today; I believe some of this was because other people interacted with me more than with her and she became accustomed to being silent. Siblings of children with disabilities need to be encouraged to participate.

As my sister grew up, she helped me with many little things, such as holding doors, fetching things, carrying things, and being a shoulder to balance on. For all of these things, I thank her. She also began to find her spot in the family by arguing with every viewpoint that I or other members of my family possessed. This may also happen with other younger siblings of children with disabilities. I am not saying that my parents neglected my sister of attention on purpose. No matter how hard parents try, the child with a disability will always receive more parental attention because he or she requires and demands it.

I would recommend that parents set aside time for the younger children to compensate for some of the quality time that is lost when in the presence of their sibling. It is also beneficial to explain to siblings that Mom and Daddy need them to be helpers. It will be easier if siblings understand that their assistance is required and they have a very specific purpose in the family.

Siblings will face many social trials because of their relationship to a child with a disability. When siblings are in public with a brother or sister who is disabled, the siblings' cohorts may tease them about their brother or sister. The siblings may also be asked questions they are afraid to ask themselves: "What is wrong with him?" "Why does he walk like that?" If my sister had a nickel for every time she had to answer on behalf or because of me, she would have quite a bank account. This is why it is essential to educate siblings about their brother's or sister's disability and prepare them for this kind of "social trial."

Sheltering Children Ensures Their Disability

My father is a sweet, gentle, caring, Christian man, who could have single-handedly made sure I was disabled for the rest of my life. My father loved his little boy so much that he was willing to protect me from all harm even if it meant doing a task for me that I should have been doing myself. Every time a task showed the littlest inconvenience, my father would do it for me. This included walking up stairs, crossing the street, getting things to eat, drinking, playing, or getting myself dressed (by 11 years of age, I was able to do all of these myself). I am not innocent in this matter. When children with disabilities learn that they can combat a difficulty with a simple request, they will do so as many times as others let them. Anytime I got lazy, I would retort with a simple "Dad will you . . . ?" He would get me whatever my heart desired. I had my own genie in the lamp.

Consequently, my father was very protective of me. Almost anything that I did was accompanied by a "Marky be careful," "Marky watch that you do not hurt your legs," or "Marky maybe you should not do that." My father's constant badgering made me think that I was unable to do things that I could have done at times. After awhile, mom got wise to our little game and began to force my father to make me do things for myself. Before she would pick me up from the floor, I would have to be hurt. Somehow the balance between my mother the dictator and my father the good Samaritan worked. (However, my father would still carry me around if I would let him.)

I believe that if my father would have been allowed to carry on, I would have ended up with far fewer abilities than I have now. I know of people with disabilities in their 20s who are unable to use a pay phone, ride public transportation, or order a meal at a restaurant because they cannot count their money. The sad part is that they are mentally capable of these skills, but their parents do not want to inconvenience the children or themselves to allow this learning to take place. I understand that taking children with disabilities into public takes a little more time and effort. I recommend that teachers and parents expose all students to as much of their environment as possible. Human interaction is the key to the children's growth.

Another idea is to involve students with disabilities in hobbies or activities, such as Cub Scouts, Wheelchair Sports, or even video games. In fact, video games are great for hand–eye coordination. My left hand was incapable of doing its job until I regained use of it through playing video games.

Society in the Presence of Disabled People

When accompanying a child with a disability in public, one must be ready for some of the longest, hardest, befuddling stares ever. No matter where I go, people look at me as if I am the bearded woman at some freakish sideshow carnival or the boogie man come to snatch up or eat unsuspecting children. You would think I was the seventh apocalyptic sign or something.

The reason for this starts very early in childhood, when curious little beings attempt to approach and question the first person with a disability whom they see. Well, this encounter lasts about 1 second until a mother realizes what her child is going to do, grabs the child, and says, "Never bother 'those people' again." In the back of their minds, many children continue to view people with disabilities as "those people." People stare not because of the severity of a person's disability, but simply because the person appears different. An important suggestion is to teach children with disabilities to understand these anticipated behaviors and how to react to them.

As I have ventured into public places, I have run (or should I say limped) into many funny little scenarios. I remember many times going into a restaurant and the waiter leaning over to ask my parents, "What will he be having?" to which they would reply, "Why don't you ask him?" because I was perfectly able to order my meal. I cannot tell you how many times I have gone into a bank or place of business and had people talk to me so slowly that I swore rigor mortis was setting in. Sometimes well-intentioned adults will explain the simplest things in such a way that I could have done them after having a frontal lobotomy. If I am in a shopping mall, the path that I wheel or walk will part like the Red Sea. It is one thing to be courteous, but quite another when people make enough room to land a Boeing 747.

It is important to teach children to feel comfortable and even to have fun with their disabilities. I believe that it is the only way to keep one's sanity in this world. For example, I was in a college English class giving a presentation at the board in my wheelchair. I leaned back just a little too far and found myself lying flat on the floor in front of 30 students who were in total shock. I quickly stood up straight, took a bow, and said, "Thank ya, thank ya very much." Although almost nobody laughed, I instantly felt better about a very embarrassing situation. When I was in high school, I used to wear a partial foot brace that was easily seen by everyone when I was in public. I got so tired of people staring that on occasion I would let my brace fall to the floor, and yell, "My leg fell off, my leg!" just to watch the expressions on their faces. I will get out of my wheelchair and walk to get something I need (I can walk very well now and sometimes go solo). People are caught so off guard that their eyes bug out of their heads and their mouths hang open. I know some of this may seem cruel, but it is some of the most genuine entertainment to be found.

Children must also learn to be open about their disabilities. Like it or not, these children need to learn how to react to the expectations of society. And, like it or not, these expectations dictate how one behaves. Think of the normal constraints of child development and adolescence, and multiply them for those with disabilities. It is partly the responsibility of the children to break these expectations by educating people. They will educate people by answering the questions that people ask and accomplishing goals that people did not think were possible. These goals do not have to be groundbreaking or highly theoretical. They could be something as simple as getting on the dance floor and doing the best possible. The reason that other people demonstrate ignorant behaviors, such as those I have mentioned, is that they are unaware of who we are and what our capabilities are. Many of these behaviors will cease to happen as we gain more exposure. This is why I said earlier in this chapter that children must be educated to make up for the deficiencies of their disability. Whether they are at the workplace or in the bowling alley, they are, or consider themselves to be, a public spectacle. If a child chooses at times not to do some things because he or she feels like a public spectacle, nobody should push the child. Give the child the right to decide; otherwise, he or she might become very self-conscious.

Personal Lives

It is difficult for many young people with disabilities to develop a relationship with a significant other. We do not fit the mold of how a "perfect" young man or woman should appear. The majority of people think that if someone is in a wheelchair, then he or she must be paralyzed. Consequently, it is very hard for people with disabilities to compete on a social level with other young teens. I know this may sound harsh, but I have seen social discrimination occur in many settings. Very rarely has a girl come up and started small talk with me as she has with some of my friends. In fact, if I am hanging out with some of my male friends, a female will not approach until I have left the scene. The reason I believe there is so much hesitation is because people without disabilities, in the back of their minds, think that going out with a person who has a disability would mean that they would have to carry around the person and the wheelchair (as well as other preconceived notions that are wrong). I have not yet met a female at the college level who can look past my disability and see what I can offer. I can only imagine what goes through the minds of students in high school when they imagine having a relationship with a person who has a disability.

Depression

There will be days when children will be angry about their disability. No matter how great a job teachers and parents have done with these children, these days will come. I do believe that if teachers and parents follow suggestions similar to those I present in this chapter, then the frequency of those days will decrease. When I was younger, periods of depression were usually triggered by certain activities that other children could do and I could not. If children with disabilities believe that there are not many things that they cannot do, then the frequency of these days decreases dramatically. However, because there will always be things that these children cannot accomplish, they are entitled to have their "this-disability-really-sucks days."

Unfortunately, there is no surefire way to heal these wounds. Coping will depend greatly on the personality of these children. For me, there was nothing that a large pizza could not cure! Some children will not be as easy to console. For the harder cases, the only thing that I can suggest is talking about the problems to ease the pain.

Now that I am older, I have my depression days about once every 6 months. These are mainly due to the sheer inconvenience of my disability. What I mean by inconvenience is having to always lug around spare accessories such as crutches and wheelchairs. It is very frustrating to constantly walk slower and take more time than everyone else. I also am sometimes depressed by the reaction that I receive from the opposite sex because of my disability (although most of my able-bodied friends seem to be depressed about the reactions they get as well). These are the main sources of my depression and rarely create more than an occasional "This sucks."

Self-Confidence

I do not think that anyone can ever promote too much self-confidence within a child. Children should be praised for every task or milestone they accomplish. Parents and teachers must work hard to give children with disabilities much-needed emotional support. Every day of my life, I must wake up and affirm to myself that I have worth not only as a person but as a person with a disability. Sometimes, even with my positive attitude, this is an arduous task. Children with disabilities must do twice as many daily affirmations as a typical child to develop the "armor" needed to protect them from danger. If supportive adults do not help to equip them with enough self-confidence to sustain them throughout life, the world will take its shots and these children will become doubtful of their abilities. It is never too late to begin building a person's self-esteem.

Conclusion

As I reflect, I now see exactly what a puzzle my life has been and exactly how many people and things had to go right in order for me to come together. I hope that this chapter will provide new insights for teachers and parents. There is one final thing that I want the reader to know: If given the chance, I would not change the fact that I have a disability. It has granted me the joy of a perspective on life that typical people will never possess. It has forced me to become more analytical, reflective, and reactive than any other life event could have. Because of my disability I have stopped to smell the flowers again, heard the songs that most strain to hear, and appreciated smiles that have gone unseen by the masses.

All children with disabilities have these options open to them. Parents and teachers must help to cultivate these options with all the suggestions I have given to start these children on the right path. Once they travel far enough, it is up to them to decide which direction they wish to go.

My disability is my greatest source from which disappointment comes, my worst enemy, my biggest fear. It is also my closest companion, my teacher, my reason to laugh, and my greatest motivation. Children with disabilities have a unique gift to see things differently.

Best Practices

Inclusion of Students with Disabilities in General Education Settings: Structuring for Successful Management

Richard L. Simpson, Brenda Smith Myles,
and Janice DePalma Simpson

Those who strongly advocate for full inclusion believe it to be the next logical step in the progression of securing appropriate services for children and youth with disabilities (Sailor, 1991; Stainback & Stainback, 1992). We are of the strong professional opinion that imprudent placement of all students with disabilities in general education settings is inappropriate. However, we believe that many children and youth with disabilities may be successfully assigned to general education settings, given the right conditions. One such condition relates to effective management support. Indeed, management of students with disabilities is a salient determinant of integration success (Braaten, Kauffman, Braaten, Polsgrove, & Nelson, 1988; Fuchs & Fuchs, 1994). In this chapter we offer suggestions for successfully managing students with disabilities in general education classrooms.

Structuring for Management Success

We contend that successful management of students with disabilities is a primary factor associated with the success or failure of inclusion programs. Thus, it bodes well for educators to have a clear understanding of management procedures, especially structuring methods, appropriate for children and youth with special needs who are assigned to regular classroom settings. Structuring of course means different things to different people. With regard to effective placement of students with disabilities in inclusionary settings, we believe that structure involves use of a variety of antecedents, contingencies, and consequences, as well as manipulation of other general education classroom variables that assist teachers in successfully meeting the demands of special needs students. In this chapter we discuss two basic management structuring considerations that we consider to be essential to the successful inclusion of students with disabilities in regular classrooms: (a) inclusion-related modifications and other regular educator supports and (b) basic general education management structuring tools.

Inclusion-Related Modifications and Other Regular Educator Supports

Parents and professionals alike have, for years, called for appropriate modifications and other supports for regular classroom teachers who assume primary instructional responsibility for children and youth with disabilities (Berres & Knoblock, 1987; Hersh & Walker, 1983; Polloway, Patton, Payne, & Payne, 1989; Salend, 1990); more recently, these same requests have been extended to students in inclusion programs (Myles & Simpson, 1992). In this regard, it is our contention that successful inclusion of children and youth with disabilities requires availability of adequate teacher planning time, paraprofessionals, appropriate staff inservice training, availability of trained support professionals, reduced class size, availability of appropriate consultants, and supportive attitudes and a positive school climate.

Availability of Adequate Teacher Planning Time

We consider adequate teacher and staff planning time to be extremely significant in successfully including children and youth with disabilities in regular classrooms. According to Myles and Simpson (1989) and Simpson and Myles (1991), approximately 50% of general educators and ancillary staff surveyed indicated that additional planning is required if one additional student with a disability were to be placed full time in a general education setting, with the majority preferring about 1 hour daily additional planning time.

Additional planning time is needed to permit teachers and other staff to develop individual and group management programs, which we contend is the greatest challenge to successful inclusion; to individualize academic programs and other activities; and to identify, develop, and evaluate alternative and innovative instructional methods. Planning time is also needed to allow regular classroom teachers opportunities to work collaboratively with others, such as school psychologists, school social workers, and so forth.

Paraprofessionals

While in no way the complete answer to the inclusion problem, paraprofessional availability is an important component in successfully managing programs and students with disabilities in general education settings (Blalock, 1991; Goodlad, 1990; Simpson & Myles, 1990). Karagianis and Nesbit (1983) noted that paraprofessionals are "a necessary adjunct to the regular classroom where the teacher has a defined responsibility for handicapped children" (p. 19). General education teachers concur with this assessment, as reflected by the finding of Myles and Simpson (1989) that 65% of the regular class teachers they surveyed perceived paraprofessionals to be minimally necessary to support students with disabilities in general education settings.

Accordingly, we recommend that to the extent necessary, paraprofessionals be made available in general education settings where children and youth with disabilities are placed. Paraprofessionals may assist with a variety of tasks, including (a) carrying out various management programs and procedures; (b) collecting and charting management-related data; (c) assisting students to practice previously taught social and academic skills; and (d) assisting teachers with daily planning, materials development, and adaptation of curriculum. We consider it inappropriate for a paraprofessional to work with a student (or students) with a disability exclusively and independently for the purpose of translating a teacher's instructions and carrying out programs. We consider the aforementioned tasks to be of a professional nature, which must be carried out by professional educators. However, we consider paraprofessional availability to be an essential resource needed to effectively manage students with disabilities in general education classrooms.

Appropriate Staff Inservice Training

Children and youth with disabilities are frequently difficult for general educators to manage and instruct; thus, regular class teachers who assume instructional responsibility for these students must receive appropriate training. Without training general educators are unlikely to use methods and procedures required for optimal student skill development and performance. In our opinion, both group and individual inservice training is needed. Group inservice workshops may be used to provide a general body of information regarding management methods, behavior intervention options, and instructional techniques associated with effective management. One-to-one or small group training is best suited for demonstrating use of specific techniques and procedures with individual students. Educators also require collaboration and consultation skills training in order to acquire and develop cooperative problem-solving skills.

A number of studies have found that inservice training programs for teachers are essential in implementing inclusion programs. Studies conducted by Myles and Simpson (1989, 1990; Simpson & Myles, 1991) reported that parents of children with disabilities, support service staff, and general educators perceived inservice training as a basic component of successfully integrating students with disabilities in regular classrooms. Indeed, Myles and Simpson (1989) reported that approximately 50% of general education teachers surveyed perceived inservice training to be minimally necessary to support students with disabilities in regular class settings.

Availability of Trained Support Personnel

We are of the opinion that the availability of collaboratively oriented and appropriately trained support service personnel (i.e., social workers, psychologists, speech pathologists, special educators, occupational therapists, physical therapists, counselors, and other professionals as needed) is essential to the successful inclusion of students with disabilities in general education settings. Thus, regular class teachers and other staff who work with students with disabilities should be able to call on professionals from various disciplines for program advice and demonstration of best practices methods, including group- and individually oriented behavior management suggestions. The importance of support staff to inclusion was demonstrated in the 1980s by Knoff (1984), who found that general education teachers were generally not supportive of integrating students with disabilities in their classrooms unless they received assistance from qualified support personnel. This still holds true today. Parents of students with disabilities and support service personnel also seem to agree that support services facilitate successful integration. Myles and Simpson (1990) found that over 50% of parents surveyed and approximately 75% of ancillary staff surveyed (Simpson & Myles, 1991) indicated that support service availability was needed to assure successful integration; general education teachers rated support services (along with class size) as the most important variable needed to successfully maintain children with disabilities in regular class settings (Myles & Simpson, 1989). Accordingly, we infer that general educators are typically willing to consider for inclusion many students with disabilities if they can rely on appropriate professionals to provide necessary services related to their respective disciplines (Larrivee & Cook, 1979; Myles & Simpson, 1992). This appears to be particularly important with regard to development and implementation of appropriate management services.

Reduced Class Size

A number of studies have clearly demonstrated that reduced class size is an essential factor in successfully supporting students with disabilities in general education settings (Harris, 1974; Simpson & Myles, 1989). The ability to implement effective behavioral, social, and academic intervention programs requires that teachers and staff not be assigned so many students that they are unable to devote necessary time to students with special needs. Simpson and Myles (1989) found that 78% of general educators considered class size to be an important inclusion issue, with most teachers believing that a class size of 15 to 19 students was needed to successfully accommodate children with disabilities. Moreover, studies have established that reduced class size is associated with increased success of children and youth with disabilities in regular class settings (Smith & Glass, 1980).

Availability of Appropriate Consultants

The need for collaborative consultation relationships to aid general educators in planning for students with disabilities is obvious (West & Brown, 1987). Myles and Simpson (1989) reported that 65% of general education teachers they polled, when asked to select classroom modifications minimally needed to mainstream a student with a disability, indicated that consultant availability was an important factor.

Relative to inclusion, we think it is important to make a distinction between consultation and collaboration. Pugach and Allen-Meares (1985) contended that consultation often denotes unequal status between professionals, with specialists providing advice to general and special education classroom teachers, while collaboration involves equal status among team members who share information and jointly engage in problem solving. While professionals vary in their willingness to accept expert advice, we contend that collaborative consultation is one of the most efficient and effective means of supporting general education teachers of students with disabilities. Thus, we endorse collaborative consultation, believing it to be a preferred approach to supporting students with special needs in regular classrooms.

Supportive Attitudes and Positive School Climate

While perhaps not typically thought of as an inclusion-related modification, a positive and supportive school climate is an undeniably important factor in fostering positive school social conditions that create management opportunities, resources, and supports. Most educators would concede this point; however, it is evident that most school programs invest little time and energy in preparing general classroom settings to accommodate students with disabilities (Reister & Bessette, 1986). Indeed, Martin's (1974, p. 150) admonition of over two decades ago—that unless educators develop strategies for creating an accepting environment for students with disabilities, "I fear we will subject many children to a painful and frustrating educational experience in the name of progress"—still rings true today. Accordingly, in our opinion, inclusion programs can be successful only to the extent that they create an educational environment in which students with disabilities are socially integrated and experience acceptance. Such a supportive environment requires use of strategies that address social, emotional, and attitudinal issues, which in turn facilitate implementation of effective management environments. Accordingly, support of administrators, teachers, parents, and normally developing and achieving students is critical to successful inclusion programs.

With respect to administrator support, O'Rourke (1980) found a significant relationship between teachers' and building principals' attitudes toward students with disabilities. Accordingly, administrative support for working with students with disabilities and positive administrator attitudes toward children and youth with special needs is crucial (Heller & Schilit, 1987). Equally important is acceptance by general education teachers (Myles & Simpson, 1989) and parents (Horne, 1985). That is, if the role models who have primary responsibility for the education, care, and development of both normally developing children and youth and those with disabilities, lack acceptable attitudes and behaviors toward individuals with exceptionalities, it is highly unlikely that management, instruction, and other program efforts will be effective.

Attitudes of normally developing students toward their peers with disabilities are an especially significant determinant of program success (Simpson, 1987). Specifically, normally developing and achieving students require information and experiences designed to familiarize them with the characteristics and needs of children and youth with disabilities, foster more accepting attitudes toward persons with exceptionalities, and promote better interactions between students with and without disabilities (Sasso, Simpson, & Novak, 1985). Positive attitudes toward students with disabilities do not naturally occur. However, curricula and procedures designed to facilitate better understanding and sensitivity toward students with disabilities have proved their worth in integration programs (Fiedler & Simpson, 1987).

It is our opinion that a salient management ingredient for students with disabilities who receive all or part of their education in regular classes is a positive and supportive environment. Without such an atmosphere, an essential underpinning of any effective management program will be missing.

Basic General Education Management Structuring Tools

A major factor in the successful integration of children and youth with disabilities is the classroom environment that teachers create. When that environment provides well thought out instruction, discipline, and motivation for students, it greatly improves opportunities for successful experiences for both children and youth with disabilities and their general education peers. Historically, general and special education literature has supported the need for classroom environments that clearly define goals, expectations, and consequences for students. The structure that surrounds the learning environment has been shown to have a significant impact on learner success. Such structure is doubly important for children and youth with disabilities as they are increasingly included in regular education settings. The following sections will discuss classroom management techniques that have been found to be effective with special populations and that may be employed to assist in development of successful inclusion programs.

Providing Physical and Environmental Structure

The ability of students with disabilities who are assigned to general education settings to organize themselves and to productively participate may be greatly enhanced by providing a physical environment that facilitates independent functioning. Such independence will be fostered by the use of routine schedules, clear expectations, and consistency. Furthermore, the physical setting itself can be designed to enhance opportunities for successful inclusion of children and youth with disabilities.

Routine schedules assist students in knowing what they should be doing at given times in the classroom, and routines reduce stress for students who are easily confused or have difficulty with transition and other changes. Because many students with disabilities, particularly those with cognitive or behavioral challenges, have difficulty with organization and concentration, routines in the classroom assist them by providing a sense of security. That is, routines may relieve the anticipation and fear of the "unknown" that often interferes with academics. Teachers can enhance existing routines for children and youth with disabilities by posting schedules for all students in the classroom, or providing an individual daily schedule with times and assignments plus advance notice of any special events that may be occurring in the school day. Verbal discussion of what the school day will encompass may be helpful to students to reduce anxiety about what will happen, especially when out of the ordinary schedule changes or special events will interrupt the normal routine. Routine scheduling of the order of academic activities in the classroom also assists teachers in promoting independent functioning by assisting students in knowing what to expect and what needs to be done.

Classroom rules are another means of implementing a structured classroom setting. In this regard, the potential for success of children and youth with disabilities is enhanced if classroom rules, regulations, and behavioral expectations are clearly known and understood. Many students with cognitive and behavior challenges do not have a clear understanding of expectations for performance and behavior in classroom settings unless such expectations are clearly explained, repeated frequently, and discussed. In some cases, appropriate models or practice of desired behaviors may be necessary to assist students in understanding how to perform expected behaviors. Statements of expectations should be as positive as possible, stressing what the student should be doing, and as often as possible positive models should be pointed out to increase comprehension of how to be successful. Canter (1989) concluded, "Teachers will never get to the content unless they know how to create a positive environment in which students know how to behave" (p. 60).

Another component of a structured classroom environment is clarification of expectations, which is greatly supported by the systematic application of discipline plans that reinforce appropriate behaviors. Consistent reinforcement of appropriate behaviors and completion of assignments through individualized management programs that clearly delineate expectations and resulting consequences, such as earning credits during each period of the day exchangeable for desirable activities, can clarify expectations and provide motivation for students who would otherwise have difficulty (Johnston, Proctor, & Corey, 1994).

The degree to which established environmental supports are consistently applied will largely determine the degree to which those supports increase student success. To minimize perceptions of the environment as threatening and confusing by students with disabilities, they need to feel that they are safe, secure, and to know what to expect. Frequent changes in expectations, routines, or the teacher's demeanor can be unbalancing experiences that negatively impact students' behavior and academic performance. Consequently, teachers in inclusive settings need to frequently self-assess the degree to which programs are consistently followed and the degree to which their own actions and affect are consistent and positive influences.

The physical setting provided in the classroom can also be an important aid in eliciting desired behaviors and academic products from children and youth with disabilities. Classrooms that are physically organized to promote attention to task and minimize distractions will benefit all students, but are particularly important for students with disabilities. For instance, students with learning and attention problems would likely not perform most efficiently if their desks were placed next to an open door leading to a hallway with traffic. Classrooms that have walls with overloaded displays of numerous interesting and distracting pictures or other materials may be overly stimulating or distracting to some students with cognitive and behavioral disabilities, and numerous cages of class "pets" scurrying through mazes may fascinate and detract students from business at hand. While classroom environments do not need to be completely sterile, teachers need to evaluate the impact of "attractive nuisances."

A classroom environment that has areas designated for certain types of activities is highly desirable as an environment for successful inclusion. To accommodate individual learning needs that may arise, classroom areas with different functions allow for the variations in large and small group instruction and other activities that may enhance learning opportunities for all students. Johnston et al. (1994) discussed the effectiveness of learning centers in general education settings as a means of addressing individual learning styles and needs and increasing successful integration of students with disabilities. Generally, a classroom that appears organized and has areas for addressing different types of learning situations will be most helpful in meeting the academic and behavioral needs of all special students.

A structured classroom setting is also implemented through use of best practices instructional techniques. The fundamental tenets of effective instruction are substantially the same for children and youth with disabilities and students without disabilities. Thus, discussion of instructional techniques in the literature supporting inclusion has pointed out the following:

> There are not two discrete sets of instructional methods—one set for use with "special" students and another set for use with "regular" students. As used here, instructional methods refer to basic instructional processes, such as the development of behavioral objectives, curricular-based assessment procedures, task analysis, the arrangement of antecedents and consequences, and open education/ discovery learning methods. While such methods need to be tailored to individual characteristics and needs, few, if any, can be clearly dichotomized into those applicable only for special students or for regular students. (Stainback & Stainback, 1984, p. 102)

Perhaps the primary difference between "special" and "regular" learners is the ability of some normally developing and achieving students to learn even when their teachers fail to adhere to effective fundamentals of instruction. However, most children and youth with disabilities require attention to the basic principles all teachers have been taught about instructional methodology. Each phase of learning is an essential building block to arrive at mastery: awareness, recognition, recall, application, generalization, and maintenance. Accordingly, preinstructional planning by teaching staff has been found to be essential in providing effective instruction in an inclusive setting, since teaching methods that are effective for some may not be for others (Dunn & Griggs, 1988). In the planning stages of an instructional unit, the individual goals and objectives for students with disabilities should be determined and supportive materials and methods planned in advance with regular and support personnel, as needed, to maximize mastery of the information. Heron and Jorgensen (1994) described successfully "frontloading" in teaching methods used with included students: "Support in the form of adaptive teaching methods, repetition and analysis, and multi-modal, multi-level sources of information are frontloaded during curriculum planning, rather than provided in a remedial or catchup method as the unit progresses" (p. 57). Such preplanning ensures attention to individual student strengths and weaknesses and provides more opportunity for students to master content in an efficient manner.

In accordance with sound instructional planning procedures, a structured design procedure for the introduction of information to students enhances the knowledge acquisition of all students, especially those with special needs. Preinstructional procedures should include creating an awareness of and context for the information to be taught, reviewing the history and background of the subject, and identifying the goals and objectives that students will be expected to accomplish. Creating a general awareness of and context for materials is an essential element not only of understanding the importance of learning about a particular subject area, but also of providing motivation for students to put their efforts into mastering the material. Accordingly, provision of clear goals and objectives assists students in focusing on the essential content necessary to attain goals and objectives.

Sound instructional techniques for students with disabilities, as stated earlier, do not differ significantly from recommended best practices for nondisabled students. However, particular attention to some specific instructional areas may prove helpful. Instruction should be provided using as many modalities as possible to reinforce learning and provide for individual learning styles. Providing models of desired products whenever possible clarifies expectations for students who may have difficulty visualizing or comprehending desired work products. Modeling examples of desired verbal products through peer or teacher models is also an effective teaching tool for students with cognitive disabilities. Supported, structured practice of desired skills that provides success experiences will provide encouragement and motivation for students to attempt independent trials. And finally, independent practice of skills or delivery of information should be encouraged and guided to provide successful completion of work products.

Secondary students with disabilities provide special challenges for planning effective general education instruction. Commenting on this challenge, Schumaker and Deshler (1994) noted the following: "While elementary students are expected to master rudimentary skills in reading, writing and math, secondary students are expected to independently use these skills in combination with more sophisticated strategies to learn large amounts of information" (p. 51). Consequently, secondary students with disabilities typically require assistance in structuring the learning process to be able to work toward independent learning. Schumaker and Deshler (1994) suggested that learning strategies information be routinely taught, or that specific classes on learning strategies be included in the secondary curriculum. They stated that practices that assist secondary students with disabilities to be effective learners include (a) daily and sustained instruction, (b) multiple opportunities for practice with the strategy, (c) individualized feedback, (d) strategy mastery, and (e) generalization opportunities.

Critical components related to the mastery of materials by students with disabilities include application, generalization, and maintenance opportunities with newly learned material. For many youngsters with disabilities, applying what they have learned to larger contexts and retaining information over time are problematic. Thus, providing these students ample opportunities for application of information both inside and outside the classroom environment assists them in generalizing and maintaining their ability to use newly acquired skills and information.

Students with disabilities can be successful learners in inclusive classroom settings if sound instructional methods are coupled with individualized instructional modifications to the regular curriculum. The goal should be content mastery as originally stipulated through the individualized goals and objectives set for the student with special needs at the outset of the instructional unit. For some students, this will require instruction and practice over and above the amount necessary for regular education peers. For others, teachers may need to assess carefully when mastery is achieved, regardless of whether intermediate instructional steps have been completed. For instance, some students with weak reading and written language skills may be very slow at producing written assignments, but may be strong auditory learners who can digest information and master it while producing fewer or shorter written products. Teachers need to assess when mastery has occurred and alter requirements that may not impact significantly the educational objective of the unit in question. In addition to promoting academic gains, use of sound instructional methodology along with creative planning to meet the individual needs of children and youth with disabilities is a salient management tool.

Structuring Inclusion Classrooms Using Surface Behavior Management Procedures and Consequences

Management of students with disabilities in general education classrooms is also accomplished through use of surface behavior management procedures and consequences. These basic general education management tools assist both in supporting other structuring components and in furthering support of students who require structure beyond that offered through use of basic physical and environmental organizational methods discussed earlier. Thus, when educators use the aforementioned basic general education management structuring tools, they significantly reduce the occurrence of behavior problems. However, in spite of the strength and general utility of these methods, it is likely that the behavior problems of some students will persist. Thus, educators must consider the use of additional management strategies.

One of the most unobtrusive of such strategies falls under the heading of surface management procedures (Long & Newman, 1976). Often students exhibit specific behaviors that may not be directly indicative of a serious impending behavior problem such as an aggressive or violent act. Nonetheless, these behaviors often disrupt the learning of the targeted student or of others, or may serve as a precursor to a tantrum or act of violence. It is easy for teachers at this stage to ignore these seemingly minor behaviors, yet these behaviors often do not subside unless teacher action is taken. Students may bite their nails or lips, lower their voices, tense their muscles, grimace, or otherwise indicate their general discontent. Students may also complain of not feeling well. Teachers can use surface management procedures, such as hurdle help, signal interference, proximity control, or interest boosting, to stop future and more serious behavior problems. Interventions at this stage do not require extensive teacher time, but it is wise to understand the events that precipitate such behaviors so that teachers can (a) be ready to intervene early or (b) teach students strategies to maintain behavioral control during these times.

Table 9.1 provides a sample of surface behavior management techniques that may be helpful. For example, a student who appears to be stressed or tense may require "antiseptic bouncing": The teacher would suggest that the student remove himself or herself from the room to "get a drink of water" or to regain his or her composure.

In some instances a structured classroom setting and surface management procedures do not provide enough support for students to control their behavior in the general education classroom. Thus, teachers and other staff need to consider other approaches to reducing behavioral excesses and deficits, a number of which fall under the realm of behavior modification. Behavior modification strategies are proposed because they have the best track record for reducing undesirable responses and increasing desired responses, and because they have been validated over many years (Nelson & Polsgrove, 1984; Nelson & Rutherford, 1988). This is not to suggest, however, that behavior modification is a panacea for all behavioral problems of students with disabilities in general education programs. However, if used properly, behavior modification seems to work better than any of the other available options. Behavioral techniques are predicated on the premise that individual behavior is influenced by what occurs immediately before (antecedent) and after (consequence) an individual's action or response. By analyzing and manipulating these variables in the general education setting, teachers can help students learn and maintain new behaviors, increase the rate of appropriate behaviors, and/or decrease the rate of inappropriate behaviors.

Identifying and Operationally Defining a Behavior of Concern

To develop a useful behavior management program, specific behaviors of concern must be pinpointed and defined in terms that are observable and measurable. The behavior selected for modification must be defined in such a fashion that it allows the individuals involved with the child to perceive the behavior in an identical manner. For example, hyperactivity to one person may denote crying, screaming, and distractibility, while to another it may mean primarily failing to complete classroom assignments. Consequently, it is essential to the success of any applied behavior analysis program that each participant define and observe the target behavior in the same way.

In addition to determining that the target behavior is observable, measurable, and defined in a manner that allows for reliability, the

TABLE 9.1
Sample Surface Behavior Management Techniques

Proximity Control—Rather than calling attention to behavior, the teacher moves near the student who is engaged in the undesirable behavior. Often standing next to a student calms disruptive behavior. This can be easily accomplished without interrupting the lesson at hand. The teacher who circulates through the classroom during a lesson is using proximity control.

Signal Interference—When an unwanted behavior is about to occur, the teacher uses a nonverbal signal to let the student know that he or she is aware of the situation. For example, the teacher can move into a position where eye contact with the student can be achieved. Or a "secret signal" between teacher and student can be used as a warning. Many teachers snap their fingers, flick a light switch, or look away to indicate that inappropriate behavior is occurring. Some of these techniques can be used to prevent behaviors from occurring.

Touch Control—Sometimes a touch can serve to stop behavior. Gently touching the foot or leg of a student who is tapping his or her feet loudly may stop disruptive behavior.

Antiseptic Bouncing—This technique allows the teacher to remove the student from a situation without punishment. If a student enters the classroom after being involved in a confrontation at home, allow the child or youth to go to an area of the room where he or she can regain composure.

Planned Ignoring—If a student is doing something merely to attract attention and is not harming himself or herself or another child, the teacher can simply ignore the behavior. Ignoring must be consistent. If the teacher decides to ignore a behavior, it must be consistently ignored. The rules for using this technique are to remain calm, grit teeth when necessary, wait for the appropriate behavior, and reinforce that behavior.

Defusing Tension Through Humor—This technique involves using a joke or humorous remark in a potentially tense or eruptive moment. The use of a joke often can prevent group contagion from occurring and salvage an interrupted lesson.

Support from Routine—Displaying a chart or schedule of expectations and events can provide security to the student. This technique can also be used in advance preparation of a change in routine. Informing students of schedule alterations can prevent anxiety and save the teacher and class from disruption.

Interest Boosting—Sometimes the teacher's showing personal interest in a student and his or her hobbies can assist a student in acting appropriately. This involves the teacher's (a) making the student aware that the teacher recognizes his or her preferences or (b) structuring lessons around a topic of interest. Interest boosting can often stop or prevent off-task or acting-out behavior.

educator implementing the program must solicit other basic information from school personnel. It must be determined whether the pinpointed behavior is under the child's control. Behaviors such as taking out the trash, fighting, and studying are typically under a child's control, whereas parasympathetic functions such as sweating, breathing, and salivating are beyond a child's influence. In most instances, the process of determining whether a behavior is under an individual's control, and consequently selecting the type of behavior analysis procedure to be employed, consists of establishing whether the problem behavior follows or precedes a controlling environmental stimulus.

Identifying Environments and Situations Where the Target Behavior Occurs

In addition to identifying an appropriate target behavior for change, the educator must seek information about the environments and circumstances surrounding the occurrence of the response. Although frequently overlooked, it is crucial to gain an understanding of the relationship of the environment to the response, including whether the response is generalized across settings or is environmentally specific. It is also necessary to determine which individuals are most frequently in contact with the students when the problem response is manifested. In few instances will the response pattern be independent of the individuals involved.

Identifying Contingencies Operating To Support the Target Behavior

According to the principles of operant conditioning, both adaptive and maladaptive behaviors are controlled by environmental conditions (Bandura, 1969). Consequently, it is essential to determine major environmental events that correlate with the occurrence of the problem behavior. Specifically, the major factors of concern include (a) the environmental circumstance that alerts the student to the fact that conditions are correct for a particular response; (b) the operant response itself (i.e., the student behavior in question); and (c) the reinforcing or consequent stimulus. In this paradigm, and in the successful construction of an applied behavior analysis program, any operant response is a function of its consequences. Therefore, understanding and modification of the contingencies that control the behavior are essential.

Although contingencies are most frequently thought of as intervention techniques, they also involve antecedent conditions. Therefore, the goal is to collect information about what happens prior to and immediately after the occurrence of the target behavior. The following types of questions may be helpful: What happens immediately before a tantrum? What happens right after the tantrum starts and ends? Also, objectively reviewing what interactions have typically occurred around a behavior, including punishment tactics and the general manner in which expectations, praise, and punishment have been used, can be helpful in determining effective behavior management plans.

Identifying, Observing, and Recording the Target Behavior

In keeping with standard behavior management procedures, educators must employ simple measurement and evaluation procedures (Simpson & Poplin, 1981). Only through measurement can a thorough analysis of the behavioral excess or deficit and its antecedent and consequent events be gained. Without such exact observation and recording activities, it cannot be determined whether the contingencies being manipulated are having the desired results. Hall (1970) identified five varieties of observational recordings, all of which can be employed by educators: continuous, event, duration, interval, and time sampling recordings.

Continuous measurements (anecdotal records) involve recording the various responses manifested by a student over a given period of time. Although this procedure allows an opportunity to record a variety of behaviors, it lacks reliability and requires great investment of resources that may be difficult for teachers.

Event recording techniques, on the other hand, are typically very functional for educators to use. These procedures consist of making a cumulative account of specific behavioral events. For example, teachers can use an event recording system to note the number of times a child follows commands or the frequency of one child kicking another. In addition to being relatively easy to understand, event recording systems are highly adaptable to use with a variety of target behaviors.

Duration recording, another observational system appropriate for classroom use, involves calculating the amount of time a child engages in a particular behavior. This alternative is preferable when the length of time a given behavior occurs is considered to be the most significant response descriptor. For example, the amount of time a child engages in tantruming may be a far more accurate descriptor of behavior than the frequency with which tantrums occur.

Interval recording systems involve dividing a predetermined observation period into equal time segments. Teachers who use this procedure should be advised to record whether the target response occurs during each interval. Although this recording technique requires the undivided attention of the person conducting the observations, it offers the advantage of allowing the person to observe more than a single target behavior.

Time sampling, although similar to interval recording, has the advantage of not requiring continuous observations. The observer determines whether the child being observed is engaging in the target behavior at the end of a specific time interval. For example, a child's study behavior might be observed for 1 hour, with recordings made at the end of each 5-minute period. Every 5 minutes the teacher would observe whether the child was studying. This procedure is efficient as it generates a significant amount of data while allowing the teacher to be involved in other activities.

Once a measurement procedure is selected, the teacher should collect baseline observations for approximately 5 to 10 days to determine the frequency of the problem behavior targeted for future intervention. Fewer observation days will provide a less than adequate picture of the behavior, whereas longer baselines may prolong classroom problems. Results should be graphed or charted in some way to provide a visual representation of the behavior in question.

Establishing and Implementing Intervention Procedures and Performance Goals

Educators involved in applied behavior analysis programs with a student are confronted with target behaviors that can be classified as either behavior deficits or excesses. That is, the student may be lacking in a particular response, such as completing classroom assignments or engaging in desirable social interactions, or the student may be viewed as excessive on some dimension of behavior, such as arguing too often. Because of the nature of the model and the manner in which problem responses are operationally defined, behavioral principles are designed to either increase or decrease the occurrence of a specific behavior under specific conditions. This goal is accomplished via systematic manipulation of reinforcers and punishers.

Reinforcement, a basic component of behavioral methodology, can be either positive or negative. Positive reinforcement is the presentation of a desirable consequence for behavior that increases the probability that the target behavior will occur again (Haring & Phillips, 1972). Negative reinforcement consists of removal of an unpleasant consequence, followed by an increase in behavior strength. For example, if a particular student dislikes being pointed out for having a messy desk, he or she may clean up the desk to avoid further negative attention. Reinforcers can also be classified as (a) social, (b) contingent activities, or (c) tangible or edible. For many students, social reinforcement that occurs naturally in the classroom may be sufficient incentive to behave in an acceptable fashion. Social reinforcement includes teacher approval or praise, or peer approval or praise, or positive feelings gained from knowledge of results or progress. Social reinforcement may be less effective for students who are less able or who do not appear to value interaction with others (Sloane, Buckholdt, Jenson, & Crandall, 1979).

Contingent activities are often used in conjunction with social reinforcement. Contingent activities are based on the Premack principle (1959), which states that high-probability behavior will reinforce lower probability behavior. Thus, students are rewarded with a preferred activity for completing an activity they may not like as well. School-related contingent activities might include serving as the lunch line leader, going to recess early, or making a decision regarding the type of activity the student will engage in next (e.g., doing math problems at the board rather than on paper, moving to a preferred seat, eating lunch with the principal).

For some students, particularly those who have had little opportunity for success in school, it may be necessary to use tangible or edible reinforcers. Tangible reinforcers, items that the student can actually touch, may consist of an immediate consequence (e.g., a sticker on each paper completed) or tokens (e.g., chips, play money) that can be redeemed later. Edible items include candy or gum. Tangible and edible reinforcers have been found to be effective, but edibles may be impractical in some settings. Out-of-school contingencies, such as parent rewards or a discount from a community merchant, may provide incentive and support for children who need motivation not readily available within the school environment (Cullinan & Epstein, 1985; Nelson & Rutherford, 1988).

If teachers are using contingent activities or tangible or edible reinforcement, they must be careful not to create teacher- or reinforcer-dependent students. The use of contingent activities or tangible or edible reinforcement must be thinned, or decreased gradually. This is often accomplished by gradually increasing the number of behaviors required to earn a reinforcer, or lengthening the time elapsed between reinforcement opportunities. Another common technique involves pairing the reinforcement with a more naturally occurring system. For example, students may be trained to graph their own accomplishments and give themselves positive messages. The contingent activity or tangible or edible reinforcer is then gradually withdrawn and the student relies on internal, self-reinforcement and the teacher's social praise.

Token Economies and Contracting

A token economy is a system of specified behaviors and consequences with a systematic method of awarding tokens and redeeming them for a reinforcer (e.g., at the end of each math period, each student who has completed his or her seatwork will earn a sticker; at the end of the week, stickers may be exchanged for various reinforcers). Token economies are typically implemented classwide and are generally based on class rules, assigned completion, or social mores. Often the management required for token economies makes them unwieldy for the general classroom. A similar approach for an individual student is a contingency contract, a predetermined written agreement between teacher and student concerning a specific relationship between a behavior and a reinforcement (e.g., When John has completed four reading assignments with 75% accuracy, he may have 15 minutes of computer time or select from a menu of reinforcers).

Extinction, another basic behavioral method that may be used with students with disabilities in general education classrooms, involves reducing and eventually eliminating problem behaviors by removing reinforcement and attention for undesirable behavior (i.e., by ignoring students) (Haring & Phillips, 1972). Although extinction may be difficult to use consistently in the classroom, it may be more effective when paired with differential reinforcement (i.e., reinforcing the target student for an incompatible behavior or reinforcing other students for demonstrating appropriate behaviors). For example, a teacher might ignore Jesse's pencil tapping while reinforcing Susan for being on task, then reinforce Jesse as soon as he quits tapping and returns to work.

Punishment is also a behavioral option that we believe has a place in managing students with disabilities in inclusionary settings. Punishment is the application of an aversive consequence for a particular inappropriate behavior in order to decrease that behavior. Punishment techniques include (a) response cost—taking away a privilege, token, or reinforcement; (b) overcorrection—requiring the student to make restitution or to practice an appropriate related behavior over and over; and (c) time-out—briefly removing the opportunity for student reinforcement (e.g, sending him to a "quiet chair" in the corner of the classroom for 5 minutes). Because of ethical and legal issues involved in using punishment techniques with children, teachers should take care to document previously unsuccessful efforts to use more positive approaches and secure permission of parents and administration before instituting punishment procedures. Table 9.2 provides definitions and classroom examples of the aforementioned punishment options.

Generally, effective classroom organization and management will minimize unacceptable or rule-breaking student behavior. Teachers should decrease unwanted behavior in the classroom by ignoring students who are seeking attention inappropriately whenever possible, while simultaneously reinforcing appropriate behaviors or reinforcing students whose behavior is more acceptable. When extinction is not feasible (i.e., the behavior is injurious or extremely disruptive), it may be necessary to use a more direct approach. Before using a more direct approach, it is important to ensure that the student clearly understands (a) the classroom rules and expectations, (b) how his or her behavior deviates from acceptable limits, and (c) the consequences for the inappropriate behavior. The teacher may then attempt to develop a written contract with the student to correct the situation. Although punishment techniques should be used only as a last resort, several (e.g., response cost, overcorrection, and time-out) have been found to reduce inappropriate behaviors (Wallace & Kauffman, 1986).

Conclusion

The Individuals with Disabilities Education Act of 1990 stipulates that students should be removed from general education programs only when the nature or severity of their disability is such that education in regular classrooms, even with the use of supplementary aids or services, cannot be satisfactorily achieved. Increasingly, this requirement has been translated to mean inclusion in general education classrooms. While we are not of the opinion that every student

TABLE 9.2
Behavior Management Terms

Term	Definition	Examples
Contingency contract	Writing an agreement between teacher and student regarding a specific contingency and behavior	Award 10 minutes free time when spelling task is completed
Extinction	Removing all reinforcement or attention from undesirable behavior	Ignore student talking out, then reward student for appropriate behavior
Negative reinforcement	Removing an unpleasant consequence to increase a behavior	Restore recess privilege for assignment completion
Overcorrection	Requiring a student to make restitution or to practice the target behavior repeatedly	Require student to clean all the desks in the class for writing on his or hers
Positive reinforcement	Presenting a pleasurable or desirable consequence for behavior	Praise student for satisfactory work
Punishment	Applying negative or aversive consequences for behavior	Require student to remain after school for detention
Response cost	Taking away a privilege, token, or reinforcement	Deduct points from student's daily sheet
Tangible/edible reinforcement	Applying a reinforcer that the student can actually touch	Award sticker, gum, or candy
Time-out	Removing the opportunity for reinforcement	Place child in a seat facing away from class for 30 seconds
Token economy	Developing a predetermined system of specified behaviors and consequences with a systematic award plan	Award stickers that can be exchanged for various reinforcers for completion of math task

with disabilities should be included in a regular classroom, we recognize that many children and youth with disabilities can and should be included in regular class settings and activities, and that inclusion will likely continue to be a trend into the 21st century. Further, we recognize that general and special educators will increasingly be required to collaborate and work together more effectively to serve the needs of all students, including those with disabilities.

Effectively and efficiently integrating and including students with disabilities in general education settings will continue to be a significant challenge for parents and professionals in coming decades. There is no reason to believe that this process will become any less of a challenge in the foreseeable future. However, structured classroom methods accompanied by individualized best practice behavioral intervention methods can significantly assist in managing students involved in integrated classroom settings.

References

Bandura, A. (1969). *Principles of behavior modification.* New York: Holt, Rinehart & Winston.

Berres, M. S., & Knoblock, P. (Eds.). (1987). *Program models for mainstreaming: Integrating students with moderate to severe disabilities.* Rockville, MD: Aspen.

Blalock, G. (1991). Paraprofessionals: Critical team members in our special education programs. *Intervention in School and Clinic, 26*(4), 200–214.

Braaten, S., Kauffman, J., Braaten, B., Polsgrove, L., & Nelson, C. M. (1988). The Regular Education Initiative: Patent medicine for behavioral disorders. *Behavioral Disorders, 55,* 21–27.

Canter, L. (1989). Assertive discipline—More than names on the board and marbles in a jar. *Phi Delta Kappan, 71,* 57–61.

Cullinan, D., & Epstein, M. H. (1985). Behavioral interventions for educating adolescents with behavior disorders. *The Pointer, 30*(1), 4–7.

Dunn, R., & Griggs, S. (1988). *Learning styles: Quiet revolution in American secondary schools.* Reston, VA: National Association of Secondary School Principals.

Fiedler, C., & Simpson, R. L. (1987). Modifying the attitudes of nonhandicapped high school students toward handicapped peers. *Exceptional Children, 53*(4), 342–351.

Fuchs, D., & Fuchs, L. (1994). Inclusive schools movement and the radicalization of special education reform. *Exceptional Children, 60,* 294–309.

Goodlad, J. I. (1990). *Teachers for our nation's schools.* San Francisco: Jossey-Bass.

Hall, R. V. (1970). *Behavior modification: The measurement of behavior.* Austin, TX: PRO-ED.

Haring, N. G., & Phillips, E. L. (1972). *Analysis and modification of classroom behavior.* Englewood Cliffs, NJ: Prentice-Hall.

Harris, J. A. (1974). Drastic proposals for educational improvement. *Today's Education, 63*(4), 5.

Heller, H., & Schilit, J. (1987). The Regular Education Initiative: A concerned response. *Focus on Exceptional Children, 20,* 1–6.

Heron, E., & Jorgensen, C. (1994). Addressing learning differences right from the start. *Educational Leadership, 52*(4), 56–58.

Hersh, R., & Walker, H. M. (1983). Great expectations: Making school effective for all students. *Policy Review Studies, 2,*147–188.

Horne, M. D. (1985). *Attitudes toward handicapped students: Professional, peer and parent reactions.* Hillsdale, NJ: Erlbaum.

Individuals with Disabilities Education Act of 1990, 20 U.S.C. §1400 *et seq.*

Johnston, D., Proctor, W., & Corey, S. (1994). Not a way out: A way in. *Educational Leadership, 52*(4), 46–49.

Karagianis, L., & Nesbit, W. (1983). Support services: The neglected ingredient in the integration recipe. *Special Education in Canada, 53*(3), 18–19.

Knoff, H. M. (1984). Mainstreaming attitudes and special placement knowledge in labeling versus nonlabeling states. *Remedial and Special Education, 5*(6), 7–14.

Larrivee, B., & Cook, L. (1979). Mainstreaming: A study on the variables affecting teacher attitude. *The Journal of Special Education, 13*(3), 315–324.

Long, N. J., & Newman, R. G. (1976). Managing surface behavior of children in school. In N. J. Long, W. C. Morse, & R. G. Newman (Eds.), *Conflict in the classroom: The education of children with problems* (3rd ed., pp. 308–317). Belmont, CA: Wadsworth.

Martin, E. (1974). Some thoughts on mainstreaming. *Exceptional Children, 41,* 150–153.

Myles, B. S., & Simpson, R. L. (1990). Mainstreaming modification preferences of parents of elementary-age children with learning disabilities. *Journal of Learning Disabilities, 23*(4), 234–239.

Myles, B. S., & Simpson, R. L. (1989). Regular educators' modification preferences for mainstreaming mildly handicapped children. *Journal of Special Education, 22*(4), 479–492.

Myles, B. S., & Simpson, R. L. (1992). General educators' mainstreaming preferences that facilitate acceptance of students with behavioral disorders and learning disabilities. *Behavioral Disorders, 17*(4), 305–315.

Nelson, C. M., & Polsgrove, L. (1984). Behavioral analysis in special education: White rabbit or white elephant? *Remedial and Special Education, 5*(4), 6–17.

Nelson, C. M., & Rutherford, R. B., Jr. (1988). Behavioral interventions with behaviorally disordered students. In M. C. Wang, M. C. Reynolds, & H. J. Walberg (Eds.), *Handbook of special education: Research and practice* (Vol. 2, pp. 125–153). New York: Pergamon.

O'Rourke, A. P. (1980). A comparison of principal and teacher attitudes toward handicapped students and the relationship between those attitudes and school morale of handicapped students. *Dissertation Abstracts International, 40*(7-A), 3954.

Polloway, E. A., Patton, J. R., Payne, J. S., & Payne, R. A. (1989). *Strategies for teaching learners with special needs.* Columbus, OH: Merrill.

Premack, D. (1959). Toward empirical behavior laws: I. Positive reinforcement. *Psychology Review, 66,* 219–233.

Pugach, M. C., & Allen-Meares, P. (1985). Collaboration at the preservice level: Instructional and evaluation activities. *Teacher Education and Special Education, 8,* 132–143.

Reister, A. E., & Bessette, K. M. (1986). Preparing the peer group for mainstreaming exceptional children. *Pointer, 31,* 12–20.

Sailor, W. (1991). Special education in the restructured school. *Remedial and Special Education, 12*(6), 8–22.

Salend, S. J. (1990). *Effective mainstreaming.* New York: Macmillan.

Sasso, G. M., Simpson, R. L., & Novak, C. G. (1985). Procedures for facilitating integration of autistic children in public school settings. *Analysis and Intervention in Developmental Disabilities, 5,* 233–246.

Schumaker, J., & Deshler, D. (1994). Secondary classes can be inclusive, too. *Educational Leadership, 52*(4), 50–51.

Simpson, R. L. (1987). Social interactions of behaviorally disordered children: Where are we and where do we need to go? *Behavioral Disorders, 12,* 292–298.

Simpson, R. L., & Myles, B. S. (1989). Parents' mainstreaming modification preferences for children with educable mental handicaps, behavior disorders and learning disabilities. *Psychology in the Schools, 26,* 292–301.

Simpson, R. L., & Myles, B. S. (1990). The general education collaboration model: A model for successful mainstreaming. *Focus on Exceptional Children, 23*(4), 1–10.

Simpson, R. L., & Myles, B. S. (1991). Ancillary staff members' mainstreaming recommendations for students with exceptionalities. *Psychology in the Schools, 28*(1), 26–32.

Simpson, R., & Poplin, M. (1981). Parents as agents of change: A behavioral approach. *School Psychology Review, 10,* 15–25.

Sloane, H. N., Buckholdt, D. R., Jenson, W. R., & Crandall, J. A. (1979). *Structured teaching: A design for classroom management and instruction.* Champaign, IL: Research Press.

Smith, M. L., & Glass, G. V. (1980). Meta-analysis of research on class size and its relationship to attitudes and instruction. *American Educational Research Journal, 17*(4), 419–433.

Stainback, S., & Stainback, W. (1992). Schools as inclusive communities. In W. Stainback & S. Stainback (Eds.), *Controversial issues confronting special education* (pp. 29–43). Boston: Allyn & Bacon.

Stainback, W., & Stainback, S. (1984). A rationale for the merger of regular and special education. *Exceptional Children, 51*(2), 102–111.

Wallace, G., & Kauffman, J. M. (1986). *Teaching students with learning and behavior problems* (3rd ed.). Columbus, OH: Merrill.

West, J. F., & Brown, P. A. (1987). State departments of education policies on consultation in special education: The state of the states. *Remedial and Special Education, 8*(3), 45–51.

CHAPTER 10

Functional Assessment and Treatment of Problematic Behavior

Gary M. Sasso, Linda Garrison Harrell, and Jane E. Doelling

O ver the last several years, professionals involved in the education of students with behavior and learning problems have been concerned with the interaction of various treatments recommended for students. Prior to this time, many programs were developed and implemented without consideration of their combined effects; that is, professionals often developed separate programs for academic skills, troubling behavior, and social skills that bore little relationship to each other and at times were incompatible. The result was too often a student treatment regimen that at best did no harm and at worst confused both the teacher and the student, resulting in an exacerbation of the very problems the program was designed to treat (Dunlap & Kern, 1994; Taylor & Carr, 1994). Current endeavors for students with emotional and behavioral disorders reflect the notion that if educators are to provide a package that achieves the desired goal, interventions across areas of functioning must be integrated, compatible with the individual goals for the student, and based on similar conceptual models to reduce the chance of implementing interventions that are ineffective. Given the current emphasis on integration and inclusion as primary goals for all students, it is imperative that integrated programs, particularly in the areas of behavior management, be developed to achieve meaningful and successful integration.

Students with learning and behavior problems often respond in ways that set them apart from other students. Some have a tendency to repeat the same antisocial, harmful, or ineffective behavior pattern repeatedly across situations and persons. One example of this is the student who reacts to all demands placed on her, whether from teacher, parents, or peers, with aggression. These students often appear to lack the array of skills necessary to respond in the diverse ways necessary to successfully achieve their goals. Similarly, there are students who, although they possess the skills necessary for appropriate interaction, consistently misperceive the demands of the situation and choose inappropriate or ineffective responses to social initiations and requests. Educators have all met or worked with the student who falls into this category. He is the one who, when asked to play a game, responds by launching into a discussion of last night's television line-up. Although these are but two examples, the pattern is clear for many students; they lack the communication skills necessary for effective interaction and learn instead to communicate in ways that get them into trouble.

To meet the needs of these students, educators must develop programs that address troubling behavior and address a student's need to communicate effectively. Our purpose in this chapter is to present a methodology for effectively decreasing student reliance on antisocial, inappropriate behavior and replacing those acts with more effective and efficient alternatives. To accomplish these goals, educators must be in a position to take advantage of empirically tested, effective interventions. Best practices in these areas include *functional analysis and functional communication training* (Iwata, Dorsey, Slifer, Bauman, & Richman, 1982; Sasso et al., 1992) approaches to the assessment and treatment of challenging behavior.

Functional Analysis and Treatment

The traditional behavior reduction model employed for years in education and psychology has been based on the treatment of specific *forms* of behavior. For example, professionals treated aggression, or disruption, withdrawal, self-injury, or stereotypy, and textbooks and university coursework reflected this focus on the form of the behavior. These books and courses were arranged to provide, by behavioral category, a list of interventions, techniques, and treatments that had been tried in the past and a notion of their effectiveness. For example, under a heading of aggressive behavior, textbooks would list such techniques as time-out, response cost, life-space interview, and differential reinforcement as being effective for students exhibiting these behaviors. In this model, the educator attends to the generic form of the negative behavior, obtains as much information about the student as possible, chooses one from a menu of interventions, and tries it. If the chosen intervention is not effective, another is selected for trials. Thus, treatment trials of this type can continue until an effective intervention is discovered. The problem has been that this method has not provided the individualization necessary for interventions that are both effective and efficient. What has been missing from these intervention protocols is one of the following critical pieces of information:

1. Why does the student engage in the behavior?

2. What environmental events motivate or maintain the behavior?

3. What does the student "get" from the behavior? How does the behavior function?

If educators are to adopt a behavior-reduction model based on the function of the response, there must be agreement on two basic issues. The first is that all behavior is purposeful. The second is that the variables originally responsible for the onset of troubling behavior may not be what is currently maintaining the response. For example, the first author (Sasso) has a son, Spencer, who began having ear infections very early in life. Almost the only times Spencer would cry were when his ears caused him pain. The typical response of his parents was to pick him up and comfort him during these times. After years of trying a variety of antibiotic medications, a doctor inserted tubes in Spencer's ears to alleviate the problem. At this time, he stopped having ear infections; *however*, he did not stop crying. The reason he still cried was that he had learned that it was the most effective and efficient way to obtain attention. For Spencer, crying communicated, "I want some attention." This was not the original function, which was to communicate discomfort and pain.

A focus on the function rather than the form of problem behavior is not a new concept. It has been discussed by Ferster (1961) and others in relation to the behavior of individuals with autism. Carr (1977) also suggested that programs designed to address the behavior of exceptional students would be more effective if professionals paid more attention to what these students were trying to communicate through their behavior. However, it was not until 1982 when Iwata et al. developed a distinct methodology for the assessment of specific environmental functions that the field began to seriously attend to the role of this variable in the management of behavior. The identification of functional maintaining variables by Iwata et al. led to a methodology using controlled clinical conditions across various proposed functions. This assessment has typically involved observing a child's behavior in several well-defined analogue (i.e., well-controlled but contrived) conditions. The physical and social aspects of each condition are arranged to allow for specific hypotheses to be made regarding the functional properties of the behavior. This assessment procedure is referred to as a *functional analysis* because of the experimental control allowed by a clinical setting.

Clinical programs that employ functional analysis methodology to determine the operant variables controlling troubling behavior generally follow a standardized assessment process designed to facilitate the gathering of relevant information concerning the behavior. The following are five generally recognized functional analysis conditions carried out in clinical settings (Durand & Crimmins, 1988; Iwata et al., 1982), and familiarity with the clinical analysis model is critical to the development of functional assessment methodology in more natural settings.

1. *Attention (Gain)*. In this condition, the examiner and client enter the therapy area together. The client is provided with a wide array of preferred toys and is told to play alone with the toys while the examiner does some work. The examiner then sits several feet away from the client, pretending to read a magazine or write a paper. The examiner attends to the child consistently only after each occurrence of the problem behavior by providing the child with some type of disapproval (e.g., "Don't throw your toys; you'll break them"). All other behaviors are ignored by the examiner. This condition is designed to assess social attention as a variable maintaining the problem behavior or behaviors.

2. *Tangible (Gain)*. A variation of the attention (gain) condition was developed to assess behavior maintained by tangible reinforcement. In the tangible condition (Durand & Crimmins, 1988), the client is usually engaged in a specific task rather than in toy play. Preferred toys, edibles, or activities are visible to the client, and each occurrence of the problem behavior results in these preferred items being made available to the client. As in the attention (gain) condition, when

problem behavior occurs at a high rate in this condition, it is likely that the response is controlled by tangible reinforcement.

3. *Demand (Escape)*. In this condition, the examiner and client are positioned at a table to work on tasks. Tasks are selected that the client is capable of completing but finds difficult to perform. A three-prompt, guided compliance procedure (Horner & Keilitz, 1975) is then used as part of the presentation of each task. In this procedure, the examiner presents the task with a verbal prompt (e.g., "Put the block in the bucket") and allows the client 5 seconds to comply. If the client fails to respond, the examiner repeats the verbal prompt and models success-ful completion of the task (e.g., "Put the block in the bucket like this [models]—you do it"). If the client fails to respond at this point, the examiner again repeats the verbal prompt and physically guides the client through the request. If the client engages in the target aggressive behavior during this condition, the task is removed and the examiner walks away. Following termination of the aggressive behavior, the examiner reintroduces the task. This condition assesses the role of neg-ative reinforcement in the maintenance of aggressive responses.

4. *Alone*. In this condition, the client is placed in a room with no sources of potential reinforcement. In a traditional alone condition, the examiner is not present. The rationale for this condition is that some behaviors are maintained by sensory reinforcement, specifically sensory induction. If the frequency of the target behavior is high in this condition, sensory reinforcement is inferred. However, this con-dition is not generally useful to the process of assessing aggressive responses, because these behaviors, by definition, rely on the pres-ence of others. A modification of this condition has been developed, an ignore condition, in which the examiner is present but does not respond to the client under any circumstances.

5. *Toy Play (Control)*. This condition is similar to the attention (gain) condition in that the examiner and client are in the room together and the client has access to a number of preferred toys. The client is allowed to play alone or cooperatively, and is occasionally prompted to engage in toy play if needed. However, rather than pro-vide social disapproval, the examiner ignores the client each time the aberrant behavior is displayed. Additionally, the examiner provides frequent (approximately every 30 seconds) social reinforcement to the client for behaving appropriately. No educational tasks or demands are presented to the student during this condition (Iwata et al., 1982). This condition is designed to act as a control for the other conditions.

In outpatient clinical settings, each condition is generally conducted for a period of 10 minutes. The order of presentation is determined by the staff during the review of client files. Thus, an initial clinical analogue sequence might be toy play–attention–demand–tangible–ignore. Visual inspection of the data obtained during each of these conditions can provide the basis for tentative treatment recommendations based on the functional controlling variables related to the problem responses. For example, Figure 10.1 shows the results of a functional analysis conducted for a 9-year-old client with aggressive behavior occurring at high frequency and intensity. The data clearly show that these behaviors are controlled by negative reinforce-

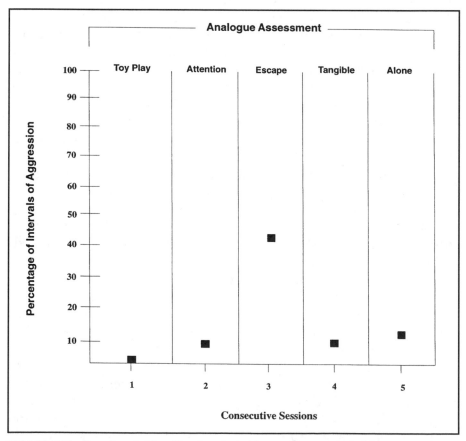

FIGURE 10.1   Experimental functional analysis of aggression conducted in an outpatient setting showing escape (negative reinforcement) as the functional variable maintaining the behavior of a 9-year-old.

ment; that is, they act to provide escape from undesirable activities or persons.

Functional Analysis and Assessment in Natural Settings

A number of naturalistic settings appear ideally suited to the use of functional analysis, and there are good reasons why these settings are, in many ways, more relevant than clinical settings to the analysis of the variables maintaining problem behavior. First, natural settings such as the home and school provide all of the antecedents (events, activities, and interactions that precede the emission of a troubling response by the student) and consequences (events and interactions that immediately follow the instance of the behavior) related to the current problem. That is, the natural environment is *where* the problem lies, and it makes intuitive sense to assess the behavior in this setting. Second, parents, teachers, and other caregivers know much more about the student (his or her preferred activities, situations in which problems occur, etc.) than any clinical staff can know. Therefore, they are in the best position to carry out meaningful assessments and interpret the results of these analyses.

The first step in any functional analysis carried out in natural settings is to determine possible reinforcers for the student. This is critical for two reasons. First, it is possible that, for many students with behavior and learning problems, there are very few current reinforcers in the environment that can be used to effect changes in behavior. Some of these students have not learned to be rewarded by common classroom reinforcers such as praise, free time, or items common to token reinforcement systems. When students do not appear to want the things available to them in the classroom, it is critical that one of two things occurs. The teacher must offer a wider variety of possible rewards in an attempt to discover those that the student desires, or the teacher or parents must work to teach the student to be reinforced by available items and activities. However, the first step should be simply to conduct a reinforcer preference assessment.

Two methods are commonly used to assess reinforcers for students. The first is the most structured and involves presenting the student with a choice of items, activities, and situations that might be reinforcing and asking the student to choose between these items

(Fisher et al., 1992; Pace, Ivancic, Edwards, Iwata, & Page, 1985). Figure 10.2 is a plan that lists possible reinforcers for the student and procedures that will allow a determination of student preference. The results suggest that the student favors free time with the teacher, computer games, and being allowed to take the lunch count to the office. The second method is informal and involves either asking the child

---

A. Student Information

    Name: Bubba
    Age: 9 years, 4 months
    Setting: Self-contained class for students with emotional and behavioral disorders; 8 other students in class, 1 teacher, 1 associate

B. Items/Activities Assessed (available in the school setting)

1. Free time alone
2. Free time with teacher
3. Free time with selected peer
4. Computer games
5. Taking lunch count to office
6. Extra recess
7. Opportunity to take break from work

C. Assessment Procedure

During 10-minute sessions at the beginning of the day, student is asked to choose between two of the items across items:
Example: "Would you like . . . ?"
a. free time or computer games
b. computer games or taking lunch count to office
c. taking lunch count to office or extra recess
d. extra recess or opportunity to take break from work
Continue until pattern of choices emerges.

D. Results

Potential Reinforcers	*Choices*
Free time alone	0
Free time with teacher	3
Free time with selected peer	0
Computer games	2
Taking lunch count to office	1
Extra recess	0
Break from work	0

FIGURE 10.2   Formal reinforcer assessment plan.

what he or she would like or completing a reinforcer inventory related to preferences. An example of a partial reinforcement inventory can be found in Figure 10.3. A document of this type should be expanded across all possible preferred activities or events for the student, to include entertainment activities, sports and games, music/arts/crafts activities, community activities, academic/classroom preferences, and domestic activities.

Once potential student reinforcers have been identified, a functional analysis can be conducted with greater accuracy. However, it is important to remember that preferences can change across time. Items and activities that are preferred on Monday may not be desired on Tuesday. Thus, it is important that the assessment of reinforcer preferences be ongoing to ensure that the items and activities offered to the student are those that he or she currently prefers.

Functional Analysis in the Classroom

One method that can be used to determine the function of behavior in natural settings is to adapt the clinical analysis of problem behavior to the classroom or home setting (Sasso & Reimers, 1988). This method is the most rigorous and will result in the most reliable data; however, it is also the most controlled assessment and thus requires a higher level of skill to successfully carry out.

There are a number of steps basic to a functional analysis of behavior, and the first two are critical.

1. *Select and operationally define the target behavior.* The teacher must state the troubling behavior(s) in observable terms to allow accurate measurement.

2. *Measure the behavior(s) in a reliable manner using a time-efficient system.* Simple frequency counts or event recording is often sufficient for discrete behaviors. For other behaviors (e.g., tantrums), the duration of the behavior is of greatest concern.

The remaining steps are specific to conducting a functional analysis through modification of classroom activities.

3. *Identify structured classroom activities to serve as functional analysis conditions.* Five structured classroom activities that resemble as closely as possible the analogue conditions previously described should be identified for each child. Although this will undoubtedly require some minor modification of each activity, it can typically be done without disrupting the other students. The composition of each

Name _____ Date of Birth _____ Date _____

Directions: The items in this survey refer to things and activities that may be reinforcing to the child. For each item, place a check in the column indicating how much the individual enjoys the item.

Potentially Reinforcing Event	*Does Not Enjoy* 1	2	3	4	*Very Much Enjoys* 5
A. *Food Items (types)*					
1.					
2.					
3.					
4.					
5.					
B. *Toys and Play Activities*					
1. Model cars					
2. Lite Brite					
3. Skateboard					
4. Trains					
5. Baseball/collector cards					
6. Legos					
7. Drawing/art activities					
8. Action figures					
C. *Social Interaction*					
1. Playing with others (Whom) _____					
2. Being praised (by) _____					
a. Mother					
b. Father					
c. Teacher					
d. Peers (list)					
3. Being hugged and kissed					
4. Being touched					
5. Having friends over					
6. Talking with others					
7. Kidding, playing around					
8. Going to a friend's house					
9. Happy faces, smiles					

FIGURE 10.3 Partial reinforcement inventory.

assessment activity will depend on the structure and organization of the classroom and will vary from classroom to classroom. We offer in the following paragraphs a number of suggestions to help facilitate the development of the functional assessment conditions. These suggestions are made under the assumption that a teacher is simulating the traditional analogue conditions described above.

a. *Alone condition.* It will likely be difficult to create a situation in a classroom in which a student is entirely alone. Modifications to the traditional analogue condition will probably need to be made for most classrooms. For example, a student could be placed in an unoccupied room to be observed, or perhaps a small part of the classroom could be sectioned off. In addition, some students will not be content to remain alone for an extended period of time. For these students it may be necessary to reduce the length of the session (e.g., from 15 to 5 minutes).

b. *Attention condition.* During this condition it is recommended that the staff person working with the student provide some type of verbal feedback that normally would be used either in the classroom or at home upon the occurrence of the target behavior. It is important to remember to respond to the student upon *each* occurrence of the target behavior. All other behaviors should be ignored. Free-time or independent work activities can be used for this condition. During this condition, the teacher should engage in some activity or task (read a magazine, work on materials, etc.) while the student is allowed to play with several preferred toys. Also, no demands should be placed on the student other than to periodically request that the student play with his or her toys while the teacher works. Ideally, this condition should be conducted with the teacher or aide and the target student only. Including other students in the activity provides a greater opportunity for extraneous variables (e.g., the behavior of other students, the inadvertent attending of the staff member to other students) to influence the student's behavior.

c. *Tangible condition.* This assessment condition is similar to the attention condition with one exception. In the tangible condition, instances of problem behavior are followed by presentation of a favorite toy or activity.

d. *Demand condition.* For this activity, a task should be selected that the student is capable of completing but finds to be difficult or frustrating. A task can usually be selected via anecdotal observations of the occurrence of the target behavior during the presentation of certain tasks. It is important that the teacher attempt to present the task at approximately the same rate from session to session. During each session we recommend that a task be presented approximately every 30 seconds. Obviously, a higher or lower rate of task presentation can be selected, as long as it remains constant through the assessment. This is important because a change in the rate of task presentation could have a positive or negative effect on the student's behavior. The student should be reinforced for compliance with each request. A three-step prompting procedure (as previously described) should be used throughout the condition. Upon any occurrence of the target behavior, the staff person allows the student to escape (to stop engaging in the task) until the next 30-second interval. As suggested for the other conditions, this activity will provide more valid information when conducted between the teacher and the student only.

e. *Toy play condition.* This condition should be the same as the attention condition, with a few exceptions. Rather than ignoring appropriate toy play and attending to inappropriate behavior, the student is reinforced for appropriate behavior and ignored for all inappropriate behavior. An attempt should be made to praise the student consistently (e.g., every 30 seconds) for *any* form of appropriate behavior. It is important not to place any demands on the student during this condition. Again, this condition should be conducted without the presence of other students or staff, if possible.

4. *Keep the properties of functional assessment activities constant.* Once the functional assessment activities have been selected and modified to resemble the traditional analogue conditions, it is important that the physical and social characteristics of each condition remain constant. These characteristics include such things as physical setting, type of task, and level of task difficulty. Holding these characteristics constant will help to rule out changes in behavior that could be caused by changes made in the assessment condition. If the room, type of task, or level of task difficulty changes periodically, it will be difficult to attribute the child's behavior to the function measured by the assessment condition. Holding these characteristics constant does not, of course, allow one to rule out other changes in the student's environment (inconsistent treatment of the behavior by parents at home, poor sleep, menstrual cycle, etc.). However, if drastic changes in the rate of a student's behavior are observed in a particular condition, the influence of events outside of the assessment condition can then be examined (assuming the properties of the assessment condition have remained relatively constant).

5. *Respond to the student's behavior in a consistent manner.* The rate and quality of the responses made to each student should be as con-

sistent as possible within each condition. This is important because any variations in the type, rate, or quality of reinforcement provided to a student could affect behavior. These inconsistencies could result in modifications of behavior that are unrelated to the predefined contingencies of each assessment condition. Thus, drastic changes in the type, quality, and rate of reinforcement within any assessment condition could confound the functional assessment, making it difficult to validly interpret the assessment data. Potential qualitative changes that might occur during a functional assessment include, but are not limited to, changing the rate of praise for appropriate toy play (e.g., from every 30 seconds to every 60 seconds); varying the quality of praise (e.g., using a flat, monotonic voice vs. praising with enthusiasm and sincerity); and changing the type of reinforcement (e.g., social praise vs. tangible praise).

As noted previously, this type of analysis requires that minor modifications be made to classroom activities. There are a number of reasons why we suggest these modifications be made. First, a traditional functional assessment facilitates the identification of those functions served by a particular behavior and also allows for a relative comparison of the impact of one function versus another. The advantage of the analogue conditions is that a relatively high degree of control is possible for the various physical and social stimuli that control behavior. This allows for assumptions to be made with greater confidence regarding the function(s) a behavior serves under the defined characteristics of a given condition. The more closely the analogue conditions resemble the natural environment, the more likely, it seems, that the assessment results obtained in these two settings will be similar (Sasso et al., 1992).

Modifying classroom activities may provide greater control over behavior; that is, isolating the various social and physical stimuli that control behavior may help to identify contingencies that maintain behavior. For example, a student who exhibits inappropriate behavior when presented with a series of difficult (demanding) tasks during a group activity might also display similar behavior to gain attention from peers. During this highly demanding activity, the student might behave inappropriately to escape the unpleasant task and to gain attention from peers. If the activity is not modified in a manner that allows the teacher to isolate the influence of demands on the student's behavior (e.g., carrying out the activity in a more secluded area, away from peers), the teacher might inadvertently attribute all of the student's inappropriate behavior to the presentation of the demanding tasks (i.e., assume that the student's behavior is being negatively reinforced). Similar discrepancies could easily be obtained within a given activity due to variations in the rate of task presentation, quality of reinforcement, type of reinforcement, and so forth. Thus, a number of contingencies can be in effect for any given activity in the classroom. Without modifications, the results obtained from the natural, unmodified activities in a classroom might not accurately assess the function(s) served by a given behavior.

ABC Assessment

A second method of assessing the functional properties of classroom behavior is to gauge the relative magnitude of each function by carefully recording each occurrence of the target behavior, as well as the antecedents (what happened before) and consequences (what happened after) of the target behavior. *Antecedent, Behavior, Consequence* (ABC) assessments (Bijou, Peterson, & Ault, 1968) have been widely used in a variety of settings.

We recommend that the antecedents and consequences of each target behavior be recorded throughout the day. Once each of the target behaviors has been operationally defined, the recording procedure requires three steps:

1. *Identify and describe the antecedents of the behavior.* Essentially, the teacher needs to describe the who, what, when, and where that occurred prior to the onset of the behavior. Examples of antecedents might be the activity in which the student was engaged, the presentation of a task by the teacher, whether the student was sitting alone or in a group, if the teacher was working with another student, if the student was being punished (e.g., time-out), the time of day, whether a request was made by other peers, or the complexity of a task.

2. *Describe the student's behavior.* The teacher simply describes the target behavior (e.g., the student had a tantrum, said "no," threw an object, hit another student, bit his or her hand).

3. *Identify and describe the consequences of the behavior.* The teacher describes what happened after the occurrence of the target behavior, that is, the measures applied by the teacher, aides, or other students. For example, the student may have been allowed to escape from the activity, given a verbal reprimand, placed in time-out, laughed at, ignored, or given a preferred toy.

The advantage of using this assessment method is that it allows a teacher to assess the target behavior throughout the day (along with the contingencies surrounding the behavior) without modifying the classroom routine. Although this procedure can be very time-consuming (especially with a high-frequency behavior), it has the potential for providing some very useful information regarding the functional properties of behavior. Some teachers might find that for high-frequency behaviors, the most frequent antecedents and conse-quences can be coded to facilitate data collection. For example, Figure 10.4 shows the ABC data for a 10-year-old student who engaged in aggression (hitting, kicking, biting peers) across the school day in both the special education class and integrated school settings. As the data show, aggression occurred most often when this student was involved in academic activities across all settings. The consequence that was used by teachers following aggression was time-out. Therefore, in this situation, the student appears to be using aggression to escape from nonpreferred or demanding situations (see the antecedents). Likewise, the intervention used to treat these responses (time-out) would be likely to further reinforce these behav-iors; that is, if the student is engaging in aggressive behavior as a means of escape from a task, then time-out reinforces the behavior by providing a cessation of the task.

Interpretation of these data is usually conducted at two levels. The first level of interpretation involves sorting the ABC data into the var-ious categories of functional control. This can be achieved by first

Name _____ Bill _____		Date _____ 2/14/95 _____	
Time/Activity	*Antecedent*	*Behavior*	*Consequence*
9:10 Reading seatwork	Working alone with worksheet	Hit, kicked peer	Time-out
10:40 Math	Problem completion at blackboard	Kicked peer	Two reprimands Time-out
11:10 Hall movement	Going to lunchroom	Hit peer	Reprimand
1:30 Integration Social Studies	Work on Valentine message	Hit, kicked peer	Time-out, removal to special education class
2:30 Reading	1:1 Reading aloud with teacher	Stuck pencil in peer's neck	Time-out

FIGURE 10.4   Completed Antecedent, Behavior, Consequence (ABC) assessment.

separating consequences (none, escape, and attention) and antecedents (none, demand, and no-demand situations) into separate categories. The demand antecedents are further separated into preferred
and nonpreferred events. Although these are fairly generic categories,
they will allow the teacher to form hypotheses regarding a behavior's
function. For example, if the target behavior occurs most often with
nonpreferred *demand* antecedents and with a high occurrence of *escape*
as a consequence, one would hypothesize that the student's aberrant
behavior is motivated by a desire to escape from unpleasant demands.
On the other hand, if the behavior occurs most frequently during *no-
demand* or preferred demand antecedents, with *attention* from staff or
peers as a consequence, it would seem likely that the student's aberrant behavior is functioning to gain some type of social attention.

A second level of interpretation involves examining the types of
activities and times of day in which the behavior is occurring most
frequently (Touchette, McDonald, & Langer, 1985). Given the varying
levels of structure across a student's school day, children will often
exhibit higher rates of behavior during certain activities or during
specific times of day. As discussed above, many of the naturally
occurring activities in the classroom resemble those conditions used
in structured analogue assessments. By recording the rate of a given
behavior across activities and times of day, a teacher can examine the
ABC data on those activities or times of day when the rate is high.
This will allow the teacher to isolate specific tasks, demands, or
sources of attention that are motivating the student's behavior.

One final method of determining the function of behavior that
should be mentioned is the *Motivation Assessment Scale* (MAS), developed by Durand and Crimmins (1988). This survey requires the
teacher, parent(s), or caregiver(s) to complete 16 separate items
related to the function of a student's problem behavior. Each item is
rated on a 7-point Likert-type scale ranging from *never occurs* to
always occurs. The following are examples of the items:

1. Does the behavior seem to occur in response to your talking to
   other persons in the room?

2. Does the behavior occur when any request is made of this person?

3. Does the behavior occur when you take away a favorite toy,
   food, or activity?

4. When the behavior is occurring, does this person seem calm and
   unaware of anything else going on around him or her?

Following completion of the 16 items, a scoring grid is used to determine the degree to which the response is related to a function or functions. For example, item 1 relates to behavior maintained by attention (gain), item 2 suggests escape-motivated behavior, item 3 is designed to capture behavior related to tangible reinforcement, and item 4 suggests behavior maintained by sensory reinforcement.

The MAS appears to be a useful screening tool in the development of an assessment that incorporates direct instruction. The accuracy of the MAS depends, of course, on the knowledge of individual raters and their ability to recall past events in the student's life.

Interventions Based on the Function of the Behavior

A functional analysis of the variables maintaining problem behavior will allow teachers, psychologists, and parents to do two very important things. The first and most direct effect will be the ability to match the intervention to the function of the behavior (Berg & Sasso, 1994). For example, if a student's behavior is maintained by attention, an intervention utilizing contingent attention will be necessary and in all likelihood more effective than an intervention that utilizes components not related to attention. The second benefit that accrues from an analysis of the functional maintaining variables related to behavior is that it provides a context for the development of proactive interventions that rely less on more intrusive, punishing contingencies. However, it is clear from the research of the past few years that these proactive interventions must include multiple components to ensure effectiveness (Dunlap & Kern, 1994; Northrup et al., 1991; Sasso et al., 1992). Thus, a number of variables should be considered in order to provide the most effective treatment for children with behavior and learning problems. Three of these treatment foci include ecological considerations, antecedent manipulations, and the direct manipulation of consequences following behavior.

Ecological Variables

The first area that should be discussed is more global in nature and refers to broader aspects of a student's life than do the other treatment foci. These interventions are related to ecological variables that can be manipulated to create an environment that acts to prevent behavior problems by enriching the experiences of the student, attending to basic needs, and ensuring physical health (Carta, Atwater, Schwartz, & Miller, 1990). Many of these techniques are related to environmental structure, and as such can be used as part of an intervention that employs the manipulation of consequences. However, we discuss them here as separate interventions related to antecedent manipulations.

Events/Activities

Students with behavior and learning problems often have restricted activity options. Some of this is undoubtedly due to the disruptiveness of their behavior. However, many of these students do not actively seek out activities, so it is critical that the teacher and parent(s) attempt to schedule additional activities to increase variety in the lives of these students. Some examples include movies, concerts, shopping, and sports activities. Other students engage in many activities outside of school, some of which are harmful, disruptive, and sometimes illegal. It is important for these children to be exposed to reinforcing, therapeutic, and appropriate activities as part of an effort to provide alternatives to problem behavior patterns. This, in turn, will often result in a decrease in the child's reliance on deviant behavior patterns.

Integration

Another variable related to problem behavior is access to appropriate models for social behavior. Chapter 12 is devoted to this issue. Research over the past several years (Chandler, Lubeck, & Fowler, 1992; Sasso, Simpson, & Novak, 1985) has consistently shown that students with behavior problems do not learn social behavior in isolation. If educators are to teach interaction skills, students must be allowed to learn these skills in the environments in which they are to be used. Models based on acquisition in isolated, special education settings with components designed to enhance generalization to natural settings have been shown to be far less effective than those that teach the skills directly in the integrated environment through modeling and repeated practice with diverse peers (Sasso, Melloy, & Kavale, 1990; Strain, 1990). However, simply placing a student in an integrated setting without the benefit of a program designed to address both troubling behavior and social interaction deficits is neither sufficient nor defensible. Inclusion of all students, all of the time, without regard for the effects of that inclusion on the student or others in the student's environment (e.g., school, peers) is at best ill-advised.

Physical/Medical Issues

Another important variable involves the biophysical determinants of behavior. In other words, is the student healthy? It is clear that issues related to an individual's physical status can have an effect on behavior. Examples of other biophysical variables related to behavior include medication side-effects and the effects of polypharmacy (e.g., multiple drug interactions), eating and food-related issues (does the child eat regularly, have food allergies, etc.), exercise habits, reaction to noise in the environment, and variables related to the child's neurological system. These variables often have an effect in conjunction with environmental variables (i.e., biobehavioral interactions) and can profoundly affect a student's behavior.

Therefore, as educators we should do what is necessary to ensure that we can determine the physical status of the student; be sure that he or she is treated for physical illness, eats and sleeps regularly, and is exposed to physical activity; and determine the optimum level of distractors in the student's environment.

Antecedent Manipulations

Another set of potential interventions that are primarily designed to prevent behavior problems are antecedent techniques. These refer to potential changes in the way educators interact with the student in order to set the stage for, or induce, positive behavior. There are a number of ways that this can be accomplished. One antecedent intervention that can be used in crisis situations (e.g., the student is engaged in high-frequency and high-intensity aggressive or self-injurious behavior) involves responding to the student based on the function of the aberrant behavior. For example, a student who engages in aggressive behavior to escape from task demands may initially be maintained in a setting by reducing the level of demands in the classroom. Or, a student who acts out to receive attention can be presented high levels of attention across the school day. This type of intervention can be considered as an initial attempt to gain some control of the behavior, to be used in conjunction with other techniques that rely on the manipulation of consequences. However, this type of intervention is possible only if there is clear evidence concerning the function that the behavior performs for the student.

In addition to the above-mentioned procedure, a number of other techniques can be used to prevent behavior problems in students. For students with significant levels of problem behavior, we often abandon these basic techniques in favor of more extreme and involved procedures based on the manipulation of consequences. However, it is our contention that, although these procedures alone will often not be sufficient to gain control of the problem behaviors of these students, they are a necessary component in any proactive intervention package.

Preferred Activities

Preferred activities is a technique in which the student is allowed to engage in a pleasurable or desired activity only when he or she has behaved appropriately (e.g., the child may watch television only when his or her homework is completed). Tangibles (e.g., stickers) may also be used. To implement this procedure, one does the following:

1. Identify the behavior that the student needs to improve.

2. Identify an activity that the student enjoys and regularly engages in (or a tangible that he or she likes to receive).

3. Explain to the student, as completely as possible, which behavior needs to be improved. Specifically state what is expected (when, where, how often, etc.).

4. Indicate to the student that he or she can engage in the enjoyable activity (or receive the reward) only when the necessary behavior has occurred. For example, "After you pick up your toys, you may _____ [name the preferred activity or tangible]."

Prespecified Reinforcers

Prespecified reinforcers is a technique, similar to preferred activities, in which the student is prompted prior to an activity for good behavior. If appropriate behavior follows, the student is allowed to engage in a preferred activity or receive some other form of reinforcement.

Examples:

- "If you will sit at the booth during dinner, we will order some ice cream."

- "It will be time to ride your bike soon. Let's hurry and clean the toy area."

To implement this procedure, one would:

1. Assess preferences and reinforcers. (Remember that an activity or item may be preferred, but the student may not be willing to complete a task in order to obtain the item.)

2. Cue the student about the upcoming desired event.

Guided Compliance

Guided compliance is a technique in which the student is physically guided through a task when he or she refuses to comply with a verbal request. To implement this procedure, one would:

1. State the request for the student (e.g., "Put on your shoes").

2. Allow him or her approximately 5 seconds to begin the activity on his or her own.

3. If he or she does not comply with the verbal request, gently but physically guide the student through the activity until it is completed. The physical guidance should be conducted in a neutral manner with as little attention as possible.

4. If the student resists the physical guidance (e.g., kicks, screams, pushes), he or she should not be allowed to escape until the task is completed.

5. Following the physical guidance, praise should be given to the student for completing the request.

Collaborative Activities

Collaborative activities is a strategy that attempts to reduce the aversive nature of a task or activity and provide positive attention. The student is told prior to the activity that help will be provided if the student voluntarily engages in the activity. This intervention is appropriate for those students who engage in challenging behavior to escape from an activity and/or to receive attention.

Examples:

- "If you will pick up three blocks, I will pick up three blocks."
- "If you will tie your shoes, I will zip your coat."

To implement this procedure, one would:

1. Identify an activity the student does not like to perform.

2. Split the responsibility of the task.

Warm-up

Warm-up is a technique in which the student is given an opportunity to do something fun (e.g., play) prior to engaging in a requested task (e.g., homework). Warm-up usually takes one of two forms: (a) engaging in a fun activity such as a game or talking about something fun or (b) talking about the requested task itself. If the student typically resists doing the task because of a preference for something else and enjoys attention, it would be appropriate to engage in a fun activity before the required task. If the student typically has difficulty understanding what he or she is supposed to do and enjoys attention, talking about the task before its occurrence would be appropriate.

To implement this procedure, one would:

1. Identify the task that the student is to complete (e.g., homework), and tell the student specifically what is expected of him or her (e.g., "You need to do problems 1 through 10 on page 72 in your math book").

2. Tell the student that you will play or talk with him or her about the task for a specified period of time (e.g., 5 minutes), then it will be time to work. It is important that the student knows exactly the length of the warm-up period in order to minimize resistance when asked to engage in the task.

3. The warm-up period is a positive time. Under no circumstances should you interact negatively with (e.g., reprimand) the student. Remember, this is the student's fun time before engaging in the task that he or she considers unpleasant.

4. Once the student's warm-up period has ended, repeat the instructions for the task. Requests from the student to continue to play or talk about the task should be denied until the task is completed.

Safety Signal

Safety signal is a procedure in which the adult prompts and informs the student of how much more of the task or activity will be completed before termination.

Examples:

- At the lunch table, the student begins to have problems. The teacher says, "Just three more bites."

- When playing a game requiring that the students take turns, Corky starts to grab the game materials. The teacher holds up his hand and says, "It's Bubba's turn and then it will be your turn."

To implement this procedure, one would:

1. Identify the situation in which the student has to wait.

2. Identify the shortest amount of time that the student will wait before exhibiting the challenging behavior.

3. Choose a signal.

4. Engage the student in the activity.

5. Wait just less than the time determined to be the student's limit.

6. Deliver the safety signal.

7. If the student successfully waits and completes the task, provide reinforcement.

8. Gradually increase the amount of time the student has to wait between the signal and the delivery of reinforcement (e.g., six bites instead of three).

Choice Making and Preferred Activities

Choice making is a procedure in which the student is allowed to determine the order of daily activities and/or to choose staff or play-mates. The choices are determined by the adult and only those choices are allowed.

Examples:

- "Do you want to go to the language center or build with blocks before you fold the towels?"

- "Do you want to work with me or work alone?"

To implement this procedure, one would:

1. Determine what it is that the student needs to complete.

2. Present the choices as clearly and completely as possible. Allow the student to respond in the easiest way possible, at least ini-

tially. For example, the student may not consistently respond verbally, but might point to the preferred area, task, or individual.

3. Be careful of order effects. The student may consistently pick the last option rather than truly discriminate.

Behavioral Momentum

Behavioral momentum is a procedure in which high-probability requests (i.e., requests for known and reinforcing things that the student is likely to do) and social reinforcement are provided prior to a prompt to engage in a low-probability activity (i.e., requests to engage in nonpreferred activities and/or tasks).

Uses:

- When moving from a desired activity to a less desired activity.

- Preventing challenging behavior during instructional tasks.

- Breaking an escalating chain of behavior (think of warm-up).

Example:

Spencer will not sit in his chair when requested to do so.

Teacher (T)	Child (S)	Consequence
Spencer, give me five.	Gives T five.	T provides praise.
Touch your ears.	S touches ears.	T provides praise.
Who's your favorite dinosaur?	S says, "Deinonychus."	T provides praise.
Sit in your chair.	S sits in chair.	T provides praise.

To implement this procedure, one would:

1. Identify those requests that the student typically will complete. These tasks should be easy and quick to complete (high-probability requests).

2. Identify those requests that the student does not comply with and that are important to his or her program (low-probability requests).

3. Validate these requests. That is, be sure that the student will comply with the high-probability requests.

4. Deliver three high-probability requests immediately prior to delivering the low-probability request.

Manipulation of Consequences

The final class of interventions that must be addressed in any multi-component intervention package based on a functional analysis of behavior includes those that rely on the contingent use of consequences to influence behavior. The instructional cycle (Cooper, Heron, & Heward, 1987) provides a model for the categorization of interventions, as shown in Figure 10.5.

We have discussed stimulus variables in the form of ecological and antecedent manipulations, which essentially set the stage for appropriate behavior. Included in that discussion has been a delineation of possible organismic variables, such as biological and medical issues, history, and the characteristics of children with behavior and learning problems. In addition, three broad classes of interventions can be used contingently to directly affect behavior: positive reinforcement, negative reinforcement, and punishment. However, as previously stated, it is not always clear what events, objects, and/or activities are reinforcing or punishing. Therefore, prior to any intervention based on the contingent use of consequences, one should conduct a reinforcer assessment of some type to provide the most effective consequences to follow appropriate behavior.

Given a student with aggressive behavior who engages in those responses to escape from demanding situations, it makes intuitive sense that if the teacher no longer allows escape from the demand following the aggressive response, a decrease in the level of aggression should result. This process is known as extinction (Hall, Grinstead, Collier, & Hall, 1980; Harris, Wolf, & Baer, 1966; Rekers &

S_D	O	R	S_R
Stimulus	*Organism*	*Response*	*Consequence*
Ecological	Biological		Positive
Antecedent	Medical		Negative
	History		Punishment

FIGURE 10.5   Operant instructional cycle.

Lovaas, 1974) and is basic to any intervention based on applied behavior analysis methodology. However, the last 10 years of research has shown that a number of other variables mitigate this process (Sasso, 1994). The first is *history*. Researchers have learned from clinical and applied work with children and adults with self-injurious and aggressive behavior that the longer an aberrant response or responses have been part of an individual's repertoire of responses, the more difficult it will be to teach the individual a more proactive replacement behavior. For example, aggression in the form of biting will be easier to treat in a 2-year-old who has been engaging in the behavior for 3 months than it will be in a 12-year-old who has engaged in the same response for 7 years. Habitual response patterns are harder to change.

Second, the *number of topographies* that form a response class of behaviors will influence the effectiveness of intervention efforts. Response class refers to a number of behaviors that all respond to the same reinforcer or share the same function. For example, the student who hits, kicks, bites, scratches, and spits to get out of work that is too difficult (an escape function) will be harder to treat than the student whose only problem behavior is kicking.

The third variable affecting the success of interventions based on consequences is *control*. One way to view the problem behavior of children is within the context of communication (Durand, 1990). Thus the student whose disruptive behavior is maintained by attention is trying to say, "Pay attention to me." The student whose aggressive responses function to escape from demands is saying, "I don't want to do this." If the teacher initiates an intervention with an extinction component that withdraws the reinforcement from the response (e.g., no attention for disruption in the first case, no escape for aggression in the second), the control the child had has been taken away. Another way of stating this is that the teacher has removed the communicative value of the behavior. The next step in this process must be to provide the student with an alternative behavior that he or she can use to gain the same reinforcers. In other words, the student must be consistently and repeatedly shown that an alternative, prosocial response can be used to obtain, as in the above examples, either attention or escape. This process is basic to any environmentally based behavior reduction intervention.

The final variable that will affect the success of intervention efforts for students with behavior and learning problems is *efficiency*. That is, the alternative response taught to the student must be easy to use, if possible, easier to use than the problem behavior. For example, if the student engages in cursing to escape from seatwork, and every time he says "shit" the teacher removes him from the room to a time-out area, then asking the student to choose an alternative, prosocial response such as raising his hand, waiting to be called on, and then asking permission to take a break following the completion of one page of the assignment, may not be effective because it takes too long, and it is too hard for the student to obtain the reinforcer. Instead, the student will likely choose the response (i.e., cursing) that in the past has been the most efficient (i.e., quickest and easiest).

With these variables in mind, most of what has been found to be effective for students is based on *differential reinforcement.* Typical interventions based on this technique include differential reinforcement of other (DRO) behavior and differential reinforcement of alternative (DRA) behavior. With these approaches, the teacher determines a schedule for the delivery of a prespecified reinforcer(s) contingent on either the absence of the troubling behavior (DRO) or the absence of the troubling behavior and emission of an alternative, prosocial response (DRA). For example, a typical DRA procedure would be to tell the student that if he or she completes a portion of an assignment and refrains from aggressive behavior, then the student can have free time away from tasks. In this instance, any emission of the aggression does not result in a removal of the task, whereas the completion of a portion of the task is the chosen replacement behavior that results in the reinforcer (i.e., cessation of the rest of the task). One problem related to the use of these types of procedures is that they do not adequately address issues related to control and efficiency. That is, it is often much easier for the student to continue to aggress given that the task takes much longer to complete and the student is required to delay the acquisition of the reinforcer.

One other intervention that is similar to techniques that rely on differential reinforcement is *functional communication training* (Doss & Reichle, 1989; Durand, 1993; Northup et al., 1991). Using this procedure, the student is prompted to emit an alternative form of communication that will function to obtain the goal that was obtained previously by the aberrant response. Using a functional communication intervention, the student in the above example would be told that he or she could receive a break from the task at any time by asking for it (e.g., "I need a break") or, for a student who is a nonoral communicator, through a manual sign (e.g., signing "Please"). Thus, the student could receive short breaks from work at any time through the use of a brief communicative response. Clinicians and educators working with students with developmental disabilities and autism have enjoyed a relatively high degree of success using this procedure in conjunction with extinction. There are several reasons for this success. First, the process is conceptually sound and appealing. The notion that all behavior is communicative allows the development of interventions that teach rather than suppress problem behaviors. It focuses attention on the teaching components related to behavior reduction. Second, functional communication deals directly with issues related to control and efficiency. That is, it is easier for educators to recognize and prompt an efficient phrase or manual sign that the student will come to understand is controlling what he or she wants rather than an alternative that may not receive a consistent response from the teacher. Finally, research over the last 5 to 7 years suggests that it can be, in a number of circumstances, a very effective intervention that allows the concurrent reduction of aberrant responses and development of prosocial, interactive behaviors (Carr, 1988; Taylor & Carr, 1994).

Conclusion

The strong relationship between a determination of the function of troubling behavior, the direct treatment of that behavior, and interventions designed to effect social responding for the purpose of inclusion cannot be overstated. Without a clear understanding of why students continue to engage in damaging behavior, professionals cannot adequately begin to develop interventions that teach functionally equivalent (Carr, 1988) replacement behaviors that allow students access to less restrictive settings. The research of the past 15 years strongly suggests that simply placing students in integrated settings will not be effective. Although it is true that some students placed in integrated settings do begin to show immediate and dramatic reductions in troubling behavior without the benefit of programs designed to treat these responses, this effect does not occur by magic. There are reasons why these events occur, and they are related to the variables or functions that the behavior serves and how these variables interact with the student's environment.

For example, there was a student whose aggressive behavior in the special education classroom was maintained by an attention function. In this segregated setting, he averaged two aggressive outbursts per day. However, he was integrated into a cooperative play group in the regular education classroom for 30 minutes twice a day. During this time, aggressive behavior did not occur, and the teachers were considering integrating this student for the entire school day. During all-day integrated trials, his aggressive behavior returned, and all integration was terminated. What happened? First, the cooperative play group in the regular classroom provided a high level of attention through peers. During this time, he interacted through a number of enjoyable activities with his peers in the regular education classroom. In this setting, the student did not need to use aggression to obtain attention because high levels of attention were present. Second, when his integration time was increased, he was placed in other activities in the regular classroom in which he did not receive high levels of attention and was required to work for extended periods of time (e.g., seatwork). These activities were not supportive of his behavior based on the attention function, and therefore he began to use aggression again to communicate his desire for attention.

This interaction between aberrant behavior and social functioning cannot be ignored. Chapter 12 will detail programs that can be used in conjunction with functional analysis to create programs for students that integrate behavior reduction variables and successful social interactive behaviors.

References

Berg, W., & Sasso, G. M. (1994). Transferring implementation of functional assessment procedures from the clinic to natural settings. In J. Reichle & D. Wacker (Eds.), *Communicative alternatives to challenging behavior: Integrating functional assessment and intervention strategies* (pp. 343–362). Baltimore: Brookes.

Bijou, S. W., Peterson, R. F., & Ault, M. H. (1968). A method of integrating descriptive and experimental field studies at the level of data and empirical concepts. *Journal of Applied Behavior Analysis, 1,* 175–191.

Carr, E. G. (1977). The motivation of self-injurious behavior: A review. *Psychological Bulletin, 84,* 800–816.

Carr, E. G. (1988). Functional equivalence as a mechanism of response generalization. In R. H. Horner, R. L. Koegel, & G. Dunlap (Eds.), *Generalization and maintenance: Life-style changes in applied settings* (pp. 221–241). Baltimore: Brookes.

Carta, J. J., Atwater, J. B., Schwartz, I. S., & Miller, P. A. (1990). Applications of ecobehavioral analysis to the study of transitions across early education settings. *Education and Treatment of Children, 13,* 298–315.

Chandler, L. K., Lubeck, R. C., & Fowler, S. A. (1992). Generalization and maintenance of preschool children's social skills: A critical review and analysis.
Journal of Applied Behavior Analysis, 25, 415–428.

Cooper, J. O., Heron, T. E., & Heward, W. L. (1987). *Applied behavior analysis.*
Columbus, OH: Merrill.

Doss, S., & Reichle, J. (1989). Establishing communicative alternatives to the emission
of socially motivated excess behavior: A review. *Journal of The Association for
Persons with Severe Handicaps, 14,* 101–112.

Dunlap, G., & Kern, L. (1994). Assessment and intervention for children within the
instructional curriculum. In J. Reichle and D. Wacker (Eds.), *Communicative
alternatives to challenging behavior: Integrating functional assessment and intervention strategies* (pp. 177–203). Baltimore: Brookes.

Durand, V. M. (1990). *Severe behavior problems: A functional communication training
approach.* New York: Guilford Press.

Durand, V. M. (1993). Causes of behavior: Functional assessment and functional
analysis. In M. D. Smith (Ed.), *Behavior modification for exceptional children and
youth* (pp. 38–60). Stoneham, MA: Andover Medical Press.

Durand, V. M., & Crimmins, D. B. (1988). Identifying the variables maintaining self-
injurious behavior. *Journal of Autism and Developmental Disorders, 18*(1), 99–117.

Ferster, C. B. (1961). Positive reinforcement and behavioral deficits of autistic children. *Child Development, 32,* 437–456.

Fisher, W., Piazza, C. C., Bowman, L. G., Hagopian, L. P., Owens, J. C., & Slevin, I.
(1992). A comparison of two approaches for identifying reinforcers for persons with severe and profound disabilities. *Journal of Applied Behavior
Analysis, 25,* 491–498.

Hall, M. C., Grinstead, J., Collier, H., & Hall, R. V. (1980). Responsive parenting: A
preventive program which incorporates parents training parents. *Education
and Treatment of Children, 3,* 239–259.

Harris, F. R., Wolf, M. M., & Baer, D. M. (1966). Effects of adult social reinforcement
on child behavior. In R. Ulrich, T. Stachnik, & J. Mabry (Eds.), *Control of
human behavior* (pp. 130–137). Glenview, IL: Scott, Foresman.

Horner, R. D., & Keilitz, I. (1975). Training mentally retarded adolescents to brush
their teeth. *Journal of Applied Behavior Analysis, 8,* 301–309.

Iwata, B., Dorsey, M., Slifer, K., Bauman, K., & Richman, G. (1982). Toward a functional analysis of self-injury. *Analysis and Intervention in Developmental
Disabilities, 2,* 3–20.

Northrup, J., Wacker, D., Sasso, G., Steege, M., Cigrand, K., Cook, J., & DeRaad, A.
(1991). A brief functional analysis of aggressive and alternative behavior in
an outclinic setting. *Journal of Applied Behavior Analysis, 24,* 509–522.

Pace, G. M., Ivancic, M. T., Edwards, G. L., Iwata, B. A., & Page, T. J. (1985).
Assessment of stimulus preference and reinforcer value with profoundly
retarded individuals. *Journal of Applied Behavior Analysis, 18,* 249–255.

Rekers, G. A., & Lovaas, O. I. (1974). Behavioral treatment of deviant sex-role behaviors in a male child. *Journal of Applied Behavior Analysis, 7,* 173–190.

Sasso, G. M. (1994, November). *Variables related to behavior reduction and social interaction.* Paper presented at the annual Teacher Educators for Children with Behavioral Disorders Conference for Severe Behavior Disorders, Tempe, AZ.

Sasso, G. M., Melloy, K. J., & Kavale, K. A. (1990). Generalization, maintenance, and behavioral covariation associated with social skills training through structured learning. *Behavioral Disorders, 16,* 9–22.

Sasso, G. M., & Reimers, T. R. (1988). Assessing the functional properties of behavior: Implications and applications for the classroom. *Focus on Autistic Behavior, 3,* 1–15.

Sasso, G. M., Reimers, T. M., Cooper, L. J., Wacker, D., Berg, W., Steege, M., Kelly, L., & Allaire, A. (1992). Use of descriptive and experimental analyses to identify the functional properties of aberrant behavior in school settings. *Journal of Applied Behavior Analysis, 25,* 809–821.

Sasso, G. M., Simpson, R. L., & Novak, C. G. (1985). Procedures for facilitating integration of autistic children in public school settings. *Analysis and Intervention of Developmental Disabilities, 3,* 233–246.

Strain, P. S. (1990). LRE for preschool children with handicaps: What we know, what we should be doing. *Journal of Early Intervention, 14,* 291–296.

Taylor, J. C., & Carr, E. G. (1994). Reciprocal social influences in the analysis and intervention of severe challenging behavior. In J. C. Taylor & E. G. Carr (Eds.), *Communicative alternatives to challenging behavior: Integrating functional assessment and intervention strategies* (pp. 63–81). Baltimore: Brookes.

Touchette, P. E., MacDonald, R. F., & Langer, S. N. (1985). A scatter plot for identifying stimulus control of problem behavior. *Journal of Applied Behavior Analysis, 18,* 343–351.

CHAPTER 11

Managing Resistance: Looking Beyond the Child and Into the Mirror

John W. Maag

"It just wasn't fair," thought Frank, as he leaned against the wall of the school scraping the mud off his shoes. It wasn't actually mud, but a combination of clay and sand from the infield of the school baseball diamond. And this stuff was sticky. The bottom of his shoes looked like a stack of pancakes that had been covered with too much syrup and then ignored. He had already broken three sticks trying to remove the stuff and was now using his last pencil which, he figured, was only good for about two scrapes. That would be another problem: When he returned to class, Mrs. Winston would give him the standard lecture of coming prepared with enough pencils. "I'm sick of her telling me what to do," Frank said aloud to no one in particular.

It was the first day that had been warm enough to go outside for recess. The bright sun had melted the last of the snow and although the ground was soaking wet, that didn't stop the children from playing games like four-square. It seemed to Frank like recess just started when the bell rang signaling its end. Mrs. Winston, his fifth-grade teacher, had recess duty this day. She spoke the routine every child new by heart: "Line up next to the wall, no talking, hands to yourself, and no bouncing the balls." It was this last rule with which Frank and the other kids had fun. Billy was standing in front of Frank holding one of the balls used to play four-square. Suddenly Frank reached over and swatted the ball out of Billy's hand. But he had not counted on Mrs. Winston turning around to face him at that very moment. A couple of kids started laughing as the ball rolled toward them. One of the kids, Randy Johnson, took this opportunity to kick the ball as hard as he could. It went flying right into the middle of the soaking wet baseball diamond. "Frank, go pick up that ball," Mrs. Winston said sternly.

"But I didn't kick it over there," whined Frank. "It's not fair that I should have to walk on that muddy baseball diamond to get a ball I didn't kick over there." From the expression on Mrs. Winston's face—a cross between marine drill sergeant and pitbull—Frank knew the discussion was over. Yet he couldn't resist making one more plea. "I'm going to get my shoes really muddy and you wouldn't want me to track mud in the classroom? Why don't we have the janitor get the ball?" Rather than responding, Mrs. Winston turned away from Frank and instructed the children to go inside.

Frank had retrieved the ball and was now scraping the mud off his shoes. "Snap," went his last pencil as a clog of mud resembling a miniature frisbee went flying off his shoe. He knew Mrs. Winston would still be angry at him as he shuffled his feet one last time on the concrete before entering the building. "Fine," he thought, "let her be angry. I don't care. She's not going to tell me what to do." When Frank entered Mrs. Winston's room, he was still determined not to let her tell him what to do again.

"Please get your reading book off the shelf, take it back to your desk, and open it to page 27," said Mrs. Winston when Frank entered the room. Frank absentmindedly picked up his reading book from the shelf and started walking back to his desk. Then he thought how Mrs. Winston was again trying to tell him what to do. He was fed up with teachers telling him what he could and couldn't do. He turned back toward Mrs. Winston, dropped the book on the floor, and glared at her challengingly.

Mrs. Winston calmly said, "Frank, please pick up your book and take a seat."

"No, I won't pick up my book. And I'm not going to sit in my chair either. You can't make me—nobody can make me!"

At this point, Frank could be considered oppositional, and Mrs. Winston must deal with his resistance. She cannot back down because her authority has been challenged. Therefore, to maintain discipline and the respect of the other students, Mrs. Winston must make Frank pick up the book and sit in his chair or suffer the consequences. Mrs. Winston responded to Frank's resistance by saying, "Frank, if you don't pick up the book right now, you'll be eating lunch by yourself in the classroom today." Frank just stood there, his bottom lip stuck out like a perch on a birdhouse, his silence communicating his answer. "Fine," said Mrs. Winston. "You can just go down to the principal's office right now and she can give your mother a call."

The situation that occurred between Frank and Mrs. Winston is fairly common, one that is repeated in many classrooms across this country each day. And it seems that with the growing number of diverse students, including those with behavior problems, being integrated into general education classes, situations like the one described here are even more likely to occur. The trend toward ensuring that all students, regardless of whether they are identified as disabled, at risk, homeless, or gifted, are educated in the general education classroom, is now referred to as the *inclusion movement* (Stainback & Stainback, 1992). With its roots in the doctrine of the least restrictive environment (LRE), this movement originally appeared in the Education for All Handicapped Children Act of 1975 (P.L. 94-142) and was later conceptualized in the 1980s as the Regular Education Initiative (REI). It is a movement that seeks to create schools where all students are educated together in general education classrooms in their communities. There are some benefits to this arrangement, such as helping students learn to understand and respect individual differences, develop communication skills and friendships, and work cooperatively with others (e.g., Madden & Slavin, 1983). However, as classrooms become more diverse, teachers will be confronted with more children who typically display oppositional behavior.

In the vignette presented above, however, Frank was not identified as a child with special needs, although most adults would view him as being oppositional or resistant. I would like to pose the following question: Who was really being resistant—Frank or his teacher? I believe Frank behaved in a very rational and purposeful way, given the situation as he interpreted it. Mrs. Winston, on the other hand, was being resistant because she was stuck using typical and unimaginative patterns of responding and, consequently, was unable to get the response from Frank that she desired (Maag, 1988). Frank did not pick up the book, place it on his desk, and sit down because of Mrs. Winston's ineffective pattern of communication. Yet, she most likely will continue to use this approach to handling student resistance even when it does not result in the desired outcome. To many people, I may seem to be espousing a fairly radical view. And if you are resistant to my assertion that children's resistance originates solely from your behavior, then you just proved my point—what I communicated to you resulted in your resistance. Here is a less cryptic way to make my point: If you never asked children to do anything, they would not be resistant!

Of course, teachers cannot effectively manage resistance simply by letting children do whatever they want. But I believe that the way teachers view, and respond to, children's resistant behavior is what prevents them from managing it effectively. In this chapter, I provide you with an understanding of resistance. Resistance may be conceptualized in various ways. However, I think Freud's view and that found in the family systems literature are particularly germane for the following reason: They point out how resistant behavior represents a rational and purposeful response to a situation. Once teachers understand that resistance serves a purpose for a child, they are better able to manage it. Resistant behavior then becomes a cue for teachers to alter their responses to a child, and to continue to alter their responses until they get the desired outcome. After providing an understanding of resistance, I present three common sources of resistance—child, environmental, and adult variables (e.g., Cormier & Cormier, 1985)—and techniques for managing resistance. Although the sources of resistance differ, my basic tenet remains the same: It is the responses to children that must be altered in order to manage resistance effectively.

Understanding Resistance

Resistance was originally described by Freud (1990/1952) in the context of psychoanalysis. Although many aspects of Freud's theory either have not withstood the test of empirical study or have few implications for teachers, his conceptualization of resistance is quite illuminating. Freud used this term to describe why many of his patients failed to participate in therapy despite their request for help. Why would a person be motivated to seek out therapy for a troubling problem but then resist the therapist's help? Freud speculated that resistance served an adaptive function: It maintained internal equilibrium and avoided emotional conflict. In other words, if an individual was to comply with the therapist, he would be exposing himself to the anxiety associated with the problem that initially prompted the need for help. However, by being resistant to therapy, he could keep the anxiety at an unconscious level which, in the short run, would be less emotionally painful that confronting it directly.

A similar explanation of resistance, but without the psychodynamic undertones, can be found in the family systems literature (e.g., Jackson, 1968). From this perspective, individuals cling to the way things are rather than exposing themselves to the uncertainty and threat that changing their behavior implies. This need to change but remain the same is at first quite puzzling. For example, why are some children who complain of not having enough friends, wanting more money, or being bored so resistant to suggestion to join a club, apply for a job, or develop a hobby? I believe the answer to this question has to do with risk: All the suggestions expose the child to the potential of being rejected or failing. Therefore, the pain implied in the risk of changing may be more severe than remaining the same, even when remaining the same is also painful. Consequently, people repeatedly engage in certain behaviors that are ineffective from time to time. In essence, individuals try to maintain *homeostasis,* a term family therapists use to describe a person's desire for consistency in life. Consistency breeds predictability which, in turn, reduces anxiety by engendering feelings of comfort and a sense of self-assurance. However, it is this perceived sense of comfort that often keeps people behaving in ineffective ways. Students repeatedly engage in the same inappropriate behavior and teachers, in turn, respond in predictable and often ineffective ways.

From the discussion thus far, one could easily conceptualize resistance as avoidance of anxiety or fear to take a risk. In addition, toward the end of the vignette appearing earlier, I described resistance in terms of the teacher's inability to communicate effectively with the student. These factors contribute to resistance and often result in children being labeled oppositional, stubborn, and inflexible. However, I would like to offer a more basic definition of resistance: any behavior that interferes with or reduces the likelihood of a successful outcome. Although this definition may seem vague, it is meant to point out that resistance can originate from a variety of factors. Traditionally, resistance is viewed as behavior a child engages in to avoid complying with a request. And sometimes this may be true—children certainly do engage in oppositional behavior with the sole purpose of trying to frustrate adults. However, it is more difficult for teachers to become frustrated if they expand their repertoire of responses to children's behavior. Therefore, although I describe three different factors accounting for resistance, the recommendations are based mostly on how teachers can alter their responses to manage resistance.

Resistance Due to Child Factors

Adults are quick to point to a child as a source of resistance. This typical child-deficit approach focuses on some condition that exists within a child. It is a conceptualization based on a medical–disease model often used in psychiatry, which considers behavior problems to be manifestations of clinical entities much like physical diseases. Although there is insufficient evidence to warrant a generalized medical model of all behavior problems or to imply that such problems exist within persons as do physical diseases (e.g., Achenbach, 1980), teachers nevertheless typically rely on deviant labels to explain why a child is being resistant. In fact, there is a psychiatric label for highly resistant children—oppositional defiant disorder—which is characterized by a recurrent pattern of negativistic, defiant, disobedient, and hostile behavior toward authority figures (American Psychiatric Association, 1994). These labels are supposed to provide information about the nature of a child's problem and to guide treatment; however, they also have the unintended effect of minimizing the influence of adults' behavior on a child's functioning. I will be describing a different conceptualization of child-specific factors—one that focuses on whether or not a child possesses the requisite skills in his or her repertoire to comply with a request.

The model of behavior appearing in Figure 11.1, developed by Howell, Fox, and Morehead (1993), can be used to understand the dynamics of resistance due to child factors. In this model, a child's resistant behavior can be examined in relation to two general categories: can't versus can. If a child can't do a behavior, it is because of one of two possible reasons. First, a child may actually lack the skill necessary to comply with a request. For example, a teacher may tell a student to stop irritating her neighbor. However, the child may not know what "irritate" means. Consequently, she is unable to comply with the request and instead appears resistant or oppositional. Second, some aspects of the environment may be reinforcing the child for continuing to irritate the peer. For example, she may receive a lot of attention, albeit negative, from the peer. Consequently, she is being reinforced for engaging in the undesirable behavior despite her teacher's directions to desist.

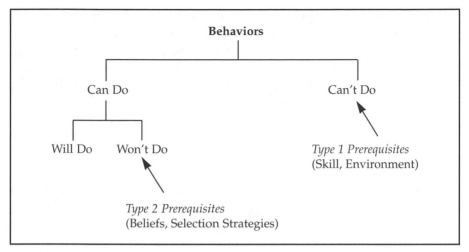

FIGURE 11.1   **Model for understanding resistance due to child factors.**

If a child can perform the requested behavior, he either will or won't perform it. If a child performs the behavior, he is not going to be considered resistant, but instead compliant. However, it is possible that a child can perform the desired behavior but nevertheless won't. There are a variety of reasons why a child won't perform a behavior he possesses. A child's perceptions about a situation may interfere with performing the desired behavior. For example, sometimes when a child gets into a playground fight, he is required to apologize to the other child. However, he may be quite resistant to making an apology—not because he lacks the skills for apologizing, but because he believes his peers will think he is a sissy for apologizing.

Another reason why children won't perform a behavior they possess is that they may select an inappropriate strategy to guide behavior. Individuals use strategies to help them analyze a given situation, select a behavior to perform based on the analysis, and evaluate the possible consequences to themselves and others of performing the behavior. For example, a child may respond to teasing from a peer by hitting her. As a result, the child receives in-school suspension for 2 days. This behavior can occur repeatedly with the same outcome because a child fails to evaluate the consequences of hitting a peer, or may have been successful using this behavior, without consequences, to get her sibling to stop teasing her.

Howell and Morehead (1987) stressed that when a child won't perform the appropriate behavior, it means he has selected, from among a variety of behaviors in his repertoire, the wrong behavior—

one that makes him appear resistant or oppositional. They are not suggesting that he consciously, and with intent to irritate adults, selected to do so. When a child purposely performs a behavior to irritate an adult, he is reacting to the adult as much as the adult is reacting to him. In this instance, I believe resistance is not due to child factors, but rather to adult factors—a point I will elaborate upon shortly. However, more often *selecting* an inappropriate behavior is not the same as *deciding* to behave inappropriately. People select behaviors automatically. Automatic responses are those that have become habitual through repeated use and are, consequently, activated unconsciously. In this instance, a child may not be purposely irritating an adult, but automatically selects an inappropriate behavior without giving conscious thought to the consequences. Given this brief overview, I will now describe in more detail resistance due to specific child factors and ways to manage them.

Children Who Lack the Necessary Skills

Some children appear resistant because they lack the necessary skills for complying. They fall under the *can't* category in Figure 11.1, although their problems also may be due to environmental factors, which I discuss in the next section. A child may experience a variety of skill deficiencies. For example, a child may seem resistant because she simply does not understand what to do or how to go about performing a behavior or task. In some instances a child is too preoccupied to understand a teacher's instructions or feels inept at carrying out the instructions. Other children may not understand a teacher's instructions or the rationale for engaging in a particular behavior or task. Resistance due to these difficulties can be managed with the following techniques.

Providing Detailed Instructions

Martin and Pear (1992) stressed the importance of providing children detailed instructions as a way to increase compliance. Instructions refer to rules that indicate that specific behaviors will pay off in particular situations. Sometimes rules clearly identify reinforcers or punishers associated with following the rules, as in telling a child, "If you finish your math assignment in 10 minutes you can be first in line for recess, but if you don't finish your math assignment in 10 minutes you will stay in from recess in order to finish it." In other cases, consequences are implied. When a teacher says to a child in an excited voice, "Wow, would you look at that!" looking in the implied direction will likely enable the child to see something interesting. On the other hand, if a teacher sternly says to a child, "Sit down right now!" the instruction carries the implication that the child's refusal to sit down is likely to lead to punishment. Martin and Pear (1992) provided the following guidelines for giving instructions:

- Instruction should be within the understanding of the individual to whom it is applied,

- Instruction should specify the behavior in which the individual is to engage,

- Instruction should specify contingencies involved in complying (or not complying) with it, and these contingencies should be applied consistently,

- Complex instruction should be broken down into easy-to-follow steps,

- Instruction should be sequenced so that it proceeds gradually from very easy to more difficult behavior for the individual being treated,

- Instruction should be delivered in a pleasant, courteous manner,

- Fading should be used as necessary to phase out instruction if you want other stimuli that are present to take control of the behavior. (p. 215)

To ensure that a child understands an instruction, the teacher can ask her to repeat it. Sometimes she will refuse to repeat an instruction, especially if she is angry at the prospect of engaging in some unpleasant activity. In this situation, as when managing *any* resistance, it is important to be flexible and exude a "matter-of-fact attitude." For example, the teacher could tell the child that, if she prefers, instead of saying it out loud, she can write down the instruction or say it into a tape recorder. If the child is still resistant, the teacher can say, in a matter-of-fact voice, that the child can choose to stay after school as long as it takes for her to paraphrase back the instruction. The teacher wants to convey to the child that it really does not matter whether she paraphrases the instruction now or after school. If the teacher really does not care that a child stays in the room after school until she is ready to paraphrase an instruction and, in fact, is pleased that the child has the opportunity to spend time thinking about the instruction, then the child will most likely not involve herself in a power struggle by refusing to paraphrase it. After all, if she does, she will not anger the teacher, but only invite some time thinking about the instruction. And if she senses that the teacher really does not care, she figures that she may as well repeat the instruction now and be done with it.

Providing Skill Training

Children who lack the necessary skills to perform a task or behavior will not comply simply because a teacher asks them to do so. Therefore, resistance is reduced when children are taught the specific skills necessary to comply and are provided with practice in the skills. Specifically, the teacher should break the skill-to-be taught into small, manageable steps of increasing difficulty; model the skill for a child; provide a child with opportunities to rehearse the skill; set up role-play scenarios to provide additional real-life practice for a child; and provide reinforcement and feedback. A variety of commercially available curricula utilizing these techniques can be used to teach children missing skills (e.g., McGinnis & Goldstein, 1984; Walker et al., 1983).

Providing Opportunities for Practice

Even after a skill is learned, a child sometimes fails to perform it for one reason or another. When this happens, additional "practice" is warranted. One such type of practice that is particularly well suited for managing resistance is called *overcorrection*. Overcorrection was initially developed to reduce inappropriate behaviors exhibited by children with autism and mental retardation. There are two types of overcorrection; restitutional overcorrection and positive practice overcorrection. *Restitutional overcorrection* requires that a child correct the consequences of his inappropriate behavior by restoring the situation to a condition greatly improved from that which existed before the misbehavior (Foxx & Azrin, 1972). For example, a child who throws food in the school lunchroom would be required not only to clean up her food but also any other food or garbage in the entire cafeteria.

Positive practice overcorrection provides a child opportunities to engage in appropriate behavior (Foxx & Bechtel, 1983). For example, a child who casually tosses a wad of paper on the floor would be required to repeatedly place the paper in the trash can. Positive practice is based on the belief that, for resistant children to learn responsibility, they must spend time and effort engaging in the appropriate behavior. In this way, they experience the inconvenience suffered by other people who must otherwise correct the disturbance.

To understand how to implement positive practice for managing resistance, I will elaborate on the example of the boy who threw a wad of paper on the floor instead of putting it in the trash can. When a child throws paper on the floor rather than putting it in the trash can, the goal is to have him assume responsibility for his behavior without imposing on others. In a matter-of-fact way, the teacher explains to the child that he or she has noticed that the child has difficulty putting paper in the trash can. Therefore, the child has to devote 1 hour after school to *practice* putting paper in the trash can. The teacher further clarifies that different people require different amounts of practice time to learn skills in different areas. The teacher expresses confidence that the child will be able to master the skill, but uncertainty whether 1 hour will be adequate time for him to practice and really learn to do it well. The teacher, appearing genuinely enthusiastic about this process, tells the child that he will be able to practice again if necessary.

The key component in getting children to comply with practicing is for the teacher to appear as if he or she really does not care; then a power struggle is diffused. If the teacher really does not care that a child is spending an hour learning how to put paper in the trash can and, in fact, is pleased that he has the opportunity to practice and master the skill, he will probably not be resistant by tossing paper on the floor, but instead will put the paper in the trash can and be done with it. And if he does toss the paper on the floor, he will not anger the teacher, thereby controlling the situation and receiving negative attention, but instead invite practice time. Remember, a child must be given a choice: either pick up the paper the first time, or receive practice. In this way, a child always has the *choice* to avoid practice. If a child chooses to practice, the teacher must never feel sorry for him. After all, practicing putting paper in the trash can for 1 hour has never caused illness, death, or permanent disability.

Children Who Have Pessimistic Expectations

Bandura (1977) described two types of expectations: efficacy expectations and outcome expectations. *Efficacy expectations* refer to a person's belief that she can perform the specific behaviors required for a desired consequence. *Outcome expectations* refer to a person's belief that a specific behavior will, in fact, lead to a certain outcome, such as reinforcement. A child might believe that asking a teacher for assistance would result in the teacher's providing help, but have little confidence that she could nevertheless successfully perform the behaviors. Alternatively, the child might believe she could successfully ask for help but believe that those behaviors would not result in the teacher's providing assistance or, worse, that the teacher would criticize her for asking for help. In either way, the child may not perform the requested behavior and, therefore, appear resistant.

Sometimes, children's beliefs are not always grounded in reality. In the previous example, the child may believe the teacher will criticize her for asking for help, without having any proof that the teacher has or will engage in such behavior. However, once a belief is formed, it attains factual status. Therefore, it is important to acknowledge children's pessimism as real. This suggestion may at first sound a little strange, or even uncaring. The typical response to children who express pessimistic ideas or expectations is to counter such beliefs with expressions of optimism. If a child is feeling some type of hurt, whether it be physical or emotional, adults naturally want to comfort him. However, in many instances, attempts to counter with optimism have the opposite effect—they elevate rather than reduce resistance. Regardless of the good intentions behind the statements, they often run counter to a child's position of pessimism. For example, take a situation where a child believes he will flunk his math test, even though his teacher knows he possesses the skills for passing. When a child has this pessimistic expectation, it is common for a teacher to counter with a statement such as, "Oh, that's ridiculous, you'll have no problem passing the test." Although this comment is meant to cheer a child up, it runs counter to his belief. Therefore, he is likely to say to himself, "My teacher doesn't understand me; she's no help at all." Instead of countering with optimism, it is better to initially acknowledge a child's pessimism. For example, the teacher could tell the child, "I can understand your point and it's probably better to be uncertain or doubtful at this time." This statement sounds strange because teachers are so conditioned to try to ease a child's emotional or physical pain. But by doing so, teachers often create resistance by saying things that run counter to a child's current beliefs.

By initially matching the comments to those of a child, the teacher is acknowledging the child's discouragement and validating it as being real. This reduces resistance, and the teacher can now move a child in a more desired direction. In the previous example, after acknowledging the boy's pessimism about not doing well on his math test, the teacher could ask, "Have there been any other math tests that you didn't flunk?" The idea behind this statement is to get a child to put his pessimistic beliefs into perspective by comparing them to past experiences. A child is more likely to reflect logically and respond honestly to this statement once the teacher has acknowledged his pessimism, however. If, on the other hand, the teacher first tries to counter with optimism, the child will think the teacher does not understand his position. Therefore, the teacher's next question is likely to fall on deaf ears—he either will not answer truthfully or will make up some reason why the question is irrelevant.

Milton Erickson, once considered an unorthodox and controversial psychiatrist, used this technique with both his parents and his children. Erickson's strategic approach to therapy has increased in popularity and is studied and taught everywhere. Since his death in 1980, Erickson has assumed the stature of a cult figure with thousands of admirers attending large conferences addressing aspects of his unique approach. It is not easy to describe Erickson's approach because of the curious way he stood on the line between healer and poet, scientist and bard. But in a nutshell, strategic therapy is a name for a variety of techniques in which the therapist takes responsibility for directly influencing people. The strategic therapist identifies solvable problems, sets goals, designs approaches for each problem, and examines the client's responses to make corrections to achieve the goals. Because it is difficult to categorize Erickson's techniques, I have instead interwoven various examples of his work throughout the remainder of this chapter.

To return to the present discussion, Haley (1993) described how Erickson handled an incident involving his son Robert who, when he was almost 4 years old, fell down the back stairs of his house, split his lip, and knocked his upper tooth back into the maxilla. The boy was bleeding and screaming with pain and fright. Erickson and his wife rushed to him and realized it was an emergency. But instead of picking up their son and comforting him, Erickson said, "That hurts awful, Robert. That hurts terrible. And it will keep right on hurting." Erickson did not try to console his son with some optimistic response such as, "Oh, Robert, it will be okay, it will stop hurting soon." Although such a comment is meant to provide comfort to a child, it usually has the opposite effect. The child knows it hurts, and by failing to acknowledge this fact, the adult creates resistance to any further efforts to move the child beyond the pain. As an adult,

Robert reflected back on this situation: "When my father agreed with me, I realized that he clearly understood the pain I was experiencing, so I was ready to listen. My father had established credibility with me" (Erickson et al., 1985, p. 628).

Children Who Have Negative or Anxious Thoughts

Some children exhibit resistance because they have negative or anxious thoughts at the prospect of changing their behavior. Such children may view the short-term negative consequences of looking foolish, not knowing what to do, or experiencing "put-downs" from peers as more significant that the potentially reinforcing long-term consequences of changing their behavior. Several techniques can be used in such situations.

Exploring Children's Expectations and Fears

It is important for teachers to encourage children to discuss their fears and anticipated reactions to changing their behavior. Contrary to what some would expect, expressing anxious thoughts actually helps children gain control over them. Sometimes adults are reluctant to have children discuss their fears, believing that talking about them will make them come true. However, children's anxieties are usually reduced when discussed in the presence of a warm, nonjudgmental teacher. Having children share their fears about changing their behavior also enables the teacher to identify and correct any irrational beliefs about the situation using cognitive restructuring techniques. Zionts (1996) described how teachers can use one such approach, rational–emotive therapy (RET), to change children's unrealistic and catastrophic beliefs that prevent them from performing desired behaviors. Briefly, children are taught to counteract irrational beliefs with more positive and realistic self-statements. To accomplish this, a teacher directly challenges a child's irrational ideas and models rational reinterpretations of disturbing events. For example, a child may be taught to tell herself that, although her situation may be annoying or inconvenient, it is not catastrophic and, moreover, there are usually things that she can do to improve it.

Setting Up a Small Alteration in Behavior

Children who hold negative beliefs are more likely to comply with a request to make a small rather than a large change in their behavior.

Therefore, the teacher should set small goals for children and then reinforce successive approximations of the terminal behavior. Behavior is not performed in one swoop, but needs to be shaped using a step-by-step process.

I was asked to help a teacher manage a student described as being highly resistant to completing multiplication worksheets. The teacher had tried sending the student to the principal, getting her additional help in math, and calling her parents. None of these techniques had worked. When I became involved, the student had about 12 uncompleted worksheets, each containing 20 problems. The student had little motivation to complete any of the worksheets—she could see no light at the end of the tunnel, so she simply refused to do any of them. Nevertheless, the teacher continued to give her a new worksheet every day, just like everyone else in the class.

Here was my solution. First, I told the teacher to throw out all the old worksheets that accumulated in the student's folder. The student probably felt overwhelmed and believed it was impossible to catch up and, consequently, had given up trying. Second, the teacher was to write one multiplication problem in the middle of a piece of white typing paper. Nothing else was to appear on the paper except a place for the student to write her name. Third, I instructed the teacher to tell the student that if she completed the problem on her "new" worksheet, she could spend the rest of the 15-minute session drawing at the free-time table in the back of the room.

The teacher looked at me with an expression of shock and dismay. She said, "Do you really expect me to let her get away with only having one problem on her worksheet when all the other students in the class have 20 problems on their worksheets? I'm not going to reward bad performance by letting this student get away with a worthless assignment." I reminded the teacher that the student was not completing any math problems, although she received a new worksheet every day. I then said, "If you get her to complete one problem— which is certainly well within her ability—she will have completed 100% more problems than she has in the last two weeks combined." I explained how the completion of one problem was only the initial step. We would double the number of problems on subsequent days until the student was able to complete the entire worksheet. By starting with small approximations of the desired outcome, the student was more likely to experience success. In addition, it became difficult for the student to be resistant since the requested change in behavior was so minor. Behavior change is like a kaleidoscope. Even if the tube is turned only a fraction of an inch, the entire pattern nevertheless changes. Requiring a small change in behavior is more likely to seem inconsequential to children, yet it has the effect of reducing resistance by setting in motion larger changes.

Using a Force-Field Analysis

Although the name of this technique sounds like something from a science fiction movie, the technique was developed by Lewin (1951) to help individuals who were resistant to change. Using this technique, the teacher assists a child in listing all possible ways to avoid complying with a request, called *resisting forces*. Although a teacher could easily list all the avoidance behaviors in which a child engages, it is more effective to have a child do it since it takes advantage of his resistant point of view. Having a child brainstorm all the possible reasons for and ways to be noncompliant with the required behavior or activity serves two purposes.

First, by listing ways to avoid the task, a child is actually being cooperative. That is, she is following the teacher's direction and, by so doing, is being compliant. Once a child is compliant in one area, it is easier to get compliance in other areas. This technique is considered paradoxical since, in order for a child to resist, she must comply (Simon & Vetter-Zemitzsch, 1985). In a force-field analysis, a child can resist engaging in a task by listing all the ways of resisting; however, by listing those ways, a child is complying with the request to list them.

Second, by having a child list ways to avoid the task or activity, the context surrounding the resistant behavior is changed. Changing the context also changes the meaning of the behavior and, consequently, the purpose for engaging in it. All behavior is purposeful and engaged in to achieve a specific outcome (Neel & Cessna, 1990). For example, a child may refuse to follow a teacher's directions because he believes his resistance will impress his peers. The resistant behavior is purposeful since it is engaged in to achieve the outcome of impressing peers. Achieving the desired outcome is dependent upon the context of resistance being unacceptable to the teacher. However, when a teacher requests that the student list all the ways of avoiding the request, the context surrounding resistant behavior is changed— it no longer serves the purpose of impressing peers.

After the child lists all possible avoidance behaviors, the teacher and child list all possible approach behaviors, called *driving forces.* Driving forces refer to behaviors a child can engage in to approach rather than avoid a task or activity. Children are more likely to list approach behaviors after first listing avoidance behaviors because the latter are more congruent with a child's resistant frame of reference.

The final step requires that the teacher and child plan ways to reduce the number and impact of the avoidance behaviors while increasing the number and impact of the approach behaviors. For example, a child may identify talking to his neighbor as an avoidance behavior rather than completing his reading assignment. An appropriate approach behavior may be allowing the child to talk to his neighbor after completing his assignment. This suggestion also makes use of the Premack principle (1959) in which access to a desired behavior or activity is contingent upon the performance of a less desirable behavior or activity.

Using Rehearsal To Practice New Behaviors

Children frequently are reluctant to try new behaviors, either because they feel unable to perform them or are unsure of the outcome. Resistance due to these two common concerns can be reduced by arranging for a child to practice the desired behaviors before actually using them in real life. Practice provides a child with confidence that she can, in fact, adequately perform the behaviors while receiving feedback about the possible reactions she will receive from others. The techniques of instruction described earlier—modeling, rehearsal, role playing, and feedback—can be used here. For example, a student was petrified to give an oral report in front of the class. Attempts to encourage him to get in front of the class were met with severe resistance; he would either cry or run from the room. Both the boy and his teacher reported that he was afraid of messing up the report and that his peers would laugh at him. A simple and straightforward method for reducing his resistance was to have him role-play giving a report under various situations.

Providing a child with repeated practice increases his confidence level and allows him to anticipate and prepare for any negative reactions he may receive from others. Initial role-play scenarios should guarantee a positive outcome. After a child becomes proficient at performing certain behaviors during a role play that guarantees a positive outcome, the scenarios can gradually be modified to include more real-life responses from others. The goal is to teach children that, no matter how socially appropriate their behavior is, they will not always get a positive response from others. By slowly interjecting more real-life responses from others, the child's ability to handle negative reactions can be built up, thereby reducing the possibility of future resistance to performing a certain behavior.

Use of scenarios that guarantee a positive reaction and then moving to more realistic responses is based on Meichenbaum's (1985) approach to dealing with anxiety, called *stress inoculation training*. The term stress inoculation was used as an analogy to medical inoculation against various diseases. For example, to inoculate a child against polio, she is given a vaccine made out of the polio virus. The idea is that when the body is injected with a watered-down version of the polio virus, it builds up antibodies that will fight any subsequent exposure to the full-strength virus. Similarly, stress inoculation is designed to build psychological antibodies by exposing individuals to situations that gradually become more stressful and that arouse psychological defenses without overwhelming them. Consequently, through experiencing success in coping with increasing but manageable levels of stress, individuals acquire what Meichenbaum called "learned resourcefulness." Maag (1994) described issues and provided recommendations for using stress inoculation training with children.

Resistance Due to Environmental Factors

The term *environment* refers to the conglomerate of circumstances and events involving both inanimate and animate objects in which individuals interact on an instance-to-instance basis (Johnston & Pennypacker, 1980). Environment exerts a powerful influence on behavior. People rely on environmental cues to help select and perform appropriate behaviors for a given situation. For example, the behaviors displayed in church are probably different from those exhibited at a major league baseball game. The baseball environment provides cues that it is appropriate to dress casually, drink beer, eat hotdogs, and yell at the umpires. In many churches, if one were to come dressed in cutoffs carrying a six-pack of beer and hotdogs and booing the preacher's sermon, one would indeed appear strange. These two environments serve as cues to help people select appropriate behaviors. However, the environment has no "personal agenda." Therefore, it can exert either a positive or a negative influence on behavior. Sometimes the negative influence it can exert results in children exhibiting resistant behaviors.

A variety of environmental factors can interfere with a child's achieving a successful outcome. However, these factors generally can be classified under two global, and somewhat similar, categories: environmental variables incompatible with change and environmental variables maintaining problem behavior.

Environmental Variables Incompatible with Change

When aspects of the environment are at odds with a desired behavior, resistance often occurs. In these instances, the environment may be failing to provide sufficient cues to activate appropriate behavior. For example, a teacher may designate a certain student to be a peer helper during an independent math practice activity. The peer helper is verbally identified by the teacher and given a button to wear. However, if the teacher forgets to give this peer the button, another student may not remember who is designated to provide help. Therefore, the student may instead talk to his neighbor, which would break the rule of no talking. Consequently, he would appear resistant. In other instances, certain aspects of the environment may be competing with a child who is displaying an appropriate behavior. For example, many students find it hard to work quietly if the norms of their peer group are to talk and write notes. That is, these norms compete with or distract the student from completing the desired responses of working quietly. A third environmental variable incompatible with change may be the negative habits children have developed. For example, some students may find it difficult to study because good study habits have never been incorporated into their daily routine. Having such a student continue the same routine and pattern with the simple addition of inserting a time and a place for studying is not likely to work because the new behavior does not fit with or is not supported by the old pattern.

A variety of techniques can be used for these three situations where the environment is incompatible with change.

Arranging Cues that Make the Desired Behavior More Likely to Occur

Cues involve anything that prompts the occasion for a desired behavior to occur. They represent the antecedents—events that precede behavior. People are confronted with a variety of cues that prompt behavior every day; traffic lights and a ringing phone are two examples. The different colors of a traffic light serve as cues to prompt behavior. As a driver approaches a traffic light and the color turns from yellow to red, for example, that cue prompts her to stop. Similarly, when a person hears a phone ring, the ring is a cue to pick up the phone. It is tempting, although inaccurate, to say that these antecedent cues *control* behavior. Instead, it is the *consequences*—reinforcement or punishment—that actually control behavior. For example, if there was never anyone on the other end of the phone when it rang, a person would quickly learn to ignore the ring. Similarly, the driver stops at a red light because of the consequences that not stopping carries—receiving a traffic ticket, getting into an accident, or injuring a pedestrian.

In some instances, however, a cue is not strong enough to set the occasion for appropriate behavior. For example, a child may not pick up on the stern look she receives from a teacher to stop talking. Therefore, resistance can often be reduced by simply providing extra cues for a child—placing messages on Post-It™ notes in a visible place is an example. Polaroid pictures also can be used to depict an activity in which a child is supposed to engage. For example, when a child sees a picture of herself asking a teacher for assistance, it may set the occasion for other appropriate responses such as trying to find the answer independently.

Reducing Competing Sources of Reinforcement

Frequently, children resist changing their behavior because of the reinforcement—attention from peers or adults—they receive for continuing to engage in the inappropriate behavior. For example, a student may continue to make animal noises in class even when he is punished for doing so or receives reinforcement for behaving appropriately. Most likely, the child continues to be resistant because of the attention he receives from his peers. It will indeed be a difficult task to reduce a child's level of resistance to engaging in inappropriate behavior when he is receiving a payoff. Therefore, efforts to manage resistance need to temporarily shift away from the child and to the people in the environment who provide attention to the inappropriate behavior.

Several techniques can be used to manage the attention others give a child for engaging in inappropriate behavior. One technique is to provide reinforcement to children who ignore the inappropriate behavior. For example, children in the class with the boy who makes animal noises could receive a sticker for every 5 minutes that passed during which they did not look at or talk to him when he made animal noises. Any children who looked at or talked to the boy when he made animal noises would lose one sticker. At the end of the class period, children could exchange their stickers for being allowed to engage in desirable free-time activities.

Two other techniques can be used to reduce competing sources of reinforcement for inappropriate behavior. Both techniques are group-oriented in that the presentation of a reinforcer to the entire group is contingent upon the behavior of either one member of the group or the entire group (Litow & Pumroy, 1975).

The first technique is a *dependent group-oriented contingency*. In this arrangement, reinforcement is delivered to everyone in the group *only* if an identified child performs the desired behavior. This technique is often referred to as the "hero procedure" because it can motivate other children to "root for" the identified child to perform the desired behavior in hopes that everyone can enjoy the reward (Kerr & Nelson, 1983). For example, the teacher of the boy who made animal noises could tell the class that for every 5 minutes that passed during which the boy did not make any animal noises, the entire class would earn a point. If the class earned 20 points by the end of the day, everyone would be able to participate in a popcorn party.

The success of this technique rests on two factors. First, the teacher must limit the degree to which the other children threaten, criticize, or harass the child whose behavior is dependent upon their getting the reward. To ward off this problem, the teacher can tally the number of scapegoating-type comments the other children make. If this number exceeds the number of intervals in which the identified child refrained from engaging in the inappropriate behavior, those children with the excessive marks for scapegoating are excluded from receiving the reward. Second, it is important to assess the extent to which the identified child finds it reinforcing to prevent others from getting a reward by purposely engaging in the inappropriate behavior. It is possible that the identified child finds it more reinforcing to prevent the group from receiving the reward than receiving the reward himself. In such situations, the teacher should either try to find a reward that is more reinforcing to the identified child than the thrill of preventing others from receiving the reward or abandon the use of this technique until an appropriate reinforcer has been found.

The second technique is an *interdependent group-oriented contingency*, whereby the group can earn a reward only if all members of the group perform the desired behavior. This approach has the potential for encouraging children to work together to earn a reward in which they all share equally. The teacher of the child who makes animal noises could say that *everyone* must refrain from making animal noises in order for *anyone* to earn the popcorn party. As with the dependent group-oriented approach, the teacher must watch out for individual children who derive pleasure from spoiling the reward for everyone by misbehaving. The teacher can combat this problem by removing points for the children doing the scapegoating as described above, or by individualizing the behavioral requirements for certain children. In the class with the boy who made animal noises, therefore, several children may also have to refrain from making such noises while other children have to refrain from teasing others. As with any group-oriented approach, if scapegoating or sabotaging persists despite efforts to stop it, the technique should be abandoned.

Changing a Child's Pattern and Routine

Children, like adults, develop patterns or routines specific to certain contexts or situations. Some individuals sit in the back of class in order to be able to daydream or write notes. As long as they continue to sit in the back, efforts at getting them to attend will be difficult. In essence, people pair certain behaviors with specific contexts or situations so that the context or situation serves as a cue to perform the behavior. Through such repeated pairing, the behavior is activated automatically with little conscious awareness of how it is prompted by the environment. Therefore, resistance often can be managed by changing a child's pattern or routine. This recommendation is based on the notion that behavior is meaningful in some but not all contexts. Thus, when the context in which a behavior occurs changes, the meaning of that behavior also changes. Consequently, it is no longer necessary to perform the behavior.

Rosen (1982) described a unique approach that Erickson used to break the pattern and routine of a woman who sought his help to lose weight. The woman weighed 180 pounds but wanted to weigh 130 pounds. In the past, when she would reach 130 pounds she would rush to the kitchen to celebrate her success, promptly gaining back the 50 pounds. Erickson told her he could help, but that she would not like the solution. At this point in her life, the woman was so desperate to lose the weight permanently that she agreed to do anything. Erickson told her to gain 20 pounds and that when she weighed an even 200 pounds she could start reducing. For every pound the woman gained, she implored Erickson to let her start reducing, but Erickson insisted that she gain to an even 200 pounds if his intervention was to be effective. When the woman reached 200 pounds, she was thrilled to finally begin reducing. And when she reached 130 pounds, she never gained the weight back. This intervention was successful because Erickson changed the context surrounding the woman's routine, which had been to reduce and gain. That is, he reversed that pattern and made her gain and reduce. Once the woman had broken the pattern, she could no longer go through the same sequence, as she had done all her life. She apparently had learned to tolerate gaining weight only up to 180 pounds. Many people with weight problems seem to have a tolerance level corresponding to a certain weight, at which point they urgently feel the need to reduce. Erickson succeeded in making the woman's tolerance level intolerable because he made her go beyond it.

An example of changing a child's pattern or routine in the classroom is the "do-nothing chair." When given an assignment, some children refuse to work on it. Instead, they doodle, talk to a neighbor, or daydream. Teacher efforts at redirecting these students are often met with resistance. As described earlier in this chapter, the context of refusing a teacher request may be meaningful to a child because it indicates he can control a teacher and, consequently, gain respect from peers. However, if a teacher responds to this resistance by saying, "If you don't want to work, you can sit in the 'do-nothing chair,'" by changing the context in which resistance takes place, the meaning that engaging in the behavior has for a child also is changed. In this example, the teacher is permitting a child to do nothing. That alteration, in and of itself, changes the context of the student's being able to control the teacher: Most children expect teachers to try and persuade them to do their work. Changing the location of doing nothing also changes the context. If a student refuses to move out of his seat, the teacher can simply make his present location the official do-nothing chair. Either way, the teacher allows the child to do nothing. Consequently, if the child is going to continue to be resistant, he must work on his assignment rather than go to the do-nothing chair, which would be seen as being compliant rather than resistant. Sometimes teachers are reluctant to tell children to do nothing since that is antithetical to what children should be doing in class. However, if traditional methods of managing resistance fail, the child is doing nothing anyway; therefore, there is nothing to lose and a lot to gain by allowing a child to do what he is doing, but changing the context around which the behavior is performed.

Environmental Variables Maintaining Inappropriate Behavior

I previously described a child who made animal noises because of the attention he received from peers and adults even though such attention was primarily negative. This begs the question, How can any child *like* receiving a verbal reprimand from a teacher or vicious comments from peers? For some children, the consequences of their behavior—the negative attention from others—serve to reinforce their belief that they can *control* others. And the perception of being able to control others represents a powerful reinforcer to many individuals.

In other situations, a child may resist changing her behavior because of the negative comments she believes her peers will make. In such cases, the consequences are considered punishing rather than reinforcing. Because most people work to avoid punishment, a child would not want to place herself in a position to be teased for complying with a teacher's request. For example, many teenagers in therapy are taught to be assertive. However, teaching them to be assertive probably results in their peers ridiculing them for engaging in behavior outside of the norm. Such ridicule is a form of punishment that, by definition, has the effect of reducing or eliminating behavior. Consequently, some children may appear resistant to trying new behaviors because they are afraid their peers will make fun of them. How many times have parents told children who are being teased by peers in school to simply tell the teacher? Children typically respond to this suggestion like this: "Oh right mom! That'll be a big help. Then I'll get teased even more for tattling on them." Several recommendations may be followed when environmental consequences are either reinforcing inappropriate behavior or punishing appropriate behavior.

Finding Effective Reinforcers for the New Behavior

Compliance is enhanced when the desired behavior is followed by reinforcement. *Reinforcement* refers to anything that follows a behavior that increases the future probability of that behavior occurring. Reinforcement *always* works. If a behavior does not increase after something was administered, then, by definition, that something was not a reinforcer. The two most difficult aspects of reinforcement are (a) finding something that is reinforcing to a child (reinforcement is individual, and what one child may find reinforcing another child may not) and (b) giving a child access to the reinforcer only *after* performing the desired behavior. For example, if a teacher wants to use a computer game as a reinforcer for assignment completion but the child has the same computer game at home, this activity will not be reinforcing since the child can play it any time.

To most effectively use reinforcement to manage resistance, the teacher should start with changes that are likely to make a child feel better in a short time, or are likely to result in dramatic or at least visible improvement. When children notice the benefits from engaging in a behavior, they are more likely to engage in subsequent behaviors that make greater demands on them and take longer to get a desired result. This recommendation follows the principle of *shaping* or *successive approximations* described previously.

Finding Alternative Sources of Reinforcement

When peers either reinforce a child for engaging in inappropriate behavior or punish her for engaging in appropriate behavior, the focus of efforts to reduce resistance needs to shift from the child to her peers. Without such a shift in focus, a child will probably be resistant to giving up the inappropriate behavior. The shift I am referring to involves getting a child's peers to ignore the inappropriate behavior and provide positive comments when she engages in the appropriate behavior. This approach is known in the literature as *promoting entrapment*. If one looks up the word entrapment in the dictionary, one is likely to find the following definition: "to catch in a trap; to lure into danger or difficulty." People often think of entrapment in negative terms. However, in the present context, the term refers to restructuring the existing reinforcement contingencies in peer interaction groups so that the new contingencies will reinforce the appropriate to-be-performed behavior of the target child (McConnell, 1987). In essence, the teacher wants to teach and reinforce peers for engaging in positive responses to a child who exhibits the desired behavior.

I had the opportunity to work with an extremely socially withdrawn fourth-grade boy whose peers teased him mercilessly on the playground at recess. Consequently, his social withdrawal was negatively reinforced in that the more he withdrew, the fewer negative comments he received. A very simple two-step program was developed to increase his socialization at recess. First, he was taught how to interact appropriately with peers during a game of four-square. Second, several fourth graders who played four-square at recess were told that, every time one of them asked the boy to join in the game and subsequently made a positive statement to him, an adult observer would make a tally mark next to that child's name. The number of tally marks each child received could be used to purchase free-time activities. This technique was effective in getting the boy to become more socially active with his peers. A common criticism of this approach is that it is "artificial." Although this criticism may be true, it is important to understand that managing resistance requires initially making small changes in the desired direction. Once a desired pattern has been established, more natural consequences can be initiated.

Teaching Adaptive Means of Attaining Reinforcement

All behavior is purposeful: Children engage in behavior to achieve some outcome. This assertion carries two implications for managing resistance. First, the outcome a child desires is most likely socially acceptable and appropriate. For example, a child may get into a fight during recess in order to impress a certain peer group. The desire to affiliate with one's peers is normal and appropriate. However, the specific behavior in which a child engages to achieve that outcome (e.g., fighting) is inappropriate. Second, by determining the desired outcome, a child can be taught a replacement behavior—one that represents an appropriate way of achieving the same outcome.

Neel and Cessna (1990) developed the Outcome Analysis Worksheet for determining the intent (outcome) of children's behavior. A running narrative is kept of a child's performance, which is then broken down into discrete incidents. From an accompanying definition sheet, a probable outcome (intent) is selected for each incident and outcomes are grouped according to certain themes (e.g., power/control, escape/avoidance, attention, acceptance/affiliation, expression of self-gratification, justice/revenge). Based on this analysis, children can be taught appropriate replacement behaviors. For example, a child who gets into a fight to impress peers may instead be taught how to initiate a conversation with the desired peers on some mutually interesting topic. By comparison, the typical approach of teaching the child an alternate behavior to fighting, such as being assertive, will be met with resistance since that behavior does not address the intent that fighting initially served.

Trying to determine the desired outcome of a child's behavior requires the teacher to engage in problem solving. Therefore, the teacher is less likely to personalize a child's resistance because the teacher is actively involved in determining the potential outcome of the behavior. Any time a teacher can avoid personalizing resistance, he or she is more likely to have access to a wider variety of options for dealing with a child. On the other hand, when a teacher personalizes a child's behavior, the teacher is more likely to respond in a stereo-typic fashion that is likely to be ineffective. This is the crux of the problem: resistance due to adult factors.

Resistance Due to Adult Factors

In many respects, humans are a stubborn and inflexible species. When a solution is not working, most people perform it even more frequently. Adults continue to respond to children in a similar fashion even when the response is not working for a couple of rea-sons. First, as I already alluded to, if teachers personalize a childs' behavior, they are more likely to overreact emotionally and engage in resistance-engendering behavior. Whenever children "push teach-ers' buttons," teachers tend to respond in similar ways as in the past—it is an automatic, habitual pattern that is difficult to break. Second, responding to children's resistance differently than one has in the past is risky, both for a child and for the adult. Teachers may be concerned about the potential outcome of risking to do something *really different* with children. Recall that a risk is threatening because it upsets the stability of the daily routine; and stability is comfort-ing, even when the habitual behavior does not result in a desired outcome.

This homeostasis results in the application of *linear intervention* (Watzlawick, Weakland, & Fisch, 1974). For example, if a student stays after school for misbehaving, the problem is presumed to have been addressed by the punishment. However, what if the student misbehaves again? The linear solution would be to keep her after school for 2 days, and so forth. These types of solutions are called "more of the same," and they rarely work. Like any intervention, if they worked, teachers would be using them less rather than more often. In essence, teachers limit the options for responding to children's oppositional behavior. Consequently, ordinary difficulties children present become more severe because the initial problem was mishandled and remains unresolved. Here is where the crux of the matter lies: Teachers need to abandon their preconceived notions about what they *should* do or say to a child and expand their perspective to adopt new patterns of behavior.

Adopting New Patterns of Behavior

Teachers generally have more knowledge than they realize of how to deal effectively with children. It is amazing what teachers could do if they recognize all of the available options. Unfortunately, teachers often follow a careful routine without realizing they are restricting their behavior. They tend to place limits on so many things and, in turn, are limited in their patterns of behavior. Every magician, for example, will not let children too near or they will see through the trick. This is not the case with adults. Adults tend to have closed minds. They think they are watching everything, but they resort to a routine way of looking. Therefore, to effectively manage resistance, it is important for teachers to be comprehensive and unrestrictive in behavior and avoid doing what they have done in the past. This recommendation is difficult to follow because teachers rely on several predictable sources to manage resistance.

First, teachers learn how to deal with students based on information received from university courses. Some of the interventions that teacher trainees heard professors lecture about or read in textbooks may be appealing, so teachers try them. Second, teachers manage students based on how other teachers manage their students. The teachers' lounge is often the setting for teachers lamenting the difficulty of dealing with resistant children. Sometimes solutions actually are shared! Third, teachers manage students based on how the teachers were managed by their own teachers—they either apply the same techniques or go to the opposite extreme because of distaste for a certain method used by a particular teacher. My point is that the sources teachers draw upon to manage students and the patterns of dealing with students are predictable, limited, and habitual. This habitual pattern is activated automatically: When a child engages in resistant behavior, the teacher relates that new information to familiar and existing information. Consequently, it is difficult for the teacher to perceive different options for managing resistance.

When speaking to a group of teachers, I often illustrate the diffi-culty of recognizing different options by asking every other person in the group to make a fist; then on the count of three, the person next to him or her must get the fist open as quickly as possible. Invariably, most people try to force the other person's fist open. I then inquire how many people simply *asked* the person to open his or her fist. After the laughter and sighs of mild embarrassment subside, I point out that *asking* is well within teachers' repertoires, yet is rarely considered as an option. Frequently, someone will respond that asking does not always result in the person's opening his or her fist. I readily agree and then stress that the important thing is doing something different and if that does not work, then try something else—*anything else.*

This approach to managing resistance goes against the grain of what most teachers have been conditioned to believe: Specific inter-ventions must be developed and implemented to handle a problem. As a result of this thinking, teachers seem to be on a perpetual search for "the intervention"—one that is practical, easy to use, and pro-duces quick results with all types of students. It is as if teachers expect that they can produce change in children's resistant behavior as eas-ily as getting the carburetor adjusted on a car. In fact, teachers possess a variety of potential techniques for responding to children's resistant behavior, based on the multitude of experiences they have encoun-tered throughout their lives. Such experiences include how a person dealt with getting lost on a vacation, putting up with Uncle Elmer's pontifications at the Thanksgiving dinner table, dealing with a slow checker at a department store, or telling a friend he has an irritating habit without hurting his feelings.

Erickson was once asked to conduct a psychiatric consultation concerning a catatonic schizophrenic who was not demonstrating adequate progress recovering (Rossi, Ryan, & Sharp, 1983). Schizophrenia is a disorder characterized by a severe disruption of thought processes that results in a sharp break with reality and a withdrawal from social interaction. In catatonic schizophrenia, the individual suddenly losses all animation and tends to remain motion-less in a single position for hours or even days. Erickson walked into the room where the patient was sitting in a catatonic state surrounded by several psychiatrists discussing various conventional psychiatric treatment approaches, such as the use of psychotropic medication, electroconvulsive shock therapy, and psychoanalysis. The psychia-trists asked Erickson for his recommendation. Without hesitation, Erickson walked up to the patient and stomped on his feet several times. The patient immediately came out of his catatonic state! I am not suggesting that teachers stomp on their resistant students' feet, but rather that many potential ways of responding to children are available if teachers would only expand their perceptions to encompass other areas of their experiences. Foot stomping was well within the skill repertoire of the other psychiatrists, but they were too narrowly focused on "psychiatric techniques" to access this approach.

Joining a Child: Accepting or Encouraging Resistance

Too often, intentionally or unintentionally, adults attempt to inculcate children with a way of looking at and dealing with the world that has worked well for adults, but that may be clumsy and inappropriate from a child's view of the world. Adults expect children to accept authority. Trying to lecture or otherwise force a child to comply with an adult version of the world will result in resistance. To deal effectively with resistance, adults must learn to join children in their frame of reference. No two people are alike, and no two people understand the same sentence the same way. Therefore, in dealing with children, adults must try not to fit them to an adult concept of what they should be. Instead, adults should try to discover what a child's concept of herself is.

I began this chapter with the story of Frank, a young boy who threw his book on the floor and refused to pick it up. This behavior was perfectly rational from Frank's perspective—he was feeling oppositional. To maintain his oppositional frame of mind, he had to resist his teacher's request to pick up his book. As I described, Frank's teacher dealt with the situation using a very traditional method. Here is another approach that *uses* Frank's oppositional frame of mind: After he responded to his teacher's request to pick up his book by saying, "No, I won't, and you can't make me—nobody can make me," his teacher could counter by saying, "You're right, I can't make you pick up that book. I can't even make you move that book one inch. And I know you *can't* move the book one foot . . . you certainly can't move the book closer to your desk. *And* I know there's no way you can put the book on your desk!"

This response acknowledges Frank's oppositional frame of reference and uses it to get him to comply with his teacher's request. To continue to be oppositional, Frank has to comply. When told he can't move the book, Frank either moves it to continue being resistant, in which case the teacher achieved the desired outcome, or he refuses to move the book, in which case he is no longer being oppositional since he is agreeing with the teacher. Although in the latter case the book still remains on the floor, Frank's oppositional frame of reference has been disrupted, which makes it easier to subsequently direct him toward the desired outcome. I described this approach earlier as being paradoxical because by encouraging or accepting resistance the teacher puts a child in a position where his attempts to resist are defined as cooperative behavior. A child finds himself following the directives no matter what he does, because what he does is defined as cooperation. Once a child is cooperating—that is, once his resistant frame of reference has been broken—it is easier to divert him into the desired outcome.

Haley (1973) described Erickson's skill at joining a 10-year-old boy's resistance to achieve a desired outcome. This boy had been brought, against his will, to see Erickson because he wet his bed every night. The boy's parents forcefully placed him screaming in Erickson's office. When the boy paused to catch his breath for a fresh scream, Erickson told him to go ahead and scream again. After the boy again screamed and paused to take a breath, Erickson screamed. The boy turned to look at Erickson and was told it was now his turn to scream. The boy and Erickson took turns screaming. After several turns, Erickson told him they could continue taking turns screaming but that would get awfully tiresome. Erickson then told the boy he would rather take his turn sitting down in his chair, which he did. He pointed to a vacant chair and the boy took his turn sitting in the other chair.

Erickson joined the boy's resistance by screaming himself—that is, he broke the boy's resistance by establishing the expectation that they were taking turns screaming. Once the boy's resistant frame of reference was changed, Erickson led the boy in another direction by changing the "game" to taking turns sitting down. He was now able to address the problem of the boy's bedwetting. Erickson described this approach as analogous to trying to change the course of a river. If people oppose the river by trying to block it, it will merely go over and around. But if people accept the force of the river and divert it in a new direction, the force of the river will cut a new channel.

Providing a Worse Alternative

One of the common themes I have stressed throughout this chapter is the influence that context has on behavior. Context is what gives behavior meaning. Lifeguards have more meaning in the context of a swimming pool than on a ski slope. Cutting open a person's skin with a knife has positive meaning in the context of a surgeon performing a life-saving operation and a negative meaning for a mugger attempting to steal someone's wallet. Many of the recommendations and stories I have presented have focused on changing the context surrounding a behavior. There are two other ways to change the context of a behavior, thereby changing the meaning and reducing resistance: providing a worse alternative and stressing the positive aspects of the behavior.

A way to provide a worse alternative is to have a child engage in what is called *negative practice* (e.g., Azrin, Nunn, & Frantz, 1980). In this technique, a child is required to repeatedly engage in the inappropriate behavior as a way to change its context and meaning. Many teachers already use this technique. For example, a teacher dealt with a child who spit on a peer by having the offending child repeatedly spit into a can for 30 minutes. Other teachers deal with children who tap a pencil on their desk by having them tap the pencil on the desk for a specified period of time. One of my graduate students told me how he used this technique when he was a substitute teacher in a class for children with emotional and behavioral problems. After the students had been assigned to complete a page of math problems, one boy was writing the name of his school followed by the word "suck" all over his paper. The substitute teacher approached the boy and told him that he had very distinctive handwriting, but that he was sure he could put it to a more creative use. He suggested trying to write the two words in a variety of print styles and colors. The boy quickly lost interest in the task and began to do his math assignment. The substitute teacher had suggested a worse alternative and by so doing changed the context and meaning that the inappropriate behavior had for the boy. The substitute teacher employed a paradoxical technique because, by asking the boy to do what he was already doing, the student was caught in the position described previously where oppositional behavior was defined as cooperation. If the boy resisted the teacher's request to write the two words on his assignment, the desired goal would be achieved. However, if the boy did as the teacher requested, he was no longer being resistant because he was complying with the direction, thus changing the context. Consequently, his desire to engage in the behavior vanished.

Rosen (1982) described how Erickson used this approach with his daughter who came home from grade school one day saying, "Daddy, all the girls in school bite their nails and I want to be in style too." He replied, "You certainly ought to be in style and you have a lot of catching up to do. Now the best way to catch up is to bite your nails for 15 minutes three times a day, every day." His daughter began enthusiastically at first. Then she began quitting early and one day she said, "Daddy, I'm going to start a new style at school—long nails." By joining his daughter in her desire to be in style, Rosen commented, Erickson proceeded to make the "stylish behavior" into an ordeal. It became more of a bother to keep the behavior than to give it up.

Stressing the Positive Aspect of a Behavior

Stressing the positive aspect of a behavior derives from the assertion I have made throughout this chapter: Every behavior is appropriate given some context or frame of reference. The name for changing the context and, consequently, the meaning of a behavior is called *reframing*. Reframing modifies a person's perceptions or views of a behavior (Watzlawick et al., 1974). For example, teachers use reframing whenever they ask children to see an issue from a different perspective. Reframing can focus on the meaning of a behavior or the context wherein a behavior occurs.

Meaning Reframe

When teachers reframe meaning, they are challenging the purpose that a child has assigned to a problem behavior. Usually, the longer a child attaches a particular meaning to a behavior, the more necessary the behavior itself becomes for maintaining consistency and predictability. In other words, the longer a particular meaning is attached to a behavior, the more a child is likely to see things in only one way or from one perspective. Reframing helps children by providing alternative ways to view a problem behavior without directly challenging the behavior itself and by loosening a child's frame of reference.

Once the meaning of a behavior changes, the person's response to the situation also changes, provided the reframe is valid and acceptable to the person. The essence of a meaning reframe is to give a situation or a behavior a new label or a new name that has a different meaning. This new meaning should have a different, and usually positive, connotation. For example, a child's "stubbornness" might be reframed as "independence," or "greediness" might be reframed as "ambitiousness." The following is an example of a meaning reframe.

Bandler and Grinder (1982) described a therapist who worked with a woman who had a compulsive behavior: She was a cleaning freak. She was a person who dusted plant leaves and venetian blinds. Her husband and three kids could handle almost all her efforts to keep the house clean except for her attempts to care for the carpet. She spent a lot of her time trying to get people not to walk on it, because they left footprints—not mud or dirt—in the pile of the rug. When this woman looked down at the carpet and saw a footprint, she experienced an intense negative reaction in her stomach, as if someone had rung it out like a washcloth. At this point, she would rush off to get the vacuum cleaner and vacuum the carpet. She vacuumed the carpet several times a day and spent a lot of time trying to get people to come in the back door, nagging them if they did not, or getting them to take their shoes off and walk delicately.

The family seemed to get along fine if they were not at home. If they went out to dinner or a movie, they had no problems. But at home, everybody referred to the mother as being a nag mainly because of her carpet behavior. After hearing this story, the therapist turned to the mother and said, "I want you to close your eyes and see your carpet, and see that there is not a single footprint on it anywhere. It's clean and fluffy—not a mark anywhere." The mother closed her eyes and began smiling contentedly. The therapist continued, "And realize fully that this means you are totally alone, and that the people you care for and love are nowhere around." The mother's expression shifted radically and she began to frown. The therapist ended by saying, "Now, put a few footprints there and look at those footprints and know that the people you care about in the world are nearby." This reframe was effective because the new meaning was acceptable to the woman. Although she valued a clean carpet, she valued her husband and children even more. Therefore, when the meaning of having a clean carpet was reframed to mean her loved ones were gone, her desire to keep the carpet clean vanished.

I used a meaning reframe with Benjamin, a 10-year-old boy I had been seeing in my private practice. At one of our sessions, Benjamin said he was angry about always having to go on errands with his mother. He related how his mother would drop off his younger sister at his aunt's house to play with their cousins, thereby insinuating the sister got the better end of the deal. I turned to Benjamin and said, "It seems to me that your mother wants you to go on errands with her because she really enjoys your company. You're like the man of the family when you're running errands with your mom. She probably depends on you. And she obviously likes talking to you more than to your younger sister who doesn't have much to say anyway. That must mean she really values your friendship and likes to treat you as an equal when you are running errands with her." His facial expression changed dramatically and a smile began to crease the corners of his mouth. I then knew he had accepted the meaning reframe. Whereas the previous meaning Benjamin had attached to going on errands was that his mother was trying to punish him, the new meaning was that his mother valued his company and treated him, on these occasions, like an equal. Benjamin bought into this new meaning because it was congruent with what many boys want from their mother—to be needed and thought of as equals.

Context Reframe

Besides reframing the meaning of a behavior, teachers can reframe the context in which a problem behavior occurs. Reframing the context helps a child explore and decide *when, where,* and *with whom* a given problem behavior is useful or appropriate (Bandler & Grinder, 1982). In essence, context reframing helps children answer the question, "In what place in your life is a particular behavior useful and appropriate?" Context reframing is based on the assumption that every behavior is useful in some, but not all, contexts or situations. Thus, when a child says, "I won't do my assignment," a context reframe would be, "In what situations, or with what people, is it useful or even helpful not to do what an adult asks?" Two situations immediately come to mind: if a child is being solicited by another child to experiment with drugs or if an adult stranger is trying to convince a child to get into his car against the child's will. Although the child may not initially comply, the teacher has effectively counteracted a child's resistant frame of reference and, consequently, it will be easier to lead her in the direction of the desired outcome.

It is easy to confuse context and meaning reframing. *Meaning reframing* involves directly trying to change the meaning of a behavior, whereas *context reframing* involves trying to find another context in which the inappropriate behavior becomes appropriate. I believe the confusion arises because typically when the context is changed, the meaning of a behavior also changes. In fact, that is the goal when using a context reframe: By changing the context to point out situations where the inappropriate behavior is appropriate, the meaning attached to the behavior in the problem situation changes and, consequently, the desire to engage in the behavior vanishes. Therefore, in both meaning and context reframing, adults try to change meaning of a child's behavior. In the former, the meaning is directly challenged; in the latter, the context is changed to elicit a change in meaning.

The following story told by Bandler and Grinder (1982) of the noted family therapist, Virginia Satir, provides an example of context reframing. The father in the family Satir was treating was a banker, professionally stuffy, but very well intentioned. He was a good provider for his family and was concerned enough to seek therapy. His wife was an extreme placater in Satir's terminology. A placater is a person who will agree with anything and apologize for everything. When you say, "What a nice morning," the placater says, "Yes, I'm sorry." The daughter was an interesting combination of the parents. Thinking that her father was the bad person and her mother the good person, she always sided with her mother. However, she acted like her father. The father's chief complaint was that his wife had not done a very good job raising their daughter because the daughter was very stubborn. At one time when he made this complaint, Satir looked at the father and said, "You're a man who has gotten ahead in your life. Is this true?"

"Yes," replied the father.

"Was all that you have just given to you? Did your father own the bank and just say, 'Here, you're president of the bank'?"

"No, no. I worked my way up."

"So you have some tenacity, don't you?"

"Yes," said the father.

Satir then got to the crux of the context reframe. "Well, there is a part of you that has allowed you to be able to get where you are, and to be a good banker. And sometimes you have to refuse people things that you would like to be able to give them because you know if you did, something bad would happen later on."

"Yes."

"Well, there's a part of you that's been stubborn enough to really protect yourself in very important ways."

"Well, yes. But, you know, you can't let this kind of thing get out of control," protested the father.

Ignoring the father's last statement, Satir went on. "Now, I want you to turn and look at your daughter, and to realize beyond a doubt that you've taught her how to be stubborn and how to stand up for herself, and that this is something priceless. This gift that you've given to her is something that can't be bought, and it's something that may save her life. Imagine how valuable that will be when your daughter goes out on a date with a man who has bad intentions."

In this example, Satir changed the context of being stubborn, which was initially viewed by the father as a bad trait in the context of the family. However, it becomes good in the context of banking and in the context of a man trying to take advantage of the father's daughter on a date. Satir changed the context the father used to evaluate his daughter's behavior. Her behavior of being stubborn with him no longer will be seen as her fighting with him. Instead, it most likely will be viewed as a personal achievement: He had taught her to protect herself from men with bad intentions.

The pattern similar in both context and meaning reframes is that every experience and every behavior in the world is appropriate, given some context or frame of reference. Much of the behavior children exhibit that adults tend to label as resistance indicates that their context is internal and based on past experiences. When, for example, a teacher says to a student, "You really did a great job completing your math problems," and the student responds with, "Fine, but I don't really care and I didn't do that good a job, so I wish you wouldn't lie to me," that is a pretty good indication that the boy is operating out of a unique internal frame of reference. Upon further exploration, it may become apparent that, from past experience, the boy takes a compliment to mean that he will just have to do more work or that teacher demands will increase in the future. A lot of teachers' ability to deal with resistance rests on realizing that what seems bizarre and inappropriate is simply a statement about the failure to appreciate the context on which the behavior is based.

Manipulating Children

The word *manipulate* probably engenders negative connotations to many people. In fact, one of the behaviors that adults find particularly troublesome is when children try to manipulate them. The classic example is when a child asks her father if she can go to a party, receives the answer "no," and then asks the same thing of her mother who says "yes." In such a situation, parents feel set up and, consequently, often get angry at each other and the child. Adults dislike manipulation just as much when it originates from other adults. Scam games and bogus contests that are commonly exposed on television journalism programs make people angry. However, the use of manipulation is not as devious as it may first appear. The very process of teaching children is manipulative. Teachers manipulate materials, curricula, and instructional techniques. Teachers manipulate children when they implement any behavior change technique. In fact, every interaction with others can be considered a manipulation since the goal is usually to elicit a response (Watzlawick, 1978). Therefore, we might as well manipulate effectively, relevantly, and constructively. By manipulating appropriately, teachers can reduce resistant behavior.

One of the easiest ways to manipulate children is through the use of surprise or shock (Farrelly & Brandsma, 1978), which helps break up rigid mental sets that all people possess. The unexpected always helps deal with resistant children—never do the expected. As a counselor at a psychiatric hospital for adolescents, I was working with a particularly oppositional boy, Allen. He hated to talk to his mother on the phone. When his mother called, he would become extremely resistant, throwing a tantrum that often escalated to the point of having to place him in a time-out room. Being placed in the time-out room was just what Allen wanted because then he could avoid talking to his mother. As part of his treatment plan, he had to talk to his mother when she called during free time so that they could begin discussing some of the issues that had resulted in his hospitalization. If he refused to talk to her, he was placed in a time-out area and lost all his daily points. One day during free time the phone rang. I told Allen the call was for him, and he immediately became resistant, saying, "No way, I'm not going to talk to her," as he started walking to the time-out area. I put the phone to my ear and loudly said, "Yes, Mr. Simmons, Allen is right here." Mr. Simmons was Allen's school principal. Allen looked at me with a terrified expression on his face. After all, it is not every day that a child gets a call from his principal. Allen slowly approached the phone and tentatively said, "Hello." Well, Mr. Simmons was not on the other end—Allen's mother was. Allen was so surprised and relieved not to have to talk to his principal that he said, "Oh, Mom, am I ever glad it's you on the phone!"

The following is a unique way a first-year teacher used surprise to diffuse a confrontation with a student. The teacher was nervous as she was calling role. As she finished she asked if there were any students whose names she had not called. A tough-looking boy in the back of the class, wearing jeans and a T-shirt with a pack of cigarettes rolled up in one sleeve, and leaning back in his chair while cleaning his fingernails with a penknife, looked up and said, "Yeah, you didn't call my name."

"And what is your name?" inquired the teacher.

The boy looked at her and said, "Fuck you."

There was a sound of students taking deep breaths before a hush fell over the room. But without changing her expression, the teacher replied, "Is 'you' your first or last name?" This unexpected response caught the student off guard and diffused his desire to be confrontational. By doing the unexpected, an adult can cause a lot of rearranging in a child's thinking.

A second way to manipulate children involves encouraging an appropriate response by initially frustrating it (Haley, 1973). Using this approach, the teacher directs a child to behave in a certain way and, as she begins to do so, cuts off the response and shifts to another area. When the teacher returns to that directive again, the child will be more responsive because she has developed a readiness to respond but was frustrated. For example, I worked with a teacher who had a student who rarely answered questions or offered much information aloud in class. The more the teacher tried to encourage the student to respond, the less she responded. I told the teacher to be patient and observe the student carefully for even a slight attempt, under any circumstances, to talk in class. Right before the student was about to speak, I instructed the teacher to briefly interrupt her. Again, when the student was about to speak, the teacher briefly interrupted. After several interruptions, the student blurted out the answer before the teacher could interrupt her. By initially inhibiting the student from talking, it was possible to increase her desire to talk.

Conclusion

Teachers should follow a simple axiom: If what you are doing is not working, try something else—*anything else.* If teachers think of managing resistance as determining children's particular frames of reference and introducing variety and richness into their lives, then the goal is to become creative and unrestrictive in interactions with them.

Hassenpflug (1983) wrote a wonderful article, "Insanity in the Classroom," describing her approach to managing resistant and disruptive students. She demonstrated an amazing ability to be flexible and creative:

> On that day when all the classroom management systems I had diligently absorbed in years of inservices completely collapsed, I tried insanity. As I approached the classroom, students were not doing

what they were supposed to be doing, and the noise level reached an ear-piercing volume. I refused to start screaming or shouting commands and threats. I simply walked into the room, looked down at the floor as if addressing a small dog, and said, "Toto, I don't think we're in Kansas anymore." As students began to turn toward me to see what was going on, I asked one of the worst offenders if he would like to take Toto out into the hall to play for a while. More heads turned and more mouths shut.

The noise and activity were still out of control, though, so I called for the ward nurse and inquired about the name of the asylum for the inmates of the room. While waiting for her arrival, I talked to an imaginary elf (but a stuffed animal or small statue would have done as well) about the unbelievable behavior of these students. When I ran out of conversation, I started watching an imaginary wasp flying around the room. Almost every one's eyes were on the teacher now.

One particularly nasty individual, however, was still putting on a show of his own. I took my clipboard and stood by him and silently noted down everything he did as if I were an entomologist studying a new species. Shortly, this student was so fed up that he sat down without my ever having to say a word. I sauntered over to another offender and began speaking politely in a mixture of French and German. The student turned red and sat down.

Class was ready to begin now, and the preliminary calming procedures had taken only five minutes in comparison to the usual ten to fifteen of yelling. (pp. 33–34).

Hassenpflug demonstrated a marvelous ability to be flexible, creative, and maintain a sense of humor about herself and her students. Teachers' ability to modify what they do by not restricting themselves to set patterns of behaving allows them to tap into and make operational all available resources in order to help deal with resistance. For example, Hassenpflug also described in her article one of her students who regularly stood by her desk and whined about not wanting to work, demanding to know why she could not be sent to the gym instead. One day, Hassenpflug jumped up, slammed down her book, and walked out of the room for 2 minutes. When she returned the student was doing her assignment. She also described how she diverted the class' attention from ongoing incidents of misbehavior by pointing out the window and describing all sorts of imaginary beings, events, and objects.

The lesson to be learned from Hassenpflug's accounts is that teachers must go beyond the standard, perceived approaches of dealing with resistance and try something new. I was in the middle of a family therapy session focusing on developing a behavioral contract when the mother stood up and said, "It sure would help the situation if my husband didn't leave his clothes around the house all the time." Although I was taken by surprise at this unexpected digression, I asked the woman how long her husband had been leaving his clothes around the house. She replied that he had been doing so for the entire 10 years of their marriage. I then asked her what she had done about it. She responded that she had yelled at him. I looked at her squarely in the eyes and said, "Congratulations, you're very persistent, really having given yelling a chance to work—10 years is a long time to try one thing. Now are you ready to try something different?"

One thing that all children teach adults is that there are different ways of looking at situations. Dealing with resistance should not be a massive job. Teachers usually know what to do, but do not always know that they know it. I close this chapter with an oriental story Watzlawick (1985) told of a father who leaves his earthly belongings, consisting of 17 camels, to his three sons with the instruction that the eldest son is to receive one half, the second one third, and the youngest one ninth. No matter how they try to divide the camels, the sons find it impossible—try and see if you can divide 17 into these fractions. Eventually, a mullah comes along on his camel, and they ask him for his help. "There is nothing to it," he says. "Here, I add my camel to yours, which makes 18. Now you, the eldest receive one half, which is nine. You, the middle son, are entitled to one third, which is six; here they are. You, the youngest, get one ninth, that is, two camels. This leaves one camel, namely, my own." And having said this, he mounts it and rides off.

References

Achenbach, T. M. (1980). DSM–III in light of empirical research on the classification of child psychopathology. *Journal of the American Academy of Child Psychiatry, 19*, 395–412.

American Psychiatric Association. (1994). *Diagnostic and statistical manual of mental disorders* (4th ed., DSM–IV). Washington, DC: Author.

Azrin, N. H., Nunn, R. G., & Frantz, S. E. (1980). Habit reversal vs. negative practice treatment of nervous tics. *Behavior Therapy, 11*, 169–178.

Bandler, R., & Grinder, J. (1982). *Reframing: Neuro-linguistic programming and the transformation of meaning.* Moab, UT: Real People Press.

Bandura, A. (1977). Self-efficacy: Toward a unifying theory of behavioral change. *Psychological Review, 84,* 191–215.

Cormier, W. H., & Cormier, L. S. (1985). *Interviewing strategies for helpers: Fundamental skills and cognitive behavioral interventions* (2nd ed.). Monterey, CA: Brooks/Cole.

Education for All Handicapped Children Act of 1975, 20 U.S.C. § 1400 *et seq.*

Erickson, L., Elliott, B. A., Erickson, A., Erickson, R., Klein, R., & Erickson, K. K. (1985). Erickson family panel: The child-rearing techniques of Milton Erickson. In J. K. Zeig (Ed.), *Erickson psychotherapy* (Vol. 1, pp. 619–637). New York: Brunner/Mazel.

Farrelly, F., & Brandsma, J. (1978). *Provocative therapy.* Cupertino, CA: Meta.

Foxx, R. M., & Azrin, N. H. (1972). Restitution: A method of eliminating aggressive-disruptive behavior of retarded and brain damaged patients. *Behavior Research and Therapy, 10,* 15–27.

Foxx, R. M., & Bechtel, D. R. (1983). Overcorrection: A review and analysis. In S. Axelrod & J. Apsche (Eds.), *The effects of punishment on human behavior* (pp. 133–220). New York: Academic Press.

Freud, S. (1952). *A general introduction to psychoanalysis.* New York: Washington Square Press. (Original work published 1900)

Haley, J. (1973). *Uncommon therapy: The psychiatric techniques of Milton Erickson, M.D.* New York: Norton.

Haley, J. (1993). *Jay Haley on Milton H. Erickson.* New York: Brunner/Mazel.

Hassenpflug, A. (1983, December). Insanity in the classroom. *English Journal, 72*(8), 33–34.

Howell, K. W., Fox, S. L., & Morehead, M. K. (1993). *Curriculum-based evaluation: Teaching and decision making* (2nd ed.). Pacific Grove, CA: Brooks/Cole.

Jackson, D. (1968). *Therapy, communication and change.* Palo Alto, CA: Science and Behavior Books.

Johnston, J. M., & Pennypacker, H. S. (1980). *Strategies and tactics for human behavioral research.* Hillsdale, NJ: Erlbaum.

Kerr, M. M., & Nelson, C. M. (1983). *Strategies for managing behavior problems in the classroom.* Columbus, OH: Merrill.

Lewin, K. (1951). *Field theory in social science.* New York: Harper & Row.

Litow, L., & Pumroy, D. K. (1975). A brief review of classroom group-oriented contingencies. *Journal of Applied Behavior Analysis, 3,* 341–347.

Maag, J. W. (1988). Two objective techniques for enhancing teacher–student relationships. *Journal of Humanistic Education and Development, 26,* 127–136.

Maag, J. W. (1994). Review of stress inoculation training with children and adolescents: Issues and recommendations. *Behavior Modification, 18,* 443–469.

Madden, N., & Slavin, R. (1983). Mainstreaming students with mild handicaps: Academic and social outcomes. *Review of Educational Research, 53,* 519–569.

Martin, G., & Pear, J. (1992). *Behavior modification; What it is and how to do it.* Englewood Cliffs, NJ: Prentice-Hall.

McConnell, S. R. (1987). Entrapment effects and the generalization and maintenance of social skills training for elementary school students with behavioral disorders. *Behavioral Disorders, 12,* 252–263.

McGinnis, E., & Goldstein, A. P. (1984). *Skillstreaming the elementary school child.* Champaign, IL: Research Press.

Meichenbaum, D. (1985). *Stress inoculation training.* New York: Pergamon.

Neel, R. S., & Cessna, K. K. (1990). Maybe this behavior does make sense. In R. B. Rutherford, Jr., & S. A. DiGangi (Eds.), *Severe behavior disorders of children and youth* (Vol. 13, pp. 18–22). Reston, VA: Council for Children with Behavioral Disorders.

Premack, D. (1959). Toward empirical behavioral laws: I. Positive reinforcement. *Psychological Review, 66,* 219–233.

Rosen, S. (1982). *My voice will go with you: The teaching tales of Milton H. Erickson.* New York: Norton.

Rossi, E. L., Ryan, M. O., & Sharp, F. A. (Eds.). (1983). *Healing in hypnosis: The seminars, workshops, and lectures of Milton H. Erickson* (Vol. 1). New York: Irvington.

Simon, D. J., & Vetter-Zemitzsch, A. (1985). Paradoxical interventions: Strategies for the resistant adolescent. In M. M. Zabel (Ed.), *TEACHING: Behaviorally disordered youth* (Vol. 1, pp. 17–22). Reston, VA: Council for Children with Behavioral Disorders.

Stainback, S., & Stainback, W. (1992). Schools as inclusive communities. In W. Stainback & S. Stainback (Eds.), *Controversial issues confronting special education: Divergent perspectives* (pp. 29–43). Needham Heights, MA: Allyn & Bacon.

Walker, H. M., McConnell, S., Holmes, D., Todis, B., Walker, J., & Golden, N. (1983). *The Walker Social Skills Curriculum.* Austin, TX: PRO-ED.

Watzlawick, P. (1978). *The language of change.* New York: Basic Books.

Watzlawick, P. (1985). Hypnotherapy without trance. In J. K. Zeig (Ed.), *Ericksonian psychotherapy: Volume 1. Structures* (pp. 5–14). New York: Brunner/Mazel.

Watzlawick, P., Weakland, J., & Fisch, R. (1974). *Change: Principles of problem formation and problem resolution.* New York: Norton.

Zionts, P. (1996). *Teaching disturbed and disturbing students: An integrated approach* (2nd ed.). Austin, TX: PRO-ED.

CHAPTER 12

Recent Developments in Social Interaction Interventions To Enhance Inclusion

Linda Garrison Harrell,
Jane E. Doelling, and
Gary M. Sasso

S ocial skills, or those behaviors that an individual exhibits to per- form competently in interactions with others (Gresham, 1981a), are typically conceptualized as part of the broader construct of social competence. Social competence has been defined behaviorally as those responses that, within given situations, increase or maximize the probability of producing, maintaining, and enhancing positive effects for the interacter (Ferster, 1961). Positive effects that are hypothesized to be the result of socially competent behavior (Gresham, 1981b) include peer acceptance, positive judgments by significant others such as teachers and parents, and other positive outcomes such as academic achievement, improved classroom behavior, play skill acquisition, high self-esteem, and improvements in cognitive functioning.

The relationship between social skills and social competence is typically conceptualized in the literature as a sequential one, with social competence occurring as a function of displaying adequate social skills. Over the past 25 years, a number of interventions have been developed to directly address the appropriate social replacement behavior of children with behavior and learning problems. These include direct instruction, teacher-mediated interventions, peer mediation, and peer tutoring (Sasso, 1987). In the sections that follow we describe two of the most recent and promising social interaction interventions, cooperative learning and peer networks.

Cooperative Learning

Cooperative learning is an instructional format that uses positive student collaboration and team goals to facilitate learning and promote content mastery. Each member of a cooperative group has a clearly defined role, and each team member's role is equally valued. Students are encouraged to seek outcomes that are beneficial to all those with whom they are cooperatively linked. Several motivational and cognitive theories support the benefits of cooperative learning (Slavin, 1995), and educators and social scientists recognize the importance of structuring positive competition through implementation of educational activities that foster student interaction and group accountability. Successful adaptation in educational, community, and vocational settings is based on coordination of the actions of many individuals to attain mutual goals. Thus, cooperative learning provides a system for preparing individuals to meet this challenge.

Effective cooperative learning models share similar principles. These principles have been discussed in some detail by Johnson and Johnson (1991) and Slavin (1995). For example, Johnson and Johnson (1991) delineated a number of differences between the typical classroom learning groups and cooperative learning groups. These include:

1. *Individual accountability*—All group members are aware of each others' progress and encourage each other, whereas in traditional groups students may not carry equitable workloads.

2. *Heterogeneous grouping*—Group members are typically diverse in regard to ability and personal characteristics, whereas traditional groups have homogeneous grouping.

3. *Positive interdependence*—Goals are structured to promote group performance as well as individual performance.

4. *Maintenance of working relationships/Direct instruction of social skills*—Skills necessary to the maintenance of effective groups are taught directly. In traditional groups, the focus is on individual task completion and collaborative skills are often assumed to have been previously learned.

5. *Teacher observation and intervention*—Teachers are actively involved in the groups to monitor comprehension and conduct

lessons related to group goals. Teacher involvement in traditional groups may be limited.

6. *Group process for evaluation effectiveness*—Teachers structure procedures and opportunities for determining student progress. Limited attention may be available in traditional groups.

Cooperative Learning Models

These principles and additional elements are incorporated in five student team learning models. Three of the models, Student Team Achievement Divisions, Teams–Games–Tournaments, and Jigsaw II, can be adapted to most subject and grade levels. The remaining student team learning methods, Team Accelerated Instruction and Cooperative Integrated Reading and Composition, focus on mastery of specific subject content. Although these models include methods appropriate to meeting the needs of individuals with disabilities, accommodations and adaptations may still be necessary. The brief discussion of student team learning models that follows is offered to illustrate application of collaborative learning concepts and to emphasize the various formats and instructional strategies used in cooperative learning activities.

Student Team Achievement Divisions (STAD)

The STAD model emphasizes the organization of the classroom rather than teaching specific subject matter. Students are assigned to four-member *heterogeneous* groups and work together to assure mastery of lesson content previously presented by the teacher. If teams achieve a designated criterion, various team rewards are received. Students may work in pairs to study, check responses, or ask each other questions; however, the success of the team depends on individual accountability, or the learning of all team members. Although emphasis is placed on helping one another learn, achieve the designated criterion, and prepare for evaluation, each student must demonstrate mastery of content through individual quiz scores. Students' quiz scores are compared to their own past performance and team points are awarded based on improvement over their previous record to ensure equal opportunities for success. This model encourages students of varied abilities to improve their own past performance and honors the contribution of all team members.

Teams–Games–Tournaments (TGT)

The TGT model includes many of the same principles as STAD; however, academic games replace quizzes as a means of earning team points, and students play games at three-person tournament tables. TGT teams are heterogeneously grouped and members are encouraged to assist each other prepare for tournaments. Team members are assigned to tournament tables based on performance in the last tournament, or through an established baseline. Students change tables depending on performance in the most recent tournament ensuring equal competition and opportunities for success. Individual accountability and attainment of group goals may be met through this format. TGT allows for an alternative method of responding and a motivational format that may appeal to students with disabilities. Additionally, individual skills and abilities are considered in the selection of tournament pairs.

Jigsaw II

In Jigsaw II, students are assigned readings that may include short books or content chapters. Each team member is randomly selected to become an expert in some aspect of the assignment. Experts from various class teams meet to compare information and return to their groups to teach the material to their teammates. Task specialization is a key element of the model, and quizzes are completed by students to assure individual accountability. While application and generalization of collaborative skills across groups is desired, accommodation and support may be necessary. The assignment of "expert" areas may need to be specific rather than random for individuals with disabilities, and strategies for comprehension of print and facilitation of oral expression should be incorporated into the model.

Team Accelerated Instruction (TAI)

The TAI program combines cooperative learning techniques with individualized instruction and was designed specifically for teaching mathematics content. Participants initially complete placement tests to determine an individualized sequence and assure equal opportunity for success. Teammates check each others' work and obtain team rewards based on the total number of units completed by the team. Emphasis is placed on student management of materials, allowing the teacher to spend more time in the presentation of lessons to small groups.

Cooperative Integrated Reading and Composition (CIRC)

CIRC is a model for teaching language arts in the middle grades. Students are assigned to teams and perform various activities with emphasis on cognition and active responding, to include summarizing, predicting, writing responses, editing written drafts for publication, vocabulary, and spelling tasks. Students complete quizzes when teammates determine they are ready, and teams receive rewards based on the average performance of all team members. To ensure equal opportunities for success, students are assigned materials corresponding with ability levels.

Other Cooperative Models

Other cooperative strategies are *Group Investigation*, in which students collaborate in groups of two to six members and select topics from a class unit for further investigation and group reporting, and the *Complex Instruction Method*, in which students may further participate in discovery-oriented projects in content areas. The latter is used in bilingual and heterogeneous classes to emphasize that each student may contribute specific skills in the development of group projects. Both Group Investigation and Complex Instruction emphasize individual accountability and task specialization through completion of a unique subtask that contributes to a final goal or product.

Implementing Cooperative Learning in Inclusive Settings

Enhanced student achievement and social skill interaction have been noted as positive effects of many cooperative learning models. For individuals who have typically experienced school failure and exclusion from integrated settings, cooperative learning methods can be powerful instructional tools. Inclusion of students with disabilities in cooperative groups in general education involves the collaborative efforts of teachers as well as students and careful consideration of a variety of ecological variables.

Although the principal elements of cooperative learning may seem simple, successful implementation of collaborative groups requires considerable work and the ongoing involvement of educational teams. Additionally, implementation of cooperative methods may involve significant changes to existing educational environments and philosophies. Prior to implementation and as a part of school improvement, educational teams should be supported with technical assistance and professional development. To ensure success, particularly with students of diverse needs, the collaborative principles applied to students must also be embraced by professionals.

Structuring the Classroom for Collaboration

Physical Accommodations. Because students with behavior and learning problems frequently exhibit processing, reasoning, and attention deficits that result in problems with organization and task completion, it is necessary to structure learning environments to meet the needs of these diverse learners and to promote the success of collaborative groups. Physical accommodations may be provided through the use of visual cuing systems and the organization and arrangement of materials.

Desks or tables should be positioned for face-to-face interaction, and the aisles should be wide enough to allow for ease of movement during transitions. Interactions between students may be facilitated by positioning of desks in quad arrangements, seating for pairs at learning centers, or less formal settings such as area rugs in the library. Further, various instructional variables enhance decisions regarding seating and material organization. For example, some collaborative models focus on interaction between cooperative pairs, whereas other activities such as tournaments and games may require seating for six or more students with rotation of team members among groups. The teacher will need to make students aware of the purpose, structure, and format of the collaborative activity.

Collaborative group areas, learning centers, and areas for whole-class instruction should be clearly identified. Visual cues may be helpful and include the use of signs, pictures, and objects, or structural barriers such as bookcases and dividers. Students with behavior and learning problems often exhibit deficits in processing and spatial orientation. Therefore, it may be helpful to have them participate in a "walk through" prior to asking them to move to cooperative groups. "Quick and quiet" points can be awarded for group members who demonstrate appropriate transition skills in preparatory activities.

Organizational Systems. Group organization and comprehension of the cooperative process may be enhanced through *individual schedules, group schedules, posters,* and *bulletin boards.* These systems provide a means of accommodating retrieval and reasoning deficits and become particularly important when new groups are formed. Group rules can be posted and collaborative skills and behaviors illustrated through classroom bulletin boards. Displays should correspond to the developmental and interest level of the class. If problems arise in cooperative groups, students should be directed to visual displays of collaborative goals or posted rules.

Prior to the initiation of collaborative activities, group schedules can be posted and reviewed, and monitoring sheets distributed to each team member. Group lesson plans or schedules may include information such as the time frame and sequence for task completion, the objectives of the lesson, materials list, and systems for monitoring progress. In addition to the group schedule, students with behavior and learning problems may benefit from individual schedule systems that provide a daily sequence of events, including the transition from individual to collaborative formats.

Materials should be organized prior to lesson implementation and positioned for easy access throughout the group activity. Cards or lists itemizing materials needed for each group can be disseminated to group members, kept in containers of manipulatives, kept in group folders, or attached to individual assignment sheets. General considerations for structuring cooperative activities include:

1. Reviewing the Individualized Education Program (IEP) to identify the needs of students in cooperative groups (e.g., response to stimuli, interaction with peers).

2. Obtaining assistance from related service personnel, such as an occupational or physical therapist, speech–language clinician, or vision specialist, to accommodate physical or sensory deficits.

3. Being consistent in regard to cues and prompts (e.g., schedules with same or similar format across settings, familiar pictures, consistent oral and written vocabulary cues).

Instructional Considerations

Several elements of cooperative group activities consistently contribute to academic or social gains (Johnson & Johnson, 1991; Slavin, 1995). Planning for cooperative groups should include incorporation of those variables known to contribute to successful student outcomes. Table 12.1 contains a number of suggestions for positive interdependence, individual accountability, task specialization, opportunities for success, and face-to-face interaction that allow for the successful implementation of cooperative learning strategies specifically for students with behavior and learning problems.

Successful cooperative lessons involve the collaborative efforts of professionals in both general and special education. The typical concerns regarding inclusion of students in general education classrooms apply to cooperative groups. Educators may believe that students with disabilities may not be successful in heterogeneous groups for many reasons, including the difficulty level of curriculum materials and the emphasis on higher order thinking. Thus, special educators often need to assure professional partners that the principles of cooperative learning complement best teaching practices noted in the professional literature for students with disabilities. Mercer (1992) provided a summary of effective instructional practices for students with disabilities that support the elements of cooperative learning noted previously. The following are instructional practices that enhance student learning:

1. Structuring the supportive environments in a manner that allows errors to be viewed as naturally occurring events with students complimented for academic and nonacademic efforts.

2. Actively monitoring progress, providing consistent individual and group feedback, and planning and changing instruction based on documented student outcomes.

3. Structuring and managing the classroom through consistent routine, posted rules, and instructional methods that promote comprehension.

4. Providing direct and systematic instruction of skills needed to complete activities. Providing explicit directions, modeling, guided practice, varying levels of practice, and reinforcement in a systematic manner.

5. Designing activities to promote academic engagement and high rates of student success.

In addition, the following general strategies for implementing cooperative learning activities may be helpful.

TABLE 12.1
Variables Related to the Successful Implementation
of a Cooperative Learning Group

1. *Positive interdependence/Group goals.* Goals are structured to promote accomplishments and success for all group members.
   a. Structure assignments so the job cannot be completed unless all team members participate.
   b. Organize materials and structure responding for group participation (e.g., team members develop group goals collaboratively, one pencil for recorder, one paper submitted by the group).
   c. Provide reinforcement for meeting group goals.

2. *Individual accountability.* Each student's mastery of the assigned content is assessed.
   a. Provide rewards and bonus points for individual improvement or progress.
   b. Conduct random comprehension checks, selecting one group member to respond to questions.
   c. Require students to check each others' work and select one paper from the group for review.

3. *Task specialization.* Students become experts on various aspects of the group assignment.
   a. A group of "experts" may be assigned specific sections of content area texts with the task of preparing a study guide to disseminate to the whole class.
   b. Let students select subtopics of a unit to be compiled by the group.
   c. Encourage students to select methods of problem solving and responding based on personal strengths (written, oral, demonstration, art project, video, etc.).

4. *Opportunities for success.* The contributions of all team members are valued.
   a. Team points are awarded based on improvement of past scores.
   b. In competitive situations (e.g., tournaments or games), students are placed with peers of similar ability.
   c. Required contributions are appropriate to individual's present level, but each contribution is valued equally (e.g., 6 math problems completed correctly for student with disability receives the same points as 12 for a typical peer).

5. *Face-to-face interaction.* Groups are structured to facilitate collaborative efforts.
   a. Structure the physical arrangement of the classroom to facilitate collaborative efforts.
   b. Select instructional methods and cooperative goals that encourage interaction (e.g., reciprocal reading and questioning, elaboration, summarizing).
   c. Award points for demonstration of positive collaborative behaviors.

Note: Adapted from *Circles of Learning: Cooperation in the Classroom,* by D. W. Johnson, R. T. Johnson, and E. Holubec, 1990, Edina, MN: Interaction Book Co. Copyright 1990 by Interaction Book Co. Adapted with permission.

Preparing for the Lesson

1. Preview academic plans at least 1 week in advance to determine appropriate goals and objectives. Match whole-class objectives to individual IEP goals and objectives. Select familiar content and, in the beginning, structure activities of relative ease to ensure success and encourage mastery of process.

2. Task-analyze the content to be mastered and structure group lesson plans accordingly. Integrate lesson content with specific elements of cooperative groups: positive interdependence, individual accountability, face-to-face interaction, opportunities for success, and adaptation to individual needs.

3. Select the cooperative format, monitoring, and reinforcement system to be implemented (e.g., points for moving quickly and quietly, rewards for group goal attainment, points for improvement of individual scores).

4. Select the group members based on class as well as IEP goals and objectives. Heterogeneous groups may be beneficial to those students having difficulty with grade-level material; however, other formats such as the use of competitive games or tournaments may require matching students of similar ability to meet some group or individual IEP goals.

5. Teach the academic and collaborative skills necessary for meeting group goals prior to implementation of the program. This will include direct instruction of specific academic content as well as social interaction skills.

6. Develop cuing systems that facilitate understanding (i.e., schedules; posters; posted group rules; hand signals, timers, or verbal cues to signal for listening, noise control, or transitions).

7. Arrange the classroom to correspond with cooperative formats and the goals of the lesson. Structure the classroom for face-to-face interaction and ease of access to materials.

Preparing the Students

1. Organize cooperative groups.
   a. Pass out cards with group members' names.
   b. Refer to poster or overhead with group schedules.
   c. Direct students to move to groups and provide points and/or praise for appropriate transition.

2. Distribute materials, lesson plans, or student monitoring sheets.
   a. Provide materials lists or cards.
   b. Prompt students to material retrieval and storage areas.
   c. Provide points and/or praise for appropriate retrieval of materials.

3. Preview the lesson with the students including the students' role in the process.
   a. Place lesson plans on overhead and review.
   b. Model student roles.
   c. Conduct guided practice as necessary.

During the Lesson

1. Conduct frequent comprehension checks and provide assistance accordingly.
   a. Clarify and reteach specific academic skills as needed.
   b. Conduct random questioning and check student assignments for progress toward group goals.

2. Prompt students to demonstrate collaborative team behaviors.
   a. If problems arise, redirect student to posted group rules and goals of lesson.
   b. Model and participate in group problem-solving strategies.
   c. Refer students to group and individual schedules, assignment sheets, student lesson plans, or other organizational cues.
   d. Set timers and/or refer to group schedules to encourage task engagement and appropriate work rate.

3. Review products and procedures for determining individual and group accountability. Do the results indicate that goals and objectives of the lesson have been met?
   a. Individual quizzes.
   b. Group or individual worksheets.
   c. Record of behavioral observations.
   d. Oral presentations and group reports.
   e. Group point totals and self-monitoring sheets.

Figure 12.1 provides an example of a cooperative learning activity that incorporates a number of the above practices.

Structuring Cooperative Groups. The formation of cooperative groups requires careful planning, including consideration of designated instructional goals and individual needs. Until students have

---

Format: Reciprocal Reading/Jigsaw Format

Objectives:

1. Students will survey passage assigned and read.
2. Students will ask each other one question based on survey and passage reading.
3. The group will design semantic map using main idea and two supporting details.

Grouping: Three (a student with disability and two typical peers)

Roles:

1. Student with disability will serve as reporter for class report based on relative strength with oral expression.
2. A nondisabled peer will serve as recorder developing a semantic map from information dictated by group members.
3. Each student will serve as prober and motivator for team members.

Positive Interdependence: Students do not accept "I don't know" as answer to question; assist peers in finding answer in text. Students will provide oral report to whole class based on assigned passage and student maps. Team points awarded for meeting group goals.

Materials: Grade-level social studies text, paper, pencil, group schedule, and group monitoring forms.

Accountability: Completed maps or sentences, and oral report to class.

Accommodation: Student may develop schematic rather than full sentence. Reading deficits accommodated by emphasis on survey of passage and questioning to enhance comprehension.

Opportunities for Success: Students assist each other within heterogeneous group and student roles determined upon analysis of individual needs.

FIGURE 12.1   Sample cooperative learning activity.

acquired collaborative skills and have gained experience with cooperative learning formats, groups should remain small. Initially, it is suggested that newly formed groups contain two or three students, gradually building to between four and six members depending on format, goals, and individual needs. To encourage generalization of skills and the development of diverse friendships, it is important to restructure groups periodically; however, the effects of change on a student with behavior or learning problems should be considered. Changes in routine and cooperative formats should be implemented gradually and with appropriate planning and student preparation.

In addition to the assignment of *specialized tasks*, it is important to consider the nature of cooperative learning and the effects on students with disabilities. Students who have experienced failure may not do well in highly competitive situations. On the other hand, competition between well-matched peers may provide incentive to complete academic tasks and reinforcement for student efforts. There will be, of course, some concerns regarding placement of students with behavior or learning problems in cooperative groups, including fears regarding behavior problems and meeting academic needs of typical peers. The literature supporting heterogeneous grouping suggests sustained academic gains for high-achieving students who participate in heterogeneous cooperative groups (Johnson & Johnson, 1991). The research in this area further suggests that typical peers gain in retention and demonstrate gains in problem-solving ability (Johnson & Johnson, 1991). However, decisions regarding placement of students within groups, assignment of student roles, and task specialization should be based on a functional analysis of a number of student variables.

Student Preparation. Interaction and involvement of the student in a collaborative group may enhance peer acceptance to a greater degree than specific academic skill mastery (Slavin, 1995); therefore, direct instruction of collaborative behaviors prior to implementation of cooperative groups is essential. A list of collaborative behaviors can be found in Figure 12.2. Student IEPs typically include goals related to the development of social and communication skills necessary for success in collaborative groups, and collaborative skill instruction is a responsibility of both the general and special educator. Figure 12.3 contains suggestions for professionals regarding structuring reinforcement in collaborative activities.

Feedback regarding the collaborative efforts of students should be provided during the lessons, with frequent opportunities to practice skills structured across various school settings. To facilitate understanding of the cooperative process, as well as individual and group expectations, schedules and lesson plans should be reviewed prior to implementation of the cooperative learning activities. Students with behavior and learning problems may have difficulty responding to time and format changes; therefore, it may be helpful

Share Ideas: Students learn how to share ideas and listen to and respect ideas from their group members.

Compliment Others: Students are encouraged to compliment each other's work and their participation within the group process.

Offer Help or Encouragement: Students assist each other in solving problems and answering questions. They encourage each other for trying and participating in the group.

Recommend Changes: Students learn how to give specific, appropriate feedback to one another in a pleasant and positive manner.

Exercise Self-Control: Students practice self-control methods such as counting to 5 when they experience difficult times within the group. They learn how accept feedback, listen to changes that are recommended, and determine whether change is needed.

FIGURE 12.2   Collaborative skills. Adapted from *The SCORE Skills: Social Skills for Cooperative Groups* by S. Vernon, J. Schumaker, and D. Deschler, 1993, Lawrence, KA: Edge Enterprizes.

to schedule collaborative activities at the same time of day and gradually build in change across time and procedures. Assignment of student roles should include similar emphasis on prior preparation and routine. Students may need to practice various cooperative roles and be given opportunities to role-play collaborative responses and participate in teacher-directed problem-solving activities.

Assignment of specialized tasks and decisions regarding the student's role within the group can be based on an analysis of individual strengths and needs. Students with disabilities may lack prerequisite skills, or have deficits specific to the disability that prohibit completion of some tasks or require appropriate accommodation. For example, recording the responses of the group may not be appropriate for a student with a written language disability, and a student with a reading deficit may need to be paired with a nondisabled peer to complete the roles of the group reader. Students must receive direct instruction in the skills required for each role prior to implementation of the program.

Cooperative learning methods require that students take an active role in the instructional process. Elements of cooperative learning, including attainment of group goals and positive interdependence, require each group member to assume various leadership and instructional roles for which they may not be prepared. A discussion

- *Provide group members with time to share information* about themselves within the group time to promote positive regard (e.g., Jennifer informs her group that she made a 90% on her reading test after last week's group time).

- *Provide nonacademic rewards,* such as extra free time, extra recess, stickers, bonus points, or edibles, when all the group members reach a designated criterion (e.g., Mrs. DeAngelo announced to the groups that 10 minutes of extra recess will be given to the groups that make 80% or better on their next reading test).

- *Provide verbal praise or affirmation* and praise the specific behavior that the student(s) are exhibiting within the group. Too many times, teachers focus on the negative behavior that students exhibit, and don't encourage or affirm the positive collaborative behavior that the students demonstrate. It is beneficial to be specific with the praise statements (e.g., As the teacher walks by the groups, he comments, "Leon, you are doing such a good job as the group's recorder. Your handwriting is very neat, and it looks like you are recording all of your group's responses. Good job!").

- *Develop a point system that allows nonacademic rewards* to be earned by the groups' performance of collaborative teaming. When group members are observed using appropriate social skills (e.g., taking turns, answering nicely, sharing materials, praising their peers), allow the group members to earn additional bonus points (separate from their academic performance) for pizza parties, in-class movies, computer games, etc.

FIGURE 12.3   Structuring reinforcement within cooperative group activities. Adapted from *Circles of Learning: Cooperation in the Classroom* (3rd ed.) by D. W. Johnson, R. T. Johnson, and E. Holubec, 1990, Edina, MN: Interaction Book Co.

of student roles and considerations in regard to accommodation and preparation for students with disabilities can be found in Table 12.2.

Peer Networks

A relatively new peer-mediated procedure related to initiation interventions is the use of peer networks to promote social competence among individuals with behavior and learning problems (Haring & Breen, 1992; Peck, Donaldson, & Pezzoli, 1990). Networks have been defined as groups of individuals who demonstrate an interest in and an understanding of the individual with disabilities and have impact on that person's life (Chadsey-Rusch, 1986; Sasso, Garrison-Harrell, & Rogers, 1994). In this context, the focus of the peer network intervention is to promote a positive social environment for the student with

TABLE 12.2
Cooperative Roles

Description of Roles	Accommodative Strategies
Recorder: Takes dictation; organizes content (phrases, sentences, paragraphs); edits and checks for group signature. *Skills:* Synthesis of oral language to written language, legible handwriting, motor coordination and speed, vocabulary and syntax that corresponds to content.	• Review text vocabulary; provide preceding questions or outline, semantic map, diagram, or other schematic. • Match content to reading instructional level, use alternative materials. • Arrange for job-sharing with peer. • Teach comprehension skills prior to group participation.
Reader: Performs oral or silent reading of assigned print, disseminates information gained to group members. *Skills:* Comprehension—main idea, details, inferential; survey skills—skimming, scanning, strategies for determining unknown words.	• Reduce writing requirements. • Provide student with partial outline or sentence stem. • Provide semantic/graphic organizers, maps or webs, time lines, compare/contrast charts. • Provide student with assistive technology: spell checks; computer/word processing; aides to assist mechanics of writing—pencil grips, felt markers, paper stabilizer.
Reporter: Gives oral presentation of group responses, presents responses to comprehension questions. *Skills:* Age-appropriate vocabulary and ability to synthesize data into cohesive thoughts; intelligible speech and appropriate rate and volume.	• Practice oral reports prior to presentation. • Use video or tape recorder to present best take to class. • Allow student to present in comfort zone (close proximity to group). • Provide with outline, schematic, or other cognitive organizer.
Business Manager: Disseminates materials, prompts students to transition at scheduled times, returns materials, obtains group signatures for monitoring sheets. *Skills:* Organization of work space, follows schedule, tells time or can respond to other signals such as a timer, knowledge of material location and storage, knowledge of routine.	• Teach organization skills *directly* related to assignments (practice with schedule; review of materials; transition cues such as hand signal, timer, etc.). • Clearly delineate areas of the class by purpose (computer center, group area, material return, etc.). • Use consistent routing and build in change gradually.

(continues)

TABLE 12.2 *Continued*

Description of Roles	*Accommodative Strategies*
Director of Collaboration: Monitors student performance and encourages reluctant members, prompts students to task when lagging, and monitors noise.	• Provide with checklist of student names to provide participation points.
	• Provide with a 3×5 card of positive statements.
Skills: Knowledge of motivational techniques and positive phrases; demonstrates enthusiam and empathy; models appropriate collaborative behaviors and demonstrates leadership; knows teacher's signal for noise control.	• Teach collaborative and social skills *directly* and provide opportunities for practice and generalization across settings prior to placement in a leadership role.
	• Use instructional methods such as role playing and scripting to teach social and collaborative behaviors.

disabilities through the creation of support systems committed to the development of social competency and friendship. For example, active school participation and increases in friendship formations have been noted in a Circle of Friends support network that included home and school support systems (Forest, 1987; Sasso et al., 1994).

Although the use of peer-mediated procedures to increase social interactions among individuals with disabilities is a well-documented strategy, the actual formation of peer networks is a relatively new development. The recent advent of networks appears to be based on the development of community support systems for individuals with disabilities. For example, Park and Gaylord-Ross (1989) taught problem-solving skills to three individuals with disabilities who were working in nonsheltered job sites. Targeted social behaviors included social initiations, conversing, and speaking clearly to peers. The typical peers were instructed to assist students in successfully interacting with others on the job site. This type of cognitive–behavioral approach was used to teach individuals with disabilities to assess the social situation, generate ideas for solutions, and converse effectively with peers.

Similarly, Horner, Meyer, and Fredericks (1987) established a network strategy that assisted individuals in obtaining and maintaining a level of social support within a community setting. Although this strategy was implemented with adults with disabilities, it provided impetus for the use of a peer network strategy for all individuals with disabilities. Horner and colleagues arranged the daily schedules of nondisabled peers and students with disabilities to allow involvement in the community. By increasing the individual's access to social contact with typical peers and maximizing the amount of social initiation and responding, they allowed individuals with disabilities to develop and maintain appropriate social skills and decrease inappropriate atypical behaviors.

Tappe and Gaylord-Ross (1990) established support networks for individuals within a supported employment placement. The network was based on the premise that a network of typical peers could assist the students with disabilities in maintaining more positive and productive employment. Several suggestions were derived from this study. First, observe the environment and identify a key individual to assist with the establishment of the network. Second, target key social behaviors and provide opportunities for social reciprocity for the individual with disabilities. Finally, advocate for the creation of shared responsibility between the individual with disabilities and his or her typical peer; that is, teach the individual with disabilities to initiate in a more typical manner toward the typical peer (e.g., send a birthday card or ask a peer to go to a movie). The need for shared responsibility among the network allows for more meaningful interactions to occur.

Cognitive–behavioral social skills instruction appears to have been instrumental in the development of networks of social support for students with disabilities. Advocates of this approach (Horner et al., 1987; Stokes & Osnes, 1986) have stressed the need for naturally occurring systems of social support that can assist in the generalization of social skills and provide a level of support that allows the development of integration activities. In the investigations cited above, this type of social skills instruction was used not only to assist the individuals with disabilities but also to teach nondisabled peers how to initiate and maintain interactions.

Others in the field have stated that support networks need to include the following: (a) the examination of the social interaction and support characteristics that naturally operate in the classroom; (b) techniques that empower an individual to more independence; (c) a school or home setting; and (d) use of the natural framework of the day-to-day interactions of the individual (Forest & Lusthaus, 1990; Stainback & Stainback, 1987). Figure 12.4 provides an example of the assessment and selection steps necessary prior to the implementation of a peer network intervention.

ASSESSMENT

1. Assess strengths and weaknesses of the target student.

2. Administer a reinforcement inventory to the target student, parent, and teacher.

3. Develop a "choice" book which contains a symbolic representation of the preferred reinforcers. Then teach the target student to indicate his or her reinforcement selection via the choice booklet.

5. Develop a visual schedule for the target student. This provides the student with a symbolic representation of the day and will assist in establishing a predictable routine of daily events in and outside of the classroom. The visual schedule will also assist in teaching the student flexibility with changes that may occur during the day.

6. Assess the target student's ability to communicate effectively with peers. If there is any doubt about a student's abilities to communicate functionally with the peer group, then augment the target student's speech.

PEER NETWORK SELECTION

1. Administer the friendship rating scale to the regular education classroom assigned to the target student.

2. Rank the students according to the status that their classmates have assigned them ("High" status versus "low" status).

3. Select at least seven students who are "High" status students and meet with the classroom teacher to make the final selection of five students for the network.

4. Establish a network time and place with the classroom teacher to meet with the network students for 2 weeks for approximately 30 minutes each session.

FIGURE 12.4   Sample assessment and selection strategies for peer network interventions.

A number of guidelines should be followed in the development of a peer network (Haring & Lovinger, 1989). In practice, the support group meets weekly for strategy sessions, support, and motivation. During these meetings, the nondisabled peers conduct an analysis of the day-to-day occurrences within the school setting that are relevant to the student with disabilities. Following this step, the network assists the student with disabilities to acquire target social behaviors that are necessary to function successfully in the school. In addition to a high level of support, the peers act as advocates for the student with disabilities and identify potential areas of concern. Figure 12.5 shows a training protocol designed to teach the skills necessary for nondisabled peers to effectively engage in a network.

The primary advantage of a social network is that it creates a high level of support for the student with disabilities within the school environment. In addition, the target student is exposed to a number of socially competent peers. Finally, relevant and individualized skills can be identified and taught to the student with disabilities using this procedure (Haring & Breen, 1992). Although there is little current research supporting the use of this intervention, descriptive and anecdotal reports have popularized the use of this procedure.

Conclusion

The successful integration of behavior management and social interaction activities is a necessary step toward effective programming for students with behavior and learning problems. Without a consideration of an array of responses that can be used to replace problem behavior, teachers cannot hope to successfully include these students in integrated environments. This chapter was designed to provide an overview of two recent social interaction interventions (i.e., cooperative learning and peer networks) that can be used to increase the inclusion of students with behavior and learning problems.

The ultimate usefulness and effectiveness of cooperative learning and peer network strategies will depend on how well these techniques support the student with behavior and learning problems in the integrated environment. It is important that the technique include components that will allow an individual to effectively obtain reinforcers natural to that environment; this will, in large measure, be determined by each child's reinforcement history. The development of any social interaction intervention for a student with behavior and learning problems must include modifications designed specifically to interface with their deficit areas.

References

Chadsey-Rusch, J. (1986). Identifying and teaching valued social behaviors in competitive employment settings. In F. R. Rusch (Ed.), *Competitive employment issues and strategies* (pp. 273–287). Baltimore: Brookes.

Session 1. Discuss likes and differences among students in their classrooms. Discuss qualities of friends who are in their classrooms (e.g., What do you need to do to be a friend? What do you want to do with your friends?). Explain the purpose of this network—that is, to have friends and to do fun activities with your friends. With each student in the network, conduct a reinforcement inventory to assist in developing games and activities that are equally reinforcing to the peers and the target student.

Session 2. Read *He's My Brother* by Joe Lasker and discuss ways that students can be friends to students who are different.

Session 3. Instruct each student to draw a circle and within that circle write the names of all of his or her close friends (people with whom the student spends time and cares about). Then have students discuss who is in their circle of friends and why. Next, diagram a circle for the target student and list the number of friends and family members with whom the target student has contact. Discuss the need for the target student to have more friends.

Session 4. Define initiating a conversation and responding to a conversation; then role-play examples of initiating and responding to conversations. Provide several positive examples of how to initiate and maintain conversations with the target student. Instruct the students to brainstorm on conversational topics that relate to their interests and the target student's interests. Place the students in dyads and have them practice these conversations with emphasis on eye contact and saying each other's names.

Session 5. Define the social skills of saying something nice and sharing. Role-play examples of these skillls, giving positive and negative examples of how to say something nice and how to share with friends. Instruct the students to discuss ways they share with their friends and how they feel when their friends say nice things to them. Place the students in dyads and have them practice these social skills with an emphasis on eye contact, saying each other's names, sharing, and saying something nice.

Session 6. Define the social skills of giving instruction and sharing ideas. Provide concrete examples of how to give instructions in a positive manner. Ask the students to practice ways in which to perform this social skill. Then review sharing ideas with them. Ask the students to brainstorm on new ideas that they could do within the network. Have the network work on sharing ideas and responding to each idea with enthusiasm and openness. Provide several examples of when sharing ideas could occur in the classroom; then ask the students how they could share their ideas with the target student.

(continues)

FIGURE 12.5   Peer network training protocol for elementary-age students.

Session 7. Review all of the previous social skills that have been instructed. Instruct the students on maintaining their conversations with the student even when the student does not indicate a verbal response back to them. Videotape the students in a small group session with the target student. Provide the network students with prompt cards regarding conversation topics. Upon completion of the activity, view the tape with the network students, discuss the level of interaction, and provide additional strategies for maintaining conversations with the target student.

Session 8. Review all of the previous social skills that have been instructed. Instruct the students on maintaining their conversations with the student even when the student does not indicate a verbal response back to them. Videotape the students in a small group session with the target student. Provide the network students with a prompt card regarding conversation topics. Upon completion of the activity, view the tape with the network students, discuss the level of interaction, and provide additional strategies for maintaining conversations with the target student. Establish specific times in the day when the network will work together. Initially, networks appear more effective when the activities are equally or more reinforcing to the typical peers than the target student.

FIGURE 12.5   Continued.

Ferster, C. B. (1961). Positive reinforcement and behavioral deficits of autistic children. *Child Development, 32,* 437–456.

Forest, M. (1987). *More education/integration: A further collection of headings on integration of children with mental handicaps into the regular school system.* Downview, Ontario: The G. Allen Rocher Institute, York University.

Forest, M., & Lusthaus, E. (1990). Everyone belongs with the MAPS action planning system. *Teaching Exceptional Children, 4,* 32–35.

Gresham, F. M. (1981a). Misguided mainstreaming: A case for social skills training with handicapped children. *Exceptional Children, 48,* 422–433.

Gresham, F. M. (1981b). Social skills training with handicapped children: A review. *Review of Educational Research, 51,* 139–176.

Haring, T. G., & Breen, C. G. (1992). A peer mediated social network intervention to enhance social integration of persons with moderate and severe disabilities. *Journal of Applied Behavior Analysis, 25,* 319–333.

Haring, T. G., & Lovinger, L. (1989). Promoting social interaction through teaching generalized play initiation responses to preschool children with autism. *Journal of The Association for Persons with Severe Handicaps, 14,* 58–67.

Horner, R., Meyer, L. H., & Fredericks, H. D. (1987). *Education of learners with severe handicaps: Exemplary service strategies.* Baltimore: Brookes.

Johnson, D. W., & Johnson, R. T. (1991). *Learning together and alone: Cooperative, competitive, and individualistic learning* (3rd ed.). Englewood Cliffs, NJ: Prentice-Hall.

Johnson, D. W., Johnson, R. T., & Holubec, E. (1990). *Circles of learning: Cooperation in the classroom* (3rd ed.). Edina, MN: Interaction Book Co.

Lasker, D. (1984). *He's my brother.* Morton Grove, IL: Albert Whitman and Co.

Mercer, C. (1992). *Students with learning disabilities* (4th ed.). New York: Merrill.

Park, H. S., & Gaylord-Ross, R. (1989). *Process social skills training in employment settings with mentally retarded youth.* Unpublished manuscript, San Francisco State University, San Francisco.

Peck, C. A., Donaldson, J., & Pezzoli, M. (1990). Some benefits nonhandicapped adolescents perceive for themselves from their social relationship with peers who have severe handicaps. *Journal of The Association for Persons with Severe Handicaps, 15,* 241–249.

Sasso, G. M. (1987). Social integration of children with autism: Issues and procedures. *Focus on Autistic Behavior, 2,* 1–15.

Sasso, G. M., Garrison-Harrell, L., & Rogers, L. (1994). Autism and socialization: Conceptual models and procedural variations. In T. Scruggs & M. Mastropieri (Eds.), *Advances in learning and behavioral disabilities* (Vol. 8, pp. 161–175). Greenwich, CT: JAI Press.

Slavin, R. E. (1995). *Cooperative learning* (2nd ed.). Needham Heights, MA: Allyn & Bacon.

Stainback, W., & Stainback, S. (1987). Facilitating friendships. *Education and Training in Mental Retardation, 22,* 18–25.

Stokes, T. F., & Osnes, P. G. (1986). Programming the generalization of children's social behavior. In P. S. Strain, M. J. Guralnick, & H. M. Walker (Eds.), *Children's social behavior: Development, assessment, and modification* (pp. 407–443). Orlando, FL: Academic Press.

Tappe, P., & Gaylord-Ross, R. (1990). Social support and transitional copying. In R. Gaylord-Ross, S. Siegal, H. Park, S. Sacks, & L. Goetz (Eds.), *Readings in ecosocial development.* San Francisco: San Francisco State University Press.

Vernon, S., Schumaker, J., & Deschler, D. (1993). *The SCORE Skills: Social skills for cooperative groups.* Lawrence, KA: Edge Enterprizes.

CHAPTER 13

Academic Equalizers: Practical Applications of Selected Strategies for Elementary and Secondary Students

Christine K. Ormsbee,
Sharon A. Maroney, and
Linda L. Meloy

S tudents with emotional and behavioral disorders (EBD) are being mainstreamed with increasing frequency. In fact, more than 45% of students with EBD receive all or a significant portion of their instruction in the general class (U.S. Department of Education, 1993). Many students with EBD exhibit poor academic skills, including low reading rates, below average math skills, and deficiencies in written language, that negatively impact the students' abilities to succeed in the general classroom (Knitzer, Steinberg, & Fleisch, 1990). However, recent studies have indicated that general educators provide relatively few accommodations or academic supports for these students (Meadows, Neel, Scott, & Parker, 1994). In order for general classrooms to be supportive environments for students with EBD, teachers should employ learning enhancements when planning for instruction, during the delivery of instruction, and during independent learning activities. In this chapter we suggest strategies teachers can use.

Teacher Planning as a Learning Enhancer

It can be said that the greatest learning enhancer is a well-planned, well-orchestrated instructional activity in which students and teachers are enthusiastic, motivated, and involved in learning. The following are examples of such activities:

- Peterson's (1990) junior high students with EBD created a television talk show with a student talk show host and students portraying characters in George Orwell's *Animal Farm* as the guests. In other classes of Peterson's, students read about the life of a homeless teen and recreated the character's living space from a refrigerator box inside the classroom; created children's books with kindergartners to donate to the school library; and played "Jeopardy" with facts from Greek mythology.

- Shatzer (1991) accomplished her goal of getting her students with EBD hooked on journal writing. In selecting their own topics to write about, Shatzer's students came up with such creations as exaggerations, riddles, eating worms, and how to itch in the classroom. One student began by writing a single six-word sentence, but a year later wrote a paragraph of three sentences and 48 words.

- In her living history curriculum, Harden (1992) had her students with EBD visit and interview residents in a nursing home, asking questions such as "What was school like when you were young?" and "Tell me about World War II." Not only did the students learn history, but many unexpected caring relationships developed between the students and the older individuals.

- While all teachers may not feel comfortable dressing up like a box of raisins and dancing to "I heard it through the grapevine," Miss Toliver (Heard, 1993) skillfully grabbed the attention of her junior high school math students and led them through a lesson on estimation.

The ability to design such engaging learning experiences for students requires not only a great deal of enthusiasm but knowledgeable planning as well. Teacher planning as a learning enhancer consists of three stages: establishing an effective teacher mind-set, planning to be effective, and devising an effective teaching lesson. A model that depicts teacher planning as a learning enhancer is presented in Figure 13.1.

Effective Teacher Mind-Set

A prerequisite to effective planning as a teacher is the development of an effective teacher mind-set; this is a positive, enthusiastic, and capable attitude toward teaching, the students, and personal teaching skills and potential for effectiveness. This mind-set is reflected in a teacher who:

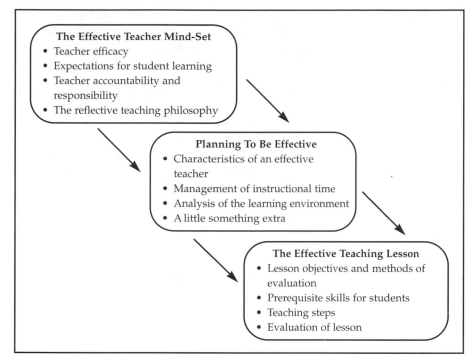

FIGURE 13.1   Teacher planning as a learning enhancer.

- Believes that all students can be taught regardless of behavioral, family, emotional, social, community, and/or environmental problems

- Believes that as a teacher, he or she has the ability to cause positive changes in the lives of students

- Believes that as a teacher, he or she is responsible and accountable for the progress of his or her students

- Utilizes a philosophy of reflective teaching

- Demonstrates an excitement for learning

The first two attributes of the effective teacher mind-set represent the concepts of teaching efficacy and teacher self-efficacy (Allinder, 1993; DiBella-McCarthy, McDaniel, & Miller, 1995). Teaching efficacy is the belief that all students can be taught regardless of outside-the-classroom variables. Self-efficacy is the degree to which a teacher believes that he or she has the skills or is able to acquire the skills needed to teach his or her students. Teachers with high levels of teaching efficacy and self-efficacy have better managed classrooms with greater levels of student academic success; elicit more correct responses from students and maintain greater levels of student engagement; persist longer with students who are struggling and are less critical of incorrect responses; work to identify the sources of student difficulty and to make needed changes; hold greater expectations for their students; and use more positive strategies, creating warmer and more humanistic classroom environments (Allinder, 1993; DiBella-McCarthy et al., 1995). Teachers can identify their own efficacy levels through informal or formal assessment procedures and design individual plans to improve personal efficacy.

The third and fourth attributes of the effective teacher mind-set refer to teachers who continually monitor student progress and view that progress as an evaluation of their teaching performance. Such teachers accept the responsibility for the progress of their students in working to identify the most effective and efficient instructional strategies for students. Strategies such as curriculum-based measurement (Howell, Fox, & Morehead, 1993) provide teachers with structured approaches to evaluate student progress frequently and accurately and to consistently assess various instructional methods. The adoption of a reflective teaching philosophy (Eby, 1992) encourages teachers to follow a cyclical approach to designing instruction, evaluating the outcomes of instruction, and making decisions regarding subsequent instruction. This approach is depicted in Figure 13.2.

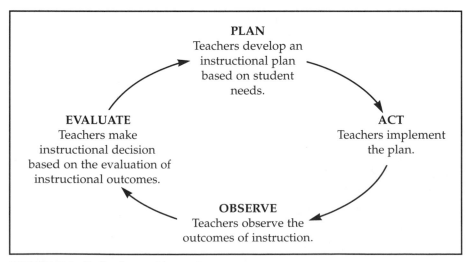

FIGURE 13.2   Reflective teaching cycle.

Responsible and reflective teachers do not immediately attribute a student's lack of progress to an identified or unidentified student disability, but work to determine those variables that are controlled by the teacher that may contribute to student progress or lack of progress. Variables such as selection of instructional materials, style of teaching presentation, level of student engagement, and distractions in the environment are a few examples of such teacher-controlled variables.

The final component of the effective teacher mind-set is a genuine excitement for learning. In motivating and engaging students and themselves, teachers must possess and demonstrate enthusiasm for teaching and learning. The brief descriptions of the four teachers, Peterson (1990), Shatzer, (1991), Harden (1992), and Toliver (Heard, 1993), illustrate teachers who are not only excited about teaching and learning, but who share that excitement with their students.

Planning To Be Effective

The second stage of the teacher planning as learning enhancer model is planning to be effective. This stage consists of four topics: (a) planning to be an effective teacher, (b) planning to employ effective time management strategies, (c) planning to analyze the components of the classroom, and (d) planning to add a little something extra into instructional lessons.

Effective Teaching

In planning to be effective, teachers must have the knowledge of what constitutes an effective teacher. With such information teachers can set goals to incorporate these characteristics in their daily teaching. In reviewing the literature on effective teaching (Englert, 1984; Mastropieri & Scruggs, 1994; Reynolds, Wang, & Walberg, 1992; Rieth & Evertson, 1988; Salend, 1994), we found that an effective teacher is one who

- Maximizes the time students are engaged in learning
- Utilizes a direct instruction approach and an interactive teaching style
- Maximizes teacher-directed instruction and minimizes the time spent in independent seatwork
- Continually and accurately monitors the effectiveness of teaching and makes necessary changes

- Carefully monitors student progress and promptly provides corrective feedback in a positive manner
- Attempts to identify the causes of student difficulty and to make accommodations
- Maintains a high level of positive teacher interactions with students
- Monitors the difficulty level and demands of instructional tasks
- Creates and maintains a classroom environment with a strong academic focus
- Provides students with options and choices
- Designs meaningful, purposeful, and functional learning activities that present variety, challenge, and motivation for students

Management of Instructional Time

For most teachers the goal of time management is to make every minute count. As noted previously, effective teachers maximize the time students are engaged in learning. The first step in accomplishing this is for teachers to allocate more time for instruction in their daily schedules. Effective teachers work to increase the amount of time devoted to teacher-led instruction while decreasing independent seatwork. Second, teachers need to plan to reduce student waiting time and interruptions during instruction. A third step in managing instructional time is to use strategies that maintain high levels of student engagement during all instructional activities. Table 13.1 describes 10 strategies for teachers to use during teacher-directed instruction to engage students in the lesson and monitor student understanding.

Analysis of the Learning Environment

A comprehensive analysis of the learning environment provides teachers with valuable information related to variables that may affect student performance or teacher effectiveness during instruction. Factors included in the physical environment, teaching style, classroom atmosphere, social interactions, instructional materials, and student response modes can affect student performance and teaching effectiveness. Analyzing the physical dimensions of the classroom can point out space limitations, obstructed views of the chalkboard, noisy circulation fans, and distracting traffic patterns.

TABLE 13.1
Ten Strategies To Monitor Student Understanding and Engage Students in a Learning Activity

1. *VCCC.* This strategy, as presented by Skinner, Ford, and Yunker (1991), requires students to Verbalize, Cover, Copy, and Compare. After having students write a definition in their notebooks, ask them to verbalize it, cover it, copy or rewrite it, and then compare their rewrites with the original definition.

2. *Mini-Lectures.* Divide lecture time into short sections of 5 to 10 minutes. Stop after each section and require some form of student interaction or response.

3. *Response Cards.* During each class period, give students a response card. Throughout the lesson, ask students to respond to various types of questions. Correct answers are given immediately, and these cards are kept by students as supplements to their class notes. Suggestions for items and questions for response cards include the following:

- Write a definition of . . .
- Give another example of . . .
- Give a nonexample of . . .
- Write a good test question for the topic of . . .
- How would you determine the best way to . . . the best advice for . . . the best reason for . . . the best leader . . . the best answer . . . ?
- What do you know about . . . ?

4. *Mini-Chalkboards.* Provide each student with a mini-chalkboard and throughout a lesson have them write words, perform math problems, and so on, on their boards and hold up their responses.

5. *Thumbs Up, Thumbs Down.* During the lesson ask students questions that can be answered with a thumbs up or thumbs down. Suggested questions include "Is the correct answer . . . ?" "Would that be the best way to . . . ?" "Given this information, would it be correct to conclude . . . ?" Requiring students to put their heads down before answering these questions reduces students' temptation to look around to see how others are responding.

6. *Make Your Own Example.* After teaching, for example, 2 digit by 2 digit subtraction with regrouping, ask students to make up their own problems of the same type. Students can exchange and solve each other's problems (Parmar & Cawley, 1991).

7. *Quickie True/False.* Frequently throughout the lesson, ask students true–false questions and have them call out their responses or use a thumbs up, thumbs down approach.

(continues)

TABLE 13.1 *Continued*

8. *Jeopardy.* At various times throughout the lesson, have students work with their neighbors to write a Jeopardy-type question and answer over the material just covered. These questions can be written on index cards and be ready to use during the Jeopardy test review game. They can also be posted on the bulletin board for student review prior to the test.

9. *Name Cards.* Create name cards for each student to be used during class when calling on students. Cards can be cut 1 inch × 3 inches so they can be easily held in the palm of the hand. Shuffle cards before each class period so that students are called on randomly. Teachers may want to make two cards for each student, so that students may be called on twice during one class period.

10. *Teach Your Neighbor.* Ask students to work in pairs, take turns being the teacher, and teach their peer the skill or information just taught by the teacher.

Analyzing the teaching methods used can identify a lack of variety in methods of teaching and student responding, the need for multisensory presentation of material, the number of academic and social demands required of students (Weade & Evertson, 1988), and a reliance on seatwork activities. Using classroom environmental checklists and setting analyses can help teachers identify changes needed to improve the effectiveness of instruction.

A Little Something Extra

A final component of this planning stage is adding a little something extra into instructional activities. Teachers need to be creative and inventive in designing different ways to teach similar skills. Teachers of students with EBD recognize the value of a "hands on, listen up, and eyes wide open" approach. Using multisensory teaching methods and student responding techniques, while adding "a little something out of the ordinary," not only adds an element of surprise and fun to classroom lessons, but also improves student learning.

The Effective Teaching Lesson

With an effective teacher mind-set, having analyzed various aspects of the learning environment and made plans to adopt the characteristics of an effective teacher and add that little something extra, teachers are now prepared to design the effective teaching lesson. The third stage of this model focuses on the actual planning of the instructional lesson. In this activity teachers address the student objectives for the lesson; the prerequisite skills needed; the teaching steps; and the evaluation of the lesson, upon its completion. The components of the effective teaching lesson, as presented in Figure 13.3, incorporate elements of effective teaching, direct instruction, lesson planning, and generalization (Hunter, 1984; Mastropieri & Scruggs, 1994; Morgan & Jensen, 1988; Reynolds et al., 1992; Rosenshine, 1986; Salend, 1994).

Lesson Objectives and Methods of Evaluating Student Achievement of Each Objective

In the first step of lesson planning, the teacher defines what he or she wants the students to learn, accomplish, or be able to do as a result of this lesson, while at the same time determining how he or she will measure whether each student has achieved those objectives. In determining lesson objectives teachers usually refer to a predetermined curriculum guide of skills and select skills that are both relevant and functional for students. The lesson objectives for students with EBD should include both academic and behavioral skills.

Lesson objectives and methods of evaluating student achievement of each objective.

Prerequisite student skills needed to achieve lesson objectives.

Teaching steps:

    Build student interest and motivation to learn

    State goals for today's lesson

    Teacher-directed instruction

    Guide students through completion of task

    Students complete task independently

    Summary of today's lesson

    Student independent practice of task

    Generalization activities

Teacher evaluation of lesson.

FIGURE 13.3   The effective teaching lesson.

The subsequent evaluation process will be easier if all objectives are written using behavioral terms, each stating the exact action expected of the students. For example, it is easier for the teacher to evaluate whether a student "can write a definition for the term freedom" than it is to evaluate whether a student "understands the term freedom." Teachers must also be sure to evaluate each student's performance on each objective. Having six students answer discussion questions does not evaluate the knowledge of the other members of the classroom. However, requiring all students to compose sample quiz questions and answers more accurately evaluates the knowledge of all students.

Prerequisite Student Skills Needed To Achieve Lesson Objectives

After defining the objectives of the lesson, teachers need to carefully identify the prerequisite academic and behavioral skills that students will need to participate in and benefit from the lesson. Constructing a task analysis (Salend, 1994) while actually completing the lesson activities can enable teachers to list the prerequisite skills students will need. These prerequisite skills may include everything from the ability to read and copy information from the chalkboard to understanding the teacher's vocabulary during instruction. For students with EBD, teachers should address academic skill and knowledge deficits (Meadows et al., 1994), attention and distractibility concerns, social and behavioral expectations, and the ability to follow oral or written directions and rules. Teachers who accurately assess student skill levels and the requirements of instructional tasks, can reduce the disruptive behaviors of students with EBD (Shores, Gunter, Denny, & Jack, 1993). In enabling all students to benefit from the lesson, teachers may need to make accommodations in the comfort of the physical environment, the variety of instructional materials used, the style of presenting information, the methods required for student responding, and the types of academic aids provided to students.

Teaching Steps

Possibly the most important step of any instructional activity involves building student interest in the lesson and motivating students to participate, put forth effort, and learn. Because many students with EBD demonstrate motivational deficits, this step is especially important. It is helpful for teachers to be aware of the classroom factors that have been found to relate to student motivation, the degree of student curiosity about the lesson content, the student's perception of the lesson's relevance and benefit, and the student's perception of personal likelihood of success (Mehring & Colson, 1990). Although many teachers of students with EBD are skilled in motivating student behavior by designing reinforcement systems for behaviors, such as following directions, completing assignments, and paying attention, there is a need to implement strategies to increase students' intrinsic motivation toward the content and the task of learning frequently (Mehring & Colson, 1990). The strategies presented in Figure 13.4, when used at the beginning of a lesson, can help teachers build student motivation for the lesson content.

In building student interest and motivation for the lesson content, teachers also state the goals of the day's lesson. In stating and posting what the students are going to be doing in the lesson, why these skills are important for the students, and what the students will accomplish in this lesson, the teacher provides the students with a sense of security in knowing what to expect and a vehicle for student recognition of personal accomplishment. Stating and posting these goals at the start of the lesson enables teachers and students to easily refer back to this information during the summary component of the lesson.

Teacher-directed instruction, especially when used for group instruction, is an effective strategy to increase both the academic gains and the appropriate behavior of students, while also decreasing disruptive behavior in the classroom (Englert, 1984; Rieth & Evertson, 1988; Shores et al., 1993). In this instructional phase, the teacher presents the new material and models using a systematic approach that ends with completion of the instructional task. The focus of instruction is to present information in such a way as to enable all students to experience success. This is accomplished through frequent monitoring of student understanding and maintaining high levels of student engagement in the learning activity. To facilitate acquisition and retention of information, it is recommended that students demonstrate a 70% to 90% accuracy level during teacher-directed instruction (Englert, 1984; Rieth & Evertson, 1988). Table 13.1, presented earlier in this chapter, lists several strategies for teachers to use during teacher-directed instruction to monitor student understanding and engage students in the lesson.

Following the modeling of the steps of the instructional task, the teacher provides a second model in which he or she asks students to

Lesson: Today's lesson will focus on transportation. Each student has previously selected a city to research and has gathered encyclopedia, chamber of commerce, and other forms of information about their city in order to prepare a city booklet. Today the students are to find out about the transportation available for persons residing in their city.

1. **Brainstorming.** Give each student a sheet of paper and have them write all the ideas/words/phrases they think of when they hear the word *transportation*. They have only 2 minutes. Have them share their ideas with a neighbor.

2. **Brainstorming.** Give each student a piece of paper and have them write as many different forms of transportation they can think of in 2 minutes. Use the blackboard or overhead to compile a class list of student ideas.

3. **Making Predictions.** Give each student a prediction card (design your own). Tell them that today they are going to research the topic of transportation in their city. Ask them to each make one or two predictions about the information they will find.

4. **Estimating Transportation Costs.** With a partner, have students think of four different forms of transportation that individuals living in a city could use to get to work and how much they think each would cost. You'll have to have some correct cost information to share with them after they make their guesses.

5. **Comparison.** Discuss with the class how people in a small town in Iowa get to work and how they think that would differ for people in large cities like the ones they are researching.

6. **Pictionary.** Write a vocabulary word related to transportation (e.g., commuter, tube [subway], rickshaw) on the board with three different definitions (one correct and two fake). Have students vote on the correct definition.

7. **Reading Bus Schedules.** Give each pair of students an actual city bus schedule and the following problem: You need to get from _____ Street to _____ Avenue by 8:30 A.M. How would you do this? How long will it take?

8. **Questions.** Give each student a question card (your design). Tell them that today they will be researching the transportation of their city and have them each write one question they would like to answer during their research.

9. **Discussion Questions.** Ask the students to discuss why some people who live in large cities drive their cars to work and others take a bus. Have them list the reasons for both sides and make a class list of their ideas. You can also have students rate or rank the reasons on each list according to areas such as cost, environmental concerns, safety, etc.

FIGURE 13.4   Building motivation to learn.

10. **Physical Activity.** Have a Nerf ball and give the class these instructions: Today we're going to learn about transportation. Each time you catch this ball you have to call out a different form of transportation. Throw the ball to a student and have them throw it to anyone they choose.

FIGURE 13.4 continued

perform each step and carefully guides them through task completion. In this step the teacher monitors to see if students understand the steps needed and can perform each step with guidance. When the teacher is satisfied with the students' progress, he or she should require the students to complete the task independently. During this stage it is important that the teacher circulates around the classroom, checking on each student's performance. In some instances, the teacher will need to reteach a task or a particular step of a task to an individual student or the entire class.

Once students have independently completed the instructional tasks required of the lesson and have met the lesson objectives, the teacher should review the previously stated goals of the lesson and involve the students in a summary activity. Sometimes referred to as closure, the purpose of the summary activity is to help the students build a sense of accomplishment and purposefulness for the completed lesson.

Once students have acquired the new skills, the teacher provides opportunities for practice. The purposes of practice activities are to reinforce procedures, facilitate memory, and improve automaticity. To be effective, practice activities, usually designed as seatwork or homework assignments, should be activities that students can complete independently at a 90% to 95% accuracy level (Englert, 1984; Rieth & Evertson, 1988).

Of particular importance in the field of special education is the need for students to generalize the skills learned in the classroom to other settings and tasks. Thus, teachers must design activities that demonstrate to students that skills learned are relevant and functional outside the classroom. For many students with disabilities, in order for generalization to occur, it must be actively planned for and taught (Morgan & Jensen, 1988). In designing generalization activities, teachers can easily apply math skills to topics such as calculating sports statistics, automobile performance ratings, and material requirements for various types of construction projects.

Teacher Evaluation of Lesson

The final step of the effective teaching lesson involves the teacher's evaluation of the lesson. In this activity the teacher, following a reflective teaching philosophy, evaluates the outcomes of the instructional activity. The teacher, in considering whether the objectives were met and/or whether any unexpected outcomes occurred during the lesson, makes decisions for future lessons. As an aid for teachers in this evaluation process, Englert (1984) suggested the videotaping of instructional activities. The videotapes provide accurate information while eliminating the need for teachers to record evaluative notes while they teach.

Learning Enhancers for Students During Instruction

In providing learning enhancers for students during instruction, the teacher needs to emphasize teaching students to assess the instructional environment and acquire information during instruction. The focus is to teach students with EBD the skills to independently perform learning tasks. These techniques are extrapolated from an adaptive instructional approach (Wang & Lindvall 1984), in that each student assumes increasing responsibility for identifying his or her own learning needs and the resources available to meet those needs, and from the concept of transenvironmental programming (Anderson-Inman, 1986). To that end, we describe two strategies that promote such student independence. These procedures are Sizing Up the Demands of the Setting (SUDS) and Zeroing In on the Presentation (ZIP).

Assessing the Instructional Environment

One of the identifying characteristics of students with EBD is their failure to independently assess the environment and lack of incidental learning, particularly in instructional settings. These students miss instructional subtleties and misread social cues. For example, students with EBD often miss the cues that teachers give during direct instruction for identifying key concepts or potential test material. Typically, these students do not model the learning behaviors and strategies of their peers during classroom activities. Therefore, instructional approaches used to enable students to maximize their learning in the mainstreamed classroom must be explicit and employ direct instructional techniques to teach specific behaviors.

The first step in preparing students for success in the mainstream is to teach them to assess the instructional environment. Sizing Up the Demands of the Setting (SUDS) offers a structured assessment procedure that students can employ. When using SUDS students assess five areas of the instructional setting: (a) instructional materials, (b) teacher presentation, (c) student responses, (d) student evaluation, and (e) classroom management.

In assessing instructional materials, students need to answer the question, What materials do I need to learn in this class? For instance, the student should identify the textbook or other materials that are used on a regular basis in the classroom, in addition to supplies needed for special assignments such as protractors, drawing paper, or crayons. Strategies for assisting students to organize and locate their materials are discussed later in this chapter. With this information and organizational strategies, students with EBD can assume the responsibility for being prepared for various class activities.

Students should also evaluate the ways that the teacher presents information. Numerous instructional methods are used in mainstreamed classes. A few examples include (a) small or large group instruction, (b) independent work, (c) cooperative groups, (d) lecture, (e) discussion, (f) laboratory experiments, and (g) demonstrations. Different modes of receiving information during instruction are best utilized with specific teaching presentation styles. For example, students require strong attending, listening, discriminating, and note-taking skills during a lecture format, whereas strong social, oral communication, and synthesis skills are needed in many cooperative group assignments. Identifying in advance the predominant instructional methods will enable students and teachers to select appropriate learning strategies to facilitate learning.

Along with how the teacher presents information, students need to identify how they will be expected to respond. Teachers may require students to read aloud, take notes, answer questions, complete worksheets, and complete group projects. Students also need to determine the number of different responding behaviors typically expected by individual teachers and whether teachers are receptive to offering students choices in responding modes. Again, it is important that an attempt is made to match the students' strengths in responding modes to the current class procedures. Teachers can assist students in identifying personal responding preferences so that they can take the responsibility for requesting accommodations from mainstreamed teachers. An analysis of student learning form that can be used to determine students' preferences is presented in Figure 13.11 and is discussed later in this chapter.

Students also should be aware of how their learning and performance will be evaluated in the classroom. Specifically, students should identify whether the teacher uses formative and/or summative procedures; whether exams are multiple choice, fill-in-the-blank, essay, or matching; or whether a portfolio approach is used. Information regarding the degree to which various matching assignments contribute to a student's overall grade is also beneficial. As with student response styles, students may perform differently when exposed to different evaluation modes due to their particular strengths and needs. Although attempts to accommodate students' response strengths may result in more accurate evaluations of skill levels, teachers need to assist students in identifying alternative evaluation modes that can assess the same skills or information as the traditional evaluation method was designed for.

The final area included in assessing the instructional environment is classroom management. For students with EBD, it is very important to define the standards of conduct established in the targeted classroom. For example, students should be very familiar with the rules and routines for the classroom and consequences for adhering to and deviating from those set expectations. With this information, students with EBD can plan their behavior choices and take responsibility for those choices.

The SUDS approach begins as a teacher-directed activity and moves to a student-directed task as the student becomes more skilled in applying the model. Two examples of teacher-prepared forms following the SUDS approach are presented in Figures 13.5 and 13.6. Teachers can help students use either of these models or design an alternative form by combining selected items depending on individual student needs. To conduct this environmental assessment, the student with EBD should visit the mainstream class and participate in activities prior to permanent placement. In some instances, teachers aware of environmental factors that affect learning may assist students in completing this assessment process.

Acquiring Information from Instruction

Students with EBD often have difficulty acquiring information from traditional classroom instruction. These students exhibit poor attention and organizational skills, and are reluctant to answer questions

---

Whose class will I be in? _____

What subject is it? _____

What do I need to have with me to be a successful learner? _____

How does the teacher teach in this classroom? _____

What kind of work do the kids in the class do? _____

What are the routines in this classroom? _____

What are the rules in this classroom? _____

Whom do I already know in this classroom? _____

Who would be a good helper for me in this classroom? _____

FIGURE 13.5   Sizing Up the Demands of the Setting (SUDS): Open-ended question format.

and ask for help. To assist them in this area, teachers need to provide instructional supports. The Zeroing In on the Presentation (ZIP) approach offers supports for improving students' attending, self-monitoring, and organizational skills in mainstreamed classes.

Attending supports can be organized by visual, auditory, and physical prompts, given by teachers, peers, or the students themselves. These procedures used to prompt students' attention to task can be subtle or quite distinct. Further, teachers can use these prompts for cuing individual students or an entire class. Table 13.2 lists examples of instructional supports for increasing student attention.

Students with EBD are often unaware of their own deficits in attending. Thus, they may appreciate the teacher's interest in their working on this goal. Simple self-monitoring sheets can be effective in helping students become more aware of their own attending behaviors and keep records of their progress toward increasing attention during instruction. However, because students with EBD tire easily of repetitive tasks, teachers may want to use a variety of self-monitoring methods, such as the following:

1. Using dot-to-dot pictures on which the student can connect 2 or more dots each time a specified behavior is exhibited.

Classroom_____   Subject_____

Instructional Materials

Book(s) used?_____   Do I have?   Yes ☐   No ☐
Other materials used?_____   Do I have?   Yes ☐   No ☐
Supplies needed? _____   Do I have?   Yes ☐   No ☐

Teacher Presentation

Lecture?   Yes ☐   No ☐
Advance organizers used?   Yes ☐   No ☐
Outlines or study guides used?   Yes ☐   No ☐
Blackboard or overhead used?   Yes ☐   No ☐
Video used?   Yes ☐   No ☐
Small/large group instruction?   Yes ☐   No ☐
Cooperative groups?   Yes ☐   No ☐
Laboratory experiments?   Yes ☐   No ☐
Independent seatwork?   Yes ☐   No ☐
Other _____

Student Responses

Reading silently?   Yes ☐   No ☐
Reading orally?   Yes ☐   No ☐
Oral responding?   Yes ☐   No ☐
Notetaking?   Yes ☐   No ☐
Homework?   Yes ☐   No ☐
Writing creatively/worksheets?
Individual products or group products?
Other _____

Student Evaluation

Types of tests and quizzes _____
Homework?   Yes ☐   No ☐
Portfolios?   Yes ☐   No ☐
Performance?   Yes ☐   No ☐
Individually or Groups?

Classroom Management

Routines _____
Rules _____
Consequences _____

Other important information that will help make a plan for being in this
class as a learner?

FIGURE 13.6   Sizing Up the Demands of the Setting (SUDS).

TABLE 13.2
Examples of Instructional Supports for Attending

Agent	Visual	Auditory	Physical
Teacher	Hand signals, such as "thumbs up" or tapping forehead	Verbal signal, such as "This is it, folks!" or "Time to zero in!"	Touching student's shoulder
	Turning on and off the lights	Tapping on the chalkboard	Pointing to page
			Establishing an attention posture
	Using a stop, look, and listen sign	Ringing a bell	Raising hand
Peer	Nod or "victory sign"	Comment such as "We really need to pay attention to this."	Tapping on desk
	Smile		Touching materials
	Modeling appropriate behavior	Whisper page number	Pointing to book
Student	Monitoring card	Ear phone with taped message	Pencil behind ear
	Picture of on-task student	Verbal rehearsal	Band on wrist
	Poster on wall	Self-talk	Monitor body position

2. Making tallies or checkmarks on a card for the occurrence of a specified behavior, preferably using recording devices with pictures or decorations to encourage attention.

3. Moving the hands of a clock face forward at each occurrence of the targeted behavior.

4. Playing Hangman on which parts of a shadow body can be added when a particular behavior is evidenced.

5. Awarding tokens, paper strips, or soft felt pompons, which are kept in a holding container for the occurrence of target behavior(s).

6. Playing "Clue," where clues to a problem or a prize are "uncovered" for tallied behaviors.

7. Writing contracts stating that targeted classroom behaviors will be checked off or assigned points.

8. Playing "Around the World," and allowing the student to collect countries or cities for occurrences of target behavior.

9. Spelling out the team name of the school (e.g., The MUSKIES).

10. Making paper clip necklaces.

11. Collecting arcade-type tickets.

Teachers can assist students in self-monitoring activities by cuing students to attend to their own behavior, to record their behavior at a given interval, or to adjust their behavior.

Students with EBD frequently exhibit deficits in organizing academic information. Graphic organizers and outlining formats, such as those presented in Figures 13.7 and 13.8, can effectively assist students in organizing information presented in classroom instruction. Students who learn better using their visual skills will benefit from graphic organizers, such as visual webs, the herringbone, story maps, Venn diagrams, and stick people. These strategies give students a schema for organizing and retrieving academic information presented in class. Students aware of the variety of outlining methods can select the most appropriate method to organize the specific information being presented by the teacher. Teachers can assist students in becoming more efficient learners by providing direct instruction and modeling in the use of these techniques.

Learning Enhancers for Students During Independent Learning

For students to benefit from instruction, they must possess effective skills for independent learning. This is a standard of behavior expected of all students in elementary and secondary classrooms. When not engaged in direct instruction, students are expected to manage their time and organize their assignments with regard to assignment format, response requirements, task deadlines, and information gathering activities. Although students with EBD who are mainstreamed may be provided behavioral modifications for their disabilities, general education teachers often hold them to the same expectations as their nondisabled counterparts with regard to those skills that make one an efficient learner. Unfortunately, students with

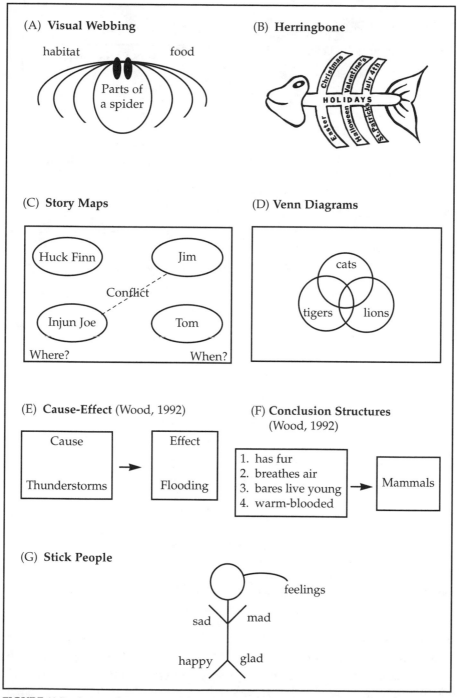

FIGURE 13.7   Approaches to organizing content presented in the instructional setting: graphic organizers.

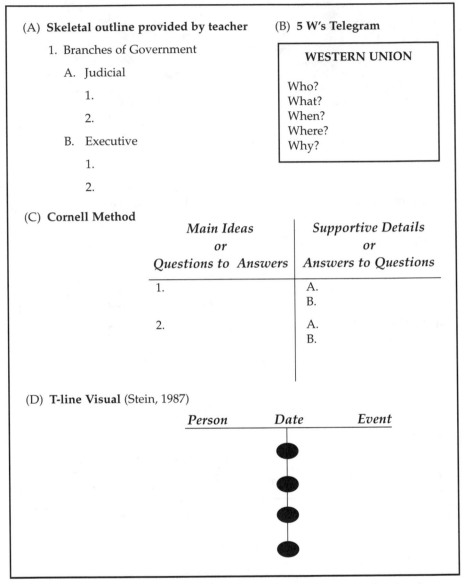

FIGURE 13.8   Approaches to organizing content presented in the instructional setting: outlining skills.

EBD often do not possess effective study skills needed to succeed in mainstream classrooms (Wong & Wong, 1986). Thus, specific help with time management, organization, good study habits, and research skills must be provided for these students to participate fully in learning activities and become lifelong learners.

Time Management

Managing time effectively seems to be a universal concern for individuals of all ages. Poor time management skills can be observed at any age. From the first day of kindergarten to the last day of senior high school, teachers can be overheard telling students to use their time more wisely. Yet, managing time seems to be a challenge for most students and even more difficult for students with EBD. General classroom teachers can employ a variety of activities to teach effective time management skills to students that will enhance their ability to complete assignments and instructional tasks in the allotted time, use unstructured time wisely, and meet assignment deadlines. One simple way to increase attention to assignment deadlines is to post a class routine for students to view. As exemplified in Figure 13.9, routines may be posted by daily activities or by weekly tasks. Daily or weekly schedules help students with EBD feel that they have more control over the activities and changes that occur in their school and home

---

Daily Schedule for February 7

    1st Period English

    8:00   Journal writing

    8:15–8:30   Review reading assignment

    8:30–8:50   Complete reading outlines and webs

Class Schedule for the week of February 10–14

Monday	*Tuesday*	*Wednesday*	*Thursday*	*Friday*
Complete spelling assignment	Read pp. 29–45 and discuss as a class	Spelling quiz Write a theme on someone you know who has contributed to the community	Review adverbial clauses Complete p. 35 in grammar book and questions 1–12 Finish themes	Spelling test Share themes with class Watch the video "Regular Lives"
Journal writing—"All people have something to contribute"	In assigned pairs–complete story web			

FIGURE 13.9   Examples of class schedules.

environments. This knowledge can translate into an increased sense of security because they know what to expect of their day.

In addition to making the general classroom more structured for mainstreamed students, teachers need to help these students generalize these time management skills to their own individual functioning. Thus, to increase mainstreamed success of students with EBD, classroom teachers should instruct students in ways to (a) make a school and study schedule, (b) estimate time to complete tasks, and (c) establish study priorities.

Many students with EBD have difficulty organizing their time and planning a schedule for completing schoolwork. One way to begin working with students on time management is to provide them with a calendar for the semester that is set up in a weekly format. This calendar can be used to help them block out class time, study time, and time for extracurricular and leisure activities. Using the calendar, teachers can have students record how they spend their school day by labeling class times as shown in Figure 13.10. By starting with the school day, all of the students in the class have a common purpose; thus, instruction can be done as a large group. After students have identified how they spend their school day, have them add their before- and after-school activities to their calendar. For example, have students note when they wake up in the morning, and approximate the time it takes for them to dress for school, eat breakfast, and travel to school. Once students have their morning and school day planned, have them indicate their after-school activities, such as clubs, athletic practices, school-sponsored activities, jobs, and so forth. They should also be encouraged to designate a specific time for completing homework, other than during in-school study halls. In particular, students should block out extra time each evening to complete unplanned homework and read class material.

Once the students have their weekly schedules completed, teachers can provide them with an estimated assignment schedule for the month and a listing of planned quizzes and exams. With this information before them, students should note on the calendar when assignments are due and plan for additional preparation and work time to complete those tasks. This activity will model for students a proactive approach to establishing a predictable and manageable plan that also has some flexibility for addressing unknown assignments and tasks as well as leisure activities.

Once students have designed their schedules, they can carry the calendars with them for several days and note when they adhered to

Time	Sunday	Monday	Tuesday	Wednesday	Thursday	Friday	Saturday
7:00							
8:00		Homeroom	Homeroom	Homeroom	Homeroom	Homeroom	
9:00		Algebra	Algebra	Algebra	Algebra	Algebra	scouts
10:00		English	English	English	English	English	→
11:00		P.E.	P.E.	P.E.	P.E.	P.E.	
12:00				Lunch			
1:00		Civics	Civics	Civics	Civics	Civics	
2:00	Homework	Art	Art	Art	Art	Art	
3:00	←			Ball practice			
4:00	→			Ball practice			
5:00				Homework			
6:00							

FIGURE 13.10 Weekly student calendar.

the schedule or strayed from the plan (Reetz & Crank, 1988). Then, the teacher and students can discuss how to deal with unexpected changes in schedules and make necessary adjustments to the overall plan. The teacher should remind students daily to use their schedules for recording their homework due dates and project deadlines. To encourage students to begin building this time management habit, the teacher can provide rewards for using the schedule regularly. The following are a few suggestions for motivating students to use a calendar:

1. Draw a student's name and check his or her calendar. If the student's calendar is up-to-date for the week, the student or class wins a prize. This can be done on an announced day each week or as a surprise.

2. Establish a competition where teams of students compete for extra credit points or prizes for the team that keeps up their calendars.

3. Have assignments for the week posted Monday morning before students enter the classroom and provide a few minutes for students to copy them down on their calendars. Chart the number of students each day who have copied this information. At the end of the week, if the class average equals or exceeds 90%, reward the students with an academic activity.

General classroom teachers can help foster time-management skills by using a variety of modeling and direct instructional practices. In fact, although it may take some class time in the beginning to establish effective time management habits in students, if this skill is given priority throughout the school year, students with EBD will be better equipped to handle the demands of the general classroom and other students in the class will also benefit from a more structured and supportive environment.

Good Study Habits

Sometimes regardless of teachers' efforts to meet mainstreamed students' academic needs, these students continue to have difficulty progressing through the curriculum with their peers. Poor achievement for many students with EBD can be attributed to inadequate study habits. That is, students with EBD often fail to develop a strategic manner of approaching schoolwork. Hence, the classroom teacher should help students to identify the most effective methods of studying and ways to use this information to plan a study program.

Study habits should be individualized to meet a student's academic and motivational needs. To determine the study needs of a student, a checklist can be used that helps delineate existing habits and those that need to be added to the student's study repertoire. One study inventory by Hoover and Patton (1995) (see Figure 13.11) has the student rate his or her skills and provides a pre- and posttest view. Based on the student's responses, the teacher can help him or her design a study program that will best fit the student's needs. When planning a study program, teachers should address the following issues: (a) where to study, (b) when to study, and (c) how to study.

A common problem for students is finding a place to study at home that is conducive to learning and completing assignments. Teachers can help students find a place to study by suggesting various sites within the home. For example, a desk in the student's bedroom is an obvious choice, but this option isolates the student from adult monitoring. For students who need regular instructional support, the kitchen table can be a good place to complete homework and review schoolwork. This gives the student easy access to parents or older siblings who can answer questions or simply check on the student's progress. Wherever the study site is, it is important that the environment is free of distractions such as stereos, toys, televisions, or windows.

Once the appropriate study site has been selected, the student must choose a time to study. Tackling homework immediately after school enables students to get the work done while they still remember the assignments from the day. It also clears their evening for other leisure and family activities. If the student requires assistance in reading or understanding directions, it is probably a good idea for that student to do homework when parents are home to answer questions. One way to accomplish this is to have the student work in the kitchen while parents are preparing the evening meal. This could provide students with 30 minutes or more of supervised studying each evening.

The last issue of studying with which students with EBD have difficulty is how to study. Students with EBD are often characterized as passive learners; that is, they frequently do not engage in active procedures to enhance the retention of information or specific skills. Thus, the teacher should provide students with a model for studying that requires their active participation. For instance, if the homework assignment is to read a chapter in the textbook, the teacher can require the students to follow a reading strategy such as SQ3R, which was designed to increase students' comprehension of text readings.

324 ORMSBEE, MARONEY, AND MELOY

Form 2.1 Study Skills Inventory

Completed by: _____ Student: _____ Date: _____

Place the appropriate number (1, 2, or 3) in the box next to each study skill subskill
(1 = Mastered—regular, appropriate use of skill; 2 = Partially Mastered—needs some
improvement; 3 = Not Mastered—infrequent use of skill).

Reading Rate
☐ Skimming
☐ Scanning
☐ Rapid reading
☐ Normal rate
☐ Study or careful reading
☐ Understands importance of reading rates

Listening
☐ Attends to listening activities
☐ Applies meaning to verbal messages
☐ Filters out auditory distractions
☐ Comprehends verbal messages
☐ Understands importance of listening skills

Notetaking/Outlining
☐ Uses headings/subheadings appropriately
☐ Takes brief and clear notes
☐ Records essential information
☐ Applies skill during writing activities
☐ Uses skill during lectures

☐ Develops organized outlines
☐ Follows consistent notetaking format
☐ Understands importance of notetaking
☐ Understands importance of outlining

Report Writing
☐ Organizes thoughts in writing
☐ Completes written reports from outline
☐ Includes only necessary information
☐ Uses proper sentence structure
☐ Uses proper punctuation
☐ Uses proper grammar and spelling
☐ Proofreads written assignments
☐ States clear introductory statement
☐ Includes clear concluding statements
☐ Understands importance of writing reports

Oral Presentations
☐ Freely participates in oral presentations

© 1995 by PRO-ED, Inc.

(Continues)

FIGURE 13.11 **Study Skills Inventory. From** *Teaching Students with Learning Problems to Use Study Skills: A Teacher's Guide* **(pp. 14–16) by J. J. Hoover and J. R. Patton, 1995, Austin, TX: PRO-ED. Copyright 1995 by PRO-ED, Inc. Reproduced with permission.**

Form 2.1 (continued)

☐ Oral presentations are well organized

☐ Uses gestures appropriately

☐ Speaks clearly

☐ Uses proper language when reporting orally

☐ Understands importance of oral reporting

Graphic Aids

☐ Attends to relevant elements in visual material

☐ Uses visuals appropriately in presentations

☐ Develops own graphic material

☐ Is not confused or distracted by visual material in presentations

☐ Understands importance of visual material

Test Taking

☐ Studies for tests in an organized way

☐ Spends appropriate amount of time studying different topics covered on a test

☐ Avoids cramming for tests

☐ Organizes narrative responses appropriately

☐ Reads and understands directions before answering questions

☐ Proofreads responses and checks for errors

☐ Identifies and uses clue words in questions

☐ Properly records answers

☐ Saves difficult items until last

☐ Eliminates obvious wrong answers

☐ Systematically reviews completed tests to determine test-taking or test-studying errors

☐ Corrects previous test-taking errors

☐ Understands importance of test-taking skills

Library Usage

☐ Uses cataloging system (card or computerized) effectively

☐ Able to locate library materials

☐ Understands organizational layout of library

☐ Understands and uses services of media specialist

☐ Understands overall functions and purposes of a library

☐ Understands importance of library usage skills

Reference Materials

☐ Able to identify components of different reference materials

☐ Uses guide words appropriately

☐ Consults reference materials when necessary

☐ Uses materials appropriately to complete assignments

(Continues)

FIGURE 13.11   continued

Form 2.1   (continued)

☐ Able to identify different types of reference materials and sources
☐ Understands importance of reference materials

Time Management
☐ Completes tasks on time
☐ Plans and organizes daily activities and responsibilities effectively
☐ Plans and organizes weekly and monthly schedules
☐ Reorganizes priorities when necessary
☐ Meets scheduled deadlines
☐ Accurately perceives the amount of time required to complete tasks

☐ Adjusts time allotment to complete tasks
☐ Accepts responsibility for managing own time
☐ Understands importance of effective time management

Self-Management
☐ Monitors own behavior
☐ Changes own behavior as necessary
☐ Thinks before acting
☐ Responsible for own behavior
☐ Identifies behaviors that interfere with own learning
☐ Understands importance of self-management

Summary of Study Skill Proficiency

Summarize in the chart below the number of Mastered (1), Partially Mastered (2), and Not Mastered (3) study skill subskills. The number next to each study skill represents the total number of subskills for each area.

Study Skill	M	PM	NM	Study Skill	M	PM	NM
Reading Rate–6				Test Taking–13			
Listening–5				Library Usage–6			
Notetaking/Outlining–9				Reference Materials–6			
Report Writing–10				Time Management–9			
Oral Presentations–6				Self-Management–6			
Graphic Aids–5							

Summary Comments:

FIGURE 13.11   continued

The steps of this strategy are Survey, Question, Read, Recite, and Review (Robinson, 1961). To monitor the students' use of the strategy, the teacher can require the students to write down the information observed at each stage. At the Survey stage, the students might write down the headings in the chapter and a brief description of each picture, chart, or diagram; at the Question stage, the students might write down several questions that were generated based on survey of the chapter; and so on through each step of the SQ3R strategy. This activity encourages students to be more active in their approach to learning and should enhance their acquisition of information.

Organizational Skills

When talking to teachers about the success of students with EBD, one of their biggest concerns is the disorganization of the students. This disorganization may manifest itself in students' coming to class without the appropriate instructional materials and homework. Although to some having a student in class without a pencil seems like a trivial issue, valuable class time can be lost if a student is searching for a writing utensil in the desk or having to return to a locker to retrieve the previous day's homework. Thus, this seemingly low-priority issue has the potential to become a large headache for students and teachers.

A relatively simple way to help students bring materials to class is to help them set up a class notebook system that has several components, including (a) a plastic utensils pouch, (b) pocket file folders that divide the notebook by subjects, and (c) a homework notebook. When notebook systems are prepared, students should put several pencils, pens, and erasers in the plastic pouch. Any other items that are used regularly in all classes should also be placed in the pouch. It is not recommended that students be encouraged to have a separate notebook for each class, but rather a large notebook that can accommodate the entire day's classes. This eliminates the problems of mixing up notebooks for different classes and serves as the primary organizational center for the student. Once the notebook is set up, teachers can encourage the maintenance of the system by checking the notebooks regularly for orderliness and neatness (Spector, Decker, & Shaw, 1991).

In secondary classrooms some learning materials are used only for a particular subject, such as compasses and protractors for math or drawing pencils and squares for drafting. As an aid for remembering to take these specific supplies to the appropriate classes, students can store these items in labeled or color-coded zip-lock plastic bags and place them in a desk or locker. If the student has difficulty remembering to bring the appropriate bag of supplies to the particular class, the teacher can consider keeping the student's materials in the classroom.

Within the notebook system, a homework log or notebook should be included for students to record daily homework assignments. Students should be reminded to note their homework, the due date, any information needed to complete the work such as directions (Reetz & Crank, 1988), and a place for the parents to sign that the homework was completed (see Figure 13.12). For students with EBD, it helps to set up a reinforcement schedule for recording, completing, and returning homework; that is, the teacher can reward the student for each day the student remembers to record the homework (see, e.g., Figure 13.13). This begins to shape the student's behavior by emphasizing the importance of writing down assignments in the homework log. Once the student has mastered using the assignment book, reinforcement should be faded by increasing the days to earn a reinforcer or shifting the focus to a higher level behavior. For instance, if the student has remembered to record homework assignments for 6 weeks consistently with weekly rewards, the teacher can change the reinforcement schedule to biweekly rewards, or the teacher can begin to reinforce completed or returned homework instead of the relatively low-level behavior of noting the homework in the log.

Although it is important for students to establish a routine for their week, they must also plan their daily activities with respect to

HOMEWORK LOG			
Date	*Assignment/Directions*	*Due Date*	*Parent Signature*

FIGURE 13.12   Homework log.

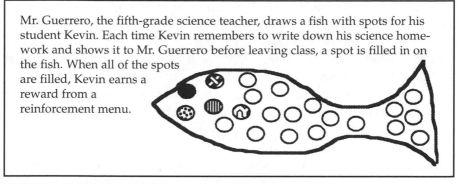

Mr. Guerrero, the fifth-grade science teacher, draws a fish with spots for his student Kevin. Each time Kevin remembers to write down his science homework and shows it to Mr. Guerrero before leaving class, a spot is filled in on the fish. When all of the spots are filled, Kevin earns a reward from a reinforcement menu.

FIGURE 13.13   Motivational idea.

daily homework assignments. To facilitate the regular completion of homework and preparation for daily instruction, the teacher should have students list everything they need to do each evening to be ready for school the following day. From the list they develop, the teacher asks the students to prioritize the items in the order in which they should complete the tasks. Thus, assignments that are not due the next day may be lower on the priority list than studying for a math exam that will be first thing in the morning. Then, the students should check off items as they complete them and record how much time they required to finish the task. This will help students learn to gauge the time it will take to complete assignments, read textbook chapters, and study for exams.

Finally, teachers should encourage students to become active decision makers in their studying. Have students consider how to organize their homework in the most effective and least disagreeable fashion. For example, if a student has three homework assignments to complete—reading a passage from *Hamlet,* doing 14 geometry problems, and comparing the nutritional labels of two canned foods—it might be best to prioritize these tasks according to the difficulty and interest level. If the student finds the geometry to be the most challenging and least likable, he might complete this first when his energy and tolerance level is highest, then pick the next assignment that would be more enjoyable to complete. This gives the student more control in completing the homework in a manner that provides the most motivation.

The focus of organizational activities should not be merely a day-to-day perspective, but rather students should be encouraged to divide larger assignments into shorter or smaller pieces over time to complete them more easily. Sometimes, particularly in secondary classrooms, assignments require work to be done over a period of several days or weeks. Long-term assignments, such as research papers, debates, and other tasks that require planning over time, can be difficult for students with EBD because of their need for structure. Hence, for mainstreamed students with EBD to successfully complete long-term assignments, teachers should provide specific, sequenced directions and monitor students' progress.

When given long-term assignments, students with EBD will benefit from a written list of the steps that must be taken to complete the task and a projected time line of when each stage should be started and finished. As shown in Figure 13.14, step-by-step guidelines make the process simpler and more manageable for the students. Also, the students can become more confident that they are succeeding because they have a measure from which to compare themselves. That is, students with EBD can use the steps and time line to gauge their progress and make decisions based on their status with regard to the model the teacher has provided.

RESEARCH PAPER GUIDELINES

Date To Begin	Task	Date Due	Teacher Signature
January 12	Pick a person from Civil War to study	January 15	
January 15	Identify five sources	January 19	
January 19	Read sources and complete note cards	January 23	
January 27	Prepare outline/map of paper	January 28	
February 1	Write draft of paper	February 4	
February 5	Edit draft	February 8	
February 9	Revise draft	February 11	
February 12	Give to peer to read and edit	February 13	
February 13	Revise draft	February 14	
February 16	Turn in final revision		

FIGURE 13.14   Example of research paper guidelines.

This time line can be given individually to the student with EBD or posted for the entire class to follow. Either way, by providing a guide to the steps that the student must follow to complete the assignment, the student is able to see that what initially may have seemed an enormous task is manageable. In addition to using a time line or step-by-step direction list, the classroom teacher should check the student's work or progress at each identified point. By monitoring the student's work at each step, constructive feedback and individual directions can be given to keep the student from falling behind or completing the tasks incorrectly.

Learning Styles

Controversy has existed for many years over the issue of learner styles. Proponents of learning styles suggest that teachers should identify how students approach learning and adjust their instructional methods for a better fit between how educators present information and how students absorb it (Carbo, Dunn, & Dunn, 1986). When addressing the learning styles of students, one must consider various dimensions, including (a) environmental factors, (b) affective issues, (c) instructional grouping issues, and (d) perceptual strengths (Carbo & Hodges, 1991).

Environmental Factors

Students report that they have preferences regarding quiet versus sound, bright or soft lighting, warm or cool temperatures, and formal versus informal setting designs (Dunn, Beaudry, & Klavas, 1989). Although meeting the specific environmental preferences of every student in a class is nearly impossible, teachers can offer some choices for students. For example, ways to make a classroom more accommodating to students with environmental preferences include having clip-on lights available to students who prefer more light or focused light, providing alternative seating structures such as chairs instead of desks, and establishing quiet zones.

Affective Issues

Some students are very sensitive to elements of motivation, persistence, conformity, responsibility, and structure. That is, many students need the classroom to be a stimulating and/or rewarding place in order for them to perform academic tasks. Hunter (1984) identified six variables that teachers could manipulate to support and enhance students' attitudes toward learning: (a) developing positive feelings about learning, (b) providing rewards for students' performance and efforts, (c) using students' interests in designing instruction, (d) designing tasks that ensure student success, (e) using the classroom structure to increase or decrease students' school-related stress, and (f) providing immediate performance feedback to students.

Instructional Grouping Issues

General classroom teachers employ a variety of instructional configurations to make learning motivational as well as to accommodate the diverse needs of students. These configurations range from individual, pairs, small groups, and whole-class groupings. Moreover, educational professionals have urged teachers to increase their use of small groups to teach heterogeneous classrooms that may include at-risk students and students with disabilities. However, not all students like to work with their peers. In fact, for students with EBD, small group or cooperative activities can be quite difficult to manage because of poor social skills and other characteristics that impede the development of effective personal relationships. Hence, teachers should consider carefully whether a student has the interpersonal skills needed to work with peers on academic tasks; if the student does not have these skills, the teacher should plan specific instruction to teach those skills. More than likely, these skills not only are lacking in those students with identified EBD but may be a problem for other students as well.

Perceptual Strengths

Students use their senses in unique ways. Some students remember what they hear, others remember what they see, and still others must manipulate the information to recall it. Knowing which modalities students prefer to use when learning helps teachers prepare instruction that is more accessible to all learners, including those students with disabilities who have been mainstreamed. Learning styles inventories are readily available to determine the range of learning styles and preferences in classrooms.

Finding Information

Students with EBD often have difficulty completing assignments that require them to access multiple sources of information found in dictionaries, encyclopedias, indexes, and library catalogs. This inability to efficiently manipulate reference materials results in poorly written and researched reports and presentations, as well as a feeling of frustration and helplessness when faced with the prospect of a trip to the library. However, if specific directed guidance is provided, the student can complete research tasks with the relative ease of peers.

Students with EBD often have difficulty finding and using resource materials for projects. Classroom teachers can do many simple things to help students find reference and other materials in the library and access those materials independently. To help students find reference materials and other types of resources, the teacher can provide a simple map of the physical layout of the library that identifies the locations of references, journals and magazines, card catalog, computerized library listings, biographies, fiction books, and nonfiction books. This library map should also indicate how the Dewey Decimal System runs and the subjects that are subsumed under each division. It would also make the student more comfortable using the library if the teacher assigned some simple tasks that required the student to find different kinds of materials in various locations in the library. For example, the teacher could assign students different topics to access using the library's computerized filing system. Much like a scavenger hunt, students can be directed to find particular information that can be located only through the computer system. In addition to having a guide of the physical layout of the library, students with EBD may need help distinguishing various reference books and their purposes. The teacher might provide a listing of various reference materials and the kinds of information contained in them to serve as a guide for students. Figure 13.15 is an example of a resource guide.

Once the student demonstrates competence in finding materials in the various sections of the library, the next concern is teaching the student how to follow a global to specific research plan. That is, most research begins with a fairly vague idea that becomes more specific as one finds information and is able to decide what is and is not needed in the paper or project. Although many students have little difficulty in following a simple format for researching a topic, students with EBD who have difficulty organizing their thoughts will have particular trouble implementing a strategic research approach. To overcome this organizational deficit, teachers can provide the student with a detailed plan for finding a topic and collecting general to specific information related to the topic. This can be accomplished by

---

GUIDE TO BASIC REFERENCES

Encyclopedia—An alphabetical set of books that cover a range of topics; provides general historical and topical information.

Magazines—A weekly, monthly, or quarterly publication that provides information on topics that are of interest to general public; can be specific to one subject or interest.

Almanacs—An annual publication containing information relating to yearly events.

Atlases—A collection of maps of states and/or countries.

Informational books—Publications that focus on one subject or event and provide detailed information.

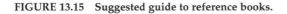

FIGURE 13.15   Suggested guide to reference books.

providing a list of pertinent guiding questions, directive statements, or actions to take with regard to working through the research process. Another way to assist students with poor research skills is to assign the student a research buddy who is doing his or her own project and can be a model of the process. Whatever option a teacher chooses to use, it is crucial that the student is monitored daily to ensure that he or she is progressing at an appropriate pace.

Study Guides

A common problem for students with exceptionalities who are mainstreamed in general classes is identifying key concepts in preparing for class discussions and formative and summative tests. One tool for supporting students' development of independent learning is the use of study guides. Study guides can be used variously to (a) lead students through independent review of academic information prior to a test, (b) introduce new content-specific vocabulary, (c) guide content-specific reading, (d) review newly introduced concepts, (e) integrate previously learned information with new content, and (f) practice specific skills (Hudson, Ormsbee, & Myles, 1994). Moreover, study guides can enhance a mainstreamed student's mastery of academic content through meaningful practice activities (Bean & Ericson, 1989; Davey, 1986; Smith, 1987).

When preparing a study guide, the teacher should organize it in the sequence in which information is presented in the textbook and in class. Items on the study guide can require a range of student responses from defining vocabulary to responding to synthesis-level questions to generating questions resulting from assigned readings. This array of activities can be useful in guiding students from low- to high-level thinking and responding (Hudson et al., 1994).

When using this format with students, it is important that the study guide be given to students at the beginning of the unit or chapter rather than at the end. This enables the students to be more proactive in their learning, reading, and attention to class activities and discussions. When preparing items, teachers may wish to provide clues such as page numbers, mnemonics, or other teacher-identified prompts designed to engage the students' memory systems. Whatever format a teacher selects, a well-developed study guide can help the classroom learning environment become more individualized by providing highly specific direction to students' learning (Wood & Mateja, 1983).

References

Allinder, R. M. (1993). I think I can, I think I can: The effect of self-efficacy on teacher effectiveness. *Beyond Behavior, 4*(2), 29.

Anderson-Inman, L. (1986). Bridging the gap: Student-centered strategies for promoting the transfer of learning. *Exceptional Children, 52,* 562–572.

Bean, T. W., & Ericson, B. O. (1989). Text previews and three level study guides for content areas reading. *Journal of Reading, 32,* 337–341.

Carbo, M., Dunn, R., & Dunn, K. (1986). *Teaching students to read through their individual learning styles.* Reston, VA: Reston Publishing. (ERIC Document Reproduction Service No. ED 281 171)

Carbo, M., & Hodges, H. (1991, May). *Learning styles strategies can help students at risk.* Reston, VA: Clearinghouse on Handicapped and Gifted Children at the Council for Exceptional Children.

Davey, B. (1986). Using textbook activity guides to help students learn from textbooks. *Journal of Reading, 29,* 489–495.

DiBella-McCarthy, H., McDaniel, E. A., & Miller, R. (1995). How efficacious are you? *Teaching Exceptional Children, 27*(3), 68–72.

Dunn, R., Beaudry, J. S., & Klavas, A. (1989). Survey of research on learning styles. *Educational Leadership, 46*(6), 50–58.

Eby, J. W. (1992). *Reflective planning, teaching, and evaluation for the elementary school.* New York: Merrill.

Englert, C. S. (1984). Measuring teacher effectiveness from the teacher's point of view. *Focus on Exceptional Children, 17*(2), 1–14.

Harden, M. L. (1992). Living history. *Beyond Behavior, 3*(3), 3–5.

Heard, S. R. (Producer). (1993). *Good morning Miss Toliver* [Video]. (Available from FASE Productions, P.O. Box 847, Los Angeles, CA 90010).

Hoover, J. J. (1988). *Teaching handicapped students study skills.* Lindale, TX: Hamilton.

Hoover, J. J., & Patton, J. R. (1995). *Teaching students with learning problems to use study skills: A teacher's guide.* Austin, TX: PRO-ED.

Howell, K. W., Fox, S. L., & Morehead, M. K. (1993). *Curriculum-based evaluation: Teaching and decision making.* Pacific Grove, CA: Brookes/Cole.

Hudson, F. G., Ormsbee, C. K., & Myles, B. S. (1994). Study guides: An instructional tool for equalizing student achievement. *Intervention in School and Clinic, 30*(2), 99–102.

Hunter, M. (1984). Knowing, teaching, and supervising. In P. L. Hosford (Ed.), *Using what we know about teaching* (pp. 169–192). Alexandria, VA: Association for Curriculum Development.

Knitzer, J., Steinberg, Z., & Fleisch, B. (1990). *At the schoolhouse door: An examination of programs and policies for children with behavioral and emotional problems.* New York: Bank Street College.

Mastropieri, M. A., & Scruggs, T. E. (1994). *Effective instruction for special education* (2nd ed.). Austin, TX: PRO-ED.

Meadows, N. B., Neel, R. S., Scott, C. M., & Parker, G. (1994). Academic performance, social competence, and mainstream accommodations: A look at main-streamed students with serious behavioral disorders. *Behavioral Disorders, 19*(3), 170–180.

Mehring, T. A., & Colson, S. E. (1990). Motivation and mildly handicapped learners. *Focus on Exceptional Children, 22*(5), 1–14.

Morgan, D. P., & Jensen, W. R. (1988). *Teaching behaviorally disordered students: Preferred practices.* Columbus, OH: Merrill.

Parmar, R. S., & Crawley, J. F. (1991). Challenging the routines and passivity that characterize arithmetic instruction for children with mild handicaps. *Remedial and Special Education, 12*(5), 23–32, 43.

Peterson, B. (1990). When nothing goes wrong. *Beyond Behavior, 2*(1), 3–4.

Reetz, L. J., & Crank, J. (1988). Include item management and learning strategies in the ED curriculum. *Perceptions, 23*(2), 26–27.

Reynolds, M. C., Wang, M. C., & Walberg, H. J. (1992). The knowledge bases for special and general education. *Remedial and Special Education, 13*(5), 6–10, 33.

Rieth, H., & Evertson, C. (1988). Variables related to the effective instruction of difficult-to-teach children. *Focus on Exceptional Children, 20*(5), 1–8.

Robinson, F. P. (1961). *Effective study.* New York: Harper and Bros.

Rosenshine, B. (1986). Synthesis of research on explicit teaching. *Educational Leadership, 43*(7), 60–69.

Salend, S. J. (1994). *Effective mainstreaming: Creating inclusive classrooms* (2nd ed.). New York: Macmillan.

Shatzer, J. R. (1991). Journal writing with emotionally disturbed children. *Beyond Behavior, 3*(1), 12–15.

Shores, R. E., Gunter, P. L., Denny, R. K., & Jack, S. L. (1993). Classroom influences on aggressive and disruptive behavior of students with emotional and behavioral disorders. *Focus on Exceptional Children, 26*(2), 1–10.

Skinner, C. H., Ford, J. M., & Yunker, B. D. (1991). A comparison of instructional response requirements on the multiplication performance of behaviorally disordered students. *Behavioral Disorders, 17*(1), 56–65.

Smith, R. (1987). A study guide for extending student's reading of social studies material. *Social Studies, 78,* 85–87.

Spector, S., Decker, K., & Shaw, S. F. (1991). Independence and responsibility: An LD resource room at South Windsor High School. *Intervention in School and Clinic, 26,* 238–245.

Stein, H. (1987, July/August). Visualized notemaking: Left-right brain theory applied in the classroom. *The Social Studies,* pp. 163–168.

U.S. Department of Education. (1993). *Fifteenth annual report to Congress on the implementation of the Individuals with Disabilities Act.* Washington, DC: Author.

Wang, M. C., & Lindvall, C. M. (1984). Individual differences and school learning environments: Theory, research, and design. In E. W. Gordon (Ed.), *Review of research in education* (Vol. 11, pp. 161–226). Washington, DC: American Educational Research Association

Weade, R., & Evertson, C. M. (1988). The construction of lessons in effective and less effective classrooms. *Teaching and Teacher Education, 4*(3), 189–213.

Wong, B. Y. L., & Wong, R. (1986). Study behavior as a function of metacognitive knowledge about critical task variables: An investigation of above average, average, and learning disabled readers. *Learning Disabilities Research, 1,* 101–111.

Wood, J. (1992). *Adapting instruction for mainstreamed and at-risk students.* New York: Macmillan.

Wood, K. D., & Mateja, J. A. (1983). Adapting secondary level strategies for use in elementary classrooms. *The Reading Teacher, 36*(6), 492–496.

CHAPTER 14

Inclusion and Diversity: Powerful Words with Powerful Meaning

Laura Zionts and Pamela Baker

Inclusion, the subject of this book, is a topic that addresses the right of every individual to actively participate in the community. The philosophy behind the inclusion movement is simple: Everybody is an equally important link in the societal chain. A challenging aspect of acting on a philosophical stance is that it challenges one to think broadly and redefine personal opinions and perspectives for consistency across one's belief system. Such is the case for those who espouse the ideals of the inclusion movement. In order that society may include *everyone*, people must examine their acceptance of the diversity of people everywhere around them. Diversity is the cornerstone of present-day society.

When speaking of diversity among student populations, educators are frequently referring to children with special needs, children of color, children for whom English is not the primary language, and children from low socioeconomic areas (Biemiller, 1993; Carnine, 1994; Grossman, 1995; Harry, 1992). It should be noted that this diversity can also include children who are homeless (Schwartz, 1995) and children who are highly mobile (e.g., children whose families are migrant farmers) (Ascher, 1991). Educators are exploring how to construct classroom environments that allow *all* students equal access to knowledge and an equal opportunity to learn and to engage in critical thought. As society enters the 21st century, these issues will only increase in importance for teachers and support staff in the public schools.

It is interesting to note the way in which educators address diversity. They address it as a subsection of the field of education rather than the integral part of education that it is. Diversity needs to be addressed within every theory and approach to which educators are exposed in teacher training programs. It should be addressed within each inservice and conference presentation educators attend, not as a postscript but as *the heart of the matter*. Educators will be able to trace progress toward meeting children's needs as fewer chapters such as this are written and the diverse backgrounds of learners are integrated *within the contexts* of theory and practice.

Many educators have been asked to teach classes of students who have very diverse learning needs. One of us (Zionts) once taught in a classroom composed of 2 children who had intense learning support needs (each had been labeled severely handicapped), 8 students who had moderate learning support needs and/or attention-deficit/ hyperactivity disorder [ADHD] (3 of the 8 were labeled as severely learning disabled, 4 were labeled emotionally disturbed, 1 was labeled mentally retarded), and 10 general education students, of whom 2 were non–English speaking students (1 spoke Spanish and 1 spoke Laotian). There were some *very* interesting days in that classroom. Thankfully, I had two part-time aides (to whom I am eternally grateful). During that year I found two ideas to be true, as many educators have: First, good teaching is good teaching, no matter who the students are. Second, sometimes good teaching is not enough; facilitating positive peer interactions is equally indispensable.

In this chapter, we offer some ideas about teaching to meet the needs of many diverse learners, and helping those learners discover the important minds within themselves and their classmates. We hope the reader will be able to take pieces of this chapter to classrooms or faculty meetings and make them work to meet the needs of each unique community.

Environmental Considerations

To create a classroom atmosphere accepting of differences among individuals, educators must pay close attention to how they model this common acceptance in all regards. This includes how teachers arrange and decorate classrooms. Room decor must represent different images of "peopleness"; that is, pictures should depict people at all ages and stages of life, people of varying socioeconomic status and occupation, people of each gender, and people with disabilities. Classroom libraries and shared literature choices should reflect acceptance of diversity among people.

In our many visits to general and special education classrooms, we have rarely seen classrooms that truly exemplify these ideals, but they do exist. Although posters, pictures, and art supplies that exemplify diversity are available, currently one still has to search for them. Two sources are the Lakeshore and Colorful World, Inc., catalogs, which contain a myriad of supplies, toys, and literature to match the characteristics of the diverse classroom. When given an opportunity to paint or color with crayons or coloring pencils, children should be able to choose from several colors representing skin tones ranging from beige to increasingly darker brown shades toward black. The "Color People" crayons from Lakeshore allow students to color people as they actually see them—not white, not black, but variations of many colors. An easy and inexpensive way for teachers to create "multicultural" colors is to mix tempera paints to create different shades.

Likewise, teachers should supplement existing classroom toys with dolls and toy figures (e.g., LEGO™ people, Fisher Price people, puzzles) of varying skin tones. One school we visited had a group of teachers who were particularly dedicated to the principle of addressing diversity with positive support in their classrooms. These teachers kept a running list of teacher supply stores in their community that offered wide selections of materials and supplies.

Students loved the multicultural art activities that one of us (Baker) used when discussing various cultures. When the class, comprised largely of African American students, did a unit on Native Americans, we discussed Native American history, conducted potlatches, made totem poles, gave ourselves Native American Indian names, and had a Kachina doll coloring contest. Many of the students had very stereotypical attitudes about Native Americans usually spurred by the media. They did not know that the music teacher at our school was Native American (in fact his father was the chief of the Powhatan Nation). At the end of the unit, he spoke to the class. The students were surprised that he was Native American because he looked and talked the way they perceived African American people. He discussed the many stereotypes that people have about Native Americans. It was an eye-opening experience for everybody.

In selecting children's literature that represents diverse populations, one must be careful. There are countless examples of literature
that inadvertently reinforce stereotypes of differences rather than
promoting acceptance of diversity. For example, through historical
and traditional inaccuracies, many multicultural literature endeavors
insult those native to the culture depicted, and foster misconceptions
among those exposed to the story. Also, literature sometimes creates
a context so far removed from children's realm of experience that it
actually interferes with their feelings of similarity with those (who
may be classmates) whose culture is depicted in the literature selection. Likewise, it is not uncommon to find a book that includes a character with a disability, for example, who is not the main character,
who depends on nondisabled peers to promote resolution of the conflict, and for whom sympathy is in some way solicited.

Multicultural literature allows children to discover that all cultural groups have made significant contributions. Multicultural literature should be well balanced and include a variety of people from
different sociometric levels, different occupations, and a range of
human characteristics (Gomez, 1991). Evelyn Moore of the National
Black Child Development Institute (1992) remarked, "Children must
come to know more about the people of the world if they are to get
the most out of life and learn to value the wonderful diversity of the
world's people."

Teachers with students who are not native English speakers or
students with low reading levels may want to contact the University
of Texas at Austin for information on literacy units that address a
wide variety of topics and techniques for exposing children to the
richness of literature while fostering those important literacy skills
within each child. The address is Research and Development Center,
Language to Literacy Project, College of Education, The University of
Texas at Austin, Austin, TX 78712-1290.

Children enjoy joining book clubs and building personal libraries
at their homes. A book club for students who speak Spanish is El
Correo de Cuentos, P.O. Box 6652, Pico Rivers, CA 90661.

The following are a few recommendations of quality children's
books that represent characters from various cultures that teachers
might include in the classroom library or choose for story sharing
time:

- *Kevin Cloud: Chippewa Boy in the City.* (Bales, 1972)—A story
  about a Native American boy growing up in modern-day
  Chicago.

- *Jamako and the Beanstalk* (Crump, 1990)—Traditional fairy tale using African American characters.

- *Someone Special, Just Like You* (Brown, 1984)—A photo story about young children with disabilities who are from many cultures.

- *Daddy and Me: A Photo Story of Arthur Ashe and His Daughter Camera* (Moutoussamy-Ashe, 1993)—A photo story about how Camera and her father lived with her father's AIDS.

- *Smoky Night* (Bunting, 1994)—A story about "cats and people who couldn't get along until a night of rioting brings them together" (Caldecott winner, American Library Association Notable Children's Book, Parent's Choice Award winner).

- *When I Am Old With You* (Johnson, 1990)—A young African American boy talks with his grandfather about life (American Library Association Notable Book, Correta Scott King Honor Book, Notable Children's Trade Book in the Field of Social Studies, National Council on Social Studies–CBS).

- *Is Your Mama a Llama?* (Kellogg, 1989).

- *Loving* (Morris, 1990)—A photo story about the ways families around the world show their love for each other.

Teachers also should review selections that are currently in the classroom from a diversity perspective. In early childhood classrooms it is not uncommon to find playful, well-intentioned books that attempt to address senses and body parts through the use of phrases such as "everybody has ears to hear with and eyes to see with, two legs to walk with and two arms to carry things with." The authors' oversight is clear and disrespectful, albeit unintentional. Teachers should take a quick inventory of "old favorites" to be certain that acceptable messages are being given to students.

In addition to these environmental considerations, an important issue is physical accessibility for some students with disabilities. Teachers should consider the classroom environment for children who have physical disabilities in terms of physical structure, furniture, and room arrangement (e.g., desk height, access to cubby/locker, storage areas, bathroom passes, homework trays, playground equipment). The U.S. Architectural and Transportation Barriers Compliance Board (ATBCB), a small independent federal agency that oversees public accessibility issues for adults and children, created official guidelines in 1995 for the accessibility of children's environments, such as day-care centers, elementary schools, and play areas. These are available from ATBCB, 1331 F Street NW, Suite 1000, Washington, DC 20004-1111. The ATBCB led the Recreation Task Force in 1993, which resulted in recommendations for playground accessibility as well.

Academic Considerations

Researchers posit that many difficulties diverse children face regarding school learning are attributable to school practices. They stress a need to provide compensatory experiences to children who are at the disadvantage of the "school agenda" at whatever point they enter the school system (Biemiller, 1993; Good & Brophy, 1987; Goodlad, 1984; McGill-Franzen & Allington, 1991; Oakes, 1992). Carnine (1994), after reviewing approximately 5,000 reports written by school psychologists to explain student learning difficulties, noted that *every* case attributed the problem to the student or the family. Not one report indicated that the source of the child's difficulty in learning was the result of weakness in school practices or teaching. Carnine and the contributing authors in a special issue of *School Psychology Review* (1994, volume 23, number 3) addressed the area of educational tools for diverse learners in specific content areas. Such tools include the use of "technology, media, and materials (books, software and video)" (p. 342). Carnine cautioned that tools must be carefully evaluated for their effectiveness before they are implemented on a wide scale with students. Most teachers have been asked to teach using texts that are outdated, biased, confusing, distracting, or illogical in layout and content.

Carnine (1994) recommended that teachers weave the following four components into any curricular area to be taught: an emphasis on understanding and extracting themes across information, rather than memorizing detail (teach the "big picture"); use of explicit strategy instruction embedded in interactive, experiential activities (carefully adjusting the level of explicit instruction to match the needs of the students; i.e., gifted students probably need less explicit instruction that others); use of scaffolding (as students become more proficient, instruction should become less teacher directed and more student directed); and providing students with continual review of previously learned themes, concepts, and skills regardless of ability levels (reviews should be at times cumulative and also in varied formats, to help students generalize what is being taught to other content areas and knowledge structures).

Teachers should also be familiar with the research into specific teaching techniques that have positive implications for learners who share particular characteristics. Although a wealth of information is available on these specific areas of instruction, in this chapter we are limited to briefly describing the directions taken by researchers in the field. We have included a few references for each area, to provide a starting place for teachers who are interested in learning more, but our suggestions merely scratch the surface. We strongly encourage teachers to take the time to learn more about these areas as they become important to the classroom population.

There are techniques that have been used successfully with students from low socioeconomic neighborhoods (to learn more, see, e.g., the research into Direct Instruction by Carnine, 1994; Grossen, 1991; Grossen & Carnine, 1992; Engelmann & Meyer, 1984) and techniques documented as effective with students who have learning and behavioral disabilities (to learn more, see Archer & Gleason's [1989] *Skills for School Success* series; Fuch's & Fuchs's [Fuchs, 1994; Mathes & Fuchs, 1991] research into classwide peer tutoring; Hallahan's or Kauffmann's [e.g., Reeve & Hallahan, 1994] literature on effective teaching strategies for students with mild to moderate disabilities; Walker's [1994] or Goldstein's [McGinnis & Goldstein, 1984] work in teaching social skills). Texts describing research into techniques that tend to work well when instructing classes of students from diverse cultural groups include Derman-Sparks's *The Antibias Curriculum* (1989); James Banks's *Teaching Strategies for Ethnic Studies* (Banks, 1991) or *Multicultural Education: Issues and Perspectives* (Banks & Banks, 1989); and Cummins's *Bilingualism and Special Education* (1984). Each of the techniques mentioned in this paragraph has been demonstrated to work well with particular populations of learners, and a teaching team with a predominance of students who are similarly diverse (e.g., students who speak Laotian, students who have learning disabilities) may well want to investigate implementing one of these approaches.

As a brief example of the information these authors may address with regard to their particular group of learners, Cummins (1984) recommended that effective instruction for bilingual students is based on reciprocal interaction models that have the following characteristics: collaborative learning, meaningful language, limited error correction, language use that is integrated across curricular content areas, continual development of higher order thinking skills, an approach that encourages intrinsic motivation, teacher as facilitator, and many opportunities for teacher–student dialogue to learn written and oral expression. He provided several reasons why traditional teaching techniques (e.g., task analysis approaches, direct instruction, drill and practice, basic skill emphasis, moving from simple to complex) are inappropriate for children who are or are becoming bilingual. Among his charges are that these techniques contradict what is known about the way language and thinking develop in young children speaking any language; reduce the context; inhibit intrinsic motivation; and limit the opportunities students have for stimulating language and interaction through language.

The inclusion movement has, regardless of our philosophical outlook on the issue, beckoned educators to examine techniques that can be used and adapted to meet the needs of many types of learners. As is evident in recent literature, including the other chapters in this book, one resource that is frequently cultivated is the use of peers to promote classroom learning. Collaborative peer strategies, when organized well, tend to work well for teaching "diverse" ability levels without catering to a specific origin of diversity. These techniques would seem well suited for use in most inclusive classrooms. Various other techniques (e.g., cooperative learning groups, peer tutoring, and ability grouping) have been outlined in previous chapters of this book.

Teaching Skills

As mentioned earlier in this chapter, good teaching is good teaching. An emphasis on examining effective teaching skills was observed nearly two decades ago in the process–product literature by studying those skills implemented by educators who have fostered high rates of student achievement and in many cases been publicly recognized at the district, state, and national levels for their contributions to teaching (see Brophy, 1986, for the landmark piece of literature in this area). This literature has been commonly called process–product because it refers to a body of research exploring relationships between the *process* of learning and the resulting *products* of learning. For the most current literature on what we perceive to be effective teaching skills to facilitate student learning, see Algozzine, Ysseldyke, and Campbell (1994), Englert, Tarrant, and Mariage (1992), Reith and Evertson (1988, for difficult to teach students), and Reynolds, Wang, and Walberg (1992).

Effective teaching skills encompass what the teacher does as well as what the teacher hopes to foster in students. Englert et al. (1992)

provided a series of checklists for teachers to evaluate their own teaching skills. They provided separate checklists for the areas of classroom management, time and instructional management, seatwork management, and examining the contexts of higher order learning. Areas for teacher consideration in the last category include creating meaningful contexts, classroom dialogues, responsive instruction, and classroom community. Reynolds, Wang, and Walberg (1992) found that a similar base of teacher-rated priorities for effective instruction exists across general and special education. On the basis of the commonalities shared by both sets of educators, the authors observed that there seems to exist a broad base upon which to build collaborative teaching and training for educators.

The following is a list of some of the teacher skills that have been recommended to facilitate student achievement:

Classroom Management

- Arrange space for ease in transition and minimal disruption from student activity.

- Create rules and procedures related to instructional events (e.g., what to do when seatwork has been completed, how to turn in homework, how to access help during a lesson).

- Clearly state in advance what will be tolerated and what will not.

- Position teacher in the room for high visibility by/of students.

- Use nonverbal signals to intervene with students in the class while working with a group of students.

- Create rules that involve respect for each class member, and frequently remind students how to meet this goal.

- Intervene and apply consequences for noncompliance with class rules/expectations immediately.

- Teach students to monitor their own behavior and foster self-regulation over time.

Time and Instructional Management

- Devote the majority of the school day to instruction.

- Keep transition times short and efficient.

- Gain attention of students before beginning lesson; maintain attention at 90% during lesson.

- Monitor and scan class during lesson and independent work.
- Ensure during seatwork that students are attending to the assignment 80% of the time.
- Make learning relevant to students' worlds, clearly explaining relevance to students during instruction.
- Relate lesson topics to students' existing knowledge.
- Model task-specific strategies and self-talk that enable students to learn the metacognitive strategies of the task.
- Point out organization, relationships, and clues in information presented.
- Encourage student involvement in learning through frequent questions to assess student comprehension of the topic.
- Require overt and active participation in lesson (perhaps through verbal interactions as well as dyad/triad assignments, cooperative groups, use of manipulatives, writing responses, etc.).
- Provide frequent reviews of learned information.
- Tell the assignment and make clear the grading/evaluation criterion.
- Assist students in generalizing skills and information across environments and topics.

Higher Order Learning

- Provide meaning for knowledge and skills by linking them to purposeful activities.
- Provide many opportunities for students to implement strategies and skills within a context.
- Model how to perform a task and include self-talk to demonstrate thought processes occurring.
- Encourage peer collaboration and problem solving.
- Create opportunities for students to self-monitor and self-evaluate.
- Continually adjust instruction to meet the needs of the students.
- Facilitate connections between what students know and do not know throughout the lesson(s).
- Provide students opportunities to make choices and to explain their thinking.

Issues in Assessing Student Achievement

Attempts to meet the challenges presented by an increasingly diverse student population have also impacted how educators measure student learning. Alternative assessment techniques, such as authentic assessment, portfolio assessment, and performance-based assessment, have gained popularity for documenting the relative successes of students from all cultures and academic standings, and to equalize success and achievement within a classroom (see the Council for Exceptional Children's mini-library on performance-based assessment, 1994, for applications and implications for special education students). The point is to provide the teacher with a means by which students are graded based on the acquisition of new knowledge and mastery of critical thinking skills rather than attempting to make a class of perhaps 35 diverse individuals conform to an antiquated system of concrete measurement of knowledge based on a white, middle class value of education.

One of the most essential differences between traditional norm-referenced assessments and alternative assessments involves the required response mode of the learner. Norm-referenced assessments require a multiple-choice or other form of "select and respond" format, whereas alternative assessments require that students produce, construct, or demonstrate knowledge and skill. In this way, educators can judge both the process and the product from the individual's effort. Alternative assessments are designed to measure the student's mastery of a variety of knowledge and skills, not limited to what the student can read or respond appropriately to in English.

Traditional assessment procedures, many professionals believe, have become inappropriate. They do not consider the many languages spoken by students, or the varied reading levels and attentional levels that may, in some cases, prevent students from demonstrating their knowledge in a particular subject. Traditional methods of assessing student achievement have included unidimensional measures of a student's passive (fact-oriented) mastery of a topic that could easily be active and demonstrative in nature. To illustrate this point, there is a world of difference in the level of mastery that can be assessed by asking a teacher to repeat the steps necessary to write a grant for additional school funding versus actually having the teacher write a grant. The same principle is applicable for assessing students' true acquisition of new knowledge and skills.

Another concern regarding overreliance on traditional testing is the cultural bias that seems inherent in many standardized tests. Many professionals also criticize the fact that traditional tests encourage students to regurgitate information rather than to apply it, and encourage teachers to teach for regurgitation rather than application. Many are looking to new methods for assessing the growth and learning of students. Specifically, they seek to identify methods for measuring student progress that foster critical thinking and analytic skills, relevance to the "real world," and demonstration of intellect in many domains.

The first type of alternative assessment mentioned at the beginning of this section is authentic assessment. This term is used to denote assessment measures that are based in the real-world application of knowledge and skills. There appears to be confusion in the field regarding an absolute definition of authentic assessment, other than that it should ultimately focus on "outside of the school" contextual applications of knowledge and skill. In authentic assessment techniques, there is an emphasis on self-evaluation and defense of that evaluation by the student. Another characteristic of authentic assessment is a greater emphasis on product than process. In this technique there is room for many "right" answers, many ways to create the desired product. Three types of authentic assessment, which were borrowed from vocational education, are direct assessment (observation) of the student interacting in the environment, work samples for which scoring is administered based on the overall quality of the final product, and simulation of a task and setting to reflect a close approximation of a real-life situation (Slater, 1980).

The second method of alternative assessment addressed in this chapter is portfolio assessment. Portfolios have two common uses: for assessment purposes and for instructional purposes. Teachers are urged to determine from the outset the goal to their use of portfolios. Assessment portfolios, according to Swicegood (1994), are intended to assist teachers in evaluating progress and making educational decisions. One of us (Zionts) used assessment portfolios, as many special educators have, to document progress toward IEP goals. Each student had a binder in which we kept evidence that the student had achieved a particular goal (e.g., the completed research report of a high school student with a learning disability, the first legible handwriting sample of a student with cerebral palsy, or the circle patterns cut with scissors by a young child with a behavioral disorder). In general education classrooms, teachers have used assessment portfolios to document curricular milestones or progress toward a level of mastery (as in writing samples for a whole language program or continued assessment of arithmetic calculations to determine level of ability).

Instructional portfolios, by contrast, are intended to motivate students, provide a framework for self-evaluation and discussion, and help students perform desired new behaviors (Nolet, 1992). The contents of the instructional portfolio are usually determined by the student and the teacher mutually. We have helped students compile instructional portfolios using Polaroid pictures of important "firsts," videotapes (of music, social interactions, dramatic play, etc.), special projects, and written or paper-related accomplishments. We have also used portfolios to create a medium for self-expression and self-esteem building, a sort of "All About Me" book that can even be appreciated by high school students. With high school students, we have used portfolios to create a job- or college-search preparation guide containing occupations or schools the student has explored, a completed resume constructed by the student, a videotaped "mock interview," writing samples, records of school participation, any achievements the student made, volunteer and work histories, personal references the student may need, as well as employment documentation records (i.e., a copy of birth certificate, work permit, driver's license or state identification card). Although portfolios are time intensive, they have been viewed favorably by teachers, parents, and students in general and special education alike. As of this point in their evolution, portfolios do not have any particularly defined evaluation guidelines. It has been suggested that they best serve their intended purpose when evaluated descriptively, as a "showcase for the student's best and most representative work" (Poteet, Choate, & Stewart, 1993).

Last, we address performance-based assessments. Most performance-based assessments focus on the creation of an end-product to validate learning and achievement. These techniques choose to place emphasis in evaluation on the process of student learning rather than the end-product itself. At times collaborative efforts are included in the assessment procedure, as social skills and ability to work jointly with others are considered valued commodities for success throughout school and after its completion. Examples of performance-based assessments include a science experiment, an article written for the school paper, solving real-life problems using math knowledge, monitoring a savings account, keeping a log and critiques of literature read throughout a school year, and solving a puzzle using logic and reasoning (Poteet et al., 1993).

A sometimes confusing issue involved in the design and evaluation of performance-based assessment procedures relates to how heavily weighted the successful completion of the assignment should be and how heavily weighted the process of the activity or project design should be. For example, one of us (Zionts) once assigned middle school students to build a simulation of a "smoking" machine to demonstrate the ill effects of cigarette smoking on the lungs. The class was divided into three groups to complete this assignment (there were five students, each with learning and behavioral disabilities, in each group). We had spent what I believed to be a significant amount of time that year learning and practicing social and collaborative skills. I decided that this project would be evaluated based on the following criteria: (a) successful completion of an operable "smoking" machine; (b) successful collaboration (as measured by observation of peaceful negotiation through the planning and implementation of this project); (c) adequate planning and preparation for the completion of this project (as measured by written/drawn drafts, lists, and assignment sheets generated by group members); and (d) joint and individual responsibility for all phases of the project (each group recorded individual assignments and group goals as well as self and group evaluations for this project). As the project resulted, I had one group that worked very well together but was unable to create an operable machine; another group that worked miserably together but created a perfect machine; and a third group that created an operable machine but only two of the five group members participated.

Assigning final grades for this project was one of the more challenging evaluative tasks I created for myself as a teacher. What grade would have been appropriate for each group? Which groups were most successful? How does one assign a value to each child's experience? These are the questions that are generated by performance-based assessment and its counterparts. These are tough questions that require subjective decision making on the part of the educator. A dedication to meeting the needs of the diverse learners who comprise many classrooms will require each educator to look into new ways of thinking, measuring, and presenting knowledge . . . and a dedication to figuring out how to do so most effectively and fairly.

Social Considerations

Respect for each person in the classroom is imperative. This respect must be modeled by adults in the room and encouraged among students. More specifically, social consideration and tolerance of difference in the classroom (and beyond) require considerable attention on many levels from teachers. Research indicates that interactions with general education peers can greatly influence the relative success or failure of students with disabilities in inclusive environments (Plumb & Brown, 1990). Stainback, Stainback, and Wilkinson (1992) found that when general education peers facilitate acceptance of students who have disabilities (through tutoring, serving as role models, and befriending), the students with disabilities gain support and encouragement in the inclusive setting.

Curiosity and interest in cultural and physical differences begin for most children about the age of 4 (Derman-Sparks, Higa, & Sparks, 1980). By the time children enter school, they already have many misconceptions and stereotypic views of people whom they perceive as different from themselves (Pang, 1991). This information is useful for teachers who find themselves teaching classrooms of children who are diverse in culture, language, race, gender, socioeconomic level, and disability. One of us (Baker) taught in a first- through sixth-grade self-contained resource class in inner-city Dallas. I was astounded when I learned that one of my African American students considered the Hispanic students in our school to be white. He responded negatively to and about our new music teacher who was white. When I asked him about other teachers he had in former grades who were white, he responded as if he never noticed their color. This indicated to me that once he knew the person, color was not an issue. Children's conceptions about race and diversity are complex and cannot be easily diagnosed or explained away.

Many variables, including cultural background, gender, and socioeconomic status, have been demonstrated in the literature to influence how well students with disabilities are accepted by their nondisabled peers. For example, students who have disabilities and come from higher socioeconomic areas are perceived more positively than those from lower socioeconomic areas (Monroe & Howe, 1971). Female students with learning disabilities are less accepted than boys with disabilities (Scranton & Ryckman, 1979). The idea of "double jeopardy" for students who have several of these variables at work in their lives is obviously supported through this information. For these children, formal intervention by educators may be their best chance at becoming welcomed and truly included members of their class. Apparently, as children grow older, they are less accepting of people with disabilities (Simpson, 1980). It is important to build tolerance of diversity and respect for others beginning as early in a child's life as possible in order to hope to positively affect beliefs and behaviors.

Celebrating diversity through difference is an important but at times painstaking process: advocating an appreciation of difference versus promoting difference and denying similarities. It is important that children learn that what makes each person different makes each special. It is also important that students appreciate that there are many similarities among all people and that people who seem very different can work together to achieve important, productive goals. The question remaining is How do educators go about teaching children to believe this?

Obviously, there is no easy answer to that question. Our first recommendation to teachers in inclusive classrooms is that they have to be or become culturally competent. A culturally competent person is one who possesses "a set of academic and interpersonal skills that allow individuals to increase their understanding and appreciation of cultural differences and similarities within, among, and between groups. This requires a willingness and ability to draw on community-based values, traditions, and customs and to work with knowledgeable persons of and from the community in developing focused interventions, communications, and other supports" (Orlandi, Weston, & Epstein, 1992).

Lynch and Hanson (1992) addressed these issues in an excellent text titled *Developing Cross-Cultural Competence: A Guide for Working with Young Children and Their Families.* This book provides specific information educators often need to be aware of with regard to learning about people of cultures other than one's own. It also includes important ideas about how to explore one's own cultural heritage, how to become comfortable about the culture with which one identifies, and how one's own culture is important and influential in a person's interpretations of the actions and beliefs of people from other cultures. It is definitely recommended reading for teachers who are trying to meet the needs of their culturally diverse students.

In addition to personally accepting diversity and having a stable sense of one's own cultural identity, teachers must view parents and the community as allies in education. Parent and community participation is a must in effective schools and classrooms. Goodson, Swartz, and Milsap (1991) stated that characteristics of effective parent involvement include the following:

1. Provision of multiple levels of parent participation—any contact is seen as positive

2. Different modes of contact that respond to different parent skills (e.g., home visits vs. working in groups)

3. Helping parents move from one type of involvement to another (e.g., from home visits to school settings)

4. Sensitivity to the literacy levels of parents

5. Use of ways to create close bonds with families, such as contracts or support groups

Many schools have established creative ways to involve parents and the community in working with the school. A school in Dallas had businesses adopt the school, forming "School–Community Partnerships." The people from the businesses came weekly to tutor students who needed extra help and provided supplies and resources for the school. The school also established a parent center (see Yates, 1993, for more details) where the parents met weekly or biweekly at a "Chat & Chew" to discuss important issues with the principal or the parent liaison. The school also met parents' needs by offering after-school programs such as computer and English classes.

At an inner-city school in San Diego, parents of special education students who were involved in a community job training and transition program met once every semester for a day-long workshop. The parents were provided lunch and child care, and for fun a few inexpensive door prizes (e.g., stationery, an attractive coffee mug). Parents had the opportunity to meet with school staff and each other, to talk about their children's program. Students and former students prepared panel presentations or round-table discussions about what was waiting in their community for them after graduation, what was important for post–high school success in that community, and what students might want to focus on now. Employers from the community who hired these high school graduates and current high school students came to talk with parents and students about priorities, skills, and abilities. Parents and students rated the students on the skills that were considered important to success in this community. After meeting for the day, school and families had established a true partnership and an agenda for the school year. The common ground made it easier for parents and teachers to collaborate throughout the year.

Assessing Levels of Student Acceptance of Diversity

Determining where, when, to what extent, and with what type of focus to address diversity with students can at first seem overwhelming. Teachers can begin by taking a look around the classroom, the school, the community. Observation is one of the most effective types of assessment to determine whether the students in a classroom have issues with difference (Ford & Jones, 1990). What should teachers look for during observations of their students? They should observe the nature and frequency of interactions between students who are different from each other (in culture, socioeconomic level, language, disability, gender); pay attention to who initiates these interactions most often and whether initiations are equally distributed; and examine which events in or outside of the classroom seem to increase or decrease the number or quality of interactions. The *Educational Assessment of Social Interaction* (Beckstead & Goetz, 1990) is a formal observation recording system that can be used by teachers to assist them in organizing and documenting their observations. Many effective ideas for addressing these assessment techniques and diversity interventions are explained in Salend's (1994) text *Effective Mainstreaming: Creative Inclusive Classrooms*. Many of the descriptions we address are a combination of his recommendations and our own experiences.

A second method teachers can use to determine acceptability of diversity within their class is a sociometric scale, the most common technique for measuring peer acceptance (Horne, 1981). A sociogram is one type of sociometric scale used to assess classroom interactions by asking peers to identify class members they would like to work with during a social activity. To construct a sociogram, teachers first devise a list of questions that require students to answer regarding students whom they would and would not like to spend time with. These questions should be clear, concise, and in language appropriate for every student to understand. Next, teachers construct a list of student names and code numbers to create anonymity for the exercise. If teachers want to target only particular characteristics, specifications can be made. For example, to study gender only, even numbers can be assigned to girls and odd numbers to boys.

Teachers should encourage students to be as confidential as possible. Salend (1994) made helpful recommendations for how to provide equal participation in this activity: review the number–name correspondences with students, create a handout for their reference, help those who cannot read by reading the questions aloud or administering it individually, put numbers on students' backs, or create a bulletin board with each student's number and picture on it. Teachers should assist students to practice completing the sociogram using several examples before beginning to be certain that students understand its function and their instructions.

After all responses have been completed, the teacher (separately from students) draws each student's name in a circle on a large sheet of paper. By drawing a solid line between each person and his or her positive choices of classmates, and a broken line between the student and his or her rejected classmates, a visual picture emerges of the patterns of interactions within the classroom. Numbers (particular students) who receive many solid lines are well accepted, those students who receive many broken lines are least accepted, and students who have few or no lines at all are considered isolated or withdrawn. It becomes easier for teachers to determine patterns of interrelation within the class.

Other informal measures are available to determine bias and acceptance within classrooms. One approach is a simple open-ended probe regarding students' individual knowledge about other cultures, people with disabilities, or gender. The teacher can have students complete a series of open-ended sentences regarding the area being explored. The following is an example of a simple probe:

Complete the following sentences: Hispanic people live _____.
I would describe them like this: _____.

A last way teachers can explore levels of acceptance within the classroom is through students' artwork (Salend, 1994). By assigning students to draw a picture about an assigned topic, teachers can gain significant insight about how students feel about one another. It is important that students write or dictate an explanation of their picture so as to avoid misinterpreting the intent of the artist.

Upon completing these various measures of peer acceptance, a teacher may find that his or her students are not experiencing any significant problems, or that problems are in areas unexpected by the teacher, or that students are misinformed and demonstrating several forms of bias within the classroom. If there are some problem areas, the teacher needs to plan a strategy for attacking the problems and get to work on it. Many Americans seem to believe that changing a person's belief is possible, but very difficult (Alexander & Dochy, 1995).

Intervention Methods for Fostering Acceptance of Diversity

Schwartz (1994) stated that a common saying among educators who are working to promote students' appreciation of diversity is that there is no gene for racism or bias. This would indicate that educators believe that, even though children may initially develop and act on intolerant attitudes, they can be educated to value human differences. Educators can positively influence the development of attitudes in children by promoting the various cultures represented among the children they teach. For example, one principal in Dallas expanded students' positive attitudes about different cultures by scheduling an exchange day. African American and Hispanic students from inner-city Dallas invited Euro-American students from suburban Plano to visit their school. Students were paired and attended classes together. A few weeks later, students in Plano invited the children from Dallas to attend their school for a day. The children decided among themselves to exchange addresses, and new friendships were formed.

It has been our experience that for younger and older students alike approaches that combine information to counter stereotypic views and bias with cohesiveness-building exercises will work most effectively to build acceptance and respect for diversity within a class. Directly addressing the topics that cause problems is an important consideration for teaching children. Poplin and Weeres (1992) found, by talking extensively with children, parents, and school staff from public elementary, middle, and secondary schools in California, that children desperately want the opportunity to talk in school about things that make them different. Teachers interviewed as part of this study were most interested in finding a way to intervene in the injustice done to students in schools. Euro-American teachers (who made up the majority of teachers) were, however, more likely to take a "color-blind" approach—that is, to express ideas such as "I try to treat every child in my class equally . . . I don't care if they are white, black, brown, purple, or green" or to blame poverty for the differences in student achievement.

Poplin and Weeres (1992) stated, "Being monocultural and often unselfconsciously so, precludes Euro-Americans from being able to think differently about the critical issues facing students of color in our schools. This leaves monocultural teachers dependent on a host of workshops often conflicting in their views on how to address issues faced by children of color" (p. 28). It seems they had a valid point. One of us (Zionts) was a teacher and part of a multicultural awareness committee at a predominantly Euro-American school. This school had put out extensive money to hire a team of mediation experts to work with the students to create a "treaty" declaring acceptance of cultural and ethnic difference. When students selected to participate in this "negotiation" process were asked to sit at tables with other students from their same culture, one female student who was of Hispanic descent refused to sit with the other Hispanic students because she claimed that she identified more closely with the Euro-American students. She felt that her family did not maintain any ties to the Hispanic community and her father was, in fact, Euro-American. She was not trying to insult the Hispanic students, but rather she felt that she would have little to contribute to their discussion and would not have much cultural identity in common with these students. The Euro-American teachers were astounded. They felt that the girl was rude and insulting and could not believe that she could ever imply that she was "white" [like us]. It was so obvious to them that she was not.

Understanding diversity and being in touch with one's own cultural identity is very important in this age of inclusion. Accepting others for how they define themselves is equally essential. Cultural identity is more than the color of one's skin. It is a culmination of experiences, values, heritage, and definition of self.

Students in the Poplin and Weeres (1992) study expressed a desire for more courses that would help them understand each other. They expressed an interest in having options available within elective coursework to study (as described by an African American high school male, p. 25) "a course in African-American Ethnic studies, a Hispanic class, an Asian class, and different ethnic background classes. Because then other ethnics would learn about different ethnic groups, and that would help a lot." In addition to learning about each other's cultures, students want the opportunity to discuss with adults the issues that surround racism and culture within society as a whole. They feel it is important to have adults they trust who can provide them with a forum to discuss and construct meaning of the outside world and who can help them construct a framework for understanding why these problems might arise. One high school student involved in their study said, "Good teachers can talk about important things such as the unfair trial that Rodney King had. Not always come to class and do the same thing over and over. They should help us understand what goes on in the world" (p. 29).

A Latina elementary teacher in the same study stated, "Students of color must learn to negotiate their own culture and try to fit into the dominant culture. This can be a difficult and painful process because students of color feel they must reject their own culture in order to assimilate. Conversely, if they choose to maintain their own culture, they may be perceived as defiant or non-conformist. . . . American schools have socialized all students to fit into one dominant culture with no regard for their own home culture" (p. 28). Indeed, this was a rich study and there is much to be learned from it.

Each person must be respected for whom each believes he or she is. Our job as teachers is to help young people begin to explore who they are and encourage them to discover the bright, responsible, and caring people inside. We can address this through the environment we construct, the curriculum we present, and the social interactions we foster. We can also teach children about our differences directly and encourage them to collaborate on projects that bring out the talents of each class member. The following paragraphs describe techniques that have been used to directly teach acceptance of difference.

The Antibias Curriculum (Derman-Sparks, 1989) provides specific interventions for young children through kindergarten; however, the activities and suggestions can easily be adapted for use with many elementary school children. The following is an example of the type of guidance provided by Derman-Sparks: "Young children are likely to ask questions about racial physical characteristics: Do not ignore, Do not change the subject, Do not answer indirectly. If you are uncomfortable, identify what gets in the way of your responding directly, matter-of-factly, and simply" (p. 33). Young children will often ask questions about how they got their hair color/texture, eye color, and skin color. Derman-Sparks recommends that the teacher's primary purpose in engaging students in discussions about racial difference changes depending upon the racial makeup of the class. She recommends that when teaching a group of racially similar students, the teacher should focus on learning about the characteristics of other races and learning that variance is desirable. When the class is racially diverse, the focus should be on learning about each other.

Zionts uses the "answer as honestly and as openly as you are able" technique in teaching both young children and adolescents. When young children notice people within the community who use wheelchairs, for example, they are likely to point at the person and ask, "What is that?" I attempt to model respect for the individual by answering, "That is a person [focus on the relevant] who is using a wheelchair to move from place to place [answer the child's true inquiry]. Probably his or her legs do not work the same as yours and mine [answer the underlying why]."

When working with older students, I still try to maintain a respect for others in my actions. When I taught high school, I had one period of students with mild disabilities in which two students with severe cognitive disabilities were mainstreamed. During one of the initial class periods, a student who from time to time had a bit of trouble adhering to *any* rules hid one of these student's jacket under a cabinet to tease him. I was a bit surprised because I had naively thought, until that point, that these students who have mild disabilities would intrinsically *know* how important it is to feel acceptance and a part of the class. Although no other students were involved in engineering this stunt, none of them admitted to knowing where the jacket was or offered to help locate it. It turned out, however, that every one of them eventually admitted to having watched the hiding take place. The student was so upset that he left class early to return to his own classroom, furious and nearly in tears.

This situation gave me cause for considerable reflection. First, I felt frustrated for the student who had had such a negative experience in school that day. Second, I felt guilty and embarrassed for having this kind of discrimination happen to a student with special needs in a *special education classroom.* Third, I felt frustrated that I had an attitude of acceptance but had missed the mark at establishing an atmosphere of acceptance (apparently, personally having an attitude of acceptance and creating an atmosphere of acceptance are not the same thing). Finally, I felt that I was not demonstrating very many effective teaching skills that day if (a) the students were not so engaged in any task that one had time to do this and the others had time to watch it happen, and (b) I was not monitoring well enough because I never saw it happen. Ouch! It was a learning experience on many levels. When the student left the room, the others immediately felt ashamed of what they had done ("We didn't mean to get him so upset"); I felt heartbroken for the student this happened to and angry at those responsible (I told them that I held them each accountable in that the person who watches injustice happen is equally to blame with the person who creates injustice). Because I was feeling angry, I calmly told the students they needed to do some problem solving about this situation and I gave myself a time-out.

The students wrote an apology letter to the student and another to his teacher. They asked the student for forgiveness and a chance to be better classmates. Every student volunteered to sign it. The letter to the teacher asked also for forgiveness and the chance to be better role models. The student who had actually taken the jacket was the author of both letters. For the next 3 days we put the math books aside and concentrated on attempting to sort out right, wrong, and moral imperative. This was in no way a lecture or punishment; it was very much a student-centered, discussion format. Information was presented nonjudgmentally, as the objective was to assist my students in developing their minds and their persons. We talked about how things can be right or wrong on many levels: (a) legally; or (b) in a parent/teacher/school way through established rules; or (c) personally, through standards each person must set for what he or she believes is right or wrong behavior for himself or herself. We looked at many situations and practiced deciding which type of situation it was and what a person would consider in deciding whether something was right or wrong (e.g., whether they could be arrested for it, whether they could be suspended, whether it could hurt someone's person or feelings, or on the other side, whether they would benefit from it through recognition, praise, money, personal power, or satisfaction). It was a true learning experience for us all. The students' participation was outstanding and their discussions and debates were sincere and challenging to each other (and in some cases to me). I hope that they took something away from the larger experience. I know I did.

Additional direct teaching techniques that can be implemented to affect a change in acceptance of differences among students include inviting guest speakers from varying cultures, races, genders, ages, and ability levels to speak about their challenges in relation to what makes them different, and sometimes in relation to a particular subject matter that simply addresses their personal expertise and the class curricula (e.g., a person who uses a wheelchair might discuss the challenges he or she has overcome to create a life that he or she is pleased with, or an African American female business person might be invited to come and address her expertise in economics). The teacher can invite a variety of people to read literature selections in younger grades, or to address their occupations in older grades. Students should get the idea that they can be or do anything, and should feel comfortable with the idea that others already are.

Teachers can use videos and literature to address difference. Research shows the most positive effects when teachers combine film and readings with cooperative learning experiences among students and give student assignments related to the video or book (reports, interviews, etc.). Teachers can also use simulation activities to teach others what it is like to be labeled or have a disability. One technique involves having everyone wear a label on their back or forehead (that they have not read). Labels may say lazy, funny, brilliant, and so on. Each person is instructed to move throughout the room reacting to the others in accordance with what their labels say. The person is to try to figure out what his or her own label says by the end of the game. Another game is to assign labels to groups of students (for today everybody in this group has green hair; this group has blue faces; etc.). Then the teacher tells what the class is given permission to do based on group designations (only people with green hair can get a drink of water right now, only people with blue faces have to complete this worksheet, etc.). In either of these activities, it is very important that a discussion follow about how people felt during the activity and how it translates to society. Students should also discuss how they fit into this picture.

Teachers can be very creative. We have seem many wonderfully creative activities aimed at teaching students about diversity, discrimination, and equality among people. Two teachers in Grand Prairie, Texas, one Euro-American and the other African American decided to give their third-grade class a lesson on cultural diversity and discrimination by describing what it was like to live in the United States when they were growing up in the 1950s. They talked to the students about segregation in schools, on buses, in restrooms, and in restaurants. Two little friends holding hands in the front row, one African American and the other Euro-American, nearly began to cry when they realized that if they had grown up then, they would not have been able to play with each other.

A student teacher I (Zionts) supervised in Denton, Texas, was placed in an early childhood education center serving Headstart and early childhood special education students. Although not an entirely inclusive environment, the teachers had wonderful collaborative efforts taking place on many levels. The student teacher asked me to observe a lesson she was planning to teach about Rosa Parks. To be honest, although I thought it was a wonderful idea, I was not sure how much her students would take from it as several were severely communicatively delayed and several had attention deficit disorder. I was very impressed with the quality of the lesson and the student involvement. The student teacher adapted the story to an appropriate language level for most of her students, and recreated the event as she told the story, using a Fisher-Price toy bus and several of the toy people figures that accompany it. Then, during center time, she had the children make individual stencil paintings of a big yellow bus, talking with the aide about it as they painted; in another center, she had gathered three sets of buses and people and let the children recreate the events themselves.

There are many ideas and many techniques by which teachers can expose students to difference and encourage respect among all class members. Additional techniques include collecting examples of famous historical and present-day people who have made significant contributions; asking students to share with the class people from their own cultures who have made significant contributions; having students create family trees and share them in class; and having them do a media search and compile examples from books, television, film, commercials, and so on, that depict people "fairly" and "unfairly" (this can be a long-term assignment). Whatever the technique, it is important that the approach be consistent, inclusive, and ongoing. Change is difficult for each of us. Derman-Sparks (1989) has these words of advice to teachers faced with discriminatory behavior in the classroom: Don't ignore—it gives implied permission for the behavior; don't excuse—it teaches the subjects of discrimination that it is okay for that to happen and that they will not be protected from it in your class; and don't be immobilized by fear—making a mistake is less serious than not doing anything at all. You can always readdress it later, if need be.

References

Alexander, P. A., & Dochy, F. J. R. C. (1995). Conceptions of knowledge and beliefs: A comparison across varying cultural and educational communities. *American Educational Research Journal, 32,* 413–442.

Algozzine, B., Ysseldyke, J. E., & Campbell, P. (1994, Spring). Strategies and tactics for effective instruction. *Teaching Exceptional Children,* pp. 34–36.

Archer, A., & Gleason, M. (1989). *Skills for school success.* North Billerica, MA: Curriculum Associates.

Ascher, C. (1991, June). Highly mobile students: Educational problems and possible solutions. *ERIC Clearinghouse on Urban Education, 73.*

Bales, C. (1972). *Kevin Cloud: Chippewa boy in the city.* Chicago: Reilly & Lee.

Banks, J. (1991). *Teaching strategies for ethnic studies* (5th ed.). Needham Heights: MA: Allyn & Bacon.

Banks, J., & Banks, C. A. M. (Eds.). (1989). *Multicultural education: Issues and perspectives.* Boston: Allyn & Bacon.

Beckstead, S., & Goetz, L. (1990). *EASI 2 Social Interaction Scale, Vol. 6.* San Francisco: San Francisco State University, California Research Institute.

Biemiller, A. (1993). Lake Wobegon revisited: On diversity and education. *Educational Researcher, 27*(9), 7–12.

Brophy, J. (1986). Teacher influences on student achievement. *American Psychologist, 41*(10), 1069–1077.

Brown, T. (1984). *Someone special, just like you.* New York: Holt.

Bunting, E. (1994). *Smoky night.* San Diego: Harcourt Brace.

Carnine, D. (1994). Introduction to the mini-series: Educational tools for diverse learners. *School Psychology Review, 23,* 341–350.

Council for Exceptional Children. (1994). *CEC Mini-Library on Performance Assessment.* Reston, VA: Author.

Crump, F., Jr. (1990). *Jamako and the beanstalk.* Nashville, TN: Winston-Derek.

Cummins, J. (1984). *Bilingualism and special education: Issues in assessment and pedagogy.* Clevedon, Avon, England: Multilingual Matters.

Derman-Sparks, L. (1989). *The antibias curriculum.* Washington, DC: National Association for the Education of Young Children.

Derman-Sparks, L., Higa, C., & Sparks, B. (1980). Children and racism: How racism awareness develops. *Interracial Books for Children Bulletin, 11*(3–4), 3–9.

Engelmann, S., & Meyer, L. A. (1984). *Reading comprehension instruction in grades 4, 5, and 6: Program characteristics, teacher perceptions, teacher behaviors, and student performance.* Eugene, OR: Engelmann-Becker Corporation.

Englert, C. S., Tarrant, K. L., & Mariage, T. V. (1992). Perspectives on good teaching. *Teacher and Special Education, 15*(2), 67–86.

Ford, B. A., & Jones, C. (1990). Ethnic feeling book: Created by students with developmental handicaps. *Teaching Exceptional Children, 22*(4), 36–39.

Fuchs, L. (1994). The nature of student interactions during peer tutoring with and without prior training and experience. *American Educational Research Journal, 31*(1), 75–103.

Gomez, R. (1991). *Teaching with a multicultural perspective.* Urbana: University of Illinois. (ERIC Document Reproduction Service No. ED 339 548)

Good, T. L., & Brophy, J. E. (1987). *Looking in classrooms.* New York: Harper & Row.

Goodlad, J. I. (1984). *A place called school.* New York: McGraw-Hill.

Goodson, B. D., Swartz, & Milsap. (1991). *Working with families: Promising programs to help parents support young children's learning.* Cambridge: Abt Associates. (ERIC Document Reproduction Service No. ED 337 301)

Grossen, B. (1991). The fundamentals of teaching higher order thinking. *Journal of Learning Disabilities, 24*(6), 343–352.

Grossen, B., & Carnine, D. (1992). Translating research on text structure into classroom practice. *Teaching Exceptional Children, 24*(4), 48–53.

Grossman, H. (1995). *Special education in a diverse society.* Needham Heights, MA: Allyn & Bacon.

Harry, B. (1992). *Cultural diversity, families and the special education system: Communication and empowerment.* New York: Teachers College Press.

Horne, M. D. (1981). *Assessment of classroom status: Using the Perception of Social Closeness Scale.* (ERIC Document Reproduction Service No. ED 200 616)

Johnson, A. (1990). *When I am old with you.* New York: Orchard.

Kellogg, S. (1989). *Is your mama a llama?* New York: Scholastic.

Lynch, E. W., & Hanson, M. J. (1992). *Developing cross-cultural competence: A guide for working with young children and their families.* Baltimore: Brookes.

Mathes, P. G., & Fuchs, L. S. (1991). *The efficacy of peer tutoring in reading for students with disabilities: A best evidence synthesis.* Nashville, TN: Vanderbilt University.

McGill-Franzen, A., & Allington, R. L. (1991). The gridlock of low reading achievement: Perspectives on practice and policy. *Remedial and Special Education, 12*(3), 20–30.

McGinnis, E., & Goldstein, A. P. (1984). *Skillstreaming the elementary school child.* Champaign, IL: Research Press.

Monroe, J. D., & Howe, C. E. (1971). The effects of integration and social class on the acceptance of retarded adolescents. *Education and Training of the Mentally Retarded, 6*(1), 20–24.

Moore, E. (1992). *African-American literature for young children: The National Black Child Development Institute (NBCD)* [Brochure]. Washington, DC: National Black Child Development Institute.

Morris, A. (1990). *Loving.* New York: Mulberry.

Moutoussamy-Ashe, J. (1993). *Daddy and me: A photo story of Arthur Ashe and his daughter, Camera.* New York: Knopf.

Nolet, V. (1992). Classroom-based measurement and portfolio assessment. *Diagnostique, 18*(1), 5–26.

Oakes, J. (1992). Can tracking research inform practice? Technical, normative, and political considerations. *Educational Researcher, 21*(4), 12–21.

Orlandi, M., Weston, R., & Epstein, L. (Eds.). (1992). *Cultural competence for evaluators: A guide for alcohol and other drug abuse prevention practitioners working with ethnic/racial communities.* Rockville, MD: U.S. Department of Health and Human Services, Office for Substance Abuse Prevention.

Pang, O. (1991). Teaching children about social issues: Kidpower. In C. Sleeter (Ed.), *Empowerment through multicultural education.* Albany: State University of New York.

Plumb, I. J., & Brown, D. C. (1990). SPAN: Special Education Action Network. *Teaching Exceptional Children, 22*(1), 22–24.

Poplin, M., & Weeres, J. (1992). *Voices from the inside: A report on schooling from inside the classroom.* Claremont, CA: Claremont Graduate School, Institute for Education and Transformation.

Poteet, J. A., Choate, J. S., & Stewart, S. C. (1993, October). Performance assessment and special education: Practices and prospects. *Focus on Exceptional Children.*

Reeve, P. T., & Hallahan, D. P. (1994). Practical questions about collaboration between general and special educators. *Focus on Exceptional Children, 26*(7), 1–10.

Reith, H., & Evertson, C. (1988). Variables related to the effective instruction of difficult-to-teach children. *Focus on Exceptional Children, 20*(5), 1–8.

Reynolds, M. C., Wang, M. C., & Walberg, H. J. (1992). The knowledge bases for special and general education. *Remedial and Special Education, 13*(5), 6–10.

Salend, S. J. (1994). *Effective mainstreaming: Creating inclusive classrooms* (2nd ed.). New York: Macmillan.

Schwartz, W. (1994, May). *Anti-bias and conflict resolution curricula: Theory and practice.* (ERIC Document Reproduction Service No. ED 377 255)

Schwartz, W. (1995, April). *School programs and practices for homeless students.* (ERIC Document Reproduction Service No. ED 383 783)

Scranton, T. R., & Ryckman, D. R. (1979). Sociometric status of learning disabled children in integrative programs. *Journal of Special Education, 12,* 44–49.

Simpson, R. L. (1980). Modifying the attitudes of regular class students toward the handicapped. *Focus on Exceptional Children, 13*(3), 1–11.

Slater, S. (1980). Introduction to performance testing. In J. Spirer (Ed.), *Performance testing: Issues facing vocational special education.* Columbus, OH: National Center for Research in Vocational Education.

Stainback, W., Stainback, S., & Wilkinson, A. (1992). Encouraging peer friendships and supports. *Teaching Exceptional Children, 24*(2), 6–11.

Swicegood, P. (1994). Portfolio-based assessment practices. *Intervention in School and Clinic, 30*(1), 6–15.

Walker, H. (1994). Social skills in school age children and youth: Issues and best practices in assessment and intervention. *Topics in Language Disorders, 14*(3), 70–82.

Yates, L. (1993, May). *Building a successful parent center in an urban school.* (ERIC Document Reproduction Service No. 358 198)

CHAPTER 15

Inclusive Practices for Preschoolers with Disabilities

Pamela Lowry Pruitt

Public Law (P.L.) 99-457, enacted in 1986 as an amendment to the Education for All Handicapped Children Act of 1975 (EHA; P.L. 94-142), extended the rights and privileges of a free appropriate public education to young children with special needs ages birth through 5. Although the law does not provide a specific definition of the term *appropriate*, it does require that individualized planning for each child include an examination of his or her unique needs and a determination to what extent these needs can be met within the regular education environment (Safford, 1989). In the area of early childhood special education, a great deal of attention has surrounded the issue of appropriateness of placement of young children with special needs. While a range of service delivery options is available for young children with disabilities, inclusion is a growing trend in early childhood special education. Salisbury (1991) maintained that inclusion is a value that is operationalized in the way teachers plan, promote, and conceptualize the education and development of young children. She stated that the underlying premise of inclusive programming is that all children should be educated in the classrooms they would attend if they did not have a disability. Further, she contended that the diverse needs of all children can be accommodated within the general education curriculum.

Because of the growing interest in providing inclusive services to preschoolers with special needs, promising early intervention practices and specific strategies that appear to facilitate the inclusion of young children with disabilities in typical settings are presented in this chapter. Specifically, this chapter has five major purposes: (a) to describe young children with special needs, (b) to present the rationale and benefits of inclusive education for young children, (c) to compare and contrast early childhood and early childhood special education practices, (d) to describe essential components of an inclusive early education program, and (e) to present specific strategies that appear to facilitate inclusion.

Description of Young Children with Special Needs

Young children with special needs are classified somewhat differently than school-age children. Preschoolers typically are divided into three areas: (a) children with identifiable conditions, (b) children with developmental delays, and (c) children who are at risk (Harbin, Gallagher, & Terry, 1991). First, EHA (reauthorized as P.L. 101-476, the Individuals with Disabilities Education Act of 1990) enabled preschool children in some states and all school-age children to receive special education services through the following diagnostic categories: mental retardation, emotional impairment, hearing impairment, visual impairment, deaf–blind, orthopedic impairment, other health impairment, speech or language impairment, specific learning disabilities, autism, multi-handicaps, and traumatic brain injury (Benner, 1992). The use of this definition, however, is problematic in that these categorical definitions refer primarily to school-age children and have limited relevance for preschoolers. For example, learning disabilities cannot be reliably determined in early childhood. Further, there is concern about possible harmful and lasting effects of labeling (Safford, 1989).

Second, P.L. 99-457 provided that preschool children may be served by special education using the term "developmental delay" rather than a specific category. According to Benner (1992), the term developmental delay is used to designate young children who are exhibiting delays in one or more areas of their development, including communication, cognition, social–emotional development, and motor development.

Third, a number of states mandated services to the at-risk preschool population using the following three categories: (a) established risk—children with genetic conditions or other diagnosed medical disorders; (b) biological risk—children with prenatal, perinatal, or postnatal histories indicating a probability of underlying problems; and (c) environmental risk—children whose early life experiences and environment may be threatening to development (Peterson, 1987).

Rationale and Benefits

The inclusion of children with disabilities in typical environments is supported by moralistic–philosophical, legal–legislative, and psychological–educational rationales (Bricker, 1978; Odom & McEvoy, 1988). From a moralistic–philosophical perspective, the least restrictive environment provision in EHA is a reflection of the normalization philosophy advanced by Wolfensberger (1972). Inclusion is considered to be a quality practice because it is based on the premise that services for individuals with disabilities should be based on circumstances that are as culturally normative as possible. Further, inclusive experiences early in a child's life maximize the value of these experiences in promoting positive attitudes about human differences (Safford, 1989).

The legal rationale for the inclusion of young children with disabilities was established by the passage of both state and federal legislation. EHA and the 1986 amendments, P.L. 99-457, support the rights of preschoolers to be included in natural environments with typical children (Bruder, 1993).

Psychological–educational arguments propose that children with disabilities benefit educationally from placement in inclusive settings (Odom & McEvoy, 1988). Research has demonstrated that inclusive settings facilitate and support the growth and development of children with disabilities in a number of ways. Recent research has suggested that children with disabilities who are included in typical early childhood programs display higher levels of social play, have more appropriate social interactions, and are more likely to initiate interactions with peers than are children in self-contained special education preschool classes (Lamorey & Bricker, 1993). Inclusive classrooms also offer more opportunities for children to rehearse newly acquired skills with peers than do self-contained special education settings

(Demchak & Drinkwater, 1992). In addition, the social environment provided by typical peers in an inclusive setting appears to be more supportive of the development of children's social competence than are the social arrangements usually found in self-contained special education classes (Guralnick & Groom, 1987). Children with disabilities enrolled in inclusive classes also have been found to make gains in language, cognitive, and motor-skill development comparable to peers with disabilities who attend self-contained special education classes (Fewell & Oelwein, 1990).

Early Childhood Education Versus Early Childhood Special Education

What constitutes quality programming for young children with special needs? Within early childhood education and early childhood special education, somewhat parallel efforts have defined what constitutes accepted practice in the delivery of intervention and services to young children with and without special needs and their families (McLean & Odom, 1993). Specifically, Cavallaro, Haney, and Cabello (1993) stated that regular preschool educators generally support a developmental model following the guidelines for developmentally appropriate practice in which programming is based on child-initiated, child-directed play that occurs in an inviting and responsive environment. In contrast, early childhood special education is based on didactic techniques that are generally carried out in intensive, structured, adult-directed learning environments that include direct instruction, adult selection of activities and goals, and limited opportunities for peer interactions.

If inclusive classrooms are to be appropriate educational settings for all children, the differences between these two approaches must be reconciled. In a comparison of accepted practices identified through the work of the Division for Early Childhood (DEC) Task Force on Recommended Practices (1993) and the National Association for the Education of Young Children (NAEYC) and the National Association of Early Childhood Specialists in State Departments of Education (1991), considerable overlap existed across recommended practices for early childhood education and early childhood special education (McLean & Odom, 1993). McLean and Odom stated that the most apparent consensus between these practices was in the development of curricular interventions, including strategies that (a) strengthen and maintain positive relationships with families, (b) appreciate cultural diversity, (c) are functional and relevant, (d) actively engage children in learning, and (e) support the physical needs of children. Cavallaro et al. (1993) proposed that a "best of both worlds" approach be taken, making use of the environments of early childhood and the technology of intervention in ways that are acceptable to both regular and special educators. The strategies presented in the remainder of this chapter will be consistent with promising practices in both early childhood and early childhood special education.

Essential Components of Inclusive Early Childhood Programs

Guralnick (1990) stated that there is an affirmative answer to the question as to whether inclusion is effective for preschoolers with disabilities. He maintained that the more contemporary question is how inclusion can be best facilitated in early childhood settings. Global practices that hold promise for effective early childhood programming include (a) an inclusive philosophy, (b) collaboration and communication among professionals, and (c) family involvement.

An Inclusive Philosophy

Stainback, Stainback, and Jackson (1992) stated that effective inclusive classrooms begin with a philosophy that everyone belongs, is accepted, supports, and is supported by his or her peers in the course of having his or her individual educational needs met. Diversity among class members is valued and is perceived to strengthen the learning opportunities. In a similar vein, Salisbury (1991) suggested that an inclusive philosophy be the foundation for all early childhood services. She further recommended that the faculty and staff develop consensus and commit themselves to a set of beliefs grounded in knowledge. She maintained that when faculty members commit themselves to these beliefs, future criticisms of practice can be more easily distinguished from faltering beliefs. Odom (1990) recommended that early childhood administrators promote inclusion by encouraging the development of an inclusive program philosophy, hiring faculty and staff who are committed to inclusion, officially recognizing teachers who participate in inclusion, providing opportunities for inservice training to support inclusion, and by ensuring teacher–child ratios that would make inclusion realistic.

Collaboration, Cooperation, and Communication Among Professionals

Peck, Furman, and Helmstetter (1993) stated that collaboration, cooperation, and mutual respect between regular and special educators are essential components of successful inclusive early childhood programs. Young children with disabilities and their families often require the services of a wide range of professionals having medical expertise, therapeutic expertise, educational expertise, and social service expertise to help establish and implement a viable intervention program. A transdisciplinary planning team in which these various professionals share roles and cross-discipline boundaries systemically has been identified as the ideal for inclusive early intervention planning (Bruder, 1993). Bruder stated that professionals from different disciplines teach, learn, and work together to accomplish a common set of service goals for a child with disabilities and his or her family. Assessment, intervention, and evaluation are done jointly by members of the team. The communication style of the transdisciplinary team involves continuous give and take among all members of the team, especially the parents, on a regular basis.

Unfortunately, struggles between professionals over issues such as classroom management, turf, activities, and interventions sometimes have resulted in resegregating children (Rose & Smith, 1993). This reality underscores the importance of effective collaboration and cooperation among faculty and staff and a guiding inclusive philosophy. Program administrators can facilitate ongoing collaboration and communication by providing educators with the time, opportunity, and encouragement to engage in collaborative relationships with other professionals. Further, workshops or inservices that focus on effective communication and collaboration skills should be provided for faculty and staff.

Family Involvement

Public Law 99-457 delineated the basic role for parents of young children with special needs. Parents and families are viewed as equal partners with professionals and also are recognized as the driving force that shapes the life experiences of the young child (Safford, 1989). McLean and Odom (1993) stated that the choice of an intervention setting for preschool children with disabilities should be a team decision with priority given to family preferences. Vincent and Beckett (1993) stated, "Families are equal members in and can take part in all aspects of early intervention systems. This includes participation in all aspects of their child's care and all levels of decision making" (p. 26).

Intervention services for young children with disabilities need to be based on the assumption that the family is the enduring and central force in the life of the child and that all services should be provided according to the family's lifestyles, values, and priorities (Turnbull & Turnbull, 1990). A number of recommendations can be made to help educators who work with families of young children with disabilities: (a) provide parent workshops on topics such as building children's self-esteem, establishing friendships between children, and behavior management (Galant & Hanline, 1993); (b) become knowledgeable about community resources such as support groups, respite care, and recreational activities for families of young children with disabilities and assist them in accessing the services (Galant & Hanline, 1993); (c) have an open-door policy so that parents can feel comfortable visiting their child's classroom; (d) become proficient at utilizing effective interpersonal skills (Turnbull & Turnbull, 1990); (e) maintain ongoing, active communication with parents either through personal interactions or written communication (Turnbull & Turnbull, 1990); (f) be flexible in scheduling to accommodate the various needs of families (Turnbull & Turnbull, 1990); and (g) be sensitive to the unique needs of families and provide intervention within the context of the family (Turnbull & Turnbull, 1990).

Interventions to Facilitate Inclusion

Research has identified a number of instructional strategies that appear to promote the success of preschoolers with disabilities in inclusive settings. The specific strategies presented are considered to be promising practices that are consistent with the guidelines for developmentally appropriate programming typically found in quality preschools and also are consistent with meeting the developmental goals of young children with special needs.

Environmental Arrangements

Bailey and Wolery (1992) stated that the environment of the preschool classroom plays an important role in teaching young children. They maintained that EHA and the 1986 amendments provide legal and ethical mandates to provide children with disabilities with an environment that is "as close to real life as possible" (p. 199).

Safford (1989), however, contended that differences exist between classrooms designed for typically developing children and those for children with special needs. For example, Bailey, Clifford, and Harms (1982) found that environmental features considered to be important in typical early childhood classrooms (e.g., furnishings for relaxation and comfort, child-related displays, dramatic play areas, sand and water play areas, free-play areas, and areas for privacy) were not nearly as likely to be present in early childhood special education settings. The following sections provide suggestions for environmental arrangements that would be appropriate preschool settings for all children.

Arranging the Physical Space

Whaley and Bennett (1991) recommended that an open preschool environment with low barriers and learning zones positively affects interactions between adults and children, leading to higher levels of child engagement. The authors stated that classrooms that are divided into zones by low barriers allow teachers to scan the environment and maximize their opportunities to respond to children's behavior and initiations.

In addition, Bailey and Wolery (1992) advised that the environment for preschoolers should be comfortable, functional, and safe for children and adults. The room should be equipped with child-size furnishings. Each child should have his or her own personal space, such as a locker, shelf, or cubby. Bailey and Wolery maintained that creating child-centered displays featuring children's work, classroom themes, or teacher-made presentations are additional strategies to add comfort to a preschool environment, as well as encouraging language interaction between children and adults.

Further, establishing activity areas or centers is a key to designing effective preschool environments (Bailey & Wolery, 1992; Whaley & Bennett, 1991). Bailey and Wolery defined activity areas as spaces that are designed to accommodate diverse types of activities, including one-to-one tutoring, small group instruction and independent endeavors. Activity areas should be designed to accommodate the ages, skills, and interests of the children. Further, Bailey and Wolery suggested that preschool environments incorporate several different activity areas, including blocks, dramatic play, art, manipulative toys, reading and language work, and sensory stimulation activities.

Whaley and Bennett (1991) suggested that adults be assigned to and be responsible for setting up and maintaining the various activity zones so that the environment is ready for children to begin play immediately upon entering the area. They further recommended that the schedule be designed so that one adult is teaching while another adult is preparing an activity area. This will ensure well-planned, smooth transitions between activities for the children.

For children who have limited mobility, Safford (1989) suggested that the following environmental arrangements would be useful: (a) classroom furnishings should be arranged to accommodate equipment the children use for mobility, (b) activities that require movement should allow all children to participate as much as possible without accentuating their differences, (c) materials should be accessible to the children, (d) safety rules should be practiced by all children, and (e) classroom materials should be arranged according to their use within distinct areas to reduce the need for unnecessary movement.

Selecting Toys and Materials

Toys and materials selected for children with disabilities should be chronologically age appropriate and the same toy choices that are made for typically developing children (Bailey & Wolery, 1992). Age-appropriate toys are more normative and allow the child with a disability to appear more similar to than different from his or her normally developing peers.

In addition, toys and materials should be selected that are inviting, interesting, and important to children (Cavallaro et al., 1993). Similarly, Bailey and Wolery (1992) recommended that toys and materials be preferred by the children for whom they are intended, relevant to the children's daily lives, and appropriate to a wide range of abilities and skill repertoires.

Whaley and Bennett (1991) suggested that developmentally appropriate materials be selected that promote a variety of play behaviors. They contended that challenging toys will increase the engagement of children with disabilities and will offer a variety of play opportunities. Bailey and Wolery (1992), however, cautioned that activities and materials be selected for children that are appropriately challenging, yet not so difficult that failure often occurs.

Toys and materials also should be chosen on the basis of goals and objectives for individual children. Materials provided by teachers can influence different types of behaviors. If the goal is to increase the socialization of a child, appropriate social interactions between children can be encouraged and enhanced by providing social toys such as blocks, balls, vehicles, puppets, dishes, dress-up clothes, and props in the housekeeping area (Whaley & Bennett, 1991). Further, Whaley and Bennett contended that board games, such as "Chutes and Ladders" and "Candyland," encourage one-to-one interactions between children, turn taking, and following directions.

Whaley and Bennett (1991) further recommended that to promote engagement, toys and materials must be accessible to children. Children who are nonambulatory may need response-contingent materials to encourage engagement. Toys may need to be equipped with electronically operated switches and other adaptations to ensure that play situations are accessible to all children. Further, placing toys and materials on low, open shelves also appears to encourage children to make choices and play independently (McGee, Daly, Izeman, Mann, & Risley, 1991).

McGee et al. (1991) recommended a systematic toy rotation plan to provide variety for students. This plan consists of dividing classroom materials into sets and varying the materials available to children in the classroom by rotating the sets. Two rotation sets are always present in the classroom, with one set being new each week. Therefore, half of the toys are familiar to the children each week, while half of the toys are new. The toy rotation plan appears to be instrumental in increasing engagement of children, increasing sharing and cooperative play, and peer modeling of imaginative and creative play—the goals of social inclusion (McGee et al., 1991).

Cavallaro et al. (1993) stated that children with disabilities may need additional experiences to learn the prerequisite skills necessary for successful engagement with materials in the inclusion setting. They recommended that observation, informal assessment, and parent interview be used to identify which toys and materials children can use independently and what prerequisite skills children have and have not achieved. Teachers can then generate additional experiences to develop the needed skills.

Designing Responsive Environments

Responsiveness and attention given to children by adults is a major indicator of quality in early childhood programs (Cavallaro et al.,

1993). Adults should attend by establishing eye contact, getting to the child's level, and using active listening as children express their needs and desires. Teachers should respond appropriately to children's communication by actively engaging in conversation, answering questions, and providing requested items. The teacher's positive response will encourage future communication attempts (Cavallaro et al., 1993). Further, Bailey and Wolery (1992) proposed that in a responsive environment, children and adults need to be able to respond to both verbal and nonverbal signals sent by others, and that independent actions of children should be valued, encouraged, facilitated, and expected by teachers.

In addition, Cavallaro et al. (1993) stated that a responsive environment responds to children's interests. Child-initiated activities provide the strongest motivators and most effective mediums for learning in young children. Cavallaro et al. suggested that adults work on children's goals and objectives within the context of child-selected and child-initiated activities by choosing and drawing upon these interests to facilitate learning. Similarly, Bailey and Wolery (1992) recommended that children's preferences be honored by teachers. They stated that the underlying assumption is that if a child can learn a skill through more than one activity, he or she will be more motivated to participate in a preferred activity. Therefore, instruction will likely be more successful utilizing an activity that children enjoy and prefer. For example, the goal of increasing peer interactions could be effectively accomplished in a number of ways (e.g., dramatic play, housekeeping, sand or water play). If the child prefers to play at the water table, the probability of achieving the goal through water play is maximized.

In a responsive environment, children are given both opportunities to interact with peers and time to be alone. Active, engaging environments are stimulating and exciting for children; however, teachers should provide a balance between stimulating activities for children and opportunities for children to have free choice and privacy (Bailey & Wolery, 1992).

Classroom schedules also can reflect a responsive environment. Predictability and routine are important aspects of an environment for young children. Early childhood programs typically have routines associated with arrival, self-care, snacks, center time, play time, and departure. Typically, times also are designated for children to choose their own activities and times for large group activities guided by the teacher (Noonan & McCormick, 1993). To the maximum extent, children with disabilities should follow the same routine of their typical peers. Separate scheduling should be avoided as much as possible.

Transitions occur when children are finishing one activity in preparation to start another one (Noonan & McCormick, 1993). Classroom schedules should provide for gradual transitions from active and vigorous activities to less active, quiet activities (Whaley & Bennett, 1991). For example, a transitional activity such as singing could provide a gradual shift from a vigorous activity such as free play to a quiet activity such as storytime.

Naturalistic Instructional Strategies

Naturalistic teaching strategies provide an instructional approach that appears to be promising for the successful inclusion of children with disabilities into preschool classrooms (Diamond, Hestenes, & O'Connor, 1994). Research has indicated that techniques associated with naturalistic teaching have appeared to be effective in teaching young children with a variety of disabilities (Fox, 1993). Through the use of naturalistic teaching strategies, individualized interventions for preschoolers with disabilities are provided within the context of naturally occurring activities in the child's environment. According to Kaiser and Warren (1988), naturalistic teaching approaches share the following characteristics: (a) teaching occurs in the natural environment of the child, (b) individual teaching interactions are brief and spaced over time, (c) instructional interactions are usually child initiated, and (d) instruction uses natural consequences. Naturalistic teaching techniques fall within the framework of developmentally appropriate practice as they focus on child interest, allow for active exploration, and provide children with opportunities to move beyond their current skill levels (Noonan & McCormick, 1993). The following strategies, incidental teaching, the mand–model technique, activity-based intervention, and individualization, are examples of naturalistic instruction.

Incidental Teaching

The incidental teaching approach involves (a) arranging the environment to increase the likelihood that the child will initiate a request; (b) selecting language targets appropriate to the child's level, interest, and opportunities; (c) responding to the child's initiation by requesting elaboration; and (d) reinforcing the child's efforts at communication (Noonan & McCormick, 1993). An incidental teaching opportunity begins when a child initiates interaction with an adult. The teacher then takes the opportunity to request a more elaborate response. If the child responds appropriately, the child is reinforced when the adult provides the requested object. If the child fails to respond, the teacher may model the request. The child's subsequent imitation is then reinforced with attention or the requested item (Noonan & McCormick, 1993). For example, a child's language goal may be to speak in three- to four-word sentences. The child's preferred toy, a red truck, is placed out of the child's reach. The child may initiate a request for the toy by pointing and saying "truck." The teacher would model the appropriate response, "I want the truck." When the child responds, "I want the truck," the verbalization would be reinforced by the teacher giving him or her the truck.

Mand–Model Technique

The mand–model technique is a variation on the incidental technique (Warren, McQuarter, & Rogers-Warren, 1984). This method also follows a child's attentional lead, but the teacher instructs the child to verbalize about the focus of his or her attention (Jones & Warren, 1991). For example, a language goal for a child is to increase basic vocabulary. During snack time, a child requests a drink of juice by pointing at the pitcher. The teacher says, "Tell me what you want." The child responds, "Drink." Teacher says, "Say 'orange juice.'" The child replies, "Orange juice." The teacher gives the child a glass of orange juice.

Both incidental teaching and the mand–model methods are based on following the child's attentional lead. These interventions are brief and dispersed through ongoing activities throughout the day. Opportunities for interaction between student and teacher can be prompted (i.e., in the incidental teaching example), or they can be used when communication teaching episodes naturally arise (i.e., in the mand–model example). These interactions should be positive and pleasant for the child (Jones & Warren, 1991).

Activity-Based Intervention

In activity-based intervention, each child's goals and objectives are addressed within the context of the ongoing classroom environment

(Diamond et al., 1994). The teacher's task is to identify specifically how the child's Individualized Education Program (IEP) goals and objectives could be met within each activity. Bruder (1993) recommended that a child's IEP be developed to include functional goals that can be embedded within daily activities and routines of the preschool environment. Specifically, critical skills that are to be taught to the child should be cross-referenced to the child's daily activities. Naturally occurring activities subsequently become instructional opportunities. Similarly, Bredekamp and Rosengrant (1992) stated that curricular strategies should be used more purposefully for children with special needs than for typically developing children, including structuring the interactions, routines, and activities of children to adequately meet specific goals and objectives. For example, a routine class activity such as fingerpainting, which often takes place in a preschool classroom, would be an opportunity for a child to work on IEP goals. The child has an opportunity to identify and experiment with colors (cognitive goal), make designs on paper (fine motor goal), and wash up after the activity (self-help goal). In addition, activities such as dramatic play, blocks, housekeeping, sand and water play, and art are examples of engaging activities that can incorporate children's individual goals into the context of an activity. For example, an activity in the housekeeping area may provide opportunities for children to engage in appropriate communication, learn to take turns, initiate social interactions, and begin to understand math concepts.

Individualization

Noonan and McCormick (1993) stated that many early childhood programs use unit plans that have goals for the class within the various activities of the unit. Specific goals for individual children with disabilities often can be incorporated within the goals for the entire class. For example, a goal for the class may be that children sequence objects by size. Children are typically given choices of groups of objects to sequence (i.e., balls, blocks, cups of various sizes). This activity can be individualized for a child with a disability by asking the child to choose the largest object in a group (instead of sequencing all of the objects). Through the use of this strategy, children with disabilities can participate in the same activity as their typical peers, while having their individual needs met.

Designing Interventions To Facilitate Social Interactions

Participation in social interactions with peers is a crucial developmental milestone for young children. A number of children with special needs, however, do not have the necessary skills to engage in appropriate peer interactions, and these children need specific social skills instruction to increase their social proficiency (Odom, McConnell, & McEvoy, 1992). Interventions must be designed, therefore, that encourage socialization among all children. Arranging the environment to facilitate socialization, teacher-mediated and peer-mediated interventions, affection training, and strategies to encourage imitation are all interventions designed to facilitate socialization.

Environmental Considerations To Facilitate Socialization

Interactions among children can be encouraged through organization of the environment (Hanline, 1985). Beckman and Kohl (1984) stated that the social interactions of children in inclusive settings can be encouraged and enhanced through the use of social toys such as balls, toy vehicles, blocks, and puppets. These toys facilitate interactive play because they can be used by more than one child at a time (Hanline, 1985). Therefore, if an IEP goal for a child with special needs is to increase socialization, teachers need to make sure an adequate number and selection of social toys are available in the setting. In addition, teachers may need to specifically direct young children with disabilities toward social types of toys and materials (Beckman & Kohl, 1984).

To further encourage social play, Hanline (1985) suggested that play sessions for children be arranged so that only two or three children can play together in one area of the classroom. She maintained that the children in these small groups should be socially compatible and similar to one another in developmental functioning. Hanline further recommended that children with special needs be seated in close proximity to typically developing peers during music, art, snack time, and large group activities to promote social interactions.

Teacher-Mediated Intervention

A powerful teacher-mediated intervention often used to promote socialization is teacher prompting and/or reinforcement (Odom & McEvoy, 1988). In this procedure the teacher gives instructions to the child with a disability to interact with his or her peers and then provides praise when the interaction occurs. For example, a child with a disability could be prompted by the teacher to share a toy with a typical child and then rewarded with verbal praise or tangible rewards when the desired behavior occurs. Similarly, Hanline (1985) recommended that teachers encourage interactions and friendships between typical children and children with disabilities with positive statements such as, "You two are playing together so nicely. You really know how to take turns!" or "Jim and Joe are sharing the blocks. They have built a wonderful house together." Further, she suggested that behaviors such as walking together and hand holding should be encouraged by verbal praise by the teacher.

Peer-Initiated Approaches

Strain and Odom (1986) recommended that educators teach typically developing children strategies to engage children with disabilities in social interactions. They suggested that typical children be taught the following specific behaviors: (a) play organizers (e.g., "Let's play with the blocks"); (b) shares—giving or exchanging an object or offering to use a toy together (e.g., "Would you like to play house with me?"); (c) physical assistance or helping the child in some way (e.g., "Can I help you with the puzzle?"); and (d) affection—hugs, pats, and hand holding. Strain and Odom stated that peer intervention training begins with the selection of a socially competent peer. They advised that the children selected should be compliant and willing to participate, have age-appropriate play skills, have regular attendance, and have no negative history with the child with a disability. Strain and Odom recommended daily work sessions of 20 to 30 minutes to teach the typical peers social initiation strategies. Daily lessons include (a) discussing the importance of making new friends, sharing, cooperating, and helping; (b) describing the target social initiation for that day (play organizers, shares, assistance, or affection); (c) modeling of appropriate behavior by the teacher; (d) opportunities for children to practice appropriate behavior with an adult giving verbal feedback on their performance; and (e) role-playing examples of incorrect uses of the strategy with prompts to help the child identify the errors.

Affection Training Procedures

McEvoy, Odom, and McConnell (1992) stated that affection activities can be used to increase social interactions of children. These activities can be used during large or small group times and consist of standard preschool songs and activities that have been modified to include prompts for interactions that usually call for some type of affectionate response. For example, McEvoy et al. suggested that, in the familiar song, "If You're Happy and You Know It," the phrase "clap your hands" could be replaced with "hug a friend." Affection activities appear to be promising in increasing social interactions of children both with and without disabilities.

Promoting Imitation

A cornerstone of the educational benefits rationale for inclusion is the premise that preschoolers with disabilities will acquire the more advanced skills modeled by typically developing peers through imitation and observational learning (Odom & McEvoy, 1988). Imitation can be facilitated by the teacher providing duplicate toys for children's use during play sessions so that children have an opportunity to imitate one another (Hanline, 1985). Imitation also can be encouraged by teacher praise through the use of statements such as, "Adam and Billy are both painting so nicely" or "Jane and Emily are both coloring red apples." Further, Hanline recommended that both verbal and motor imitations can be encouraged by the teacher through the use of statements such as, "Robert, can you say 'please' like Sam did?" or "Sally, try to hop on one foot like Tommy."

The Role of Play in Learning Social Skills

The Association for Childhood Education International (ACEI) recognized the need for play and confirmed the role of play in children's healthy development, believing that play is a necessary and integral part of childhood and that teachers must take the lead in articulating the need for play in children's lives (Isenberg & Quisenberry, 1988). Philosophical and theoretical differences exist, however, between early childhood and special educators regarding the role of play in the classroom. Bordner and Berkley (1992) stated that early childhood educators consider play to be a critical component of developmentally appropriate programs for young children. In contrast, special educators, being heavily influenced by behavioral principles emphasizing direct instructional approaches, often view play as either a reinforcement of or a break from a learning task.

Teachers can encourage and facilitate peer play through a variety of methods. Rogow (1991) suggested that the play environment be structured to initiate children's play by giving play choices and through the use of appealing and novel props to encourage pretend play, such as dress-up clothes or a pretend grocery store. Play can be prolonged by additional props and by making sure that each child has an appropriate play prop.

In addition, Rogow (1991) asserted that teachers can demonstrate and model appropriate play by sometimes taking play roles themselves and participating in children's play. This practice may be particularly effective in involving children who are more insecure in group play. Teachers also can encourage play by demonstrating interest and enjoyment, thereby communicating to the children that play is important. Teacher comments reinforce prosocial behavior. Children's awareness of the joys of pretending is heightened by teacher statements. Further, teachers can facilitate a child's entry into group play by physically bringing him or her to the group and staying close by, if necessary, to offer assistance in including the child in social play (Rogow, 1991).

Teachers can structure play activities by assisting children to select toys and materials and by assigning roles to the children (DeKlyen & Odom, 1989). After assisting in the structuring of the activity, the teacher should withdraw to observe and allow the children to follow through with their play. Through the use of this strategy, the individual objectives and needs of a child with disabilities may drive the play activity, or a play theme may be developed based on observations of children's initiations. DeKlyen and Odom found that children's play is facilitated by the teacher's structuring the play activity.

Bordner and Berkley (1992) contended that teachers may need to help children with disabilities engage in play and learn social play skills. It may be necessary for teachers to provide direct instruction through modeling and/or physical or verbal prompts to children who are displaying inappropriate play behaviors such as taking away other children's toys or not taking turns.

Conclusion

Inclusive programming for young children with disabilities is a growing trend in early childhood special education. Research indicates that preschoolers with special needs benefit both academically and socially from placement in inclusive settings. Successful inclusion will not be realized, however, by simply placing young children with special needs into typical settings. Professionals need to embrace an inclusive philosophy that welcomes and supports all children within typical settings. Educators need to refine their communication and collaboration skills to effectively work with parents and other professionals to plan and implement programs for young children with special needs in typical settings. Further, educators must take an active role in ensuring young children's success in inclusive settings by designing appropriate educational environments, choosing materials and activities that facilitate interaction and learning, and utilizing teaching strategies that promote the cognitive and social development of all children.

Early childhood appears to be the optimal time to begin including children with special needs in typical settings. The task for early childhood professionals is to provide children with quality programs that incorporate promising practices from both early childhood education and early childhood special education to maximize success for all children in typical settings.

References

Bailey, D. B., Clifford, R. M., & Harms, T. (1982). Comparison of preschool environments for handicapped and nonhandicapped children. *Topics in Early Childhood Special Education, 7*, 73–88.

Bailey, D. B., & Wolery, M. (1992). *Teaching infants and preschoolers with disabilities.* New York: Macmillan.

Beckman, P. J., & Kohl, F. L. (1984). The effects of social and isolate toys on the interactions and play of integrated and nonintegrated groups of preschoolers. *Education and Training of the Mentally Retarded, 19*, 169–174.

Benner, S. M. (1992). *Assessing young children with special needs.* New York: Longman.

Bordner, G. A., & Berkley, M. T. (1992). Educational play: Meeting everyone's needs in mainstreamed classrooms. *Childhood Education, 68*, 38–42.

Bredekamp, S., & Rosengrant, T. (1992). *Reaching potentials: Appropriate curriculum and assessment for young children.* Washington, DC: National Association for the Education of Young Children.

Bricker, D. D. (1978). A rationale for the integration of handicapped and nonhandicapped preschool children. In M. Guralnick (Ed.), *Early intervention and the integration of handicapped and nonhandicapped children* (pp. 3–26). Baltimore: University Park Press.

Bruder, M. B. (1993). The provisions of early intervention and early childhood special education within community early childhood programs: Characteristics of effective service delivery. *Topics in Early Childhood Special Education, 13,* 19–37.

Cavallaro, C. C., Haney, M., & Cabello, B. (1993). Developmentally appropriate strategies for promoting full participation in early childhood settings. *Topics in Early Childhood Special Education, 13,* 293–307.

DEC Task Force on Recommended Practices. (1993). *DEC recommended practices: Indicators of quality in programs for infants and young children with special needs and their families.* Reston, VA: Council for Exceptional Children.

DeKlyen, M., & Odom, S. L. (1989). Activity structure and social interactions with peers in developmentally integrated play groups. *Journal of Early Intervention, 13,* 342–352.

Demchak, M. A., & Drinkwater, S. (1992). Preschoolers with severe disabilities: The case against segregation. *Topics in Special Education, 11,* 70–83.

Diamond, K. E., Hestenes, L. L., & O'Connor, C. E. (1994). Integrating young children with disabilities in preschool: Problems and promise. *Young Children, 49,* 68–75.

Education for All Handicapped Children Act of 1975, 20 U.S.C. §1400 *et seq.*

Education of the Handicapped Act Amendments of 1986, 20 U.S.C. §1400 *et seq.*

Fewell, R. R., & Oelwein, P. L. (1990). The relationship between time in integrated environments and developmental gains in young children with special needs. *Topics in Special Education, 10,* 104–116.

Fox, L. (1993). A preliminary evaluation of learning within developmentally appropriate early childhood settings. *Topics in Early Childhood Special Education, 13,* 308–327.

Galant, K., & Hanline, M. F. (1993). Parental attitudes toward mainstreaming young children with disabilities. *Childhood Education, 69,* 293–297.

Guralnick, M. J. (1990). Major accomplishments and future directions in early childhood mainstreaming. *Topics in Early Childhood Special Education, 10,* 1–17.

Guralnick, M. J., & Groom, J. M. (1987). The peer relations of mildly delayed and non-handicapped preschool children in mainstream playgroups. *Child Development, 58,* 1556–1572.

Hanline, M. F. (1985). Integrating disabled children. *Young Children, 40,* 45–48.

Harbin, G. L., Gallagher, J. J., & Terry, D. V. (1991). Defining the eligible population: Policy issues and challenges. *Journal of Early Intervention, 15,* 13–20.

Individuals with Disabilities Education Act of 1990, 20 U.S.C. §1400 *et seq.*

Isenberg, J., & Quisenberry, N. L. (1988). Play: A necessity for all children. *Childhood Education, 64,* 138–145.

Jones, H. A., & Warren, S. F. (1991). Enhancing engagement in early childhood language teaching. *Teaching Exceptional Children, 23,* 48–50.

Kaiser, A. P., & Warren, S. F. (1988). Pragmatics and generalization. In R. L. Schiefelbusch (Ed.), *Language intervention strategies.* Baltimore: University Park Press.

Lamorey, S., & Bricker, D. D. (1993). Integrated programs: Effects on young children and their parents. In C. A. Peck, S. L. Odom, & D. D. Bricker (Eds.), *Integrating young children with disabilities into community programs* (pp. 249–270). Baltimore: Brookes.

McEvoy, M. A., Odom, S. L., & McConnell, S. R. (1992). Peer social competence interventions for young children with disabilities. In S. L. Odom, S. R. McConnell, & M. A. McEvoy (Eds.), *Social competence of young children with disabilities* (pp. 113–133). Baltimore: Brookes.

McGee, G. G., Daly, T., Izeman, S. G., Mann, H. M., & Risley, T. R. (1991). Use of classroom materials to promote preschool engagement. *Teaching Exceptional Children, 23,* 44–47.

McLean, M. E., & Odom, S. L. (1993). Practices for young children with and without disabilities: A comparison of DEC and NAEYC identified practices. *Topics in Early Childhood Special Education, 13,* 274–292.

National Association for the Education of Young Children & National Association of Early Childhood Specialists in State Departments of Education. (1991). Guidelines for appropriate curriculum content and assessment in programs serving children ages 3 through 8. *Young Children, 46,* 21–38.

Noonan, M. J., & McCormick, L. (1993). *Early intervention in natural environments: Methods and procedures.* Pacific Grove, CA: Brooks/Cole.

Odom, S. (1990). Mainstreaming at the preschool level: Potential tasks and barriers for the field. *Topics in Early Childhood Special Education, 10,* 48–61.

Odom, S. L., McConnell, S. R., & McEvoy, M. A. (1992). Peer-related social competence and its significance for young children with disabilities. In S. L. Odom, S. R. McConnell, & M. A. McEvoy (Eds.), *Social competence of young children with disabilities* (pp. 3–35). Baltimore: Brookes.

Odom, S. L., & McEvoy, M. A. (1988). Integration of young children with handicaps and normally developing children. In S. L. Odom & M. B. Karnes (Eds.), *Early intervention for infants and children with handicaps* (pp. 241–267). Baltimore: Brookes.

Peck, C. A., Furman, G. C., & Helmstetter, E. (1993). Integrated early childhood programs: Research on the implementation of change in organizational contexts. In C. A. Peck, S. L. Odom, & D. D. Bricker (Eds.), *Integrating young children with disabilities into community programs* (pp. 187–205). Baltimore: Brookes.

Peterson, N. L. (1987). *Early intervention for handicapped and at-risk children: An introduction to early childhood-special education.* Denver: Love.

Rogow, S. (1991). The dynamics of play: Including children with special needs in mainstreamed early childhood programs. *International Journal of Early Childhood, 23,* 50–57.

Rose, D., & Smith, B. (1993). Public policy report. Preschool mainstreaming: Attitude barriers and strategies for addressing them. *Young Children, 48,* 146–155.

Safford, P. L. (1989). *Integrated teaching in early childhood: Starting in the mainstream.* White Plains, NY: Longman.

Salisbury, C. L. (1991). Mainstreaming during the early childhood years. *Exceptional Children, 58,* 146–154.

Stainback, S., Stainback, W., & Jackson, H. J. (1992). Toward inclusive classrooms. In S. Stainback & W. Stainback (Eds.), *Curriculum considerations in inclusive classrooms: Facilitating learning for all students* (pp. 3–17). Baltimore: Brookes.

Strain, P. S., & Odom, S. L. (1986). Peer social initiatives: Effective interventions for social skill development of exceptional children. *Exceptional Children, 52,* 543–552.

Turnbull, A. P., & Turnbull, H. R. (1990). *Families, professionals, and exceptionality: A special partnership.* New York: Macmillan.

Vincent, L. J., & Beckett, J. A. (1993). Family participation. In DEC Task Force on Recommended Practices, *DEC recommended practices: Indicators of quality in programs for infants and young children with special needs and their families.* Reston, VA: Council for Exceptional Children.

Warren, S. F., McQuarter, R. J., & Rogers-Warren, A. K. (1984). The effects of mands and models on the speech of unresponsive socially isolate children. *Journal of Speech and Hearing Disorders, 47,* 42–52.

Whaley, K. T., & Bennett, T. C. (1991). Promoting engagement in early childhood special education. *Young Children, 46,* 51–54.

Wolfensberger, W. (1972). *The principles of naturalization in human services.* Toronto: National Institute on Mental Retardation.

Author Index

Subject Index

About the Authors

Pamela Baker, PhD, is a special education teacher with the Dallas Public Schools. She has taught children with autism, serious emotional disturbance, learning disabilities, and mental retardation for the past 9 years. Her areas of expertise include working with children and youth with serious emotional disturbance, understanding multicultural and urban education issues, and using computer technology to enhance classroom learning. Currently, she is a doctoral candidate in the field of special education with a minor in criminal justice. She anticipates completing her doctorate from the University of North Texas in August 1996.

Jane E. Doelling, EdD, is an associate professor in the Department of Special Education, Southwest Missouri State University. She received her doctorate in 1986 from the University of Missouri. Her research interests include traumatic brain injury and inclusive strategies for students with disabilities.

Regina M. Foley, EdD, is an associate professor of special education in the Department of Educational Psychology and Special Education at Southern Illinois University at Carbondale. She received her bachelor's and master's degrees in special education from the University of Nebraska–Lincoln and her doctorate in special education from Northern Illinois University. Foley has served as codirector of a federally funded staff development project, Interdisciplinary Collaboration Training for Secondary School Personnel. Her research interests include collaboration activities in secondary schools and strategies for integrating adolescents with learning and behavior disabilities in general education classrooms.

Linda Garrison Harrell, PhD, is an assistant professor in the Department of Special Education, Southwest Missouri State

University. She received her doctorate in 1996 from the University of Kansas. Her research interests include academic and social engagement strategies for students with disabilities in inclusive settings.

Jennifer Gildner, MA, has taught children with emotional and behavioral disorders in a self-contained classroom in Charleston County, South Carolina. She has developed and implemented a team teaching inclusionary program for sixth-grade students with learning disabilities and emotional and behavioral disorders in Kearsley Community Schools in Flint, Michigan. She is currently a teacher consultant implementing early intervention with students in kindergarten and first grade.

Nancy S. Hartshorne, EdS, has been a school psychologist for the Gratiot–Isabella Regional Education Service District in Michigan for 4 years. She has given presentations on the topics of CHARGE syndrome, inclusion, 3-year reevaluations, and Individualized Education Programs for parents and professionals. She has been a member of the National Association of School Psychologists, the Michigan Association of School Psychologists, The Association for Persons with Severe Handicaps, and the National Family Association for Deaf–Blind. She sits on advisory boards for Michigan's 307.11 state grant for Services for Children and Youth with Deaf–Blindness, Michigan State University's Teacher Preparation Program for Vision and Hearing Impairments, and the Children's Lending Locker of Michigan. She is an advocate for quality education in the least restrictive environment for her son as well as for the children with whom she works daily.

Timothy S. Hartshorne, PhD, is professor and chair of the psychology department at Central Michigan University. He is co-author of *Ethics and Law for School Psychologists* and numerous book chapters and journal articles. His current research focuses on the relationship between parents of children with disabilities and service providers, and how that relationship influences outcomes for families and children. He is a member of the American Psychological Association, the National Association of School Psychologists, the American Counseling Association, and the North American Society for Adlerian Psychology. He has recently completed a research fellowship at Renwick College, University of Newcastle, Sydney, Australia.

Sandra M. Keenan is administrator of special services for Narragansett School Department in Narragansett, Rhode Island. She was previously assistant director of special education for Westerly Public Schools, educational director in private schools for behaviorally disordered students, a consultant and trainer, and a classroom teacher. She has numerous professional affiliations in education and special education, and is currently the governor for Council for Children with Behavior Disorders on the Council for Exceptional Children. Keenan serves on the Rhode Island Task Force for Improving Services to Behaviorally Disordered Students and those at risk and on the local coordinating council for Wraparound Mental Health and Community-Based Services. She also is chairperson for the Rhode Island Statewide Conference on Students with Behavioral, Emotional and Social Needs. Keenan has presented conference presentations, and published articles on inclusion of students with behavior problems in the public schools.

John W. Maag, PhD, is a behavioral consultant to agencies, school districts, and businesses on best practices for motivating individuals, managing resistance and conflict, and improving relationships with others. His two most popular seminars are *Controlling Your Emotions and Behavior—Forever* and *Managing Resistance: Looking Beyond the Child and into the Mirror.* His professional interests include the study of effective self-management techniques, development of comprehensive behavior management packages for organizations, and the treatment of depression and attention deficit disorders. Maag has published over 50 articles and book chapters dealing with these topics. He is the author of *Parenting Without Punishment,* a book designed to help parents develop proactive methods for managing children's challenging behavior. Maag serves as a field reviewer for several journals and is a consulting editor to two journals: *Behavioral Disorders* and the *Journal of Emotional and Behavioral Disorders.* In addition, Maag is a licensed professional counselor and has a private practice where he treats children, adolescents, adults, couples, and families.

Sharon Maroney, PhD, is a former special educator who currently teaches undergraduate and graduate courses in mental retardation and assessment. Currently an associate professor at Western Illinois University, she has been very active in the Council for Children with

Behavior Disorders serving in various capacities. She is now midwest regional representative.

Lisa Matts, MA, is a teacher of middle school students with emotional and behavioral disorders in Gaylord Community Schools, Gaylord, Michigan. This teaching experience has included many different opportunities for teach teaching in order to provide services for students with emotional and behavioral disorders.

Linda L. Meloy, PhD, NCSP, is a former regular and special education teacher who is now an associate professor, teaching graduate courses in special education. She is also a practicing school psychologist, specializing in curriculum-based measurement and effective teaching strategies for all learners. Meloy is a frequent inservice presenter in the Midwest, and is involved in programs for gifted Hispanic students and their families.

Nancy A. Mundschenk, PhD, received her doctorate in special education from the University of Iowa. She is an assistant professor in the Department of Educational Psychology and Special Education at Southern Illinois University, where she served as codirector of a 3-year federally funded project to train teachers in collaborative strategies. In addition to collaboration, her research interests include the development of social competence of students with behavior disorders and autism.

Brenda Smith Myles, PhD, is an assistant professor of special education at the University of Kansas. She is codirector of the combined behavior disorders/autism doctoral training program and codirector of the masters training program in autism. Myles is the author of numerous books and articles related to education of children and youth with disabilities.

Christine K. Ormsbee, PhD, is a former secondary special educator with experience teaching in urban and rural settings. Currently associate professor/associate chair in the Division of Psychology and Special Education at Emporia State University, she coordinates a multicategorical graduate training program, teaches undergraduate and graduate methods courses, and consults with special and general educators on curriculum and management issues of students with learning and behavioral concerns.

Pamela Lowry Pruitt, PhD, is an assistant professor in the Department of Counseling and Special Education at Central Michigan University. She received her doctorate in special education from Indiana University. She currently teaches courses in parent and professional relationships, mental impairments, and learning disabilities. Her professional interests include transition, inclusion, early childhood special education, and family issues.

Gary M. Sasso, PhD, is a professor in the Department of Special Education and in the Department of Pediatrics at the University of Iowa. He received his doctorate in 1984 from the University of Kansas. His research has included work with individuals with autism related to social competence and the functional variables related to problem behavior. He is currently editor of *Behavioral Disorders.*

Janice DePalma Simpson earned a PhD in educational policy and administration and a master's degree in special education from the University of Kansas. She is the director of therapeutic education for the Behavioral Health Services Unit of Bethany Medical Center in Kansas City, Kansas, and consults with schools, agencies, children's mental health programs, and private practitioners regarding education and mental health issues. She has 20 years experience as a teacher, special education administrator, and university instructor in addition to her current professional activities. Her research interests include mental health and education collaboration, inclusion of students with behavior disorders, and attention deficit disorders.

Richard L. Simpson, EdD, is professor of special education and school psychology at the University of Kansas. He is also codirector of the combined behavior disorders/autism doctoral training program and codirector of the masters training program in autism. Simpson is the author of numerous books and articles related to education of children and youth with disabilities.

Mark Tovar is presently a junior at Central Michigan University and is seeking degrees in psychology and broadcasting. He hopes to continue on to graduate school to attain a doctorate in psychology. Mark is now walking and considers himself almost 100%. He still on occasion uses a wheelchair or crutches but for the most part is normal (no matter what others might say).

Jo Webber, PhD, is associate professor of special education at Southwest Texas State University. She is a past president of the National Council for Children with Behavioral Disorders and regularly consults with public school personnel nationwide regarding appropriate programming for students with emotional or behavioral disorders. For the past 20 years, she has conducted inservice training in the areas of behavior management, special education programming, and team building. She has worked in the public schools as a special education teacher, staff development director, and special education administrator and has directed programs for dropout prevention and for children and youth with autism. Webber's current interests include self-management and special education advocacy.

Laura Zionts, PhD, has taught general and special education in urban settings. Her teaching experiences have been primarily in early childhood special education and secondary level transition for students with mild disabilities. Zionts has developed expertise in multicultural and diversity issues in education and is interested in the impact of the educational environment on social development in young children. Currently a doctoral candidate at The University of North Texas, she anticipates completing her doctorate in special education in September 1996.

Paul Zionts received his PhD in educational psychology from the University of Connecticut and is a professor of special education at Central Michigan University. He has taught and applied the principles of Rational–Emotive Therapy in his roles as a teacher in a reform school and an inner city high school, a program director, consultant, and a teacher trainer. He has lectured and provided training in local, state, and national events and has conducted hundreds of workshops that have included teachers, counselors, psychologists, social workers, administrators, parents, secretaries, and bus drivers. He has authored *Teaching Disturbed and Disturbing Students (2nd edition)* and coauthored with Richard Simpson, both *Autism* and *Understanding Children and Youth with Emotional and Behavioral Problems*. He is currently preparing a series of Rational–Emotive Therapy lesson plan books.